AMERICAN WOMEN

images and realities

AMERICAN WOMEN
Images and Realities

Advisory Editors
ANNETTE K. BAXTER
LEON STEIN

A Note About This Volume

By correct count, Ann Eliza Webb Young (1844-?) was the twenty-seventh wife of Mormon prophet Brigham Young, who led his people to the founding of an industrious city on the edge of the Great Salt Lake. Polygamy, as practised by the Mormons and a number of other sects, based marriage on religious spiritualism rather than on civil license—and it outraged most Americans. The prophet had wooed Ann and they were secretly married. But like her mother, the first of her father's five wives, she found polygamous life unbearable. In 1873, she astounded the nation by seeking divorce. She told her story from the lecture platform and in this widely sold book. A second book in 1908 failed; the Mormon church had already abandoned polygamy in 1890. Ann Young herself quickly disappeared from view.

WIFE No. 19

ANN ELIZA YOUNG

ARNO PRESS

A New York Times Company
New York • 1972

Reprint Edition 1972 by Arno Press Inc.

Reprinted from a copy in The State Historical
Society of Wisconsin Library

American Women: Images and Realities
ISBN for complete set: 0-405-04445-3
See last pages of this volume for titles.

Manufactured in the United States of America

- - - - - - - - - - - - -

Library of Congress Cataloging in Publication Data

Young, Ann Eliza (Webb) b. 1844.
  Wife no. 19.

  (American women: images and realities)
  1. Mormons and Mormonism. 2. Polygamy. I. Title.
II. Series.
BX8641.Y7 1972   289.3'3   72-2634
ISBN 0-405-04488-7

WIFE No. 19

Sincerely Yours
Ann Eliza Young

WIFE No. 19,

OR

THE STORY OF

A LIFE IN BONDAGE,

BEING A

Complete Exposé of Mormonism,

AND REVEALING THE

SORROWS, SACRIFICES AND SUFFERINGS OF
WOMEN IN POLYGAMY,

BY

ANN ELIZA YOUNG,

BRIGHAM YOUNG'S APOSTATE WIFE.

WITH INTRODUCTORY NOTES BY

JOHN B. GOUGH AND MARY A. LIVERMORE.

———

ILLUSTRATED.

———

SOLD BY SUBSCRIPTION ONLY.

DUSTIN, GILMAN & CO.
PUBLICATION OFFICE: HARTFORD, CONN.
BRANCH OFFICES: CHICAGO, ILL., CINCINNATI, OHIO.
1875.

TO THE

MORMON WIVES OF UTAH.

I Dedicate this Book to you, as I consecrate my life to your cause.
As long as God gives me life I shall pray and plead for your deliverance from the worse than Egyptian bondage in which you are held.

Despised, maligned, and wronged; kept in gross ignorance of the
great world, its pure creeds, its high aims, its generous motives, you
have been made to believe that the noblest nation of the earth was truly
represented by the horde of miscreants who drove you from State to State,
in early years, murdering your sons and assassinating your leaders.

Hence, you shrink from those whom God will soon lead to your
deliverance, from those to whom I daily present your claims to a
hearing and liberation, and who listen with responsive and sympathetic
hearts.

But He will not long permit you to be so wickedly deceived; nor
will the People permit you to be so cruelly enslaved.

Hope and pray! Come out of the house of bondage! Kind hearts
beat for you! Open hands will welcome you! Do not fear that while
God lives you shall suffer uncared for in the wilderness! This Christian
realm is not "Babylon," but THE PROMISED LAND!

Courage! The night of oppression is nearly ended, and the sun
of liberty is rising in the heavens for you.

ANN-ELIZA YOUNG.

INTRODUCTORY NOTE,

BY

JOHN B. GOUGH.

Since Mrs. Young's pleasant visit to us, I have thought much of the important mission to which she has devoted herself, and I wish to say, and I do it most cordially, that having been reared and educated in Mormonism, from her experience and the sufferings she has endured, she is fully competent to expose the whole system, and show to the public the true side of it, as no other person can or will. I need not assure her of my entire confidence in her sincerity and ability to carry out the work to which she has devoted herself, and the talents God has given her. I believe she has been called to this mission, and by her experience and intense sympathy with the sufferings of her sex, has been wonderfully qualified, and prepared for the work.

The sympathy of our entire household is with her, and we earnestly pray that she may be enabled to overcome all opposition, and that God may give her abundant success, and that the blessing of many ready to perish may rest upon her.

JOHN B. GOUGH.

WORCESTER, MASS., July, 1875.

INTRODUCTORY NOTE,

BY

MRS. MARY A. LIVERMORE.

———∘∘⦂∘⦂∘∘———

I HAVE read the advance sheets of Mrs. Ann-Eliza Young's book with painful interest, which has deepened into disgust and pity. Disgust at the hypocrisy, brutality, and diabolism of the Mormon leaders; pity for the wasted, joyless, sacrificial lives of the poor women who immolate themselves on the shrine of Mormonism, in the holy name of Religion.

Born and reared in the midst of these deluded people, removed from all counteracting influences, it was inevitable that Mrs. Young should accept their beliefs, and be drawn into their practices. And it must have required heroic resolution in her to break away from the Mormon Church, even when her vision was unsealed to its rottenness, knowing as she did that she would be compelled to flee from home, leaving a beloved mother and precious children in the hands of the enemy. I congratulate her on her complete emancipation, on her reunion with her beloved, whose obvious peril weighed so heavily on her filial and maternal heart, and on the possession of ability to give to the world an exposé of the Mormon horror, such as it has

never before received. My sympathies are entirely with
her in the work to which she has consecrated herself.
With her awakened conscience, she could not do otherwise than seek the disintegration of the Utah community,
whose foundations are laid in the degradation of woman.
May she have the largest success compatible with human
effort.

MARY A. LIVERMCRE.

MELROSE, MASS., Oct. 1875.

TO THE WIVES OF BRIGHAM YOUNG.

SHOULD this book meet your eyes, I wish you most distinctly to understand that my quarrel is not with you. On the contrary, the warmest and tenderest feelings of my heart are strongly enlisted in your favor. As a rule, you have been uniformly kind to me. Some of you I have dearly loved. I have respected and honored you all. My love and respect have never failed, but have rather increased with separation. I think of you often with the sincerest sympathy for your helpless condition, bound to a false religion, and fettered by a despotic system; and I wish from the depths of my heart that I could bring you, body and soul, out from the cruel bondage, and help you to find the freedom, rest, and peace which have become so sweet to me since my eyes have been opened to the light of a true and comforting faith.

Since I have left Utah, I know that some of you have censured me severely, and have joined in personal denunciations. But I know that you are actuated by a mistaken zeal for the cause which you feel yourselves bound to sustain. You, no doubt, regard my course with horror. I look upon your lives with pity.

I have taken the liberty of describing your characters and situations. I was not prompted by the slightest animosity toward you, but because the public are interested in you, and curious concerning you, and I felt that I could give to the world a true story of your lives, and, at the same time, do you justice, and let you be seen as you are in my eyes, which are not dimmed by prejudice.

I was driven to the course I am pursuing by sheer desperation, as some of you, with whom I have exchanged confidences, well know. The motives which have been attributed to me, and the charges that have been made against me, are as utterly false and foreign to my nature as darkness is to light. You, at least, should not misjudge me. You should know me better, and you do. Even your bitter prejudice, and your disapprobation of the step I have taken, cannot make you believe me other than I am. You know that apostasy from Mormonism does not necessarily degrade a person, and sink them at once to the lowest depths of infamy.

If, as is taught,— and as I suppose you believe, — I have lost the light of the gospel, and departed from "the faith once delivered to the saints," am I not rather deserving your compassion than your censure? Your own hearts and consciences must answer that.

The women of Utah should know that I shall vindicate their rights, and defend their characters, at all times and in all places. Their sorrow has been my sorrow; their cause is my cause still. My heart goes out to them all, but more especially to you. *You* have been my companions and my sisters in tribulation. Now our paths diverge. I go on the way that I have chosen alone, while you stay sorrowing together. I wish I had the power to influence you to throw off the fetters which bind you, and to walk triumphantly forth into the glories of a faith, whose foundation is in God the compassionate Father, whose principles are those of a tender mercy, whose ruling spirit is love. Alas! I cannot do it; but I pray that the good Father in His infinite mercy may open your eyes to His glory, and lead you forth His children to do His blessed will.

ANN-ELIZA YOUNG.

CONTENTS.

CHAPTER I.

THE DAYS OF MY CHILDHOOD. — WHY I EVER WAS A MORMON.

An Important Question. — Born in Mormonism. — Telling my own Story. — Joseph Smith's Mission. — He preaches a New Dispensation. — My Parents Introduced to the Reader. — The Days before Polygamy. — My Mother's Childhood. — Learning under Difficulties. — First Thoughts of Mormonism. — Received into the Church. — Persecution for the Faith. — Forsaking all for the New Religion. — First Acquaintance with the Apostle Brigham. — His Ambitious Intrigues. — His Poverty. — His Mission-work. — Deceptive Appearances. — My Mother's Marriage. — A Brief Dream of Happiness. — That Sweet Word "Home." — The Prophet Smith turns Banker. — The "Kirtland Safety Society Bank." — The Prophet and Sidney Rigdon Flee. — A Moment of Hesitation. — Another "Zion" Appointed. — Losing All for the Church. — Privation and Distress. — Sidney Rigdon and his "Declaration of Independence." — He Excites an Immense Sensation. — Mobs Assemble and Fights Ensue. — Lively Times among the Saints. — The Outrages of the Danites. 31

CHAPTER II.

FOUNDING THE NEW RELIGION. — ASSASSINATION OF JOSEPH SMITH.

The Saints expelled from Missouri. — They cross the Mississippi into Illinois. — Forming a New Settlement. — Arrival in Quincy. — A Kind Reception. — The City of "Nauvoo" Founded. — A New Temple Begun. — Great Success of the Foreign Missions. — The Saints flock from Europe. — Thousands assemble in Nauvoo. — The Prophet Joseph applies for a City Charter. — Nauvoo Incorporated. — The Saints Petition the National Government. — The Prophet visits Washington. — His Interview with President Van Buren. — He Coquets with Politics. — He Stands on the Edge of the Precipice. — The Saints in Danger. — The Prophet Smith nominated for President. — He tries to find the "Golden Way." — Mormon Missionaries preach Politics. — The Prophet looks towards the Pacific Coast. — The Blind Obedience of the Saints. — The Real Devotion of their Faith. — Gentile Opinions. — How Boggs was Shot in the Head. — The Spiritual-Wife Doctrine. — Dr. William Law Protests. — Terrible Charges against the Prophet. — The "Nauvoo Expositor." — The Prophet Surrenders. — He is Murdered in Jail. . . 49

CHAPTER III.

THE "REVELATION ON CELESTIAL MARRIAGE."—TROUBLE AMONG THE SAINTS.

The Announcement of Polygamy. — " *Celestial* Marriage." — Joseph " sets himself Right." — Mrs. Smith is very Rebellious. — Mrs. Smith's Adopted Daughter. — The Prophet too fond of Fanny. — Mrs. Smith takes her in Hand. — Marital Storms. — Oliver Cowdery called In. — He goes and " Does Likewise." — Joseph first Preaches Polygamy. — The Saints Rebel. — The Revelation given in Secret. — Eleven "Adopted *Daughters*" sealed to the Prophet. — A Domestic Squall in the Prophet's House. — Nancy Rigdon Insulted by Joseph. — Sidney's Zeal Grows Cold. — How Celestial Marriage was Introduced. — Mr. Noble begins to Build Up his Kingdom. — The first Plural Marriage. — False Position of the Second Wife. — John C. Bennett. — His Profligacy and Crimes. — He Apostatizes and Writes a Book. — Joseph Defends Himself. — Apostasy of an Apostle's Wife. — The Prophet in Difficulties. — The Revelation on " Celestial Marriage." 65

CHAPTER IV.

AFTER JOSEPH'S DEATH. — BRIGHAM YOUNG ELECTED PROPHET.

Kindness of the Gentiles. — Strangers in a Strange Land. — My Parents join the Saints in Nauvoo. — They Purchase Land in the City. — Are shamefully Defrauded. — Joseph's Unfaithful Friends. — My Parents left almost Destitute. — I am Born in the Midst of Troubles. — The Saints Bewildered. — Who should Succeed Joseph? — Sidney Rigdon's Claims to the Presidency. — He returns to Nauvoo. — Has Dreams and Visions. — He Promises to " Pull Little Vic's Nose." — The Apostles hear of the Prophet's Murder. — They hasten to Nauvoo. — Brigham begins his Successful Intrigues. — He Settles Sidney Rigdon. — An Extraordinary Trial. — Brigham's Idea of Free Voting. — Women's Suffrage in Utah. — Why Brigham gave the Franchise to the Women. — My own Experience as a Voter. — Brigham Dictates what I'm to Do. — I obey Quietly. — How Sidney Rigdon was Deposed. — Brigham Rules the Church. . . . 87

CHAPTER V.

MY FATHER'S PLURAL-WIFE. — CHILDHOOD IN POLYGAMY.

Childhood in Mormondom. — A striking Contrast. — The Sorrows of my Earliest Years. — How my Mother received Polygamy. — Submitting to the Rod. — Clinging to Love and Home. — Resigning all for Religion. — Strange ways of glorifying God. — The Reward of Faithfulness. — The Prophet Joseph imparts a New Religious Mystery. — The Breaking-up of a Home. — Fears of Rebellion. — The Struggle of Faith against Nature. — Seeking Rest, but finding None. — Brigham's " Counsels." — A New Wife Selected. — My Parents enter into Polygamy. — The New Bride, Elizabeth. — The Marriage Ceremony. — My Mother Sealed. — She is to become a Queen. — Domestic Arrangements in Polygamy. — Bearing the Cross. — A First Wife's Sorrows. — " Where does Polygamy Hurt?" — The Mormon Husband; his Position and Privileges. . . 98

CHAPTER VI.

FORSAKING DEAR ZION. — WE FIND A NEW HOME IN THE FAR WEST.

A New Home in the Far West. — Dangerous Neighbors. — Some very Unpleasant Stories. — Seeking a New Home. — Preparing to Depart. — Life at Winter-Quarters. — A Lively Time in the Temple. — "Little Dancin' Missy." — Bound for Salt Lake Valley. — Life by the Way. — Songs of the Saints. — A False Prophecy. — "The Upper California." — Saintly Profanity. — A Soul-stirring Melody. — The Saints Excited. — Beside the Camp-Fires. — The Journey Ending. — Entering Zion. — The Valley of the Great Salt Lake. 110

CHAPTER VII.

OUR WELCOME TO "ZION." — UTAH IN EARLY DAYS.

Our Welcome to Zion. — Housekeeping under Difficulties. — Our First Home in Utah. — The Second Wife's Baby. — The Young Mother. — A very Delicate Position. — Doctors at a Discount. — Brigham's Wife turns Midwife. — An Obedient Woman. — Taking Care of the Baby. — Practising Economy. — The Path of the Crickets. — Too much Cracked Wheat. — Building the First Mill. — Brother Brigham Speechifies. — Tea at Five Dollars per Pound. — Californian Gold Discovered. — Building up Zion. — Brigham's "Dress Reform." — A Rather Queer Costume. — The Women "Assert" Themselves. — Clara Decker Rebels. — How the Prophet treats his Wives. — I ask for some Furs, and am Snubbed. — How the Prophet doled out his Silk. — Eliza Snow and Fanny's Finery. — The Prophet Snubs Eliza. — He Combats the "Grecian Bend." — Dancing among the Saints. — Polygamy Denied. — How the Saints received It. — A Nice Little Family Arrangement. . . . 123

CHAPTER VIII.

TROUBLES UNDER THE NEW SYSTEM.

The Sorrows of My Uncle. — "It's a Hopeless Fix." — A Woman's Argument about Polygamy. — My Mother "labors" with a First Wife. — Wife No. 2 "Walks Off." — Marrying a Widow and her Two Daughters. — Mrs. Webb becomes a Wife No. 2. — Wife No. 1 throws Brickbats into the Nuptial Chamber. — She clears the Field of Extra Wives. — "Building up the Kingdom." — The Atrocious Villanies of Orson Pratt. — How he has Seduced Innocent Girls. — Brigham's Nephew Rebels. — Trouble in the Prophet's Family. — Forgetting a Wife's Face. — A Woman who liked Polygamy. 142

CHAPTER IX.

THE HARDSHIPS AND PERILS OF LIFE IN A NEW COUNTRY.

"Killed by the Indians." — How Apostates Disappeared. — A Suspicious Fact. — How Brigham "took care" of the People's Property. — The Mormon Battalion. — Brigham Pockets the Soldiers' Pay. — How Proselytes were Made. — Scapegraces sent on Mission. — My Father goes to

Europe. — How Missionaries' wives are Left. — Collecting funds for the Missionaries. — Brigham Embezzles the Money. — The "Church Train." — Joseph A. Young as a Missionary. — His Misdoings in St. Louis. — What Brother Brown said of Him. — The Perpetual Emigration Fund. — How the Money was Raised. — Cheating the Confiding Saints. — How Brigham Manages the Missionaries' Property. — The "Church" makes Whiskey for the Saints. — The Missionaries bring home new Wives. — How English Girls are Deceived. — My First Baptism. . 160

CHAPTER X.

THE UTAH "REFORMATION." — "A REIGN OF TERROR." — THE BLOOD-ATONEMENT PREACHED.

The Beginning of the Reformation. — The Payson Saints Stirred Up. — What the Wicked " Saints " had been Doing Secretly. — The Old Lady who stole a Radish. — Confessing the sins of Others. — A System of *Espionnage*. — Brigham bids them "Go Ahead!" — The Story of Brother Jeddy's Mule. — The Saints receive a terrible Drubbing. — Great Excitement in Mormondom. — How the Saints were Catechized. —Indelicate Questions are put to Everybody. — My Mother and Myself Confess. — The Labors of the Home Missionaries. — Making Restitution. — Everybody is Re-baptized. — " Cut off *Below their Ears.*" — The "Blood-Atonement" Preached. — Murder recommended in the Tabernacle. — Cutting their Neighbors' throats for Love. — A " Reign of Terror" in Utah. — Fearful Outrages Committed. — Murdered " *by the Indians*"? — Brigham advises the Assassination of Hatten. — Murder of Almon Babbitt, Dr. Robinson, the Parrishes, and Others. — Bloodshed the Order of the Day 181

CHAPTER XI.

"DIVINE EMIGRATION." — THE PROPHET AND THE HAND-CART SCHEME.

Early Emigration to Utah. — The Prophet Meditates Economy. — The "Divine Plan" Invented. — How it was Revealed to the Saints. — They Prepare to " Gather to Zion." How the Hand-Carts were Built. — The Sufferings of the Emigrants. — On Board Ship. — An Apostolic Quarrel. — Base Conduct of the Apostle Taylor. — The Saints arrive in Iowa City. — How the Summer-time was Wasted.. — Beginning a Terrible Journey. — Suffering by the Way. — " Going Cheap." — They reach Council Bluffs. — Levi Savage Behaves Bravely. — Lying Prophecy of the Apostle Richards. — How the Emigrants were Deceived. — Brigham Young sends Help to Them. — Two Apostles are Denounced. — The Prophet in a Fix. — He lays His own Sins on the Backs of Others. — Preparing to Receive the Emigrants 200

CHAPTER XII.

BRIGHAM'S HAND-CART SCHEME, CONTINUED. — FAILURE OF THE "DIVINE PLAN."

Arrival of the First Train. — Fearful Sufferings of the Emigrants. — Women and Girls toiling at the Carts. — The Prophet's "Experiment." —Burying the Dead. — Greater Mortality among the Men. — Arrival of

Assistance. — Hand-Cart Songs. — Scenes in the Camp of the Emigrants. — How every Prophecy of the Elders was Falsified. — How the Tennant Family were Shamelessly Robbed. — One of the Vilest Swindles of the Prophet. — Mr. Tennant's Unhappy Death. — His Wife Views the "Splendid Property" Bought from Brigham. — Brigham Cheats her out of her Last Dollar. — She is reduced to Abject Poverty. — The Apostle Taylor Hastens to Zion. — Richards and Spencer are made Scape-goats. — Brigham evades all Responsibility. — Utter Failure of the "Divine Plan.". 213

CHAPTER XIII.

THE MOUNTAIN MEADOWS' MASSACRE. — "VENGEANCE IS MINE: I WILL REPAY."

The Results of the Reformation. — The Story of a Fiendish Deed. — The People's Mouths Closed. — How the Dreadful Crime was Hushed Up. — Judge Cradlebaugh's Efforts to Unravel the Mystery. — Who were the Guilty Ones? — The Emigrants on the Way to Utah. — The People Forbidden to sell them Food. — They Arrive at Salt Lake City. — Ordered to Break Camp. — In need of Supplies. — Who was Accountable? — Why the Mormons hated the Emigrants. — The Story of Parley P. Pratt. — How he Seduced McLean's Wife. — Their Journey to Cedar City. — Hungry and Weary, but still Pressing On. — They Reach the Mountain Meadows. — Attacked by "the Indians." — The Emigrants Besieged. — Dying of Thirst. — Two little Girls shot by the Mormons. — An Appeal for Help. — The Last Hope of the Besieged. — Waiting for Death. . 228

CHAPTER XIV.

BETRAYED AND MURDERED. — TRIAL OF JOHN D. LEE.

The "White Flag of Peace." — Friends in the Distance. — A Cruel Deception. — Mormon Fiends plan their Destruction. — John D. Lee's Crocodile Tears. — " Lay down your Arms, and Depart in Peace." — A Horrible Suspicion. — The Massacre. — The Scene of Blood. — No Mercy for Women and Children. — Robbed and Outraged. — Murdered by Lee's Own Hand. — The Field of Slaughter. — Dividing the Property of the Murdered Ones. — Brigham Young Demands his Share. — Haunted by Spectres. — John D. Lee's Trial. — Instigated by Brigham. — No Justice in Utah. — Lee's *Confession* made to Shield the False Prophet. — Eight Mormon and Four Gentile Jurors. — What was to be Expected? 245

CHAPTER XV.

THE BLOOD-ATONEMENT. — THE DESTROYING ANGELS. — DANITES AND THEIR DEEDS.

Sweet, Saintly Sentiments. — "He ought to have his Throat cut." — Too many Gentiles About. — The Spirit of "Blood-Atonement" Still Cherished. — Present Position of Apostates. — How they used to be "Cut Off." — " *Cutting Men off below the Ears*." — How " *Accidents* " hap-

2

pened to People who "Knew too Much." — How Mr. Langford expressed his Opinion too Freely. — Mormon Friends kindly advise him
to "Shut Up." — "Be on your Guard!" — Poetry among the Saints :
a Popular Song. — *Human Sacrifices Proposed!* — How Saints were
taught to Atone for their Sins. — "*Somebody*" ready to shed their
Blood. — "*The Destroying Angels:*" who they were, and what they
did. — Saints told to do their own "Dirty Work." — People who "ought
to be *Used up*." — Murdering by Proxy! — Brigham Young *proved* to
be the Vilest of Assassins. — Hideous Crimes of Porter Rockwell and
Bill Hickman. — How Rockwell tried to Murder Governor Boggs. —
Hickman Confesses his Atrocious Crimes. — Six Men Robbed of
$25,000, and then "Used Up." — Another Frightful Assassination. — A
Council of Mormon Murderers. — The "Church" orders the Assassination of the Aikin Party 262

CHAPTER XVI.

FRIGHTFUL DEEDS OF BLOOD. — MORMONISM IN ITS TRUE LIGHT.

The Yates Murder. — Brigham and the Leading Mormons Arrested for the
Crime. — Mr. Yates accused of being a Spy. — He is Arrested, and his
Goods Seized. — Bill Hickman takes possession of the Prisoner's Body.
— Brigham Embezzles his Gold. — Another Saint steals his Watch. —
Hickman carries him to Jones's Camp. — He is Murdered there while
Asleep. — Hickman asks Brigham for a Share of the Spoil. — The
Prophet refuses; sticks to every Cent. — Hickman's "faith" in Mor-
monism is Shaken. — His fellow-murderer Apostatizes Outright. — How
Bill was finally "paid in Wives." — He tries a little matter of Seven-
teen. — Fiendish Outrage at San Pete. — Bishop Snow contrives the
Damnable Deed — The fate of his Victims. — A Mysterious Marriage. —
The Feather-beds and the Prophet. — Mrs. Lewis comes to Live
with Me 277

CHAPTER XVII.

TROUBLES IN OUR OWN FAMILY. — LOUISE COMES UPON THE SCENE.

Increase of Polygamy. — Marrying going on Day and Night. — "Taking
a Wife and Buying a Cow." — A Faithful Husband in a Fix. — How
Men get "Married on the Sly." — How Wives were Driven Crazy by
their Wrongs. — My Father Marries Considerably. — He "Goes in" for
the Hand-Cart Girls. — Marries a Couple to Begin with. — Takes a
Third the same Month. — Rapid Increase of his "Kingdom." — How
the Girls Chose Husbands. — Instructing the New Wives in our Family.
— Louise doesn't want to Work. — My Father goes on Mission Again. —
Louise Flirts and Rebels. — She is Scolded and Repents. — Goes to Bed
and Weeps. — Bestows her Goods on the Family. — "Lizzie" Interviews Her. — She Poisons Herself. — Is a "Long Time Dying." — She
gets a Strong Dose of Cayenne. — Is sent on her Travels. — The Last
we Heard of Her 290

CHAPTER XVIII.

INCREASE OF POLYGAMY. — MIXED-UP CONDITION OF MATRIMONIAL AFFAIRS.

Christ alleged to be a Polygamist. — The Men to save the Women. — Making "Tabernacles" for little Spirits. — The Story of certain Ladies who were Deceived. — They Discover a Mystery. — Their Fate. — Orson Hyde's False Prophecy. — Throwing Mud at Apostates. — Death preferred to Polygamy. — Frightful Intermarriages. — Married his Mother-in-law. — A Man who Married his Wife's Grandmother, Mother, and All. — Marrying a Half-Sister. — Marrying Nieces and Sisters. — How Emigrant Girls were Married Off. — Frightful Story of a Poor Young Girl. — Polygamy and Madness. — One Woman's Love too Little. — How English Girls were Deceived. — How Claude Spenser committed a Damnable Wrong. — A Girl who was Martyred for her Religion. — How the Bereaved Husband Acted. — A Man with thirty-three Children. — "They never cost him a Cent." — A Many-Wived Saint. — Mixed-up Condition of Marital Affairs. 306

CHAPTER XIX.

THE MYSTERIES OF POLYGAMY. — WHAT THE WIVES COULD TELL.

Incestuous Intermarriages. — A Widow and her Daughters married to the same Man. — "Marrying my Pa." — The "U. S." Government Conniving at Mormon Iniquities. — Beastly Conduct of Delegate George Q. Cannon. — Polygamists legislating for Bigamists. — Mother and Daughter fighting for the same Man! — It is Wicked to Live with an Old Wife. — A *Young* lover Ninety Years Old! — A Bride *Eleven* Years Old. — Brides of Thirteen and Fourteen Years! — I receive an "Offer" when Twelve Years Old! — Old Ladies at a Discount: Young Women at a Premium. — Respect for the Silver Crown of Age. — Heber gives his Opinion. — "Why is She making such a Fuss?" — Seeing One's Husband Once a Year. — The Rascality of Orson Hyde towards his Wife. — When Rival Wives make Friends. — A Very Funny Story about an Apostle and his Wife. — Rights of the First Wife: Brigham Young in a Fix. — He treats an Early Wife to a Dance. — Amelia in the Shade. — The Prophet becomes Frisky. — Poor, neglected Emmeline. — How Polygamy was once Denied. — A Mistake which a French Lady Made. — Milk for Babes. 320

CHAPTER XX.

BRIGHAM BUILDS WAGONS BY "INSPIRATION." — THE CHURCH SETS UP A WHISKEY-STORE.

Saying "Yes" under Difficulties. — A Woman who Meant to have her Way. — Two Company: Three None. — Building Wagons by Inspiration. — My Father despatched to Chicago. — He gets rid of his New Wives. — My Brother sent to the Sandwich Islands. — My Mother tells her own Story. — She Returns to Salt Lake City to see my Father. — Wifely Considerations. — She finds two other Ladies at her Husband's Bedside. — He likes a good deal of Wives about Him! — A Heart dead

to Love. — Brigham "asks no odds of Uncle Sam or the Devil." — He
proclaims Martial Law. — Fiery Speeches in the Tabernacle. — Preparing for War. — Government Troops Arrive. — The Saints quit Salt Lake
City. — The Church Distillery. — Brigham shamelessly Robs my Father.
— He fills his own Pockets. — My Father, being without Funds, takes
his Sixth Wife. 333

CHAPTER XXI.

GOING THROUGH THE "ENDOWMENT-HOUSE." — I TAKE THE MYSTERIOUS BATHS.

No Physic among the Saints. — I am taken Sick. — Heber C. Kimball
recommends "Endowments." — How Brigham Murdered his little
Granddaughter. — The Prophet wants a Doctor. — Being "administered"
To. — I am Re-baptized. — Receive my Endowments. — How Saintly
Sins are Washed Away. — Undignified Conduct of Elders. — The Order
of Melchisedec. — How I was "Confirmed." — To become a Celestial
Queen. — I go down to the Endowment-House. — The Mysterious Ceremonies Described. — The Veil at last Lifted. — The Secrets of the
Endowment-House Exposed. — I enter the Bath. — Miss Snow Washes
Me. — She Anoints Me All Over. — I dress in a Bed-gown. — The " Peculiar Garment" of the Saints. — What the Mormon Girls do about It.
— " Going through" without a Husband. — " A Great Shouting for
Sarah !". 349

CHAPTER XXII.

WE CARRY ON THE ENDOWMENT DRAMA. — I AM FULLY INITIATED.

In the Endowment-House. — How the "Kings and Priests" appeared in
their Shirts. — The Poor Fellows "feel Bad!" — The "Gods" hold a
Conversazione. — Michael is sent down to Earth. — The " Tree of Life."
— How Raisins grew instead of Apples. — Not good to be Alone. — The
Rib abstracted and little Eve made. — The Devil dressed in "Tights." —
John D. Lee once a Devil. — Eve's Flirtation. — She eats Forbidden
Fruit. — Tempts her Husband. — Fig-leaves come into Fashion. — We
hide in Holes and Corners. — The Devil is Cursed and we are Lectured.
— The Second Degree. — Story of a Pugnacious Woman. — The Terrible Oaths of the Endowment-House. — Pains and Penalties. — Signs
and Grips. — " Good-bye ! " — Brother Heber gives me Advice. . . . 362

CHAPTER XXIII.

THE PROPHET MAKES LOVE TO ME. — I HAVE OTHER VIEWS.

The Prophet Casts his Eye on Me. — He Objects to my Beaux. — "A Low
Set Anyway." — I Didn't Want to Marry the Prophet. — He Considers
Himself an Irresistible Lover. — My First Drive with the Prophet. — I
Join the Theatrical Corps. — How We "Got Up" our Parts. — How
" Fun Hall " was Built. — The Prophet Erects a Theatre out of Temple
Funds. — How Julia Deane, the Actress, Fascinated the Prophet. — How
Brigham Cheated the Actors in his Theatre. — The Girls Grumble over
their Scanty Fare. — They want Something Good to Eat. — My New
Beau. — Love at First Sight. — I am Engaged to My First Husband. 373

CHAPTER XXIV.

MY FIRST MARRIAGE. — A LIFE'S MISTAKE.

My First Marriage. — Wedded to James Dee. — Marriage Rites in the Endowment-House. — The way in which Plural Wives are Taken. — Brigham sends for Me to help in the Theatre. — Repenting of Matrimony. — I get tired of it in a Month. — Cruel Conduct of my Husband. — He flirts considerably with the Young Girls. — I am greatly Disgusted and furiously Jealous.— He threatens to take another Wife. — The Ownership of Women in Utah. — How Newspaper Reporters are humbugged by Brigham. — How Visitors to Salt Lake are Watched. — The Prophet's Spies. — How People are misled about Utah Affairs. — The Miseries of the Women Overlooked. 387

CHAPTER XXV.

EARLY MARRIED LIFE. — MY HUSBAND AND MY MOTHER.

My early married Life. — We go to live with my Mother. — Incompatibility of Temper. — How my Mother had opposed our Marriage. — My Husband does not Admire Her. — He goes after the Girls. — I don't like it at All. — I become extremely angry with Him. — He is advised to "increase his Kingdom." — How Promises to Wives are broken by Mormon Men. — How Women are Snubbed and Undervalued. — I become anxious and Watchful. — How Heber comforted his Wives. — My Husband subjects me to personal Violence. — He is afraid of Results. — My first Baby is Born. — Zina Young marries into Polygamy. — Contrast between Mormon and Gentile Husbands. — "The Bull never cares for the Calves." — My Husband nearly strangles Me. — I leave him, and go to my Parents. — Brigham gives me some good Advice. — I obtain a Divorce. — I rejoice at being free Again. 398

CHAPTER XXVI.

AFTER MY DIVORCE. — AFFAIRS AT HOME.

After my Divorce from Dee. — " Is Polygamy good to Eat?" — Curious Experiences among the Saints. — A Man who thought his Heart was Broken. — How Two Wives Rebelled. — The Husband in a Fix. — He Runs Away from Home. — Dismisses his Plural Wife. — Being " Sealed " to Old Women for Eternity. — Nancy Chamberlain's Story. — Who is to be Brigham's Queen in Heaven? — An Old Wife Dresses up as a Ghost. — How Brother Shaw Replenished his Exchequer. — The Battles between my Father's Wives. — My Mother Enjoys his Troubles. — The Story of a Turkey. — A First Wife Asserts Her Rights. — My Life at South Cottonwood. — I Receive Offers of Marriage. 412

CHAPTER XXVII.

A WALK WITH THE PROPHET. — HE MAKES LOVE TO ME.

How Brigham Travels through the Territory. — Triumphant Receptions Everywhere. — Trying to Establish the " Order of Enoch." — How the Prophet Insulted his Faithful Followers. — " Rheumatism " in the Tem-

per. — Grand Doings in the Settlements. — We go to meet the Prophet.
— How the Saints were Lectured in the Bowery. — How Brigham *gave*
Howard a Piece of Land. — Howard Insulted by the Prophet. — Over-
looking the Prophet's Lies. — Van Etten becomes Brigham's "Friend."
— He Helps Him to Steal a Hundred Sheep. — He makes a Big Haul,
and Escapes to Canada. — The Prophet Ogles Me during Service-Time.
— We Take a Walk Home Together. — He Compliments My Good
Looks. — Makes Love to Me. — Matrimonial Advice. — Brigham Wishes
Me to Become His Wife. 426

CHAPTER XXVIII.

HOW BRIGHAM YOUNG FORCED ME TO MARRY HIM.

Brigham's Offer of Marriage. — I think the Prophet too Old. — My Parents
are Delighted with the Honor. — They Try to Persuade Me. — I am
Very Obstinate. — Arguing the Matter. — How Brigham Found Means
to Influence Me. — My Brothers get into Trouble. — The Prophet and
the Telegraph-Poles. — He takes a Nice Little Contract. — Then Sells it
to his Son. — Bishop Sharp makes a *Few* Dollars out of It. — My
Brother Engages in the Work. — He Becomes Involved in Debts and
Difficulties. — Brigham Threatens to Cut Him Off for Dishonesty. —
My Mother Tries to Excuse Him. — Hemmed In on All Sides, I Determine to Make One Last Appeal. — I fail, and Consent to Marry Him. 440

CHAPTER XXIX.

MY MARRIAGE WITH BRIGHAM YOUNG. — HOW THE OTHER WIVES RECEIVED ME.

The Prophet Rejoices at my Yielding. — My Family Restored to Favor. —
The Webbs Reconstructed. — My Prophet-Lover Comes to See Me. —
He Goes Courting " on the Sly," for Fear of Amelia. — We are Married
Secretly in the Endowment-House. — I am Sent Home Again. — Brig-
ham Establishes me in the City. — Limited Plates and Dishes. — We
Want a Little More Food. — The Prophet's " Ration-Day." — How the
Other Wives Received Me. — Mrs. Amelia Doesn't Like Me. — How the
Wives of the Prophet Worry and Scold Him. — The Prophet Breaks his
Word. — My Father Remembers the Thousand Dollars. 455

CHAPTER XXX.

THE PROPHET'S FAMILY CIRCLE. — HIS WIVES AND CHILDREN.

The Prophet Marries his First and Legal Wife. — How she lives, and how
Brigham has treated Her. — The Prophet's Eldest Son. — The Story of
his Life. — His Wives and Families. — Mary and Maggie. — The Favor-
ite Wife, Clara. — Young " Briggy " and his Expectations. — What the
Saints think of Him. — His Domestic Joys. — How he visited me when
Sick, and Scolded the old Gentleman. — Brigham and " Briggy" make
love to Lizzie. — Briggy Wins. — " John W." — He neglects his " King-
dom." — " Won by the Third Wife." — The Story of Lucy C. — The
Prophet's Daughters. — Alice and Luna. — Miss Alice's Flirtations. —
Sweet Language between Father and Daughter. — Tragic Death of
Alice Clawson. 468

CHAPTER XXXI.

THE WIVES OF THE PROPHET. — BROTHER BRIGHAM'S DOMESTIC TROUBLES.

The Wives of the Prophet. — Lucy Decker. — A Mysterious Disappearance. — Lucy's Boys. — Brigham's Wife, Clara. — Her Busy Household Work. — About the Girls. — Harriet Cook. — She Expresses Unpleasant Opinions. — Brigham is frightened of Her. — He Keeps out of the Way. — Amelia and the Sweetmeats. — How one of Brigham's Daughters Scandalized the Saints. — How Mrs. Twiss Manages the Prophet's House.. — The Work a Woman can Do. — Martha Bowker and her silent Work. — Sweet and saintly Doings of the Prophet. — Concerning Harriet Barney. — The Wife who " Served Seven Years " for a Husband. — Another English Wife of the Prophet. — The " Young Widow of Nauvoo." . 484

CHAPTER XXXII.

THE PROPHET'S FAVORITE WIFE. — HOW HE CONDUCTED HIS LOVE AFFAIRS.

The Prophet's Favorite Wife, Amelia. — How Brigham made Love in the Name of the Lord. — How he won an Unwilling Bride. — A Lady with a Sweet Temper. — How she Kicked a Sewing-Machine down the Prophet's Stairs. — She has a new House built for Her. — Rather Expensive Habits. — Her Pleasant Chances for the Future. — Mary Van Cott Cobb. — A Former Love of the Prophet's. — Miss Eliza-Roxy Snow. — The Mormon Poetess. — Joseph Smith's Poetic Widow. — Versification of the Saints. — Mrs. Augusta Cobb. — Emily Partridge. . 497

CHAPTER XXXIII.

THE DEAD WIVES OF THE PROPHET. — HE NEVER WAS KNOWN TO SHED A TEAR.

The Discarded Favorite. — The Story of Emmeline Free. — A Stupendous Humbug. —·A " Free" Opinion of Mormonism. — Amelia comes upon the Scene. — How Brigham Insulted Emmeline Free. — Brigham is Ashamed of his Cowardice. — I tell him a little of my Mind. — Joseph A. Expresses his Opinion. — Apologizes for his Father. — Death of Emmeline Free. — The Story of Clara Chase. — The Prophet's Maniac Wife. — Ellen Rockwood, and the Cause of her Neglect. — A Wife who was visited once in Six Months. — Margaret Alley. — How the Prophet treated his Dead Wife. — He steals his Children's Property. — How he Scandalized another Wife, and sent her Home. — He " Never shed a tear at a Wife's Death." 506

CHAPTER XXXIV.

THE PROPHET AT HOME. — HOW HE LOOKS, LIVES, AND ACTS. — MORMON PHILANTHROPY AND EDUCATION.

Brigham at Forty-five and at Seventy-five. — Slipping the Yoke. — The Salt Lake Tribune. — Books on Mormonism. — Prophetic Philanthropy. — The New Temple. — Paying the Workmen. — The Tabernacle. — Ad-

vantages of the Presidency. — Free Schools and Liberal Education.
— Sharp Practice. — The Rich and the Poor. — Unconscious Sarcasm. —
Looking into the Future. — The Spectacles of Ignorance. — Personal
Habits. — The Prophet's Barber. — Dinner at the Lion House. — The
Good Provider. — Helping Herself. — Prophetic Cunning. — Evening
Devotions. — A Gift in Prayer. — Advice to the Deity. — Fatherless
Children. — The Bee Hive. — Monogamist *vs.* Polygamist. 517

CHAPTER XXXV.

BRIGHAM AS A FARMER. — MY NEW HOUSE. — TAKING BOARDERS.

One Year after Marriage. — Life at the Farm. — House-keeping Extraordi-
nary. — Bread and Milk Dinners. — Brigham Tries to Catch us Nap-
ping. — Hours of Labor. — Dejection. — My New House. — Parlor
Stairs. — "Wells Wanted." — My Mother receives Notice to Quit. — My
Elder Brother Pays her Board. — Failing Faith. — Taking Boarders. —
The Prophet's Contemptible Meanness. — Brigham's Neglect. — Rev.
Mr. Stratton. — I open my Heart. — The New Religion. — Woman's
Sphere. — First Glimpses of the Outer World. — Forming Resolu-
tions. 532

CHAPTER XXXVI.

BREAKING THE YOKE. — I LEAVE MY HOME.

The Workings of Destiny. — A Noble Lawyer. — A Small Stove and a
Large Family. — Last Interview with Brigham. — A Startling Proposal.
— Sickness and Gentile Care. — Brigham's Police. — A Moral Thunder-
bolt. — My Third Baptism. — A Religious Farce. — I Decide to Escape.
— A Memorable Day. — Removing in Forty Minutes. — The Walker
House. — Among the Gentiles. — A Perilous Situation. — New Hopes. —
Interviewed by Reporters. — Unwelcome Notoriety. — A Touching Let-
ter. — A Visit from my Father. — The Paper War. — Overshooting the
Mark. — Sueing for a Divorce. — A Tempting Offer, $15,000 and my
Freedom. — The Prophet Astonished. 542

CHAPTER XXXVII.

THE DIVORCE SUIT. — PROCEEDINGS IN COURT. — BRIG-HAM'S AFFIDAVIT.

I bring an Action against the Prophet. — My "Complaint" against Him.
— What the "Complaint" Stated. — My Birth and Early Life. — My
Marriage with the Prophet. — Exile to Brigham's Farm. — Cause of
Action for Divorce. — The Question of Alimony. — My Own Affidavit.
— Corroborative Testimony. — Opinion of Judge McKean. — Brigham
Young's Reply and Affidavit. — The Prophet states the Value of his
Property. — Wonderful Difference of Opinion. — Proceedings in Court.
— Judge McKean Sums Up. — Order for Allowance and Alimony. —
Judge McKean Removed. — His Order Quashed by the New Judge. —
The latest Proceedings. 553

CHAPTER XXXVIII.

MY ESCAPE FROM SALT LAKE CITY. — MY PUBLIC CAREER.

Thoughts of the Future. — The Gentile Papers. — A Private Audience at the Walker House. — Hopes and Fears. — I Resolve to Take the Platform. — Sneers and Ridicule. — Brigham is made Acquainted with my Plans. — Packing under Difficulties. — My Perilous Escape from Utah. — A Noble Woman. — Arrival at Laramie. — Denver. — My First Public Lecture. — A Grand Success. — Brigham at Work. — A Scandalous Article in the Chicago Times. — A Mean Lawyer. — Lecture at Boston. — Kindness of the Members of Boston Press. — Opposed by George Q. Cannon. — Washington Lecture a Success. — First Glimpses of the True Faith. — Conversion to Christianity. 566

CHAPTER XXXIX.

CHURCH GOVERNMENT. — MORMON APOSTLES. — THE ORDER OF ENOCH.

Mormon Administration. — The Earthly Trinity. — Filling Vacancies. — Mormon Apostles. — Polygamy made Profitable. — The Seventy. — Two-Dollar Blessings. — Astounding Promises. — Bishops and Spies. — The Order of Enoch. — All things in Common. — An Apostolic Row. — How Enoch Works. — A Stupid Telegram. — Logic Extraordinary. — A Gigantic Swindle. — Zion's Co-operative Mercantile Institution. — Brigham's Revelations. — The Saints Laugh in their Sleeves. — "It pays to be a Mormon." — Beginning to see through It. — The Apostate President. 577

CHAPTER XL.

THE CONDITION OF MORMON WOMEN. — HIGH AND LOW LIFE IN POLYGAMY.

Increasing Light. — The Equality of the Sexes. — Exaggeration Impossible. — Likely Saviours. — The Present Condition of Mormon Women. — The Prospects for the Future. — Polygamy Bad for Rich and Poor. — A Happy Family. — The Happiness Marred. — Sealed for Time Only. — Building on Another Man's Foundation. — The New Wife. — How the Old One Fared. — The Husband's Death a Relief. — Asa Calkins's English Mission. — What Came of It. — How to Get Rich. — Two Sermons from One Text. — Dividing the Spoil. — No Woman Happy in Polygamy. 589

CHAPTER XLI.

MY RETURN TO UTAH. — SECRET OF BRIGHAM'S POWER. — UTAH'S FUTURE.

I Return to Utah. — Reception at the Walker House. — Greeting old Friends. — My Love for the Place. — Six Lectures in the Territory. — Brigham's Daughters make Faces at me. — My Father and Mother in the Audience. — The Half not told. — Multitudes Pleading for Freedom. — Eastern Newspaper Reports. — Indiscretion. — The Poland Bill. — Increase of Polygamy. — The Secrets of Brigham's Power. — The Pulpit and Press on Mormonism. — The Salt Lake City Tribune. — A Word to the Sufferers. — Calls for Help. — The Future of Utah. 598

ILLUSTRATIONS BY STANLEY FOX, 391 CANAL ST. N.Y.

PAGE

Portrait of Ann Eliza Young (*Steel*), ... Frontispiece.
Turned out of Doors, ... 31
Preaching the New Religion, ... 37
Joseph Smith, the Founder of Mormonism, ... 40
The Night of Terror, ... 46
Nauvoo Temple, ... 49
Burning of the Newspaper Office, ... 62
Assassination of Joseph Smith and his brother Hyrum, ... 64
Emma Smith, "The Elect Lady," 65
The Indignant Wife, ... 69
The First Plural Marriage, ... 72
Arrival at Quincy, Illinois, ... 87
Sidney Rigdon, ... 90
My First Vote, ... 95
My Father's First Plural Marriage, ... 98.
"Do you think *I* have no Trials?". 107
Winter Quarters, ... 110
A Blessing from Brigham, ... 115
Singing the Rallying Song, ... 120
The Journey to Zion. — Crossing the Plains, ... 121
Brigham Imitating the "Grecian Bend," 123
Anointing the Sick with Oil, ... 125
The Deseret Costume, ... 130
Brigham Refuses my Request, ... 133
The Ball in the Bowery, ... 137
The Dissatisfied Wife, ... 142
The Apostle Orson Pratt, "The Champion of Polygamy," 150
Joseph Young, Brother of Brigham, and President of the Seventies, 151

PAGE

Brigham's Brotherly Love, ... 153
Discouraging Apostasy, ... 160
Brigham Seizing Cattle for the Church, ... 163
Apostle Lorenzo Snow, ... 166
Apostle C. C. Rich, ... 166
Apostle A. Carrington, ... 166
Apostle Joseph F. Smith, ... 166
Apostle Erastus Snow, ... 166
Joseph A. Young Preparing for Missionary Work, ... 171
E. Hunter, Presiding Bishop Mormon Church, ... 172
Doing Missionary Work, ... 178
Awakening the Saints, ... 181
"Scene during Reformation," 185
Dealing with a Weak Brother, ... 191
Brutal Assault upon Mrs. Jarvis, ... 193
Blood Atonement. — Scene during Reformation, ... 198
The Emigrants' Landing-Place, "Castle Gardens, New York," . . . 200
Apostle Franklin D. Richards, "Husband of Ten Wives," 202
Mormon Emigrants on Shipboard, ... 205
The Hand-Cart Train, ... 210
"Some will Push, and some will Pull," 213
Relief in Sight, ... 215
Arrival of "Hand-Cart Companies" at Salt Lake City, ... 221
"Vengeance is Mine," 228
Parley P. Pratt, ... 235
Assassination of Parley P. Pratt, ... 237
John D. Lee (Has nineteen wives and sixty-four children), ... 238
The Murder of Two Little Girls, ... 241
Murdered by Lee's Own Hand, ... 245
Murdering the Women and Children, ... 247
The Mountain Meadows Massacre, ... 248
Scene after the Massacre, ... 249
Using up an Apostate, ... 262
Brigham's "Destroying Angel," "Port" Rockwell, ... 269
Murder of the Aiken Party, ... 272
Brigham Young's Farm-House, ... 277
Bill Hickman, Brigham's "Destroying Angel," 279
Brigham Wooing Widow Lewis, ... 284
Only a Wife out of the Way, ... 290
Life a Burden, ... 293
Bird's-Eye View of Salt Lake City, ... 295
The New Addition, ... 297
Scene in Polygamy. — Greeting the Favorite, ... 305
The Maniac Wife, ... 306
The Happy Home of a Polygamist, ... 313

PAGE

Broken-Hearted, ... 317
Orson Hyde and Forgotten Wife, ... 320
Apostle George Q. Cannon, Member of Congress (Has four Wives
    and thirteen Children), ... 322
Apostle Orson Hyde, ... 324
Brigham in a Quandary, ... 327
Apostle John Taylor (Husband of Six Wives), ... 330
Mormons Burning a Government Train, ... 333
A Good Deal of Wives. — Too much Attention, ... 339
Remains of Adobe Defences, ... 341
Mormons Selling Provisions to United States Troops, ... 343
Brigham's Folly, "The Prairie Schooner," 347
Taking my Endowments Behind the Curtain, ... 349
Mormon Baptism, ... 352
Mormon Confirmation, ... 354
The Endowment House, ... 356
The Devil of the Endowment House, ... 362
Apostle Willard Woodruff ("Timothy Broadbrim"), ... 364
Receiving the Endowments, ... 366
Apostle Heber C. Kimball, ... 371
My First Appearance in Brigham's Theatre, ... 373
My First Ride with Brigham, ... 376
Brigham's Theatre, ... 379
A Life of Unhappiness, ... 387
Family Jars, ... 398
My Baby Boy, ... 403
Strangled by my Husband, ... 407
"Grandma, what is Polygamy?" 412
No Peace with Polygamy, ... 415
Old Farm-House at Cottonwood, ... 422
Brigham on his Travels, ... 426
Brigham Preaching at South Cottonwood, ... 430
Breaking the News, ... 440
Chauncey G. Webb ("My Father"), ... 444
Eliza C. Webb ("My Mother"), ... 445
Brigham's Stormy Interview with my Mother, ... 452
Amelia tries to Keep Me Out, ... 455
Amelia's Display of Temper, ... 463
Insulted by her Father, ... 468
Joseph A. Young, ... 471
Maggie Young (Joseph A.'s Discarded Wife), ... 472
"Briggy" (The Prophet's Successor), ... 474
John W. Young, ... 477
Lucy Rebellious, ... 479
Kissing Libbie Good Night, ... 480

PAGE

Mrs. Alice Young Clawson (Brigham's Eldest Daughter), ... 482
Emmeline Serving Brigham and Amelia, ... 484
Clara Decker (Wife of Brigham), ... 486
The Lion House (Brigham Young's Residence), ... 490
The Lion House and Brigham's Offices, ... 493
Brigham Looks Amazed, ... 497
Amelia Folsom (Brigham's Favorite Wife), ... 498
Miss Eliza R. Snow (Mormon Poetess), ... 501
Zina D. Huntington (Wife of Brigham), ... 502
Zina Williams (Brigham's Daughter), ... 503
A Little Conversation with Brigham, ... 506
Waiting for Brigham to Keep his Promise, ... 509
The Disgraced Wife, ... 515
Dinner at the Lion House, ... 517
Brigham Young (Full Page Portrait), ... 520
Mormon Temple (now Building), ... 523
Interior of Tabernacle on Sundays, ... 524
Family Prayers at Bee Hive House, ... 529
Toiling for Brigham, ... 532
Relating my Story to Mr. and Mrs. Stratton, ... 540
Alone at the Hotel, ... 542
Carrying my Furniture to the Auction Room, ... 546
Excitement in Salt Lake City, ... 548
Brigham Fined and Imprisoned for Contempt of Court, ... 553
Flight at Night, ... 566
Escape from Salt Lake City, ... 570
View of Salt Lake City, showing Tabernacle, ... 571
The Co-operative Store, ... 577
George A. Smith, First Counsellor, ... 578
Daniel H. Wells, Second Counsellor, ... 579
The Old Mormon Tabernacle, ... 580
Mormon Tithing Store, and Office of Deseret News, ... 585
View of Brigham's Canal, ... 587
Polygamy in High and Low Life, ... 589
Driven from Home, ... 594
Receiving my Friends at the Walker House, ... 598
Reception at Salt Lake City, ... 599
"Not Afraid of the Poland Bill," 603

CHAPTER I.

THE DAYS OF MY CHILDHOOD. — WHY I EVER WAS A MORMON.

An Important Question. — Born in Mormonism. — Telling my own Story. — Joseph Smith's Mission. — He Preaches a New Dispensation. — My Parents Introduced to the Reader. — The Days before Polygamy. — My Mother's Childhood. — Learning under Difficulties. — First Thoughts of Mormonism. — Received into the Church. — Persecution for the Faith. — Forsaking All for the New Religion. — First Acquaintance with the Apostle Brigham. — His Ambitious Intrigues. — His Poverty. — His Mission-work. — Deceptive Appearances. — My Mother's Marriage. — A Brief Dream of Happiness. — That sweet word "Home." — The Prophet Smith turns Banker. — The "Kirtland Safety Society Bank." — The Prophet and Sidney Rigdon Flee. — A Moment of Hesitation. — Another "Zion" Appointed. — Losing All for the Church. — Privation and Distress. — Sidney Rigdon and his "Declaration of Independence." — He Excites an Immense Sensation. — Mobs Assemble, and Fights Ensue. — Lively Times among the Saints. — The Outrages of the Danites.

TURNED OUT OF DOORS.

URING the somewhat public career which I have led since my apostasy from the Mormon Church, I have often been asked why I ever became a Mormon. Indeed, I have scarcely entered a town where this question has not been put by some one, almost on the instant of my arrival. It is the first query of the newspaper reporter, and the anxious inquiry of the clergymen, who with one accord, without regard to creed or sect, have bid-

den me welcome into the light of Christian faith, from out
the dark bondage of fanaticism and bigotry; and I have
often answered it at the hospitable table of some enter-
tainer, who has kindly given me shelter during a lecture
engagement.

Curiosity, interest, desire to gratify a wondering public
by some personal items concerning me, are the different
motives which prompt the question; but surprise is almost
without exception betrayed when I tell them that I was born
in the faith. Sometimes I think that the people of the outside world consider it impossible that a person can be born
in Mormonism; they regard every Mormon as a deluded
proselyte to a false faith.

It is with a desire to impress upon the world what Mormonism really is; to show the pitiable condition of its women, held in a system of bondage that is more cruel than
African slavery ever was, since it claims to hold body and
soul alike; to arouse compassion for its children and youth,
born and growing up in an atmosphere of social impurity;
and, above all, to awaken an interest in the hearts of the
American people that shall at length deepen into indignation, — that I venture to undertake the task of writing this
book. I have consecrated myself to the work, not merely
for my own sake, but for the sake of all the unhappy women of Utah, who, unlike myself, are either too powerless
or too timid to break the fetters which bind them.

I intend to give a truthful picture of Mormon life; to veil
nothing which should be revealed, even though the recital
should be painful to me at times, coming so close, as it necessarily must, to my inmost life, awakening memories which
I would fain permit to remain slumbering, and opening old
wounds which I had fondly hoped were healed. Neither
shall I intentionally tinge any occurrence with the slightest
coloring of romance; the real is so vivid and so strange
that I need have no recourse to the imaginary.

All the events which I shall relate will be some of my

own personal experiences, or the experience of those so closely connected with me that they have fallen directly under my observation, and for whose truth I can vouch without hesitation.   To tell the story as it ought to be told, I must begin at the very beginning of my life; for I have always been so closely connected with these people that I could not easily take up the narrative at any intermediate point.

I was born at Nauvoo, Illinois, on the 13th of September, 1844, and was the youngest child and only surviving daughter of a family of five children.

My father and mother were most devout Mormons, and were among the very earliest of Joseph Smith's converts. They have, indeed, been closely identified with the Church of the Latter-Day Saints almost from its first establishment.   They have followed it in all its wanderings, have been identified with its every movement, and their fortunes have risen or fallen as the Church has been prosperous or distressed.   They were enthusiastic adherents of Joseph Smith, and devoted personal friends of Brigham Young, until he, by his own treacherous acts, betrayed their friendship, and himself broke every link that had united them to him, even that of religious sympathy, which among this people is the most difficult to sunder.

My father, Chauncey G. Webb, was born in 1812, in Hanover, Chatauqua County, N. Y.   He first heard the Mormon doctrine preached in 1833, only a very short time after Joseph Smith had given the Book of Mormon to the world, and had announced himself as another Messiah, chosen by "the Lord" to restore true religion to the world, to whom also had been revealed all the glories of "the kingdom" that should yet be established on the earth, and over which he was to be, by command from the Lord, both temporal and spiritual ruler.

They — the old folks — embraced the new faith immediately, and prepared for removal to Kirtland, Ohio, which

3

was to be the nucleus of the new church, the "Zion" given by revelation to Joseph Smith as the gathering-place of the Saints. They were naturally anxious to gather all their children into the fold, and they urged my father, with tearful, prayerful entreaties, to accompany them to the city of refuge prepared for the faithful followers of the Lord and His prophet Smith.

Like many young people, he had at that time but little sympathy with religion He had given but very little thought to the peculiar beliefs of the different churches. This world held so much of interest to him, that he had considered but very little the mysteries of the future, and the world to come. Of a practical, and even to some extent sceptical turn of mind, he was inclined to take things as they came to him, and was not easily influenced by the marvellous or supernatural. If left to himself, he might, probably, never have embraced Mormonism ; but he yielded to the entreaties of his parents, and joined the Mormon Church more as an expression of filial regard than of deep religious conviction. The Saints were at that time an humble, spiritual-minded, God-fearing, law-abiding people, holding their new belief with sincerity and enthusiasm, and proving their position, to their own satisfaction at least, from the Bible. They had not then developed the spirit of intolerance which has since characterized them, and though they were touched with religious fanaticism, they were honest in their very bigotry. The Mormon Church, in its earliest days, cannot be fairly judged by the Mormon Church of the present time, which retains none of its early simplicity, and which seems to have lost sight entirely of the fundamental principles on which it was built. My father, although not entering fully into the spirit of his new religion at that early period of his saintly experience, yet found nothing of the insincerity which he claimed to have met in other beliefs ; and having embraced the new faith, he was prepared to hold to it, and to cast his lot with it. So he went with his parents to Kirtland, in 1834, where he found the first romance of his life in the person of Eliza Churchill, my mother, then a young girl of seventeen, just blossoming into fairest womanhood.

Never was there a greater mental or spiritual contrast between two persons. My mother was a religious enthusiast, almost a mystic. She believed implicitly in personal revelation, and never doubted but that the Mormon faith came directly from "the Lord." She "saw visions and dreamed dreams," and at times it would have taken but little persuasion to have made her believe herself inspired. It was a religious nature like hers, dreamy, devoted, and mystical, that, in other conditions and amid other surroundings, had given to France a Joan of Arc. It must have been the attraction of opposite natures that brought together in so close a relationship the practical, shrewd, somewhat sceptical man, and the devoted, enthusiastic, religious girl. It was probably the very contrast that made the young man feel such tenderness and care for the homeless orphan girl, and made her cling to him, trusting her helplessness to his strength.

Her early life had by no means been so sheltered as his, and to her the thought of tender care and protecting watchfulness, through all the rest of her days, was unutterably sweet and restful. If her dream could only have been realized! But polygamy cursed her life, as it has that of every Mormon woman, and shattered her hopes before she had but a taste of their realization.

She was born at Union Springs, Cayuga County, N. Y., on the 4th of May, 1817, but only lived there until she was two years old, when her parents removed to Livingston County, in the same state. When she was four years old her mother died, leaving three little children, the youngest a mere baby. Her father, finding it impossible to obtain any one to take care of the three as they should be cared for, was obliged, much against his will, to separate them, and put them in the charge of different persons, until such time as he was in a situation to make a home for them together. But that was destined never to be, and these children were never reunited, although they have never lost sight of one another; and to this day the hearts of the Gentile and Mormon sisters yearn towards each other, and the more fortunate one suffers in sympathy with her sister's sufferings.

My mother was given into the care of a family of the name of Brown, with whom she staid twelve years. Her life with them was rendered most unhappy by the treatment which she received, and from lack of sympathy. Ambitious, and craving knowledge most ardently, she was denied all means of procuring a proper education, and was reduced to the position of a mere drudge. But her perceptions were keen, her memory retentive, and in spite of all drawbacks she managed to learn something; enough, indeed, to lay the foundation for the knowledge which she afterwards acquired, and which stood her in good stead as a means of support for herself and her children, after the arrival of the Saints in Utah. Whatever came in her way in the shape of reading-matter she eagerly devoured, whether it was the torn bit of an old newspaper, the inevitable "Farmer's Almanac," or some odd volume of history, biography, or fiction, which had found its way mysteriously to the New York farm-house of other days; but above all, the Bible and Methodist hymn-books. These she had read and re-read until she could repeat large portions of them from memory. Wesley's beautiful hymns, with their earnest, fervid tone, were her special favorites among these religious songs, and her young heart glowed as she listened to the poetic inspirations of Isaiah and those other prophecies, which she believed, although she could not understand.

When she was fifteen years of age, she united with the Methodist Church; and it was while she was in the first

flush of her religious experience that the Mormon missionaries came to Avon, the town in which she lived,
preaching their new doctrines.   My mother had very naturally a great deal of curiosity concerning this new religion, which was railed at as a delusion, and its prophet
and founder, Joseph Smith, who was called a hypocrite, a
false teacher, a blasphemer, and every other opprobrious
name that could be heaped upon him, in the bitterness of
religious persecution.   But she was forbidden to attend
their meetings, and it was many months before she was
able to listen to one of the sermons.   During this time she
had grown somewhat into sympathy with these people, and
had come to feel an interest in them greater than she
would have felt had she not met with such persistent, and,
what seemed to her, unreasonable opposition to her often
expressed wish to hear them and judge of their sincerity
and truth for herself.

PREACHING THE NEW RELIGION.

After a time, however, she found an opportunity of attending a two days' meeting, without the knowledge of her
friends ; and she listened eagerly to Joseph Young as he
expounded the new doctrine and dwelt upon the glories
of the "kingdom" which was to be speedily set up upon
the earth.   Predisposed as she already was in its favor, it

is not strange that she was readily convinced of its divine origin, and accepted it at once as the true religion. Before the meeting was over, she was numbered among Elder Joseph Young's converts, and was received into the Mormon Church, being baptized by the apostolic hands of his brother Brigham.

When it became known that she had become a convert to the obnoxious faith, she was the object of bitter persecution. The family with whom she lived were especially intolerant, and in their anger resorted to every expedient to force her to give up her new faith. They confined her in a cellar for several days, kept her upon bread and water, and subjected her to other severities of a like nature. All this opposition did not move her one particle. She remained firm in her chosen faith, and was steadfast and true to her convictions of right. All this severity of treatment she rather gloried in. Was it not worth while to suffer persecution, and be treated with contumely and contempt, for the sake of the church that had been specially called by the Lord to "build up the waste places of Zion"? Would not her reward be the greater by and by? So filled was she with the new enthusiasm that nothing had power even to render her unhappy; as she says, she triumphed in persecution and rejoiced in suffering.

When her persecutors found that neither arguments nor threats could move her, they turned her out of doors, considering that they were doing only their duty, since it would be a sin to harbor a Mormon. The thought of her extreme youth and her unprotected situation did not move them in the slightest degree. Their doors were shut against her, as their hearts had always been.

Instinctively she turned towards the people with whom she had so lately connected herself, and for whose sake she had left home and friends; they received her kindly and hospitably, and she went with them to Kirtland, where my father found her when he arrived a few months later.

It was at this time that the friendship began between my mother and Brigham Young, which lasted so many years — a faithful friendship on her part, met, as a matter of course, by unkindness and treachery on his side. At that time he was young and zealous, and seemingly sincere. He was one of the most successful of the early Mormon missionaries, and was considered specially gifted. He was an ardent supporter and personal friend of Joseph Smith, and young as he was, had attained a high position in the Church of the Saints, being the second of the twelve apostles, all of whom were chosen by the Prophet Smith himself.

Some have considered that his zeal was assumed, and that beyond the ambition of attaining a high position he had no personal regard for Mormonism. It is believed by many of the old Mormons that he always entertained the hope of becoming Joseph's successor, and standing at the head of the church. He has no natural religious nature; indeed, he is at times a positive sceptic. He has made the church a stepping-stone to temporal prosperity, and the Mormon people have been the pliant tools with which he has carved his fortune.

In those days he was struggling with poverty, going on missions, as the apostles of old were commanded to do, and as all these new apostles did, in their first days of apostleship, "without purse or scrip;" and to my mother the "Apostle" Brigham was invested with all the attributes which belong to an earnest nature, intensified by deep religious faith. In short, he was, as she regarded him, a creature of her imagination, and utterly unlike his real self as she came at length to know him.

The year following my father's arrival in Kirtland, and his first meeting with my mother, they were married. The first few months of their married life were peculiarly happy, and they prospered beyond their most sanguine expectations. My father was a wheelwright by trade, and directly on reaching Kirtland built a wagon manufactory, and started in business for himself. He was eminently successful in his undertaking, and made money sufficiently fast to suit his own ideas and ambitions. He built a cosy little house, and carried my mother to it; and there, for the first time since she was a little child, she knew what it was to have a home — a genuine home! not a mere resting-place, where she felt herself an intruder, but a place in which she was mistress, over which love and she held absolute and undisputed sway.

It was during that happy period, the only happy time in her whole life, that she fitted herself to teach. She was an indefatigable student, and she made the most and the best of her time. At that time she studied to satisfy her intense craving for knowledge, and as a pleasant recreation, with no thought that she might some day have to turn her studies to practical account. She had not then been introduced to the doctrine of "plural wives," and its attendant "glories," which, being defined, meant miseries and torture. And the definition has never been altered, and never will be, until women's natures are most radically changed.

JOSEPH SMITH, THE FOUNDER OF MORMONISM.

As I said before, my father was prospering in worldly affairs, and when it was "revealed" to Joseph Smith that in addition to the profession of "Prophet," he should add that of banker, he assisted Smith in founding the "Kirtland Safety Society Bank," by promising to deposit all his money therein; in short, giving Smith all that he possessed outside of his house and shop towards completing the amount necessary for a capital on which to start the new enterprise. When the

bank failed, which it did very shortly after its establishment, my father, of course, lost every cent which he
had invested. He was intensely disgusted with the whole
proceeding, which, if it had happened in the Gentile
world, would have been termed swindling, and Smith
would not have been easily let off by the mere calling of
names. Many Gentiles, who had suffered by the failure,
were not so lenient as Smith's followers, and demanded
that the Prophet should answer to the complaint of swindling before the United States court. But, as usual, he
eluded the officers of justice, and all attempts to arrest him
were unavailing.

The poor Saints, although losing, many of them, all
their hard-earned savings, were still loyal to their leader,
and excused him on the ground that " he had lost the Spirit "
for the time, and the revelation was not of divine origin;
although he was unconscious of that fact, and received it
in good faith. My father, however, not so ready to excuse
what seemed to him an act of premeditated dishonesty, and
having very little faith in "revelation" at any time, was
very bitter in his denunciations ; and it was only by my mother's influence, who still clung fondly to her faith, that he
did not then renounce Mormonism. Although she has
never openly acknowledged it, I think that my mother has
since often regretted her steadfast adherence to the church
at that time. Her loyalty and persistence brought upon her
the unhappiness of her life, and finally plunged her into
such utter misery as only polygamous wives can experience. Her religion, that was to be so much to her, brought
her not one ray of comfort, but in after years blighted her
domestic life, and laid upon her a cross almost too heavy
to be borne. But I must do her the justice to say, that
through it all she has never complained, but has endured
her sufferings in silence, and met her woes with patience.

This unfortunate revelation of the Prophet's, together with
other somewhat questionable business transactions, and the

consequent growing prejudice of the people of Ohio against
him and his followers, made it necessary for the Saints to
seek some other place, where they might build their "Zion."
It was certain that the Lord did not favor Ohio; and about
that time he "revealed" to Joseph that the place he had
selected in which to establish His temporal kingdom was
Missouri. This was to be the Mormon Canaan, the land
which they — the chosen people of the Lord — should enter
and possess. To be sure, He had revealed the very same
thing concerning Kirtland; it was there that he declared
"He had established His name for the salvation of the nations." But according to the Prophet's later explanation,
Satan was striving to break up the kingdom, and the spirit
of "apostate mobocracy" raged and grew hotter, until
Smith and his confederate, Sidney Rigdon, were obliged
"to flee from its deadly influence, as did the apostles and
prophets of old;" and "as Jesus had commanded his followers, when persecuted in one city, to flee to another," so
these two worthies left the "chosen city of the Lord" most
unceremoniously, under cover of darkness, pursued by officers of the law, and never returned to it again. But from
Missouri Smith sent messages and exhortations to those of
the Saints who still remained faithful, "to gather quickly
to Zion."

Very many members of the church apostatized at that
time, and the numbers of the faithful "chosen" were decidedly lessened. Among those who remained unshaken was
my mother, who in her almost fanatical blindness, accepted
the Prophet's explanations, and was still willing to be led
by his revelations. My father was held by his affection for
her rather than by any conviction of the "divine leading"
of Smith, whom, indeed, he distrusted almost entirely; and it
was in compliance with my mother's ardent wish to follow
her prophet, and to establish herself and family in Zion
amidst the Saints, that my father finally decided to emigrate with the remnant of the church to Missouri.

He settled in Daviess County, about thirty miles from Far-West, where the body of the Saints were located, and was again tasting the sweets of prosperity and domestic comfort, when the Missouri war broke out, and he was obliged to remove his family, in the greatest haste, to Far-West for their safety, leaving house and property to be confiscated by an angry mob.

This was the second time, since casting his lot with the Saints, that all my father's possessions had been suddenly swept away, and this last would have discourged him sadly had it not made him so indignant to see the injustice which was shown by Gentiles to the Mormons; and he assisted in guarding the lives of the Mormon people, and the remant of property which was left to them, until such time as they could find another home.

During this time my mother's sufferings were intense. Many of the houses had been burned by mobs, and she, and many other women in as severe straits as herself, were compelled to live as best they could, exposed to the wind and rain, and without any proper shelter, during almost the entire winter, with two little children, one a baby only a few months old, the other about two years old. In addition to all the discomforts of the situation, she was always in constant terror of an attack by the infuriated mobs, who were waging a genuine war of extermination with the suffering Saints. As is always the case with a religious war, the feeling was intensely bitter. The Gentiles had no charity for the Mormons, and would neither tolerate their faith nor them. The Mormons returned the hatred of the Gentiles with interest, and considering themselves the chosen of the Lord, selected by Him to the exclusion of all the rest of the world, of course argued that whatever they did could by no possibility be wrong, and they returned their ill-treatment with interest.

Although there had been, always, a strong prejudice against the Mormons in Missouri, as in other states where they had lived, it was not until after Sidney Rigdon made his famous incendiary speech, at the commencement of the foundation of the new Temple at Far-West, on the 4th of July, 1838, that the feeling broke into anything like aggressive hostilities.

Rigdon had embraced Mormonism in 1830, and had been ever since that time an ardent Saint. He was a Campbellite preacher in Ohio at the time of his conversion, which was accomplished under the teachings of Parley P. Pratt, a man who played quite an important part in the early Mormon history. Rigdon was a very fluent speaker, much revered by the Saints on account of his eloquence, which, it must be confessed, was decidedly of the "buncombe" order. For a long time he was the intimate friend and chief counsellor of Joseph Smith, was connected with him in the Kirtland Bank swindle, and escaped with him to Missouri.

It had been revealed to the Prophet Smith that another temple must be built to the Lord in the new Zion, since the one at Kirtland had been desecrated by falling into Gentile hands, and Rigdon was chosen to make the speech on the occasion of laying the first foundation-stone of this sacred edifice.

The "Champion of Liberty," as Rigdon was called by his admirers, was more bombastic and more denunciatory than usual. He surpassed himself in invective, and maddened the already prejudiced Missourians, who were only waiting for some excuse to quarrel with their unwelcome neighbors. Among other absurd things, he said:

"We take God and all the holy angels to witness, that we warn all men to come on us no more for ever. The man or set of men that attempts it, does so at the expense of their lives. The mob that comes to disturb us we will follow until the last drop of their blood is spilled, or else they will have to exterminate us. We will carry the war into their own homes and families. No man shall come into our streets to threaten us with mobs; if he does, he shall atone for it before he leaves the place. We this day proclaim ourselves free, with a purpose and determination that can never be broken. No, never! No, never!! No, never!!!"

This speech fired the excitable nature of the Saints, and they were aroused to a high pitch of warlike enthusiasm. Already, in imagination, they saw Missouri conquered, and the church in possession of the entire state. There could be no doubt of the final result, for this was the Promised Land into which they had been led by the hand of the Lord.

With the superstition which characterizes this people, they turned every accident or occurrence into some sign from Heaven, and it was always interpreted to promise success to them and confusion to their enemies. On this day of celebration the Mormons had erected a liberty-pole in honor of the occasion; in the afternoon it was struck by lightning, shivered to atoms, and fell, its flag trailing in the dust. There was rejoicing among the Mormons; that was certainly an omen of the speedy downfall of their enemies. It seems now as though — if it must be considered an omen of anything — that it was prophetic of the uprooting and scattering of this people, so soon was it followed by their expulsion from the state.

The feeling of bitterness between the two contending factions grew more intense daily, and each party was eagerly watching for some acts of violence from the other. The next month, at the election, the war commenced in earnest. A man named William Peniston was candidate for the legislature. The Mormons objected to him on the ground that he had headed a mob against them in Clay County. The Missourians, aware of this objection, endeavored to prevent the Mormons from voting, and a fight ensued, in which the latter proclaimed themselves victorious. Gallatin, the court town of Daviess County, was soon after burned by the Mormons. Then commenced robbing, plundering, and outrages of every kind by both parties. It was a season of the wildest confusion, and both sides were blinded with passion, and lost sight of reason, toleration, and, above all, Christian forbearance. It was a positive reign of terror. Houses, barns, and haystacks were burned, men shot, and all manner of depredations committed.

THE NIGHT OF TERROR.

It is impossible for me to say which party was the principal aggressor; probably there was equal blame on both sides; but I have been informed that Joseph taught his followers that it was right, and " commanded of the Lord," for them to take anything they could find which belonged to their enemies, in retaliation for the wrongs which they had suffered at their hands. I can the more easily believe this to be true, because the spirit of the Mormon Church has always been that of retaliation. The stern old Mosaic law, "An eye for an eye, and a tooth for a tooth," is in full force among them, and is not only advised by the leaders, but insisted upon by them. Indeed, they have added to its severity, until now it stands, "A life for an offence, real or suspected, of any kind." In support of this they refer to the Israelites "borrowing" jewelry from the Egyptians before they took their flight from Egypt; and they quote, "The earth is the Lord's, and the fulness thereof;" and as they claim to be the Lord's particularly favored children, — in fact, his only acknowledged ones, — they seem to consider this text peculiarly applicable to the situation, and all the excuse they need to give for any irregularities in the way of appropriating other people's property. They are merely coming into their inheritance.

At all events, the people were not slow to obey the command of the Lord and the counsel of Joseph, and they displayed their spirit of obedience by laying hold of every kind of property which came within their reach. In the midst of these troubles, Joseph came out to Daviess County to a town called "*Adam-ondi-Ahman*," named, of course, by revelation, and meaning, when translated, "The valley of God in which Adam blessed his children;" said to be the identical spot where Adam and Eve first sought refuge after their expulsion from Eden. Upon his arrival, he called the people together, and harangued them after this mild and conciliatory fashion : "Go ahead! Do all you can to harass the enemy. I never felt more of the spirit of God at any time than since we commenced this stealing and house-burning." My parents were living at Adam-ondi-Ahman at that time, and were present when Joseph delivered this peculiarly saint-like address.

About this time the Danite bands were first organized, for the purpose of plundering and harassing the people of the surrounding country. I have been told this by a person who heard the oaths administered at a meeting of the band in Daviess County. They were instructed to go out on the borders of the Settlements, and take the spoils from the "ungodly Gentiles;" for was it not written, "The riches of the Gentiles shall be consecrated to the people of the house of Israel?"

Joseph Smith always denied that he had in any way authorized the formation of the Danite bands; and, in fact, in public he repeatedly repudiated both them and their deeds of violence. At the time of which I speak, however, Thomas B. Marsh, who was then the president of the "twelve apostles," together with Orson Hyde, who now occupies that post, apostatized. Both subsequently returned to the bosom of the church, making the most abject submission. Poor Marsh died, crushed and broken-hearted. Hyde's heart was of tougher composition, and he still lives; but Brigham will never forget or forgive his apostasy.

While both Marsh and Hyde were separated from the church, they made solemn affidavits against Joseph and the Mormons in general, accusing them of the grossest crimes and outrages, as well as of abetting the Danites and their deeds. The cowardly Apostles afterwards declared that these affidavits were made under the influence of fear. That is very probable, but at the same time there can be no real doubt that there was a larger amount of truth in what they affirmed than jealous Mormons would be disposed to admit.

The outrages committed by these Danites, and others like them, caused the expulsion of the Saints from Missouri. Joseph and about fifty of his followers were taken prisoners, and between his arrest and imprisonment, and the final exodus from the state, there was great suffering among the Mormon people.

CHAPTER II.

FOUNDING THE NEW RELIGION. — ASSASSINATION OF JOSEPH SMITH.

The Saints expelled from Missouri. — They cross the Mississippi into Illinois. — Forming a New Settlement. — Arrival i. Quincy. —A Kind Reception. — The City of "Nauvoo" Founded. — A New Temple Begun. — Great Success of the Foreign Missions. — The Saints flock from Europe. — Thousands assemble in Nauvoo. — The Prophet Joseph applies for a City Charter. — Nauvoo Incorporated. — The Saints Petition the National Government. — The Prophet visits Washington. — His Interview with President Van Buren. — He coquets with Politics. — He Stands on the Edge of the Precipice. — The Saints in Danger. — The Prophet Smith Nominated for President. — He tries to find the "Golden Way." — Mormon Missionaries preach Politics. —The Prophet looks towards the Pacific Coast. — The Blind Obedience of the Saints. — The Real Devotion of their Faith. — Gentile Opinions. — How Boggs was shot in the Head. — The Spiritual Wife-Doctrine. — Dr. William Law Protests. — Terrible Charges against the Prophet. — The "*Nauvoo Expositor.*" — The Prophet Surrenders. — He is Murdered in Jail.

NAUVOO TEMPLE.

AFTER this, crime succeeded crime, and the state of affairs grew worse daily. The Mormons were getting decidedly the worst of the warfare, and their opponents showed them no mercy. At the massacre at Haun's Mills, for instance, men, women, and children were shot down in cold blood by a company of the Missouri militia, the houses plundered and burned, and the clothing even stripped from the dead bodies.

There had been inhuman murders in other places, men

and women alike falling victims to the fury of the mobs;
there had been a battle fought at Crooked River, and several skirmishes between the Mormons and Missourians,
exaggerated reports of which had spread through the country like wildfire. The whole state was in arms against the
Mormons. The governor issued an order of expulsion,
thinking it the surest way to quell the disturbance, which
had almost grown beyond him, and gave the Saints three
months in which to leave the state. Every Mormon was
to be out of the state at the end of that time, except those
who were in prison. Of them the governor said, " Their
fate is fixed; the die is cast; their doom is sealed."

As on the occasion of the removal from Ohio, there was
considerable apostasy in the church. Many persons grew
discouraged, and their faith wavered. In following Smith
they had been led from difficulty into danger, had suffered
persecution and poverty, and were now driven from their
homes to seek refuge in some more hospitable spot. Every
man's hand seemed turned against them, and they had
grown tired of perpetual warfare. If God had ever called,
He had surely deserted them now, and there was no use in
their longer undergoing trial and suffering.

Those who remained firm were still strong in the faith;
stronger, if possible, than ever. Joseph was their Prophet,
and they clung to him and his revelations with unshaken
confidence. "Blessed are they who are persecuted for
righteousness' sake," was a favorite and comforting quota-
tion at that time. They were cheered by frequent letters
from Joseph, written in prison, as they journeyed towards
Illinois, which was the next point towards which they turned
their feet, already weary with wandering. On receiving
the order of expulsion, the Saints pledged themselves never
to cease their exertions until every one of their faith was
out of the state; and to accomplish this within the time
required, they worked unceasingly, through sickness, poverty, and privation.

My mother has often described to me this enforced journey. She was always deeply moved, and never spoke of
it that the hot tears did not rush to her eyes, and her voice
quiver with indignation. The journey was taken in the
dead of winter. Many of the women and children were
already ill from exposure, yet they were obliged to leave
the state with the rest; and although everything was done
for their comfort that could well be done, yet their sufferings were most intense. They were robbed of their horses,
and were obliged to make their escape with ox-teams, crossing those twenty-mile prairies, facing cold, wintry winds
without even a cover to the wagons. My mother held her
two infants close in her arms during all the long, tedious
journey, to keep them from perishing. She had but one
dress to wear, as she had to leave Daviess County in great
haste, taking only her children with her; and on her arrival
in Illinois she was entirely destitute, her clothing being literally torn in pieces. In the spring of 1839 all were safely
landed across the Mississippi River, where they were joined
in April, soon after their arrival, by Joseph and his fellow-
prisoners, who had "miraculously," as Joseph said, made
their escape from their enemies.

The joy of the Saints was very great at his arrival. The
waning courage was restored, wavering faith was strengthened, and they were all ready to enter the next scheme
which his prophetic soul should propose, and to follow
blindly and unquestioningly the next "revelation."

The feeling of the Mormon people towards the Missourians is very bitter to this day, and they have never lost an
opportunity in all these years of injuring them whenever it
became possible. The memory of the indignities heaped
upon them, and the sufferings to which they were subjected,
is still most vivid. Even my mother, notwithstanding the
fact of her having apostatized, and having now no interest
or faith in the Mormon Church, can never forgive the Missourians. She says, "If the Mormons were the greatest

fanatics on the earth, the Missourians cannot be justified in
the course which they pursued.   There is no doubt they
were exasperated by the actions of the Mormons, and suffered loss of property, and even life, at the hands of the
Danite bands ; but they need not, in the cruel spirit of revenge, punish the innocent women and children, for it was
on these that the blow fell the hardest.   It was they, who
had no part in bringing on the trouble, who were to suffer
in retribution for the misdeeds of others."

Notwithstanding all that had taken place in Missouri,
some of the more enthusiastic Saints believed that it was the
promised land, and that some time they should come in and
possess it.   Indeed, that belief has prevailed among some
of the older Mormons until within a very short time.   Brigham has preached it and promised it; but now he says very
little about it, and when he does he is wise to add, " if the
Lord shall will it so."   The present indications are, that the
Lord will not " will it so," and all the Saints have content-
edly accepted Utah as " Zion," in the face of " revelation."

In giving, thus briefly, a sketch of the " Missouri war," I
tell the story as I have always heard it, since I was a child,
from my parents, who were in the midst of it, and who
were rendered homeless and poor by it.   Although always
hearing it from the Mormon side, I must, to do the narra-
tors justice, say they have never attempted to hide any part
of the provocation which the Saints gave ; and they now
hold Joseph responsible for it, by his, to say the least, unwise
teachings.

It is not very long since I was talking with a person who
was with the Mormons in Missouri and Illinois.   He said
that Joseph not only advised his people publicly to plunder
from the Gentiles, but privately ordered them to do so.   At
one time he was himself sent by the Prophet to steal lumber for coffins.   He went with a party of men down the
river, loaded a raft with lumber from a Gentile saw-mill,
and brought it up to the " City of the Saints."   Another man,

now a bishop in the Mormon Church, told my mother that
he was deputed by Joseph to go and take some cattle, and
drive them to the city. As he was entering the town on
his return from his successful marauding trip, he was called
into a house, where there were sick persons, to anoint and
pray for them in connection with another elder. On meeting this elder afterwards, he remarked, "I have often wondered that the Lord listened to our prayers in behalf of the
sick under such circumstances. The elder replied, quietly,
"*I* had not been stealing."

Had such teachings been given by the Gentiles, and followed by their people, it would have been sin. But with the
Mormons it was always "the will of the Lord," and in His
name they committed the crimes that produced disaster and
disgrace among the people of Missouri, and finally resulted
in their own expulsion from that state. Thus it was that
at length we find them driven out by violence from among
a people who at first had received them with the utmost
friendliness, and forced to seek refuge on the farther shore
of the Mississippi, despite the promise which Joseph had so
often given them, "in the name of the Lord," that Missouri
should be the abiding-place of the Saints.

Joseph, however, still continued to assert that the Saints
"should return again and build up the waste places of
Zion," and pointed out Missouri as the spot which was to
be the "central stake" from which he was eventually to
rule all America; but the fact remained that the people
must have homes until such good time as they might be
allowed to "come again to their own."

They had landed at Quincy, Illinois, and had been very
kindly received by the residents. On their arrival they at
once commenced searching for a place to settle, and build
another "stake;" and the place finally selected by the
Prophet was situated on the Mississippi River, about forty
miles from Quincy. It was first called Commerce; but this
name being considered altogether too matter-of-fact and

practical, it was named, by inspiration, NAUVOO, which, being translated from the " Reformed Egyptian, " — the language in which all revelations were first given, — means " The Beautiful."

The new city grew rapidly ; another Temple was commenced by command of the Lord, and the people were adjured not to cease work upon it until it was finished ; all the Saints were commanded to gather there as soon as it was practicable. Missionaries were sent to Europe, and converts flocked from thence to Zion. Never were missions crowned with greater success than those that were established in Europe by the Mormon Church. The elders went first to England, from there to Norway, Sweden, Denmark, Switzerland, France, and they even attempted Italy, but with so little success that the mission there was speedily abandoned. Indeed, the southern countries of Europe did not seem to have taken kindly to the new doctrine of the Saints, and evinced but slight interest in the establishment of a " spiritual kingdom on the earth," and paid no heed whatever to Joseph's revelations. But hundreds of converts were made among the English and Scandinavian people, and they all evinced a strong desire to " gather to Zion," and considered no sacrifice too great to be made to facilitate their emigration. Most of them were from the poorer classes, but some among them were persons of considerable wealth, and many were from the comfortable middle class of farmers and trades people.

The people of Illinois were inclined to be very friendly with the Mormon people, and to make up by sympathy and kindness for the treatment which the Saints had received in Missouri. But, as has invariably been the case, the Mormons, by their own acts, managed to turn these friends into enemies, and to embroil themselves in more quarrels.

The people in the surrounding towns found them troublesome, and most undesirable neighbors ; for in spite of their kindly reception, Joseph did not cease his injunctions to "get all you can from the wicked Gentiles," and the consequence was perpetual trouble and constant complaint.

Early on his arrival at Nauvoo, Joseph applied to the Illinois legislature for a city charter, which was granted at once. This charter was extremely liberal, and by its ambiguous wording deceived the legislature, they considering it straightforward and honorable, while really it gave Joseph unlimited power in the government of the city, without regard to state or national laws, and rendered it impossible that he could be held prisoner, even if arrested. He had the right to release himself: the charter provided for that.

Before the establishment of the city it was "revealed" to Joseph that his people must importune at the feet of all in authority for a redress of their wrongs in Missouri. They commenced with the justices of the peace; from them they went to the state officers; finally to the President himself. They prepared very carefully, and, as far as possible, very accurately, a statement of the losses of the Saints in Missouri, and Joseph Smith, Sidney Rigdon, and Elias Higbee went to Washington with it, to endeavor to seek redress through the agency of Congress.

Martin Van Buren, who was President at that time, received them with that peculiar suavity of manner for which he was specially noted, that impressiveness which expressed so much and meant so little, and listened to them with the most courteous patience. But his answer was: "Gentlemen, your cause is just, but I can do nothing for you." The party returned to Nauvoo disappointed, but in no wise discouraged, and exceedingly indignant with the government and the entire American people, whom they considered their enemies from that moment. From the lowest officer to the highest, they considered that they had failed to meet with the slightest sympathy, and there was no desire shown to make any amends to these people. Joseph and the elders indulged in more incendiary talk than ever; but this was now devoted entirely against the government.

"In the name of the Lord God of Israel," prophesied
Joseph, "unless the United States redress the wrongs committed upon the Saints in Missouri, in a few years the government will be entirely overthrown." And again : "They
all turned a deaf ear to our entreaties, and now the Lord
will come out in swift fury and vex the nation."

The troubles in Illinois culminated, as they had in Missouri, in political difficulties. The people of Illinois were
growing exceedingly tired of their new citizens, whom they
had welcomed so warmly, since their kindness had been
returned with so much ingratitude by the Mormons ; but
the political leaders of the state endeavored to curry favor
with Joseph, and obtain his influence, since it had been discovered that the Mormon vote was solid. Whigs and Dem-
ocrats had each tried to secure them, but Smith had his
own purpose to serve, and he used either Whigs or Demo-
crats as best suited him. Neither party could rely on him
or his promises, and consequently both became exceedingly
hostile towards him, and were equally zealous in endeavoring to limit his power. He was, indeed, rendered perfectly
independent of the state laws by the charter which the governor so readily signed, without being aware what a blunder he was committing ; and the exertions of the Illinoi-
sians were directed towards getting this charter repealed.
Anti-Mormon organizations were formed for the purpose
of inducing the legislature to cancel the charter, disband
the Nauvoo Legion, a military organization, of which Joseph was commander-in-chief, and, if possible, to eventually
get rid of the Mormons altogether. The feeling ran quite as
high as it had done in Missouri, although there were no such
deeds of violence as that state witnessed. It remained, for
some time at least, a political rather than a personal warfare,
and Joseph seemed for many months to maintain his position
in spite of every exertion of his enemies ; and, in fact, got
decidedly the best of them in every way.

Joseph's political career was, to say the least, an intricate

and an ambitious one.   He aimed at the very highest position which the country could give him.   He inaugurated a
legislature at Nauvoo, in opposition to that of the state; but
he took good care that it should be kept from the knowledge of all persons outside of the city, and this same legislature did, in its way, the most remarkable work.   One of
its acts was to nominate Joseph for the Presidency of the
United States.

Clay and Calhoun were at that time rival candidates for
the Presidency, and Joseph wrote to both of them, asking
them what course they would pursue towards the Mormons
in case they were elected.   Neither of them answered in a
manner to please him; they were altogether too indefinite,
refusing in any way to commit themselves to the Mormon
cause; and he gave them both a severe castigation, and
withdrew his support and countenance from both parties;
and with him, of course, went the whole body of the Mormons.

He published his own views on the national policy in a
pamphlet, and announced himself as Presidential Candidate.
His followers confidently believed that he would be elected.
They had no idea that he could fail to attain whatever he
attempted.   Missionaries were sent all over the United
States, proselyting and electioneering, and the Saints certainly worked faithfully to further their Prophet's ambition.

In the legislative assembly he had those friends and allies
in training who were to form his cabinet when he should
reach the White House.   Of this assembly, Brigham Young
was an important, active, and favorite member, and Joseph
prophesied wonderful things of him.   It is said that he even
named him as his successor as leader of the Mormon
people.   But I think that that story is a little more than
doubtful.

In the midst of all this seeking after political influence,
Joseph Smith must, I think, have had some idea of the
hopelessness of it all, and some presentiment at least that his

failure must be followed by another exodus of the Mormon people, for as early as 1842 he began to talk of the superior advantages of the Pacific valley as a settlement, and the "Lord's finger" seemed turning slowly but surely in that direction, and it was not long before the Prophet sent a company of men to explore that, then, almost unknown country, and not long after he began prophesying that in five years' time the Saints would be located "away from the influence of mobs."

The Saints, as usual, received the prediction in good faith, and were ready to follow him wherever he should lead, notwithstanding that doing so meant giving up home, and property, and becoming poor, exiled wanderers. The devotion of this deluded, persecuted people to their false Prophet was almost sublime. In answer to his "Leave all and follow me," came the self-sacrificing words, "Whither thou goest we will go; thy God shall be our God."

Mistaken, deceived, deluded as they were, the great body of this people deserve some charitable regard, since they obeyed the dictates of their consciences, and were willing to suffer martyrdom for their religion. The great body of them are not answerable for most of the crimes committed by the command of the leaders, since they were ignorant of them, and their hatred of the Gentiles is not so greatly to be wondered at, since they suffered the persecution without even knowing that there was the slightest cause for it, except their objectionable belief. I feel that I must pay this tribute to the Mormon people. Naturally, they were a law-abiding, peace-loving, intensely religious people; their peculiar natures, touched a little with fanaticism, having that mental organization that not only accepts the supernatural, but demands it, made it the more easy for them to become the victims of a man like Joseph Smith.

The belief that they were the very chosen of God; that He revealed Himself to them through their Prophet; that He took special note of their in-comings and out-goings; that He

led their way in all their wanderings, sometimes in thorny
paths, sometimes through pleasant places, — made them positively heroic in their devotion. I hold that their earnestness
and singleness of purpose ought to win them a certain degree of respect, mingled with the intensest pity that they
could become the dupes of such unscrupulous, overbearing,
unprincipled men as their leaders have proved themselves
to be. They have been blinded by fanaticism, and led by
false representations. Kept in a community by themselves,
forbidden any intercourse with the outside world, they
have known nothing outside of Mormonism except what
their rulers have chosen to tell them, and that has never
been the truth. They have believed that every man's hand
was against them; that they were literally "persecuted for
righteousness' sake;" and they have been taught that the
Lord commanded them to hate all persons not of their belief,
and that it was an act pleasing to Him whenever a Gentile
was put out of the way. Without being murderers at heart,
they have been taught that murder is a part of their religion,
a vital portion of their worship. I shall explain that belief
more fully presently, when I come to speak of the "Blood-
Atonement."

The Gentiles have had very little opportunity, until lately,
of mingling at all with this people; and they have, quite as
naturally on their part, judged the Mormons to be a bloodthirsty, cruel, dishonest, and licentious people, who not only
did not merit toleration, even, but ought, indeed, to be utterly exterminated. No good could possibly come out of
Nazareth, they thought; and a person avowing himself a
Mormon has not been so much an object of hatred as of
loathing and contempt.

Mind you, I am not upholding the Mormon faith; I consider it the falsest, most hypocritical, and most cruel belief
under the sun. Although its founder arrogated to it the
title of the "Church of Jesus Christ," there is nothing Christ-
like in its teachings or in its practice. Its leaders always

have been, and still are, supremely selfish, caring only for their personal aggrandizement, disloyal to the government under which they live, treacherous to their friends, revengeful to their foes; insincere, believing nothing which they teach, and tyrannical and grasping in the extreme, taking everything that their lustful eyes may desire, and greedy, grasping hands can clutch, no matter at whose expense it may be taken, or what suffering the appropriation may cause. But the people themselves have no part in the treachery, revengefulness, hypocrisy, or cupidity of their leaders, and should be judged from an entirely different standpoint.

In 1842 Governor Boggs, of Missouri, was shot at and wounded severely in the head. This act was suspected to have been done at the instigation of Joseph, and the feeling against him grew stronger than ever. It was with considerable difficulty that his followers prevented his seizure and forcible abduction into Missouri. He was very nearly in the power of his enemies several times; but the devices of the Missourians were nothing compared to the wiles and cunning of the crafty Prophet and his officers. The governor of Illinois attempted to arrest him, but found the warrant of apprehension set aside by the charter which he himself had signed. In fact, it was found that the law was powerless to touch the Prophet, and he could afford to set it at defiance. With that charter to uphold him, and the "Nauvoo Legion" to defend him, he, for a time, completely baffled his enemies.

About this time an added reason was found for hating and dreading the Mormon people and their influence. The "Spiritual-Wife" doctrine was hinted at just at this juncture, and this created even a greater disturbance than the political difficulties had done, since this caused a large apostasy, and divided the church against itself. The accusations that some of the apostates brought against Smith were damaging in the extreme.

One of his chief accusers was a man named William Law, who had been his earnest friend and one of his counsellors. The Prophet had had no stancher friend or warmer defender than Law, and he was also highly esteemed by all the Mormon people, as well as by Smith himself. He strongly disapproved of some of Joseph's acts, and finally felt obliged to withdraw from him altogether.

After his apostasy, he, with some other disaffected Mormons, among whom were his brother, Wilson Law, Dr. Forster, William Marks, and the Higbee brothers, all men of standing and influence among the Saints, commenced to hold meetings in a grove on Sundays. This grove was a mile from the place where the Mormons held their regular services; yet parties of the Saints were accustomed to go to the other meeting to hear what was said and report to the Prophet. So he was kept well informed of the movements of the apostates, and their attitude towards him and the church.

At one of these meetings, William Law electrified and almost stunned his listeners by testifying that the Prophet had made dishonorable proposals to his wife, Mrs. Law, making the request under cover of his asserted "Revelation," that the Lord had commanded that he should take spiritual wives, to add to his glory. He also stated that Smith made his visit to his wife in the middle of the night, when he knew her husband to be absent. Mrs. Law was present, and her husband called upon her to testify as to whether he had made the statement correctly. She corroborated all that he had said, and added that Joseph had asked her to give him half her love; she was at liberty to keep the other half for her husband.

The Higbees testified, at the same meeting, to having frequently seen Joseph's horse standing for a long time before the door of certain improper resorts. This statement was certainly untrue, and was probably made under a mistake. The greatest excitement prevailed after this meeting, and the feeling ran very high between the contending factions of the church.   Joseph and his adherents, on their part, charged some of the apostates with gross immorality, and they retaliated by saying they had only followed the teachings of Smith.   Criminations and recriminations were hurled furiously at each other by the two parties.

BURNING OF THE NEWSPAPER OFFICE.

Law and some of his associates started a paper called the "*Nauvoo Expositor*," which they intended to devote to the criticism of Smith's policy, and the denunciation of his character.   As may be imagined, it was not a very long-lived sheet, only one number being issued.   Enraged by its plain speech, Joseph and some of his followers destroyed the building, broke the machinery, and threw away the type, in their strenuous endeavors to suppress "the freedom of the press."

Affairs had reached such a crisis, that to allay the excitement and to explain some of his "peculiar" moral weaknesses, the Prophet found it necessary to produce the famous "Revelation," giving the most unbridled license to all the worst passions of their nature.   This "Revelation" was intended to silence the noisy clamorings of the Saints; for who of them would venture to question the convincing "Thus saith the Lord."

It was only given to the faithful in Zion. Its existence was denied loudly, if in any way a whisper of it reached the outside world, and the missionaries were cautioned to keep utter silence upon the subject. Among the Saints it was received most reluctantly. The women, especially, felt that a cross was being laid upon them greater than they could bear, and many openly rebelled. They felt that some great trouble was come upon them, but they did not then know the intense bitterness of it, nor what the moral results would be. The majority of them did not believe that they would suffer personally from it; but, alas! they little knew how easy it would be to convince a man that positive wrong would become moral right, when all legal restrictions were removed, or when the conscience could be so easily soothed by the opiate of "Revelation."

Joseph's career, after producing his "Celestial Marriage" cheat, and palming it off on his followers with the blasphemous "Thus saith the Lord," was very short. He was induced to surrender himself to the authorities, and with his brother Hyrum, the Apostle John Taylor, and the Apostle Willard Richards, was placed in the Carthage jail.

It was feared by the Mormons, and by some of the Gentiles, that attempts would be made to massacre him in prison; but Governor Ford, under whose protection he was, seemed to apprehend no danger, and placed no extra guards about the prison. He himself went from Carthage to Nauvoo, to see personally into the condition of affairs there, and also to assert his authority, but took no measures for a redoubled care and watch over the prisoners. While he was away the jail was attacked, and the Prophet and his brother Hyrum assassinated. Their companions escaped with wounds.

The history of Joseph Smith is one of the most remarkable on record. From an ignorant, superstitious farmer's boy, he became "Prophet, Seer, and Revelator," founder of a new religion, which was to make his name known, not only in his own country, but over the world; made by "Divine appointment" "God's Vicegerent upon the earth, and Religious Dictator to the whole world." So much for his spiritual titles. He was no less fortunate in earthly honors; being President of the "Council of Fifty," chief of the legislature of Nauvoo, and Mayor of the city; and at last he aspired to the Presidency of the United States — a position, it is needless to say, which he did not attain.

ASSASSINATION OF JOSEPH SMITH AND HIS BROTHER HYRUM.

It is safe to believe that no one man can wear all these "honors" without growing somewhat dizzy under them; and it is no wonder that the Prophet Smith overreached himself at last, and fell a victim to his overweening ambition and stupendous self-esteem, which probably made him believe that he could accomplish impossibilities.

CHAPTER III.

THE "REVELATION ON CELESTIAL MARRIAGE." — TROUBLE AMONG THE SAINTS.

The Announcement of Polygamy. — "*Celestial* Marriage." — Joseph "sets himself Right." — Mrs. Smith is very Rebellious. — Mrs. Smith's Adopted Daughter. — The Prophet too fond of Fanny. — Mrs. Smith takes her in Hand. — Marital Storms. — Oliver Cowdery called In. — He goes and "Does Likewise." — Joseph first Preaches Polygamy. — The Saints Rebel. — The Revelation given in Secret. — Eleven "Adopted *Daughters*" sealed to the Prophet. — A Domestic Squall in the Prophet's House. — Nancy Rigdon Insulted by Joseph. — Sidney's Zeal Grows Cold. — How Celestial Marriage was Introduced. — Mr. Noble begins to Build Up his Kingdom. — The first Plural Marriage. — False Position of the Second Wife. — John C. Bennett. — His Profligacy and Crimes. — He Apostatizes and Writes a Book. — Joseph Defends Himself. — Apostasy of an Apostle's Wife. — The Prophet in Difficulties. — The Revelation on "Celestial Marriage."

EMMA SMITH, "THE ELECT LADY.

AFTER the Revelation on Celestial Marriage was publicly announced, in 1852, it was stated that Joseph Smith first produced it in 1843 ; but there were, no doubt, hints of this new doctrine at a much earlier date. It is generally believed, and in fact well known by many of the old Nauvoo Mormons, that he had it in contemplation at a much earlier date ; certain indiscretions rendering it necessary that he should find an excuse of some kind for acts that were scarcely consistent

5

with his position as "Vicegerent upon earth," and set himself right, not only with his followers, but with Mrs. Emma Smith, his wife, who objected very decidedly to some of his prophetic eccentricities.

Mrs. Smith had an adopted daughter, a very pretty, pleasing young girl, about seventeen years old. She was extremely fond of her; no own mother could be more devoted, and their affection for each other was a constant object of remark, so absorbing and genuine did it seem. Consequently it was with a shocked surprise that the people heard that sister Emma had turned Fanny out of the house in the night.

This sudden movement was incomprehensible, since Emma was known to be a just woman, not given to freaks or caprices, and it was felt that she certainly must have had some very good reason for her action. By degrees it became whispered about that Joseph's love for his adopted daughter was by no means a paternal affection, and his wife, discovering the fact, at once took measures to place the girl beyond his reach. Angered at finding the two persons whom most she loved playing such a treacherous part towards her, she by no means spared her reproaches, and, finally, the storm became so furious, that Joseph was obliged to send, at midnight, for Oliver Cowdery, his scribe, to come and endeavor to settle matters between them. For once he was at his wits' end; he could face an angry mob, but a wronged woman made a coward of him at once.

The scribe was a worthy servant of his master. He was at that time residing with a certain young woman, and at the same time he had a wife living. He had taken kindly to Joseph's teachings, although he by no means coveted publicity in the affair; and after seeing Mrs. Smith's indignation he dreaded exceedingly lest Mrs. Cowdery should discover that he was practising his new religious duties with another woman.

The worthy couple — the Prophet and his scribe — were

sorely perplexed what to do with the girl, since Emma refused decidedly to allow her to remain in her house; but after some consultation, my mother offered to take her until she could be sent to her relatives. Although her parents were living, they considered it the highest honor to have their daughter adopted into the Prophet's family, and her mother has always claimed that she was sealed to Joseph at that time.

The first public announcement Joseph ever made of his belief in the plurality of wives was at Nauvoo, in 1840. In a sermon one Sunday he declared that it was perfectly right in the sight of the Lord for a man to have as many wives as he pleased, if he could evade the laws of the land. Said he:

"People of polygamous nations will be converted to the church, and will desire to gather with the Saints to Zion; and what will they do with their wives? We must have polygamy among us as an established institution, and then they can bring all their wives with them."

He referred to the Bible to sustain his position, and grew very eloquent on the subject. He seemed determined not only to maintain the doctrine to his own satisfaction, but to convince his people of its truth and its desirability.

As may readily be imagined, it caused the greatest excitement and indignation in the church; and many threatened to abandon the faith. The women most especially were aroused, and they declared they never would accept a doctrine so hateful. It was the first open rebellion against any of the Prophet's teachings by his most devoted followers, and he was wise enough to see his mistake, and to rectify it. Evidently, as he said to certain followers, it was " too soon for the Lord to reveal Himself upon this subject."

The following Sabbath he arose, and said he wished to retract what he had said the Sabbath before; he was at that time only trying the Saints, to see what they could bear. The Revelation at first was made known only to a few of

Joseph's most intimate friends, and they were solemnly bound to keep its existence a secret; but in some way it became known very generally that there was such a Revelation, although it was not given to the world until 1852. It is on this ground that Smith's sons endeavor to palm the Revelation on to Brigham, and deny that their father ever intended to have polygamy become a church institution. The elder Mormons, who were at Nauvoo, among whom are my parents, know better than this, however, and also know the exact time when the "Revelation" was first talked of. If Smith was not a polygamist, his sons must allow that he was a libertine, or an advocate of free-love principles. It makes little difference which; the results are the same.

The wife of the Prophet took no more kindly to this new doctrine of Celestial Marriage than did the rest of the Mormon women, and no woman of them all allowed her objections to become so widely known as Mrs. Smith. She knew her husband's nature too well to believe in the Divine origin of the system, and she fought it persistently during his lifetime.

At one time he had eleven young ladies living in his family as adopted daughters, to whom he had been sealed without the knowledge of his wife. She for some time supposed that his object in having them there was purely a charitable one. To be sure, some of them had parents living; yet there was some plausible reason always given for having them under his roof, which none of the Saints dared to question, although many of them, especially those who were growing disaffected, were dissatisfied with his reasons, and suspicious of his motives. Very little was said about it openly, until his wife saw something which aroused her suspicions, and she remonstrated with Joseph for having the girls there; but with no effect. The girls should remain — on that point he was decided.

Unlike many of the Mormon women, Mrs. Smith was not one to accept a cross of this kind submissively. She by no means bowed her head, broke her heart, and silenced her lips, and allowed her husband to pursue his licentious course without opposition. When Joseph would not send away the girls, she said very quietly, but with a determination which showed she was making no idle threat, —

" Either those girls leave this house to-night, or I do."

" Very well," replied her husband, in a passion at having his authority questioned ; " you may go, then, for I intend them to stay."

THE INDIGNANT WIFE.

Without another word she left the house. No sooner had she gone than he began to consider the consequences of her departure directly it should be known, and she would keep neither it nor the cause which provoked her to the step a secret. The publicity of the affair was more than he dared meet. He was not yet ready to encounter the storm it would raise. Great as was his influence over his people, he did not dare risk his popularity by such a bold movement as this. Consequently he followed his wife, and prevailed upon her to return, by promising to dismiss the girls, which he did the next morning. This was her second triumph over his practice of the divine ordinance.

Emma Smith was, as may be supposed from the above-narrated incidents, an energetic, strong-minded woman, possessing a great influence over Joseph, whose superior she was, both mentally and socially, when he married her. She was fond and proud of her husband during the first years of his success ; but when there was any disagreement between them, she generally got the better of him, being less passionate in temper, and more quietly decided in manner. She forced her husband to respect her and her opinions, although he was notoriously unfaithful to her during all their married life.

Several young girls left the church in consequence of the dishonorable proposals which the Prophet made to them. One of these was a daughter of William Marks, another a daughter of Sidney Rigdon. Both these men — Rigdon especially — had been his warm friends and supporters; but this insult offered to their daughters exasperated them beyond measure, and both withdrew from him. Marks joined William Law and his apostate circle, and was as bitter in his denunciation as Law himself. Rigdon removed from Nauvoo, but still avowed himself a "true Mormon," while he repudiated Joseph and his teachings. Other young girls made affidavits to his offers of "Celestial Marriage," and their statements were published in many of the leading papers all over the country, creating the most intense excitement.

Joseph not only paid his addresses to the young and unmarried women, but he sought "*spiritual* alliance" with many married ladies who happened to strike his fancy. He taught them that all former marriages were null and void, and that they were at perfect liberty to make another choice of a husband. The marriage covenants were not binding, because they were ratified only by Gentile laws. These laws the Lord did not recognize; consequently all the women were free.

Again, he would appeal to their religious sentiments, and their strong desire to enter into the celestial kingdom. He used often to argue in this manner while endeavoring to convince some wavering or unwilling victim: "Now, my dear sister, it is true that your husband is a good man, a very good man, but you and he are by no means kindred spirits, and he will never be able to save you in the celestial kingdom; it has been revealed by the Spirit that you ought to belong to *me*."

This sophistry, strange as it may seem, had its weight, and scarcely ever failed of its desired results. Many a woman, with a kind, good husband, who loved her and trusted her, and a family of children, would suffer herself to be sealed to Joseph, at the same time living with the husband whom she was wronging so deeply, he believing fondly that her love was all his own.

One woman said to me not very long since, while giving me some of her experiences in polygamy : "The greatest trial I ever endured in my life was living with my husband and deceiving him, by receiving Joseph's attentions whenever he chose to come to me."

This woman, and others, whose experience has been very similar, are among the very best women in the church; they are as pure-minded and virtuous women as any in the world. They were seduced under the guise of religion, taught that the Lord commanded it, and they submitted as to a cross laid upon them by the divine will. Believing implicitly in the Prophet, they never dreamed of questioning the truth of his revelations, and would have considered themselves on the verge of apostasy, which to a Mormon is a most dangerous and horrible state, from which there is no possible salvation, had they refused to submit to him and to receive his " divine " doctrines.

Some of these women have since said they did not know who was the father of their children; this is not to be wondered at, for after Joseph's declaration annulling all Gentile marriages, the greatest promiscuity was practised; and, indeed, all sense of morality seemed to have been lost by a portion at least of the church. Shocking as all this may appear, women that were sealed to Joseph at that time are more highly respected than any others. It is said, as the highest meed of praise which can be given, that they never repudiated any of the Prophet's teachings, but submitted to all his requirements without a murmur, and eventually they will be exalted to a high position in the celestial kingdom.

Among the earliest converts to the doctrine of plural wives was a Mr. Noble, who, more impressible, or, according to Joseph, "more faithful" than any others, opened his heart very readily to receive the teachings of the Prophet, and was willing to reduce the teachings to practice. Joseph had paid his addresses to Mr. Noble's sister-in-law, a very worthy woman, and had succeeded in overcoming her scruples so far that she had consented to be sealed to him.

THE FIRST PLURAL MARRIAGE.

He then advised Noble to seek a second wife for himself, and to commence at once to "build up his kingdom." He was not slow in following his Prophet's advice, and together the two men, with their chosen celestial brides, repaired one night to the banks of the Mississippi River, where Joseph sealed Noble to his first plural wife, and in return Noble performed the same office for the Prophet and his sister. These were the first plural marriages that ever took place in the Mormon Church, and they were obliged to be very secretly performed, and kept hidden afterwards.

The young girl that Mr. Noble married went to live with his first wife, and, as a matter of course, this arrangement produced the greatest misery to both. Outwardly they were compelled to keep a semblance of regard; but they hated each other with an intensity of hatred that cannot possibly be felt outside of polygamy. The first wife pined gradually away, until she was a mere shadow of her former self. Life for her was utterly wrecked. Compelled to share her home, her husband's affections, and his attentions with another woman, and to keep the strictest silence through it all, it is no wonder that the poor woman longed eagerly for death as a release from all her woes.

The condition of the second wife was, if possible, less enviable. A son having been born to her after her marriage to Noble, she was compelled to see herself pointed out as an object of pity, and her child branded as illegitimate. She was in a cruelly false position before the world, and she was powerless to justify herself; her lips were sealed, and she, too, must suffer in silence. Her parents were heart-broken at their daughter's shame. They were living in one of the eastern states, but they came instantly to Nauvoo to take their child home. She was compelled to turn a deaf ear to all their entreaties to return with them, and she could not tell them her secret. Her mother was nearly distracted when she was obliged to return home without her daughter, heart-broken and disconsolate, and bowed down with shame at her supposed dishonor. She remained at Nauvoo, and the burden of her life becoming greater than she could bear, she became insane, — a common fate of polygamous wives, by the way, — and remained a maniac until her death. Her son, now a man grown, and living in Utah, was the first child born in polygamy. She was an innocent, engaging young girl, and a great favorite until this sad affair occurred; her sensitive spirit could not endure the torture of existence, and she died — the first martyr to polygamy.

The first wife died soon after, literally broken-hearted. The husband has had many wives since then; indeed, he has been an indefatigable disciple of the Celestial Marriage system ; but his many wives have died one by one, until he has been left alone. He is living still, and is pointed out and referred to with praise as the first man brave enough to respond to the call of Joseph Smith and become a polygamist.

One of the first persons to be initiated into the plural-wife doctrine, if not indeed Joseph's confederate in producing it, was Dr. John C. Bennett, at that time Mayor of the city, Major-General of the Nauvoo Legion, and a very great friend of Joseph. It is said that the pupil fairly outran the teacher, and his success as special pleader for the system of Celestial Marriage was so decided that he incurred the displeasure of the Prophet, and they quarrelled violently. He taught the doctrine to some ladies whom Smith had intended to convert himself, and thus coming directly in contact with the Prophet and his schemes, a rupture was caused between the worthy co-workers.

Bennett apostatized, left Nauvoo, and wrote a book called "Mormonism Exposed," in which he fully ventilated the doctrine of spiritual wives which Joseph was about to introduce into the church, and accused the Prophet of the grossest immoralities. This exposé created a wide-spread feeling of indignation, and, to save himself and his people, Joseph was obliged to deny all Bennett's statements ; and several of the leading men and women denied them also, although they knew perfectly well that the greater portion of them was true. It is probable that the book would have had a much wider influence had not Bennett's character been so well known. He was a notorious profligate, and was pronounced by Gentiles who had known him before he embraced Mormonism to be "the greatest villain unhung."

Joseph's only method of defending himself from Bennett's attacks was to assail him in return. The raven was taunting the crow for being a blackamoor. He coupled Bennett's name with that of a lady of high standing in the

Mormon community, in the most disgraceful manner, and published the scandal to a large congregation of the Saints, causing the utmost consternation and dismay. The lady in question had always been considered above reproach; never before had suspicion touched her name by even a breath, and the accusation which Joseph brought against her seemed too horrible to believe. But the Saints could more easily credit the scandal than they could believe for one instant that their Prophet could be guilty of misrepresentation; and the general conclusion was, that the lady had fallen from her virtuous estate, broken her marriage vows, and become a creature unworthy of countenance or sympathy.

Her husband was away from home when the trouble first commenced, but returning while the excitement was at its height, his indignation and rage at the position in which his wife was placed knew no bounds. He realized the situation at once, and saw that his wife was suffering from the Prophet's jealous anger, and was simply being used as a means of revenge and retaliation on his enemy Bennett. This has been the Mormon leaders' manner of doing things from the beginning; they believe most implicitly in vicarious suffering, and it is with them always the innocent and help-less who are punished for the wrong-doings of the more powerful.

The husband of this unfortunate lady came at once to the rescue of his injured wife's reputation. He " bearded the lion in his den," and defended his wife's character in public, hurling the lie at his leader's head, and incurring anathemas in return. He did not mind them, however, but still main-tained his wife's honor in the face of everything. He was nearly insane with grief and rage, but he behaved nobly through the whole affair. He was greatly attached to the church, and could not make up his mind to forsake it, and he grieved over this action of his Prophet, but yet found an ex-cuse for him on the ground that he had " lost the Spirit," and had been taken possession of by evil influences for a while.

He loved his wife, and considered her terribly wronged and sinned against, and he tried by all the tenderness in his power to heal the cruel hurt which she had received. His own regard for and belief in her turned the tide of public opinion again in her favor, and she has been, if possible, more highly esteemed than ever since that unfortunate accusation. In course of time her husband, who is none other than Orson Pratt, one of the twelve apostles, took several plural wives, and became so warm in his advocacy of the system that he is called "the defender of polygamy." Mrs. Pratt has since apostatized, and is working nobly against Mormonism and its peculiar system. No woman is more highly regarded by Gentiles and Mormons than she. Her husband even, although she has steadfastly refused to live in polygamy with him, and has fought it from its first introduction, still has a high regard for her, although he looks upon her as lost beyond redemption. She is now an elderly woman, but her energy has not abated one whit, and she declares she will never relax her exertions towards putting down polygamy while she lives. If her husband is its "defender," she may be called its "denouncer;" and her work is the most certain of being crowned with ultimate success.

The days that preceded the Revelation were exciting ones in the church. Apostasy prevailed to an alarming extent, and the numbers of the faithful were sadly depleted, and many more threatened to leave the church, who were finally prevailed upon to remain. So intense was the feeling that in the summer of 1843 the Prophet, moved by pressure on every side, dissatisfaction within the church and hatred and indignation without, heightened by Bennett's exposé and the corroborating accounts given by apostates, was compelled to intrench himself behind a divine "revelation" to shield himself from public odium and restore the wavering confidence of his people.

It had always been a practice of Joseph, whenever he

met with any difficulty, to receive a "Revelation," which immediately put everything straight. On the present occasion he was equal to the emergency, and received that celebrated " Revelation " which then and since has constituted the sole authority in the Mormon Church for the practice of polygamy. It was at first only communicated to a chosen few, and it was not until long after polygamy had been practised more or less openly in Utah that Brigham Young delivered it to the world in 1852. It was then published in the " *Seer*," and also in the "*Millennial Star*," under the title of

CELESTIAL MARRIAGE.

A REVELATION ON THE PATRIARCHAL ORDER OF MATRIMONY, OR PLURALITY OF WIVES.

Given to Joseph Smith, the Seer, in Nauvoo, July 12th, 1843.

Of all the extraordinary "revelations" given by Joseph Smith during his eventful career, this is, perhaps, the most remarkable. It certainly produced a deeper and more lasting influence upon his deluded followers than all his other effusions put together, although its language is as ungrammatical as its tendency is immoral. The opening clause is peculiarly absurd. The Book of Mormon, the Book of Doctrine and Covenants, and countless " revelations" had denounced polygamy, and stated how offensive the conduct of some of the patriarchs in this respect had been to "the Lord." Yet here Joseph is made to ask that same "Lord" how he "justified" the very principle that Joseph had all along proclaimed that "the Lord" held to be "an abomination"! The Prophet's sons of course point to this fact, and say that it was impossible for their father to be guilty of such an unparalleled contradiction. The clause reads thus : —

" Verily, thus saith the Lord, unto you, my servant Joseph, that, inasmuch as you have enquired of my hand to know and understand wherein I, the Lord, justified my servants as touching the principle and doctrine of their having many wives and concu, bines: Behold, and lo, I am the Lord thy God, and will answer thee as touching this matter: Therefore, prepare thy heart to receive and obey the instructions which I am about to give unto you; for all those that have this law revealed unto them must obey the same; for, behold, I reveal unto you a new and everlasting covenant, and if ye abide not that covenant, then are ye damned; for no one can reject this covenant and be permitted to enter into my glory; for all who will have a blessing at my hands shall abide the law which was appointed for that blessing and the conditions thereof, as was instituted from before the foundations of the world; and as pertaining to the new and everlasting covenant, it was instituted for the fulness of my glory; and he that receiveth a fulness thereof must and shall abide the law, or he shall be damned, saith the Lord God."

Having made this very pleasant announcement, the Revelation goes on to declare that all contracts — matrimonial or other — were null and void unless ratified by the Prophet: —

2d. "And verily I say unto you, that the conditions of this law are these: All covenants, contracts, bonds, obligations, oaths, vows, performances, connections, associations, or expectations, that are not made and entered into and sealed by the Holy Spirit of promise of him who is anointed both as well for time and for all eternity, and that, too, most holy, by revelation and commandment, through the medium of mine anointed, whom I have appointed on the earth to hold this power, — and I have appointed unto my servant Joseph to hold this power in the last days, and there is never but one on the earth at a time on whom this power and the keys of the priesthood are conferred, — are of no efficacy, virtue or force in and after the resurrection from the dead; for all contracts that are not made unto this end have an end when men are dead."

The third clause is simply a reiteration of the sentiments contained in the preceding; but the fourth announces one of the most peculiar tenets of Mormon theology. The reader will see that in it the assertion is distinctly made that if a man and woman are married by civil contract or accord-

ing to the usage of any of the ordinary sects, although they
may be among the most faithful members of the Mormon
Church in every other respect, yet, after death, they shall
not enjoy exaltation in heaven, they shall not become gods,
shall not marry or have children, shall have no kingdom or
priesthood, but shall simply be as the angels — servants and
messengers of the Saints. It reads thus : —

4th. " Therefore, if a man marry him a wife in the world, and
he marry her not by me nor by my word, and he covenant with
her so long as he is in the world, and she with him, their covenant
and marriage is not of force when they are dead, and when they
are out of the world ; therefore they are not bound by any law
when they are out of the world ; therefore, when they are out of
the world they neither marry nor are given in marriage, but are
appointed angels in heaven, which angels are ministering servants
to minister for those who are worthy of a far more, and an exceeding and an eternal weight of glory ; for these angels did not
abide my law, therefore they cannot be enlarged, but remain
separately and singly, without exaltation, in their saved condition,
to all eternity, and from henceforth are not gods, but are angels of
God for ever and ever."

Thus far the Revelation sets forth the uncomfortable fate
of those who do not strictly conform to the teachings of the
Prophet in matrimonial affairs. We now come to the other
side of the question — the rewards which are to crown the
faithful. The reader will observe that the strictest obedience is required to be paid to " him who is anointed," and
who carries the keys.

6th. " And again, verily I say unto you, if a man marry a wife
by my word, which is my law, and by the new and everlasting
covenant, and it is sealed unto them by the Holy Spirit of promise
by him who is anointed, unto whom I have appointed this power
and the keys of this priesthood, and it shall be said unto them,
Ye shall come forth in the first resurrection, and if it be after the
first resurrection, in the next resurrection ; and shall inherit
thrones, kingdoms, principalities and powers, dominions, all
heights and depths, then shall it be written in the Lamb's Book

of Life, that he shall commit no murder whereby to shed innocent blood. And if ye abide in my covenant, and commit no murder whereby to shed innocent blood, it shall be done unto them in all things whatsoever my servant hath put upon them, in time and through all eternity, and shall be of full force when they are out of the world, and they shall pass by the angels and the gods which are set there, to their exaltation and glory in all things, as hath been sealed upon their heads, which glory shall be a fulness and a continuation of the seeds for ever and ever.

7th. "Then shall they be gods, because they have no end; therefore shall they be from everlasting to everlasting, because they continue; then shall they be above all, because all things are subject unto them; then shall they be gods, because they have all power, and the angels are subject unto them."

This is the reward of the faithful. The Revelation, however, was intended to be comprehensive and final; it was to meet every case, and there was to be no appeal from its decisions. The married couple being united in strict accordance with the Revelation, they are now assured of salvation and exaltation in the world to come, provided they commit no unpardonable sin. In the following paragraph that sin is defined, but the reader must bear in mind that the blood of Gentiles is *not* " innocent" blood; the shedding of it, therefore, is no crime: —

9th. " Verily, verily I say unto you, if a man marry a wife according to my word, and they are sealed by the Holy Spirit of promise according to mine appointment, and he or she shall commit any sin or transgression of the new and everlasting covenant whatever, and all manner of blasphemies, and if they commit no murder wherein they shed innocent blood, — yet they shall come forth in the first resurrection, and enter into their exaltation, *but they shall be destroyed in the flesh*, and shall be delivered unto the buffetings of Satan unto the day of redemption, saith the Lord God.

10th. " The blasphemy against the Holy Ghost, which shall not be forgiven in the world nor out of the world, is in that ye commit murder, wherein ye shed innocent blood and assent unto my death after ye have received my new and everlasting covenant, saith the Lord God; and he that abideth not this law can in no wise enter into my glory, but shall be damned, saith the Lord."

In the italicized words, "but they shall be destroyed in the flesh," is foreshadowed that terrible doctrine — the Blood-Atonement; of which I shall presently speak more. It was not long before the Saints were taught openly that it was their duty to "destroy in the flesh" all upon whom the leaders of the church frowned.

We come now to the examples which were held up for the Saints to follow: —

12th. "Abraham received promises concerning his seed and of the fruit of his loins, — from whose loins ye are, namely, my servant Joseph, — which were to continue so long as they were in the world; and as touching Abraham and his seed, out of the world they should continue; both in the world and out of the world should they continue as innumerable as the stars, or if ye were to count the sand upon the sea-shore ye could not number them. This promise is yours also, because ye are of Abraham, and the promise was made unto Abraham; and by this law are the continuation of the works of my Father, wherein He glorifieth himself. Go ye, therefore, and do the works of Abraham; enter ye into my law, and ye shall be saved. But if ye enter not into my law ye cannot receive the promises of my Father which he made unto Abraham.

13th. "God commanded Abraham, and Sarah gave Hagar to Abraham to wife. And why did she do it? Because this was the law, and from Hagar sprang many people. This, therefore, was fulfilling, among other things, the promises. Was Abraham, therefore, under condemnation? Verily, I say unto you, Nay; for I, the Lord, commanded it. Abraham was commanded to offer his son Isaac; nevertheless it was written, Thou shalt not kill. Abraham, however, did not refuse, and it was accounted unto him for righteousness.

14th. "Abraham received concubines, and they bare him children, and it was accounted unto him for righteousness, because they were given unto him and he abode in my law. As Isaac

6

also and Jacob did none other things than that which they were commanded, and because they did none other things than that which they were commanded, they have entered into their exaltation, according to the promises, and sit upon thrones; and are not angels, but Gods. David also received many wives and concubines, as also Solomon, and Moses my servant; as also many others of my servants, from the beginning of creation until this time; and in nothing did they sin, save in those things which they received not of me.

15th. "David's wives and concubines were given unto him of me, by the hand of Nathan my servant, and others of the prophets, who had the keys of this power; and in none of these things did he sin against me, save in the case of Uriah and his wife; and therefore he hath fallen from his exaltation, and received his portion; and he shall not inherit them out of the world; for I gave them unto another, saith the Lord."

The audacity of Joseph Smith in stating as a *Revelation* from God, that "David's wives and concubines were *given him of me by the hand of Nathan . . . in none of these things did he sin against me,*" is scarcely conceivable, when it is remembered that in the "divinely inspired" Book of Mormon it is written, "David and Solomon truly had many wives and concubines, *which thing was abominable before me, saith the Lord.*" "The Lord," however, whom Joseph served, seems to have been as inconsistent in this as in many other matters. But in case of difficulty, Joseph was specially commissioned "to restore all things." Celestial Marriage was more exactly defined, and that the whole concern should run more smoothly, the keys of the kingdom on earth and in heaven were handed over to the Prophet.

16th. "I am the Lord thy God, and I gave unto thee my servant Joseph, an appointment, and restore all things; ask what ye will, and it shall be given unto you, according to my word; and as ye have asked concerning adultery, verily, verily I say unto you, if a man receiveth a wife in the new and everlasting covenant, and if she be with another man, and I have not appointed unto her by the holy anointing, she hath committed adultery, and shall be de-

stroyed. If she be not in the new and everlasting covenant, and
she be with another man, she has committed adultery ; and if her
husband be with another woman, and he was under a vow, he
hath broken his vow, and hath committed adultery; and if she
hath not committed adultery, but is innocent, and hath not broken
her vow, and she knoweth it, and I reveal it unto you, my servant Joseph, then shall you have power, by the power of my Holy
Priesthood, to take her, and give her unto him that hath not committed adultery, but hath been faithful, for he shall be made ruler
over many ; for I have conferred upon you the keys and power of
the priesthood, wherein I restore all things, and make known unto
you all things in due time.

17th. " And verily, verily I say unto you, that whatsoever you
seal on earth, shall be sealed in heaven ; and whatsoever you bind
on earth, in my name, and by my word, saith the Lord, it shall
be eternally bound in the heavens ; and whosesoever sins you remit
on earth shall be remitted eternally in the heavens ; and whosesoever sins you retain on earth shall be retained in heaven.

18th. " And again verily I say, whomsoever you bless I will
bless ; and whomsoever you curse I will curse, saith the Lord ; for
I, the Lord, am thy God."

After all this preamble, — the keys committed to Joseph,
the relation of husbands and wives under the new dispensation defined, " Celestial Marriage " instituted, and a great
many other matters discussed, we come to what was, no
doubt, prominent in the Prophet's mind all the while he was
dictating the Revelation to Elder Clayton, — namely, how to
manage " the Elect Lady," Mrs. Emma Smith. Accordingly she is made the subject of a special address. She
is told to " receive all that have been given to my servant
Joseph." She is forbidden to leave the Prophet, as she had
threatened to do if he carried out his " celestial " system,
and certain other very useful hints are given for her guidance if she would remain in peace. One particular passage
is said to refer to a matrimonial scene in which a threat was
held out that the life of the Elect Lady should be terminated

by poison. She is here commanded to "stay herself, and partake not" of that which Joseph had offered her. It is, however, only right to add that the Mormon exponents of the Revelation say that this passage refers to an offer which Joseph had made to sacrifice his own personal feelings, and to accede to a divorce between Emma and himself. In these few lines more is disclosed of the Prophet's domestic life and difficulties than he probably was aware of. I give these paragraphs in full, that the reader may judge for himself.

20th. "Verily I say unto you, a commandment I give unto mine handmaid Emma Smith, your wife, whom I have given unto you, that she stay herself, and partake not of that which I commanded you to offer unto her; for I did it, saith the Lord, to prove you all, as I did Abraham; and that I might require an offering at your hand, by covenant and sacrifice; and let mine handmaid Emma Smith receive all those that have been given unto my servant Joseph, and who are virtuous and pure before me; and those who are not pure, and have said they were pure, shall be destroyed, saith the Lord God; for I am the Lord thy God, and ye shall obey my voice; and I give unto my servant Joseph, that he shall be made ruler over many things, for he hath been faithful over a few things, and from henceforth I will strengthen him.

21st. "And I command mine handmaid Emma Smith to abide and cleave unto my servant Joseph, and to none else. But if she will not abide this commandment, she shall be destroyed, saith the Lord; for I am the Lord thy God, and will destroy her if she abide not in my law; but if she will not abide this commandment, then shall my servant Joseph do all things for her, even as he has said; and I will bless him and multiply him, and give unto him an hundred fold in this world, of fathers and mothers, brothers and sisters, houses and lands, wives and children, and crowns of eternal lives in the eternal worlds. And again, verily I say let mine handmaid forgive my servant Joseph his trespasses, and then shall she be forgiven her trespasses, wherein she has trespassed against me; and I, the Lord thy God, will bless her, and multiply her, and make her heart to rejoice."

The concluding clauses speak for themselves. The reader will see that in the twenty-third the Prophet is completely set free from all responsibility, and left at liberty, without let or hinderance, to follow the dictates of his own sweet will. In the two concluding paragraphs the wildest licentiousness is permitted, in the name of "the Lord," to the masculine portion of humanity, — if believers in Joseph, — and the weaker sex are sternly warned of the penalties of doubt and disobedience.

23d. "Now as touching the law of the priesthood, there are many things pertaining thereunto. Verily, if a man be called of my Father, as was Aaron, by mine own voice, and by the voice of him that sent me, and I have endowed him with the keys of the power of this priesthood, if he do anything in my name, and according to my law, and by my word, he will not commit sin, and I will justify him. Let no one, therefore, set on my servant Joseph; for I will justify him; for he shall do the sacrifice which I require at his hands, for his transgressions, saith the Lord your God.

24th. "And again, as pertaining to the law of the priesthood: If any man espouse a virgin, and desire to espouse another, and the first give her consent; and if he espouse the second, and they are virgins, and have vowed to no other man, then is he justified; he cannot commit adultery, for they are given unto him. For he cannot commit adultery with that which belongeth unto him, and to none else; and if he have ten virgins given unto him by this law, he cannot commit adultery, for they belong to him; and they are given unto him — therefore is he justified. But if one or either of the ten virgins, after she is espoused, shall be with another man, she has committed adultery, and shall be destroyed; for they are given unto him to multiply and replenish the earth, according to my commandment, and to fulfil the promise which was given by my Father before the foundation of the world; and for their exaltation in the eternal worlds, that they may bear the souls of men; for herein is the work of my Father continued, that He may be glorified.

25th. "And again, verily, verily I say unto you, if any man have a wife who holds the keys of this power, and he teaches unto her the law of my priesthood, as pertaining to these things; then shall she believe, and administer unto him, or she shall be destroyed, saith the Lord your God, for I will destroy her; for I will magnify my name upon all those who receive and abide in my law. Therefore it shall be lawful in me, if she receive not this law, for him to receive all things whatsoever I the Lord his God will give unto him, because she did not believe, and administer unto him, according to my word; and she then becomes the transgressor, and he is exempt from the law of Sarah, who administered unto Abraham according to the law, when I commanded Abraham to take Hagar to wife. And now, as pertaining to this law; verily, verily I say unto you, I will reveal more unto you hereafter; therefore let this suffice for the present. Behold, I am Alpha and Omega. Amen."

When Joseph released all other wives from their marriage contracts, of course Emma was also released. It is said she thought of making another choice, and would have done so, but the Revelation came in time to prevent it. Joseph offered to make the sacrifice, but the Lord told Emma to " abide and cleave to my servant Joseph," who had been cunning enough to insert these clauses in his " Revelation," so as to hold her more closely. It is said that she was shown the first copy of it, and burned it; if so, there must have been another in existence, for the one that Brigham Young gave in 1852 as Joseph's revelation was identical with that given a few of the chosen Saints in 1843.

I have entered somewhat more into detail regarding the early history of Mormonism than I intended in the beginning; but I have considered it necessary to do so, in order to show to my readers more fully the doctrines I have been taught from my infancy, and to give them some idea of the Mormon stand-point. They can easily see how things may become distorted when looked at from such a one-sided position.

CHAPTER IV.

AFTER JOSEPH'S DEATH. — BRIGHAM YOUNG ELECTED PROPHET.

Kindness of the Gentiles. — Strangers in a Strange Land. — My Parents join the Saints in Nauvoo. — They Purchase Land in the City. — Are shamefully Defrauded. — Joseph's Unfaithful Friends. — My Parents left almost Destitute. — I am Born in the Midst of Troubles. — The Saints Bewildered. — Who should succeed Joseph? — Sidney Rigdon's Claims to the Presidency. — He returns to Nauvoo. — Has Dreams and Visions. — He Promises to "Pull Little Vic's Nose." — The Apostles hear of the Prophet's Murder. — They hasten to Nauvoo. — Brigham begins his Successful Intrigues. — He Settles Sidney Rigdon. — An Extraordinary Trial. — Brigham's Idea of Free Voting. — Women's Suffrage in Utah. — Why Brigham gave the Franchise to the Women. — My own Experience as a Voter. — Brigham dictates what I'm to Do. — I obey Quietly. — How Sidney Rigdon was Deposed. — Brigham Rules the Church.

ARRIVAL AT QUINCY ILL.

PON the arrival of the Saints in Illinois they made Quincy their first stopping-place, and thence the majority of them went at once to Nauvoo, the new gathering-place.

My parents did not accompany them, but remained in Quincy two months. They reached that city in a state of almost utter destitution, with barely clothing enough to render them decent, certainly not enough to make them comfortable. Their reception by the residents of the city, indeed by the people of Illinois generally, was very cordial, and my mother often says she shall never forget the kindness she received at their hands. Literally, she "was a stranger and they took her in, hungry and they fed her, naked and they clothed her." And not only her, but her little ones.

My mother was energetic and willing, and she found work in plenty, and managed to get together some of the comforts and necessaries of life, when, after a two months' sojourn amid these hospitable people, they removed to Payson, where my father built a carriage manufactory and once more commenced business. After three years of remunerative labor, during which time he had got his business fairly established, he concluded to leave it and join the Saints at Nauvoo; he and my mother both — the latter more especially — desiring to be once more in Zion with the "chosen people." My father had purchased five acre-lots in the City of Nauvoo, and felt that he had a material as well as a spiritual hold upon Zion. The deeds were properly executed, and after making sure that everything was right during a visit to the city, he made instant preparations to move his family thither.

When he returned with his family and prepared to take possession of his property, he found it claimed by Dr. Foster, a friend and favorite of Joseph Smith, who pretended to have made a verbal contract for the land two years before. This, of course, brought the property into a dispute which could only be settled by the church authorities, Joseph himself presiding. As a matter of course, there was but one decision, and what that would be my father knew very nearly as well before it was given as he did afterwards. Joseph would not decide against his friend; the rest, seeing how his mind was made up, dared not; and the land was declared to belong to Foster, who, by the way,— such were his regard and gratitude for his leader,— apostatized not very long afterwards, attached himself to Law and his party, and finally removed from Nauvoo, denouncing the religion and its Prophet, and, indeed, carried his enmity so far that he joined those miscreants to whose violence may be attributed the death of Joseph Smith.

My father was again stripped of his property, by the treachery and unjust ruling of the very man whom he had so faithfully served. He had enough money remaining, however, to purchase other lots, and on the land thus obtained he built two very comfortable houses, in one of which I was born, as I before said, on the 13th of September, 1844, at the most tempestuous and most critical period in all Mormon history.

Joseph Smith had been assassinated the previous July, and his death, sudden and violent as it was, had almost paralyzed the people, who were thus left without a leader, and who were ill fitted to govern themselves, since they had for so long a time given up their wills to the Prophet, following his instructions as obediently as the most tractable children do their parents' behests. They had for so many years depended upon him to guide them that they were unfitted almost to think for themselves. Life was a hopeless muddle, and they saw no way of making it clearer. Then their former friends had turned to enemies, and they began to fear that they should be driven from their pleasant homes in Illinois, as they had been from Missouri. And with all the disturbance outside the church, there were heresy and schism among themselves.

The question who should be the leader in Joseph's place was exercising the church. The "First Presidency" was composed of Joseph Smith, his brother Hyrum, and Sidney Rigdon. Hyrum Smith was killed in prison with his brother, and Rigdon, although he had not apostatized, had grown cool in the faith, left Nauvoo, and was living at Pittsburg, Pa., enjoying life outside of Mormondom, and seemingly finding much pleasure in Gentile society. After the Missouri episode his enthusiasm was very much chilled, and he indulged in fewer rhodomontades against the government. When Joseph made his advances to his daughter

Nancy, Rigdon was very much offended, and left Nauvoo at once. As soon, however, as he heard of Joseph's death he made all haste to return and secure for himself the "office" of "Prophet, Seer, and Revelator," to which he claimed he had been ordained. He was not received with enthusiasm by the Saints, and he very soon discovered that whoever might step into the dead Prophet's shoes, he, for a certainty, would not be allowed to wear them. There was nothing then remaining for him to do but to assume that Joseph's mantle

SIDNEY RIGDON.

of prophecy had fallen upon his shoulders; consequently, he revelled in visions and dreams of the wildest and most fanatical kind. His prophecies were the most wonderful that ever were heard, and were so very incoherent and inconsistent that serious doubts of his sanity were entertained. There were to be tremendous battles; blood was to flow until the horses waded in it up to their very bridles. All the powers of the earth were to assail the Saints, but Rigdon was to lead the faithful to certain victory. All the strength of earth was to bow before this little band of people and their consecrated leader, and he was, as a final act of triumph as he returned from the battle of Armageddon, to call in England and "pull the nose of little Vic."

What the young queen, then in the full flush of popularity, had done to raise this modern Bombastes' ire, remains to this day a mystery. It is needless to say that the battles have never been fought, nor has her majesty's nose been maltreated by Rigdon or any other crazy Mormon fanatic.

At the time of the assassination of Joseph Smith nearly all the apostles were away on a mission. On hearing the evil tidings from Zion, they hastened there without delay, and Brigham Young, Parley P. Pratt, Orson Hyde, and Heber C. Kimball arrived soon after Rigdon made his appearance, and while he was in the midst of his "revelations." From the moment of their arrival his chances were smaller than ever, although he still maintained, but in not so public a manner as at first, that he held "the keys of David," and that he intended to persist in the maintenance of his claims, even if obliged to do so forcibly.

The man for the situation appeared at this juncture in Brigham Young. Ambitious himself for the position which Rigdon so earnestly coveted, fortune seemed to have placed him exactly in the situation to attain it. He was — so it happened by the merest chance — the senior apostle, and that gave him authority. Thomas Marsh, who was at one time the senior, had apostatized; Patten, the second apostle, had been killed by the mob, and this made the third apostle the first or senior of the "twelve." The third happened to be Brigham Young; so that, after all, it was a mere chance that placed him where he is. Both the Pratts were far superior to him in intellect; and they and Orson Hyde were far ahead of him in mental attainments, such as they were. He was a very plain man, entirely uneducated, and had been noted for nothing except his fidelity to the Prophet and the church and his hard-working disposition. But he was shrewd enough to see his opportunity and to seize it, and yet to do it in such a manner that neither his associates nor the church itself had the least suspicion of his real plan.

The first move was to have Rigdon's case settled. He was summoned for public trial before the High Council, and eight of the apostles appeared as witnesses. Brigham Young played a very important part in this trial; he opened proceedings by accusing Rigdon of a determination to rule the church or ruin it, and followed up the accusation by declaring that he should do neither. All the events of his life were passed in review, and although he was not present, being detained, it was said, by illness, the case was by no means deferred, and he was tried without an opportunity of defending himself. At the motion of Brigham, he was "cut off from the Church of Latter-Day Saints, and delivered over to the buffetings of Satan, in the name of the Lord; and all the people said, Amen."

There were about ten persons who ventured to vote in favor of Rigdon, and they were immediately "suspended" from the church for their temerity. This is the way in which persons are served even now who venture to disagree with Brigham Young. There is absolutely no such thing known among the Mormons as a free expression of opinion. Whether it be on religious or political subjects, the decision of the people is governed by the wishes of the President. The manner of voting in public assemblies is never varied. Brigham prefaces all ceremonies of the kind by an address, in which he manages to let the people know exactly how he feels upon the subject under discussion, and they understand that they are to feel exactly the same way ; and as there is no question of choice, they make themselves fancy they do believe exactly as he does. If they have any question of doubt, they stifle it very quickly, and, if they are very good Mormons, take themselves to task for their wickedness in entertaining a thought contrary to the opinion of their Prophet. After the address, Brigham calls for a show of uplifted hands, and requests every one to vote. The "contrary minds" are then called; but such is the singular unity of this people that there is never a "contrary" mind among them. To make this ceremony of voting more humorous, the Prophet, in requesting all the people to vote, wittily adds, "in one way or the other." This piece of pleasantry on Brigham's part is quite appreciated by the Mormons, and the "one way" receives all the saintly votes, to the utter exclusion of "the other." Let any one attempt to take the

Presidential joke *au sérieux*, and it becomes anything but pleasant for him.   He is looked upon with suspicion, regarded as an enemy of the church and its ruler, and if he escape serious persecution he may be considered especially fortunate.

In politics there is about the same freedom of opinion, or of its expression, rather.   Although a semblance of independent action is kept up, since the people are not publicly told which way they must vote, yet the bishops and ward-teachers manage to make it understood very decidedly what is expected of "the Faithful" at the elections.   The expectations, it is perhaps needless to state, are always realized.

I have often heard ladies in the East say that they considered Utah way in advance of the age in one respect at least; that there the equality of the sexes was so far regarded that the ballot was in the women's hands, and that there they had received the right of suffrage.   And I know that for this one act Brigham Young is commended by some of the leaders of the Woman Suffrage party, and he is viewed by them with a lenient eye, in spite of all his other acts of gross injustice.   If these same radical reformers only understood the reason that the franchise was extended to Utah women, and the peculiar "freedom" and intelligence with which they are allowed to exercise this privilege, I think they would not be so scathing in their denunciations of the Poland bill.   To the men and women engaged in this reform there seems to be no possibility that there can be cases where positive harm would ensue when the ballot was given to women; they evidently believe that with universal suffrage will be ushered in the millennium.

It may have that effect in other portions of the States, but in polygamous Utah, ruled over by a treacherous tyrant, this very right, which they claim will loosen the legal and political shackles by which women are bound, and render them absolutely free, only binds the chains the tighter and makes them greater slaves than ever.   And the most hateful part is, that they are helping to tighten their own bonds, and are doing it, too, under compulsion.

The reason of this wonderful act of "justice" on Brigham Young's part can easily be given. When the Union Pacific Railroad was completed, and the influx of miners and other outsiders from the Gentile world began to flood the Territory and make homes for themselves in the very midst of Mormondom, the chiefs of the Mormon hierarchy grew very fearful and apprehensive lest the power should pass from their grasp into Gentile hands by the gradual change of population. By adopting female suffrage they would treble their voting power at once. There was no longer any hesitation ; the measure was adopted, and so general and generous was it, that in Utah to-day every person of the female sex, from the babe in the arms to the oldest, bed-ridden, imbecile crone, has the right of elective franchise, and is compelled to use it.

To illustrate the intelligence with which women vote, and the freedom of opinion in political matters which is allowed them, I think I can do no better than give my own first experience in exercising the prerogative of a free woman.

It was the first election-day that occurred after the right of suffrage had been, not granted, but commanded. I was standing in front of my husband's office, talking with a friend, when he came out. His first question, put before he had offered either myself or my friend any greeting, was, —

" Have you voted to-day ? "

" No, Brother Young, I have not."

" Then I suppose you intend doing so at once."

" Not at all," I replied ; " I have no intention of voting at all."

" And why not ? " he asked, somewhat angrily.

" Because I have not yet become sufficiently acquainted with the political situation to understand what it is best to do, and I prefer not to vote ignorantly."

" But I wish you to vote," was his peremptory reply.

"Excuse me, please, Brother Young," pleaded I; "I don't know who or what to vote for, and I really had much rather not." I was quite in earnest. I did not know anything then of politics, and I must confess I had no interest in them.

"Get into the carriage," commanded he, so sternly that I knew I must obey, and further parley would be useless. "I want you to vote, and at once. Mr. Rossitur will take you to the polls and tell you how to vote."

Mr. Rossitur, to whose care I was committed, was Brigham's coachman, and was to be my political instructor. All the information I gained will never harm nor help me very

MY FIRST VOTE.

materially. I was driven to the polls, a ticket was handed me, and hustled along without the opportunity of examining it, and to this day I am in blissful ignorance of what or who I cast my only vote for. I know, however, that among other officers they were electing a delegate to Congress, and I suppose I must have voted for George Q. Cannon. There is an encouraging and inspiring picture for the advocates of female suffrage, who are jubilant over the triumph of their cause in Utah. A polygamous wife of the President of the church conveyed to the polls by her husband's coachman, and compelled to cast the vote he gives her without an opportunity of exercising her judgment or her choice, and ignorant even of what she is doing. By all means let us have the suffrage in Utah, in spite of Judge Poland.

After the Council had disposed of Sidney Rigdon to its satisfaction, and "all the people" had signified theirs by saying "Amen," he turned about and prepared to fight them. His resistance, however, was short and feeble, He returned to Pittsburg, and attempted to resurrect the "*Latter-Day Saints' Messenger and Advocate*," a Mormon publication that had died some years before. His attempt was futile, and he gave up the contest with his failure to revive that sheet, and Mormonism has known little or nothing of him since.

In the mean time the Twelve Apostles were to rule over the church until such time as a change in the Presidency should seem necessary. This was Brigham's first step, and the rest came easily and naturally enough. To all intents and purposes he was as much the ruler of the Mormons as he is now, although he did not then arrogate so much to himself. He knew very well that it would not do to declare himself too suddenly; so he quietly worked and waited until he found himself in the position which he now holds — a position which has never been contested by his followers.

He was always a hard worker, quite successful in making converts, and the steady determination of his character, which amounted to decided obstinacy, united with a scheming cunning, helped him very much at this period of his life.

He was shrewd enough not to attempt, as Rigdon had done, to play the prophet; he knew very well that in that rôle he would not meet success. He announced that no one should take Joseph's place, and to this day he maintains to those who remember what he said then, and contrast his past assertions with his present position as head of the church — "No one can take the place of Joseph; he is in his place as the spiritual head of the church, and will always be there, through time and eternity."

"I am no prophet and revelator, as Joseph was," he used to say to the Saints: "but Joseph left revelations enough for you to follow for twenty years; in the mean time, the Lord will reveal Himself to those among you whom He may

choose so to honor, and there is no reason why you should
not all have revelations."

But, revelations or not, one thing he insisted upon: that
was, that the Saints were to "build the kingdom up for
Joseph," and that he kept constantly before them. He next
proceeded to make the church self-sustaining in a pecuniary
sense. Each member was to tithe himself or herself one
tenth of all their property, and place it in the hands of the
"Twelve" for the use of the church. This tithing fund Brigham had absolute control of—a control that he has taken
pains never to lose. He instituted other "reforms" in the
church, and everything he proposed the people acquiesced
in with a surprising readiness. They yielded to him,
seemingly, without being aware that they were yielding,
and he had his own way without opposition, while the poor
deluded Saints thought he was carrying out their ideas, in
part at least. They came under Brigham's yoke without
knowing when they bent their necks to receive it, and in less
than six months after the Prophet's death his mastery over
the church was as assured as it is to-day.

7

CHAPTER V.

MY FATHER'S PLURAL WIFE. — CHILDHOOD IN POLYGAMY.

Childhood in Mormondom. — A striking Contrast. — The Sorrows of my Earliest Years. — How my Mother received Polygamy. — Submitting to the Rod. — Clinging to Love and Home. — Resigning all for Religion. — Strange ways of glorifying God. — The Reward of Faithfulness. — The Prophet Joseph imparts a New Religious Mystery. — The Breaking-up of a Home. — Feais of Rebellion. — The Struggle of Faith against Nature. — Seeking Rest, but finding None. — Brigham's " Counsels." — A New Wife Selected. — My Parents enter into Polygamy. — The New Bride, Elizabeth. — The Marriage Ceremony. — My Mother Sealed. — She is to become a Queen. — Domestic Arrangements in Polygamy. — Bearing the Cross. — A First Wife's Sorrows. — " Where does Polygamy Hurt ? " — The Mormon Husband ; his Position and Privileges.

MY FATHER'S FIRST PLURAL MARRIAGE.

OFTEN wonder if there is a child in Mormondom, born under the blight of polygamy, who knows what it is to have a happy, joyous childhood, rendered more happy and more joyous by the smiling, calm content of the mother in whose arms its tiny infant form lies cradled. I fear the cases are as rare as happy women are.

True, childhood always has a certain careless happiness of its own, that even the saddest surroundings cannot wholly repress ; but even this happiness is embittered by the tearful eyes that gaze into trustful baby ones, and the lips that quiver with pain, as they try to smile back into laughing baby faces.

In the happy homes which I have visited since I broke the chains that bound me, and came forth a free woman, unshackled in thought and untrammelled in action, although a wanderer on the face of the earth, with no abiding-place where to stay my weary feet, I have been compelled to contrast the difference between childhood in a monogamic country and in a polygamous one; and when I have seen the mother's face grow almost divine in its radiant content as she smiled down into the face of the little one sheltered so closely in her heart, I have felt my heart throb and ache with jealous anguish for the little ones in Utah, and above all for their weary-hearted mothers, to whom maternity brings no such joy, and added love, and tender care.

I was consecrated to sorrow by the baptism of my mother's tears upon my baby brow. I never remember on her face one such look as I see daily upon mothers' faces now. My baby hands wiped away tears, my baby fingers stroked a cheek furrowed by them, and my baby eyes never saw beyond the mist in hers. I came to her when the greatest misery of her life was about to fall upon her; and that misery came to her, as it came to all the women then, under the guise of religion — something that must be endured "for Christ's sake." And as her religion had brought her nothing but persecution and sacrifice, she submitted to this new trial as to everything that had preceded it, and received polygamy as a cross laid upon her, but which strength would be given her to bear.

She had never questioned any of Joseph Smith's "revelations," and she did not dare do so now, although this one came to her like a sudden and heavy blow, hurting heart and soul, and rendering the thought of life unendurable. Hitherto, although her sufferings had been severe, and her privations many, yet through them all she had been sustained

by her husband's love. That was hers, and together they
had shared poverty and tasted plenty. Their sufferings
had brought them closer together, and whether in plenty
or poverty, they had been happy in each other and in their
children, and had made a home, and a cheerful one,
wherever they had been, one in which the spirit of love
ruled supreme. Now, her religion told her that she was
selfish and wicked to try and keep this home and husband.
The one must be broken and desolated, the other shared
with some one else. "The Lord commanded it." What a
blasphemy and satire on Him who is the God of Love,
that He should make His children unhappy, and wreck
all hopes of peace and content, for His glory! It seems as
though this one act of Smith's alone should have opened
the eyes of this deluded people, and shown them that their
false Prophet was not taught of God, as he pretended, and
they so fondly believed, but that he was impelled by the
demons of covetousness and lust. But their eyes were
blinded, and they could not see; their reason was inthralled,
and they did not know it was bound; their wills were obedient to his, and he held them soul and body, and played
with them as though they were so many puppets, helpless
and lifeless out of his hands.

Being accounted among the specially "faithful," my parents were among the first to whom polygamy was taught
by Joseph Smith himself, and my father was commanded
by him to "live up to his privileges," and to take another
wife.

At first, the thought of taking a second wife to share his
home with the one whom he had first loved, who had been
the object of his youthful dreams and of his manhood's
devotion; who had stood by him, through every reverse,
with the courage, and consideration, and love which only a
strong-natured, tender-hearted, earnest-souled woman could
show under such circumstances; who was, in every sense,
a helpmeet, and, above all, the mother of his children, — was

hateful to him. It took a long time, too, to overcome his
aversion to the new system. He and my mother had many
a long, tearful talk over it; and although they received the
doctrine, believing that it must be right, they could not for
some time make up their minds to put it in practice. In
the mean time Joseph was assassinated, and for a little time
they were left to each other in peace. But Brigham Young
was bound to carry out Joseph's revelations, and this one
relating to the plural wife system was strongly, though secretly, urged upon the Saints. Both my father and mother
were visited by Brigham, and "counselled" in regard to
the matter. My mother has often said that the "Revelation"
was the most hateful thing in the world to her, and she
dreaded and abhorred it, but she was afraid to oppose it,
lest she should be found "fighting against the Lord." The
thought that she might be obliged to live in a polygamous
relation with another woman filled her with horror and fear;
but she was assured by her religious leader, that the feeling was merely the effect of her early training, which she
would soon outgrow under the benign influences of the
gospel. For several months she struggled with herself over
this subject, before she could think patiently of it for even a
minute. She wanted to have it made easy and plain to
her, for she could not bear to repudiate any of her beloved
Prophet's teachings. She agonized over it day and night;
she prayed incessantly to be given the true "spirit" of submission; if it was God's will, she wanted strength to endure
it; and she believed she should have it, for surely the kind
and loving Father would not impose upon his children burdens greater than they could bear. She had not learned,
as she has since, that the God of the Mormon belief was
not the heavenly Father whose love the Saviour taught, but
a jealous God, a cruel, avenging Spirit, who demanded
blood-offerings to appease his awakened wrath. He was
not the tender Parent, all-wise, all-powerful, and all-lov-
ing, whom she reverenced and adored. There was little

use in looking towards her people's God for help or comfort. Retribution, and justice untempered by mercy, were all He had for His subjects, not children.

During all these months of wavering doubt and untold misery, my father never attempted to influence my mother's decision in the least; she had her battle to fight, and he his; the end was inevitable for both; but for all this the contest was no less severe. Brigham's "counselling" began to assume the form of commands, which at last grew so imperative that they were obliged to be obeyed. My mother did not rebel; she looked upon it as duty, and she was determined to do it silently and uncomplainingly, if not willingly and cheerfully. My parents consulted together regarding the choice of the new wife, and fixed upon the person with surprising unanimity. They were each anxious to help and comfort the other in this as they had been in every other emergency of their lives. My father wished, if he must take another wife, to choose one who should be agreeable to my mother, or rather as agreeable as one woman could be to another under such circumstances; and my mother was, for her part, equally determined not to oppose him in his selection. But opposition was not necessary, as his choice fell upon the very person whom my mother would have selected, had the task rested with her alone.

A short time after my birth, a Miss Elizabeth Taft came, with a younger sister, to live in our house. She was a very pleasant, cheery, affectionate person, and all the family became very much attached to her. Father, mother, children, all quoted "Elizabeth," and she became almost a part of our very selves. She was thoughtful of my mother, and tender to us little ones, petting us and indulging us in our childish whims, and we, in return, loved her very dearly. She was a good woman in its highest interpretation, and devotedly religious. Naturally enough, seeing her so constantly, both my parents thought of her as the new wife. If they must enter polygamy, they knew they could do no better than to take her into the family, if she could be induced to consider the subject in the same light. My father made proposals to her, and my mother seconded them. The thought of living in a polygamic relation with any one was very unpleasant to her, as indeed it is to every true woman; but she desired to live her religion, and believing this to be a part of it, accepted my father's proposal, and became his first plural wife when I was about a year old.

Her parents were in Michigan at the time, and Elizabeth wished to wait until their arrival; but Brigham, who, as a matter of course, was interested in the affair, counselled the marriage to proceed, and of course it was considered right and prudent to obey his counsel; and as he was hurrying forward the endowments in the Nauvoo Temple, preparatory to leaving for the West, the parties most nearly concerned in the matter thought it best to hasten the nuptials.

My mother was to be "sealed" at the same time, as, according to Joseph's Revelation, her former marriage, having been performed in the Gentile form, was not binding. The place of sealing was the Temple; and there, one midwinter day, in the beginning of the year 1846, my mother was sealed to my father for "time and for all eternity," after which she gave him Elizabeth as his wife according to the Mormon marriage formula. It was with a steady voice and calm composure that she pronounced the words that gave another woman a share in her husband's love; but it was none the less with a heavy, breaking heart. Think of it, wives, who are happy in undivided homes, and in your husbands' unshared love! What if your religion commanded you to give another woman to your husband as a wife; who was to have an equal right with you to his attention and his love; who should bear his name, and be a mother to his children; that all this should be done "in the

name of the Lord," and without shrinking or complaint on
your part. Take this home to yourself, and you will be
able to appreciate as never before the horrors of Mormonism.

It was in January that my father obeyed the "counsel" of
his Prophet and leader, and in March his new wife's parents returned, and were shocked and grieved beyond measure to find their daughter married into polygamy ; yet, being
strong in the faith, and much attached to their church and
their religion, submitted without a murmur, like the good
Saints they were.

My mother was so quiet and uncomplaining in the position which she had voluntarily assumed, that she was praised
by the officious brethren and sisters for submitting with
such good grace, and was told by them that great glory
awaited her as a reward, and also, as she had so readily
made the great sacrifice, she would always be recognized
as the first wife, which, among the Mormons, is considered
an exceeding great honor. One of the sisters, who was a
strong advocate of the new "Celestial" system, said to her :
"You will stand at the head of your husband's kingdom
as a queen ; no one can ever take your place from you, but
you will be honored to stand by his side through the endless
ages of eternity." It was by such nonsensical talk and
absurd promises as these that the Mormon leaders tried
to make polygamy attractive to the women who were already married, and render them more willing to enter it.
Such absurdities may have weight with some women, but
they did not affect my mother, nor render the cross she had
assumed any more easy to bear. Her husband's undivided
love during time was better than royal honors in eternity.

The new wife lived in the family, and to outward appearance everything was unchanged. Only a few of the "very
faithful" knew of the new arrangement ; it was deemed
best to keep it a secret from the majority of the people, to
whom polygamy was not a fixed fact, and who were waver-

ing slightly in the faith on account of it. The time had not yet come to promulgate the doctrine freely, and many left Nauvoo for the West quite ignorant that the system really existed in their midst. I think many of them never would have crossed those endless plains, and sought shelter under the shadow of the Rocky Mountains, had they known what unhappiness awaited them. But unchanged as our family circle was to those outside it, within was unhappiness and bitterness of spirit. It was much harder to endure, even, than my mother had anticipated. Terrible as was the thought, the reality was much more horrible. She thought she had counted the cost; she found she had, in her ignorance, been unable to estimate it. Every hour of her life her heart was torn by some new agony. She was compelled to see many of the tender, wifely little offices, trifles in themselves, that she had been accustomed to perform, done by other hands, and she herself always turned off with the excuse, "You see, dear, you have the children to attend to, and I did not wish to give you trouble." Trouble! as though anything done for him, with a heart full of love, could be accounted as such! That hurt her almost as much as to see another doing what it had always been her delight to do.

As is the custom of men in polygamy, my father fell more easily into the new arrangement, and even found a certain comfort and content in it, and he wondered very much that my mother could not be happy as well. Indeed, he was a little impatient, after a while, that she would not say she was content and satisfied in the new relation.

"I don't understand it," he would say; "you were willing at first. What is the difficulty now? Don't you think Elizabeth a good, true girl?"

"Yes, indeed," was always the reply; for my mother was too just a woman to do even a rival a wrong.

"Don't you believe in polygamy, then?" he would ask, determined to get to the bottom of the mystery.

"Yes, I suppose so. I wish to live *my* religion," was the dreary reply.

"Well, what is to be done about it?" was the next anxious question.

"O, I don't know," my mother would say, in bitter despair; "but I can't endure this life."

"And yet you entered it voluntarily. I don't understand you; you are strangely inconsistent."

Her remonstrance and his comfort never went beyond this point. There was nothing more to be said. She had protested with unutterable anguish against the life that she felt was false and in direct contradiction to every law of moral right, although she was told to look upon it as "divine;" and the only answer she could get was, "You are inconsistent; you entered the relation voluntarily." The very truth of this reply silenced her, but it did not make her burdens any lighter or easier to bear.

She saw that patient endurance was all that was required of her, and all she could give. Her husband was hers no longer; she herself had given another woman the same right to his care that she had; and now she turned to all that was left her in life that she could call her own — her children. Had it not been for us she would have prayed to die. I was the baby, and she has said that at that time I was the strongest tie which held her to life. If it had not been for me, lying helpless in her arms, she would have taken her life into her own hands, and put an end to it then and there. But she could not endure the thought of leaving me, her only daughter, — her baby girl, — alone and unshielded by a mother's care. My brothers, who were quite large boys at that time, she thought would not miss her, nor need her so much; and many a time she has knelt with me clasped fast in her arms, the tears falling on my wondering face, and prayed frantically that we both might die. The thought that she had brought a girl into the world to suffer as she was now suffering, to find her whole life's happiness

made a wreck by the religion which should be a stay and
a comfort, drove her almost wild. She had buried one
little girl, and I have often heard her thank God that He
had taken her to Himself before life became a terrible bitterness and burden. She often says, in referring to her
sufferings at that time, and the desperate state she was in,
she wonders she did not commit suicide; what kept her
from it she cannot tell to this day, unless the thought that
these polygamous relations did not end with time, but were
carried on through all eternity.

She had to keep a double guard on her tongue and on
her actions. She did not like to vex her husband, and
neither did she wish to grieve the young wife, whose position
was no pleasanter than her own. Besides, a husband in
polygamy is very sensitive regarding the treatment of the
last wife by those who have preceded her, and she knew
that no act of hers would escape her husband's notice, even
had she been inclined to ill-treat her rival.

"DO YOU THINK *I* HAVE NO TRIALS?"

Once, very mildly and kindly, she tried to tell some of
her troubles to Elizabeth, and begged her not to add to her
sorrow by bestowing so many marks of affection on my
father in her presence. The young wife turned on her
quickly, and demanded, bitterly, —

"Do you think *I* have no trials?"

"God forgive me, and help us both ; *I know you have,*" was my mother's quick and sympathetic answer.

After all, what could she say or do? She had influenced the girl quite as much as my father had, believing she was only doing what was right, and that the act, hard as it was, would bring its own blessing with it. Instead, it brought what polygamy always does bring — the curse of a wrecked home and a life's unhappiness.

A gentleman visiting Salt Lake City for the first time once asked me where polygamy hurt the most.

"It hurts all over, body and soul, mind and heart," was my reply. "I can't tell a spot that it does not hurt."

"It is even worse than I thought," he replied, with a shudder.

The reply which I gave then I would give again. Never, until a woman ceases to love her husband, can polygamy cease to be anything but a series of cruel stings, alike to pride and conscience.

I have tried to portray a little something of the misery that fell upon our family by the introduction of polygamy into it, but I have utterly failed to give an adequate idea of it. No pen can possibly depict the heart-breaking sufferings that are endured by women in this relation, and no one can imagine or understand them who has not experienced them. And yet, in spite of all this unhappiness, we were accounted a model family, and were pointed out as the best exponents of the system. "They are so united!" was the admiring verdict. This was due a great deal to my mother's exertions and her conscientiousness. Having taken this new mode of life as a religious duty, she was determined not to be found wanting in readiness to perform whatever it required of her. A happy, contented spirit she could not give ; but she could show patience, long-suffering, and a calm, though by no means cheerful, face and manner.

Then, my father was very just in the treatment of his wives. One did not fare better than the other in any re-respect. If he purchased an article of wearing apparel for one, he got its counterpart for the other; in every particular they shared alike. His position was by no means an enviable one; still it was preferable to that of either of his wives. Men, as I said before, always get the best of it in polygamy, and always become more easily reconciled to it than do the women. At meetings and all social assemblies, my father appeared with both wives, and they deferred to each other in the most charming way, both of them being too sensible and too proud to show the slightest feeling where it might be commented on. Then, too, in spite of the natural bitterness of feeling between them, there was a mutual respect and regard between them, and each was too just to lay her troubles at the door of the other. Had these two women, with their generous natures and firm principles, met on any other ground, they would not only have "got along" amiably and quietly as they did, but they would have been warm, earnest friends, and the respectful regard would have grown into positive affection. As it was, they had nothing but kind words for each other, my mother, especially, pitying the young wife as she did herself. Elizabeth was still kind to us children, and gained the love which she has held ever since, and which she fully deserved. Still the introduction of polygamy into our midst was not a pleasant thing, and we little ones, even, felt instinctively its baleful influence.

But we were to be diverted from the contemplation of its miseries by a new and absorbing excitement. The Mormon people were again compelled to move, leaving their beautiful new city in the "defiled hands" of the Gentiles; and in the very midst of our first family trouble and unhappiness came the command to seek another Zion, since this could no longer be a shelter for the Saints.

CHAPTER VI.

FORSAKING DEAR ZION. — WE FIND A NEW HOME IN
THE FAR WEST.

A New Home in the West. — Dangerous Neighbors. — Some very Un-
pleasant Stories. — Seeking a New Home. —Preparing to Depart. —
Life at Winter-Quarters. — A Lively Time in the Temple. — " Little
Dancin' Missy." — Bound for Salt Lake Valley. — Life by the Way. —
Songs of the Saints. — A False Prophecy. — " The Upper California." —
Saintly Profanity. — A Soul-stirring Melody. — The Saints Excited. —
Beside the Camp-Fires. — The Journey Ending. — Entering Zion. —
The Valley of the Great Salt Lake.

N the spring of 1846 our
family left Nauvoo, with
the large body of the
Saints, to find a new home
in the West. The Mor-
mon people had become
quite as unpopular in Illinois as they had been in
Missouri; and collisions
between them and the
Gentiles were very fre-
quent.

Sometimes it was one
side that was the aggressor, sometimes the other. The
Saints were indignant at the treachery which resulted in
Joseph Smith's death. They held the United States government responsible for it, as well as for the troubles in
Missouri, and taught disloyalty to the government, and personal revenge on all who molested them.

The people of Illinois, in their turn, regarded the Mormons as dangerous neighbors, and getting a hint of the
new doctrine of polygamy, looked upon them as grossly

immoral, and accused them of much greater crimes than they really committed. All sorts of horrible rumors were rife, and the indignation of the people outside knew no bounds.

The Mormon people realized, very soon after Joseph's death, that they must seek a new home, and they looked with a feeling of positive relief to the unexplored region beyond the Rocky Mountains. They believed that there they would find a realization of all that had been promised them by their murdered Prophet. At least they would be beyond all interference and molestation, and after all they had suffered, they did not care how much space they put between themselves and the Gentile world.

All through the winter of 1845 and '46, my father was very busy building wagons for the purpose of transporting the Saints and their property to their new and yet unknown home ; for their destination was not definitely known to any of them at that time. The Apostle Taylor advocated California, and, indeed, announced that it would be the Saints' objective point when they should leave Nauvoo. He wrote an emigration song about it, and all the way from Nauvoo to Winter-Quarters, some of the emigrating party were tunefully averring, —

"The Upper California, O, that's the land for me !"

Yet, in spite of Taylor's prophecy and the saintly singing of it, they never reached California.

It mattered little to me, at that period of my existence, where we went. Home was home wherever my mother was, whether it was east, west, or camping on the prairies between. Of course I remember but little respecting the exodus of the Saints from Nauvoo ; still there are indistinct recollections of things that happened as early as that which sometimes cross my mind, although they are very dim. My first distinct remembrance was of Winter-Quarters, which were then where Council Bluffs now stands.

My father built a log-house there, and we were comparatively comfortable. Our family consisted of my father, mother, two brothers, myself, and Elizabeth, the new wife. We were together nearly all the time, but when my father went into Missouri to work a while at his business, and get a little money ahead to take us to our new home, and settle us, he took my mother, my younger brother, and myself, leaving Elizabeth — the new wife — and my oldest brother at Winter-Quarters.

Notwithstanding the facts of the enforced emigration, the uncertainty of their future, and sacrifices they had been compelled to make, the migrating Mormons were not an unhappy party, and they managed to make their stay in Winter-Quarters lively, if not merry. As a people, they have always mixed amusement with their religion in the most amusing manner. Dancing was a favorite recreation with them, and all their balls were commenced with prayer. That custom, by the way, is still continued, and the blessing of "the Lord" invoked at every dancing party which takes place in Mormondom. The Temple at Nauvoo (I have heard) was used for dancing parties, and it was then given out that the exercise was a religious one. It was taught to the Saints that recreation was positively necessary. Everybody dances among the Saints — president, counsellors, apostles, elders, and all; and they dance with an unction, too, that is very amusing, and frequently ridiculous.

It was while on the way to Salt Lake, when I was only about three years old, that I learned to dance. It was when I was living in Missouri that I had my first lessons. Dancing was the common amusement there, and I remember the negroes used to play. I was active and lithe, and very ready at imitations, and had, besides, a quick ear for music. I was petted by everybody, and the negro musicians took a special fancy to "little dancin' missy," and they taught me several negro dances, which I used to execute to the intense delight of my sable instructors, and the amusement of my friends.

That winter, in Missouri, is one of the bright spots in my childhood, to which I am especially fond of looking back. It is, indeed, the only really happy time I can recollect. My father was busy most of the time, and we lived very pleasantly and comfortably, for that section of the country at that early day; my mother was more cheerful than I had ever known her to be, and the atmosphere of our home was peaceful. The second wife had been left at Council Bluffs, and my mother had her husband's sole care and attention, as she had had it in the old days before the curse of polygamy was thrust upon her to embitter her whole life, and rob her of all that a woman holds most dear, and guards most jealously. Its shadow was over her still, and she knew she could not escape from it; but she would take what comfort she could, and think no more of past or future sufferings than she could possibly help.

In 1847 a party of the Saints left Winter-Quarters for the Salt Lake Valley. My parents had intended to accompany them, but my father was obliged to remain on account of business, and to assist in the final departure of the main body of the church. Brigham Young and his family went, necessarily, with the first party. Brigham was now absolute in authority, and he managed the affairs of the Saints so arbitrarily that no one dreamed of interfering with him, or gainsaying him in the least. He decreed that my father should remain at Winter-Quarters, and as a matter of course he obeyed. We were there another winter, and all the while my mother's heart was setting most strongly Zionward.

It was the 4th of May, 1848, when at last we were fairly started for our Rocky-Mountain home. The hearts of all the people were filled with eager anticipation, and they said "good-bye" cheerfully and heartily to the civilized world,

8

in which were centred all the memories of their past, and
turned gladly towards that unknown country beyond the
wild plains and pathless deserts in which were all the hopes
of their future.

My father took provisions that would last a year, by
practising economy, and we had two wagons and three
yoke of oxen ; there were six of us in the family — our own
selves and Elizabeth. We joined with a train of two hundred wagons, which was afterwards divided into companies of fifties. I suppose the journey must have been a
tiresome one to the older members of the party, but I enjoyed it extremely. I ran along, during a portion of the
day, by the side of the wagons, picking the flowers by the
way, and talking to the different members of the train, for
I knew everybody, and was petted almost as much by my
fellow-travellers as I had been by my negro friends in Missouri. It is a wonder that I was not completely spoiled ; I
daresay I should have been, had it not been for my mother's sensible and judicious training. I was her idol, the
one object for which she cared the most in the world ; but
for all that, she ruled me wonderfully, and I yielded her the
most implicit obedience, while giving her the most passionate childish love and devotion.

I remember her so distinctly on this journey ! She occupied herself a great deal with writing, keeping a literal
transcript of all that befell us on our journey, mingled with
the deepest religious meditation and poetic fancies. She
always wrote in a large book, which she afterwards destroyed, when we arrived at Salt Lake City. I have always
regretted the destruction of that book, as I should have
liked it as a *souvenir* of that journey to the "Promised
Land." But she was so shy of having her feelings known,
and so fearful lest it might fall into some person's hands
who would not understand her, but who would jeer at her
for a sentimentalist, that she put it out of the way at the
very earliest opportunity. Among other things, she wrote

a song, which used to be sung in camp, and was a great favorite; but even that is lost. I cannot recall it to memory, and my mother will not, as she says it is much better forgotten.

We rested every Sabbath, and always held services. Sometimes we staid a week in camp, resting our tired oxen, and recruiting our own strength. It was a pleasant season of the year, and we could afford to travel leisurely,

A BLESSING FROM BRIGHAM.

as we had left Winter-Quarters so early that we had ample time to reach Salt Lake Valley before the weather became disagreeable, even if we made frequent stops. We had plenty of provisions, too, and there was no fear of their becoming exhausted.

Brigham Young had returned from the new settlement to accompany the emigrants and show them the way. We travelled in company with him, and I attracted a great deal of his attention. The two families, Brigham's and our own, had lived in adjoining houses in Nauvoo, and I had known "Brother Young" from my birth; he blessed me in my infancy, and I was at one time as great a favorite of his as any child ever could be; which isn't speaking very enthusiastically of his affection, to be sure, since he is not noted for fondness for children, even his own. I little thought then what relation I should one day hold to this man, who was older than my father. My future was not foreshadowed in that summer journey in search of a home.

The Saints used to cheer their tedious journey by singing from some point or other in the train. I could always catch snatches of song; and on Sunday, while we were encamped, the whole body of the Saints would sing their hymns and local songs together. Some of these I recollect very distinctly, and, even now, find myself humming snatches of them, having taken them up quite unconsciously. One of them I referred to before, by the Apostle Taylor, who at that time was a famous hymn-writer for the Saints. This one especially was a great favorite of the younger men in the company, and if one voice began it while we were journeying on, it would be taken up the whole length of the train and sung with great unction. I give it as a specimen of the style of hymns that was popular in the church.

"The Upper California, O, that's the land for me!
It lies between the mountains and the great Pacific Sea;
    The Saints can be supported there,
    And taste the sweets of liberty,
In Upper California — O, that's the land for me!

We'll go and lift our standard, we'll go there and be free,
We'll go to California, and have our jubilee;
    A land that blooms with endless spring,
    A land of life and liberty,
With flocks and herds abounding — O, that's the land for me!

We'll burst off all our fetters, and break the Gentile yoke,
For long it has beset us, but now it shall be broke;
  No more shall Jacob bow his neck;
  Henceforth he shall be great and free
In Upper California — O, that's the land for me!

We'll reign, we'll rule and triumph, and God shall be our King;
The plains, the hills, the valleys shall with hosannas ring;
  Our towers and temples there shall rise
  Along the great Pacific Sea,
In Upper California — O, that's the land for me!

We'll ask our cousin Lemuel to join us heart and hand,
And spread abroad our curtains throughout fair Zion's land.
  Till this is done, we'll pitch our tents
  Along the great Pacific Sea,
In Upper California — O, that's the land for me!

Then join with me, my brethren, and let us hasten there;
We'll lift our glorious standard, and raise our house of prayer;
  We'll call on all the nations round
  To join our standard and be free
In Upper California — O, that's the land for me!"

Another one that the Saints used to sing a great deal — and one that was composed in Nauvoo, to be sung in the Temple before the exodus — was set to the pathetic air of "Old Dan Tucker." I give what I can remember of it.

  "In '46 we leave Nauvoo,
  And on our journey we'll pursue;
  We'll bid the mobbers all farewell,
  And let them go to heaven or hell.

  Old Governor Ford, he is so small
  There is no room for soul at all;
  He neither can be damned nor blest,
  Though heaven or hell should do their best."

This song, profane as it may seem, was sung, not once, but many times, in Nauvoo Temple, and religious exercises in camp were never considered complete without it. Why these two songs stand out more prominently in my memory than any others — with one exception, which I shall presently mention — I do not know, unless it was because the airs pleased me; the first was bright, stirring, and very easily caught; the other was familiar to me in Missouri. When I think of it now, two scenes always come to my mind: one, of a little blue-eyed girl, dancing merrily under the trees while a band of delighted negroes sang the gay tune which the tiny feet were beating out; another, of the same little girl, running along by the side of a covered emigrant-wagon, with her hands full of half-withered flowers which she had picked by the wayside, listening to the old song with the new words, which she only half comprehended, and involuntarily making her steps keep time to the music.

The other hymn which I remember was a great favorite with the Saints, and whenever they sang it, it had the power of awakening the wildest enthusiasm. It is of a style entirely different from either of the other two. I can't help quoting here a verse or two, it is so much a part of the memory of this portion of my life.

"The Spirit of God, like a fire is burning!
    The latter-day glory begins to come forth;
  The visions and blessings of old are returning;
    The angels are coming to visit the earth;
        We'll sing and we'll shout, with the armies of heaven;
        Hosanna! hosanna to God and the Lamb!
      Let glory to them in the highest be given,
        Henceforth and for ever.   Amen and Amen!

The Lord is extending the Saints' understanding,
    Restoring their judges and all as at first;
  The knowledge and power of God are expanding;
    The veil o'er the earth is beginning to burst.

We'll call in our solemn assemblies in spirit,
    To spread forth the kingdom of heaven abroad,

That we through our faith may begin to inherit
The visions, and blessings, and glories of God.

We'll wash and be washed, and with oil be anointed,
Withal not omitting the washing of feet,
For he that receiveth his penny appointed
Must surely be clean at the harvest of wheat.

Old Israel that fled from the world for his freedom,
Must come with the cloud and the pillar amain ;
A Moses, and Aaron, and Joshua lead him,
And feed him on manna from heaven again.

How blesséd the day when the lamb and the lion
Shall lie down together without any ire,
And Ephraim be crowned with his blessing in Zion,
As Jesus descends with his chariots of fire.
We'll sing and we'll shout, with the armies of heaven :
Hosanna ! hosanna to God and the Lamb !
Let glory to them in the highest be given,
For ever and ever. Amen and Amen."

This hymn always stirred the Saints to the very depths
of their natures. It was as appealing and sonorous as a
battle-cry, as exultant as a trumpet-note of victory. Without
understanding it, I was powerfully affected by it ; my cheeks
would glow, my eyes flush with tears, and my little heart
grow so large that I would almost suffocate. The sublime
exaltation of the Saints, as they sung this, was felt by me,
child as I was, though I could not comprehend it. I shut
my eyes now, and see a large company gathered together,
in a fast-falling twilight, on a wide plain, that seems as endless as the ocean ; the blue of the star-studded sky is the
only covering for the heads of this company. In the dusk
the white-covered wagons look weird and ghostly. Camp-
fires are burning ; men, women, and children are clustered
together, and the talk goes back to the old days and the trials
and persecutions which these people have borne, and forward

to an independent and happy future, blessed of God and unmolested by man.   In the glow of anticipation, some one strikes up this fervid hymn,— the rallying-song of the Mor-

mons, — and the wide plains echo back the stirring strains. I nestle by my mother's side, awed and subdued, but content to feel the clasp of her hand and meet the loving light of her eyes.   The song is over, and "hosannas" and "amens" resound on every side, and out of the blue sky the stars smile down on the wanderers with a calm, hopeful light.

Never, to the very last, up to the time of my abandoning Mor-monism and leaving Utah, could

SINGING THE RALLYING-SONG.

I hear this hymn unmoved ; and even now the very thought of it thrills me strangely.   I have heard it sung again and again since then ; but it is, nevertheless, indissolubly con-nected with that journey across the plains and over the mountains.

Towards the last of the journey some of the Saints began to be somewhat impatient, and begged to hasten onward. We had occupied nearly the whole summer with the journey, and probably crossed the plains more comfortably and with less trouble or loss than any train which followed us.   Start-ing as early as we did, we could move as slowly as we liked, with no dread of winter storms overtaking us.   The last stop we made of any length was at Weber River, where we remained a week in camp, fishing, and getting ready for the final part of our journey.   Our wanderings were nearly at an end ; only a few days more and we should reach our new home — the " Zion " of the promises, the resting-place for God's people.   Brigham, who did not often indulge in

CROSSING THE PLAINS—JOURNEYING ZIONWARD.

"revelations," said the place had been pointed out to him in
a vision, and in the shadow of the mountains the Saints
should hold their own against the entire world. The pictures of the mountain-fastnesses which he drew for the
wandering people, and his assurances of their future safety
and constantly increasing power, filled them with anticipation and exultation. Already they saw the masses of the
converted from the Gentile world knocking at their doors
for admission; this yet unbuilt city in the wilderness was to
be the Lord's dwelling-place on earth, and to Him here,
from every nation on the globe, sinners were to come flock-
ing, whose future glory would add to the brightness of His
kingdom here and swell His kingdom in heaven.

From their stronghold in the mountains they were to reach
out and grasp the whole world. "The fulness of the earth"
was to be the Lord's through them. Like the Covenanters
of old, they might have sung, —

> "For the strength of the hills we bless Thee,
>   Our God, our fathers' God!
> Thou hast made Thy children mighty
>   By the touch of the mountain sod.
> Thou hast placed the Ark of Refuge
>   Where the spoiler's foot ne'er trod;
> For the strength of the hills we bless Thee,
>   Our God, our fathers' God."

In spite of all that this devoted people had passed through,
they still believed they were the "Chosen of God," to whom
it was given to "build the waste places of Zion, and make
the desert blossom as the rose."

There was general rejoicing when at last the camp at
Weber's River was broken, and we were again on our way.
The spirit of prophecy broke loose and fairly run riot among
the leaders. The "Promised Land" was near, the "City of
Refuge" for the weary-footed Saints was nearly reached,
where God Himself would cheer his people. The rest of

the journey was accomplished quickly; lagging footsteps hastened and heavy hearts grew light as they neared the Mormon Canaan. It was destined not to be a land over-flowing with milk and honey, but they had little care for that, when, on the 20th of September, 1848, they reached the Salt Lake Valley, and were welcomed to the Fort by the little band who had preceded them into the wilderness. They were travel-stained and weary; but here was home at last — the " Zion " of their hopes.

CHAPTER VII.

OUR WELCOME TO "ZION."—UTAH IN EARLY DAYS.

Our Welcome to Zion. — Housekeeping under Difficulties. — Our First Home in Utah. — The Second Wife's Baby. — The Young Mother. — A Very Delicate Position. — Doctors at a Discount. — Brigham's Wife turns Midwife. — An Obedient Woman. — Taking care of the Baby. — Practising Economy. — The Path of the Crickets. — Too much Cracked Wheat. — Building the First Mill. — Brother Brigham Speechifies. — Tea at Five Dollars per Pound. — Californian Gold Discovered. — Building up Zion.— Brigham's "Dress Reform." — A Rather Queer Costume.— The Women "Assert" Themselves . — Clara Decker Rebels. — How the Prophet treats his Wives. — I ask for some Furs, and am Snubbed. — How the Prophet doled out his Silk. — Eliza Snow and Fanny's Finery. — The Prophet Snubs Eliza. — He Combats' the "Grecian Bend." — Dancing among the Saints. — Polygamy Denied. — How the Saints received It. — A Nice Little Family Arrangement.

BRIGHAM IMITATING THE "GRECIAN BEND."

UR own immediate family were welcomed by Elizabeth's parents, who had gone on with the first body of the Saints, and were living as comfortably as they could under the circumstances, in the Fort. We were their guests but a short time; then we moved into a tent and our covered travelling-wagon, which constituted our first housekeeping establishment in Utah.

We were quite in the fashion, however, as nearly all our
friends were living in the same way. My father commenced
immediately to build an adobe house, hoping to get us into
it before the winter set in. When it was finished it was regarded with admiration, and ourselves with envy, since no
one else had so fine a place. The reason of its superiority
was, that it was the second house in the place, and the
other was a miserable affair of a log-cabin, in contrast with
which our adobe structure was quite a palatial affair.

Shortly after our arrival at Salt Lake, Elizabeth added a
son to the family. This was a time and an occurrence to try
my mother's spirit; but she bore it bravely, and showed herself a true Christian, and a brave and sympathetic woman.
She took all the care of the mother and child, and was as
devoted to the former as though she had been a daughter.
If there was any bitterness in her heart towards her, she
certainly did not show it at this crisis of her life. It was a
trying position for her to be placed in, as any woman can
realize who will give a thought to the circumstances, — a
woman caring for another during the birth of a child whose
father is her own husband.

For many years the Mormons rejected the aid of physicians altogether. They applied oil, and "laid hands" on
all sick persons, without regard to their ailments. If a
person was ill, the elders were called, and they anointed him
with consecrated oil; then they rubbed or manipulated him,
much after the manner of the modern "magnetic treatment,"
the elders praying audibly all the time. In cases of child-
birth, women used to officiate, and Brigham Young compelled one of his wives, Zina Huntington, to learn mid-
wifery, in order that she might attend her husband's other
wives during their *accouchements*. The task was extremely
distasteful to her, as she was not particularly fond of nurs-
ing; and as those to be cared for were her own rivals, she,
of course, relished the work still less. But she was a good,
conscientious woman, and her reverence for her husband —

for, strange as it may seem, she *did* reverence him —
would not allow her to resist any commands he might place
upon her; and her generous nature and strict sense of
justice would not allow her to neglect any one under her
care, no matter how distasteful the person might be to her.
She never carried her personal feelings into a sick room,
and always gave her patient the tenderest, most watchful,
and motherly care. The world, Mormon or Gentile, does
not hold a nobler, truer woman than Zina Huntington
Young.

ANOINTING THE SICK WITH OIL.

In the absence of physicians, almost the entire responsibility and care of Elizabeth and the boy, my half brother,
fell upon my mother. She has often said that in the care
she gave her at that time, she tried to make amends for
some of the bitterness of feeling she had shown before.
She never expected to be reconciled to the family arrangement; but as it was inevitable, she was determined to do
everything in her power to help everyone concerned in it,
and to make the new home in Zion as peaceful and har-
monious as possible. It was a difficult task; but then po-

lygamy is made up of difficult tasks and trying situations.
There is nothing else in it, — no one palliation for all the
woe. My mother grew very much attached to the child,
and he clung to her with loving affection. He is twenty-
six years old now, but he has always kept his love for
"Auntie," as he calls my mother, and she has an unflagging
interest in him. Indeed, all Elizabeth's children are fond
of my mother, and our two families have been more united
than polygamous families usually are. This has been due
to the common-sense of the two mothers, who, the dupes of
a false system and a still falser religion, nevertheless knew
each that the other was not to blame for the mutual suffering. For twelve years they lived together under one roof,
eating at the same table, with not an unkind word passing
between them. It was a matter of conscience with both;
they were neither of them resigned to the situation, but
they believed that it was right, and they must endure it.

When we arrived at "the Valley" we found the people
practising the most rigid economy. The crickets had been
very numerous, and had almost entirely destroyed the
crops, devastating whole fields, until they looked as though
they had been scorched by fire. A few had managed, by
most desperate exertions, to save some of their wheat; but
as there was only an apology for a mill, with no bolting
apparatus, this wheat was obliged to be eaten without being
sifted. When I have seen persons eating cracked wheat
as a delicacy, and heard them speaking of it with the subdued enthusiasm which some people manifest when talking
of food, I have thought of the time when this delicacy was
the only thing that was seen on the tables at Utah for breakfast, dinner, or supper, and I have come to the conclusion
that "delicacies" may, in time, grow monotonous.

To be sure, we brought flour and other necessaries from
the Missouri River in considerable quantity, — enough to
have lasted us a long time, had we kept them exclusively
for our own use; but on our arrival we divided with those

who had none, and ate our share of the coarse bread. As soon as possible a good mill was built, and the year after we arrived we had our wheaten flour again. Of course when once our small store of groceries was exhausted, it was quite impossible to procure more in the Territory. Everything was used most sparingly, and what had, in the States, been looked upon as actual necessaries, were now positive luxuries. It was a year of deprivation and self-denial, but the Saints bore every cross with patience, and were brave to the end. During the time no word of complaint was heard, and not one seemed to regret the step he had taken. There was an exultation and a spirit of freedom that amounted to bravado. Brigham added to this spirit by his Sunday discourses in the Bowery, by such language as the following : —

"We are now out of reach of our enemies, away from civilization, and we will do as we please, with none to molest. The Gentiles cannot reach us now. If they try it they will find themselves in trouble."

During the first year we had only the groceries we brought with us ; but the following year some kinds were brought in from the States, and although the prices demanded were fearfully high, yet buyers were found for all the articles. Tea sold for five dollars a pound, sugar for one dollar and fifty cents a pound ; potatoes brought their weight in silver, and potato-balls were brought from California, at a great expense, to be used for seed.

It was at this time that the California mines were discovered, and the gold-dust actually was more plentiful than food or clothing, for a while.

The first winter was filled with a variety of occupations, the men going to the cañons for timber, building houses, and taking care of stock ; the women knitted, repaired the dilapidated clothing, and attended to the household duties, necessarily in a very primitive fashion. There wasn't a pair of idle hands in the entire settlement. The yarn which the women used for knitting was made from buffalo wool, which we picked from the sage-bush on the journey. The carding and spinning were also done by the sisters. Our principal food, the first winter, was dried buffalo-meat, very poor beef, and the coarse bread of which I have spoken, made from the unbolted wheat. Occasionally, as a very great luxury, we had dried fruit and a cup of tea; but this was only on state occasions, and at very long intervals.

I am sorry to say that bickerings among this Saintly people were no more infrequent than among the Gentiles, and that there were as many disputes over land and other claims in "Zion," as ever there had been in "Babylon." They were not above jealousies, either, this "chosen people;" and, indeed, on our arrival at Salt Lake we found trouble between the Apostle John Taylor and Bishop Smart, the two men whom Brigham Young had left in authority when he left Utah for the States to fetch the remainder of the Saints. Each had become jealous of the other, and envious of his authority, and it required considerable skill and tact to settle the apostolic quarrel and make matters smooth again. Jedediah M. Grant was presiding, and holding the two factions apart when Brigham arrived; and so well did he manage this most difficult task, that, as a reward for his faithfulness and patience, Brigham made him his second counsellor. It took some time to settle this and other disputes, and often the entire Sunday service was devoted to the adjustment of difficulties between the brethren.

The Fort was by no means large enough to hold all the people who had already arrived, and tents would be comfortable for only a few weeks. The work of building went on as rapidly as possible, those who were able having log or adobe houses, while others of less extensive means were obliged to content themselves with "dugouts," which were nothing more or less than holes dug in the ground and covered with willow boughs and earth.

When the clothing wore out, as there was no cloth there, and no wool to make it from, the men wore clothes made of deer and antelope skins. It was at this time that Brigham undertook to inaugurate a "dress reform" among the women, and introduce a most unique style of dress of his own invention. If the dress reformers of the East are likely to fail in their attempts to present a sufficient quantity of novelties to meet the demands of their patrons, I would most respectfully recommend to their most favorable notice President Young's "inspired" dress, which was called the "Deseret costume."

It is a marked peculiarity of the Mormon Mogul, that he is extremely fond of interfering. No matter is too trivial for his mind to dwell upon and consider. Nothing is of too private or personal a nature for him to refrain from meddling with it. From the *cuisine* of the poorest family in the Territory to the wardrobe of the richest, nothing escapes him, and whatever he may say or do, no one dares resent his interference.

Not long after the arrival of the Saints in Utah, Brigham conceived the idea of a uniform dress, by which the sister Saints should be distinguished from the rest of the world, and for a while he was enthusiastic on the subject of this "dress reform." He not only introduced the idea of this dress, but he planned it himself, and was as proud of his costume as Worth is of any one of the most gorgeous gowns which he sends out from his world-famed establishment. Several of the sisters had adopted the Bloomer costume in Illinois, and President Young had warmly approved of it. He now wanted something more pronounced, and he held meetings with the leading ladies who favored his plan, for the purpose of deciding in what manner to introduce the new costume. There was much excitement over it, and most of the sisters were intensely curious concerning the proposed style of it, when suddenly it was revealed to them in all its beauty.

9

The costume consisted of a short dress, which did not fit the figure at all, but resembled very closely the modern gored wrapper, such as is worn at the present time. It reached about half way between the knee and ankle, and was worn with long pantalets, made of the same material as the dress itself. Over this was worn a long, loose sacque, of antelope skin. This costume was certainly peculiar and distinctive enough; but it did not quite suit the Mormon Worth; it was not complete enough; so he added a hat eight inches high, with a straight, narrow brim; and then he viewed his achievement with complacent admiration.

THE DESERET COSTUME.

It must be confessed, however, that the large majority of the sisters did not share his admiration; and even he, although he strenuously urged the general adoption of this costume, could induce but very few of the sisters to wear it. Even Mormon women will assert themselves in matters of the *toilette*, and they refused, most persistently, to make perfect guys of themselves. It was a very unbecoming dress, both to face and figure; there was nothing graceful or beautiful about it, and probably the female Mormons have never, in all their lives, come so nearly being actually indignant with their Prophet as they were when he endeavored to induce them to disfigure themselves by wearing this hideous costume.

Some of the sisters, however, were quite energetic in their efforts to bring about the desired dress reform, and they cut their silk dresses and other expensive materials after this pattern. It is true, silk was not very common in Utah at that time, but a few of the more wealthy had brought materials with them for future use; and the first use they made of them was to sacrifice them to one of President Young's whims. They did it with an earnestness, and even eagerness, that was beautiful to behold — or would have been, had not one been pained at their delusion.

But the "Deseret Costume" was not a success. The high hat killed it at its birth. It is possible that without this addition the rest of the dress might have been tolerated; but as every one who wore it was expected to don the hat also, the short-dress mania was of brief existence. Of course the material that was used for one of these dresses was utterly worthless after that, as nothing could be done with it. The dress was in so many pieces that the cut-up cloth was good for nothing.

One or two of the Prophet's wives — who wished to serve the Lord and glorify Brigham, and who were determined to live by "every word that proceeded out of his mouth" — persevered in wearing the dress, hat, pantalets and all, long after every one else had abandoned it; until at last they were compelled to succumb to popular opinion and a more prevailing fashion. That was the first and last attempt of Brigham Young to institute a "dress reform," although he has never ceased inveighing in the strongest terms against the follies and vanities of the feminine world, and assailing the women who followed the fashions. It is, indeed, a pet occupation of his when he is in exceedingly bad temper; and the Saints can easily tell when anything has gone wrong with him during the week by the ferocity with which he attacks the sisters on the subject of dress, in the Tabernacle on Sunday. He does not seem to make a very decided impression on his listeners, however; even his wives and daughters following their own inclinations rather than his teachings. The truth is, he says so much about it that it is altogether an old story, and has lost all its impressiveness from its frequent repetition. His chief topic is retrenchment in dress, and he pleads for it as earnestly as though it were a vital matter with him. And he not only preaches economy in the Tabernacle to his people, but he practices the most rigid parsimony at home with his wives. Except by Amelia, a request for any article of wearing apparel is the signal for all sorts of grumbling. Once in a while, however, some of his wives will turn suddenly and give him an answer; though, I must confess, the occasions are rare.

Clara Decker, one of his numerous wives, was sadly in want of some furs, and she did not hesitate to ask Brother Young to supply her needs. He became positively furious, and declared that her extravagance was beyond all endurance; she wanted to ruin him; she was determined to ruin him; all his wives were banded together for his financial downfall; and so on, with endless abuse. She listened to him patiently for a few minutes; then getting tired of all this abuse, she interrupted him : —

"If you think, Brigham Young, that I care anything for you, except for your money and what little I can get from you, you are mistaken. I might have cared more once; but that was a long time ago."

She then turned and left the room, leaving him petrified with amazement. A few hours after a set of furs was sent to her room. She quietly took them, and the subject was never referred to again.

The winter after my marriage with the Prophet, I myself preferred a similar request, and was met by a similar torrent of abuse. Not knowing that this was his usual manner of meeting a request from his wives, and not having Clara Decker's experience, I was perfectly overcome, and felt as though I had committed the unpardonable sin in daring even

to think of a set of furs, which, by the way, are actual necessities in a Utah winter. I burst into tears, and sobbed out, —
" O, don't, Brother Young ! "

I left the office and went home, puzzled and astonished at this new revelation of my Prophet-husband's meanness and coarseness. The next time he came to see me he brought me my furs. I used them two seasons, when the muff needed re-lining, and I ventured to ask him for silk for

BRIGHAM REFUSES MY REQUEST.

the purpose, thinking, of course, he could find no fault with so modest a request as that. But it seems I had not even then tested his full capacity for fault-finding. He treated me to a tirade, longer and more abusive than ever. He had got my furs for me, and yet I was not satisfied, but I must come bothering him again. I knew that he had several trunks full of silks, velvets, and laces, that he was keeping for some purpose or other, and consequently the material for re-lining my muff would cost him nothing; so I did not feel that I merited the lecture I was receiving. I said nothing, however, beyond making my request, and when he had finished he cut off *a quarter of a yard* of narrow silk from an entire piece which he had in one of the trunks, and gave it to me with as many airs and as much flourish as though he were presenting me with a whole dress pattern. It is needless to say that my muff was not lined with *that* piece of silk.

The trimming of dresses also comes in for a full share of Brother Brigham's condemnation; but he likes to have all the scolding and fault-finding to himself. If any one else ventures to express a like opinion, he is more than likely to disagree with them, probably from pure contrariness. I remember an incident that illustrates this, which took place at family prayers at the Lion-house one evening. One of the Prophet's daughters, Fanny, a very pretty, stylish girl, came into the parlor wearing a black wrapper trimmed with rows of red braid. The sight of this seemed very greatly to exercise Eliza Snow, — a proxy wife of Brother Brigham, — and she exclaimed in a shocked tone, —

"Is it possible that I see one of Brigham Young's daughters in a dress trimmed with red? I am more surprised than I can tell."

Brother Brigham couldn't stand this invasion of his province, and called out peremptorily, —

"That dress is well enough. Let the girl alone; she shall wear whatever she chooses. I've seen you in more ridiculous finery than that." And this to the woman who was the first to adopt, and the last to relinquish, the hat, pantalets and short gown of the "Deseret Costume!" Such is Prophetic gratitude!

On one occasion he was holding forth on the subject of long dresses; reviling them, of course, and holding up to ridicule and contempt the women who wore them.

"The very next time," said he, growing warm with his

subject, "that I see one of my wives with a dress on sweeping the ground, I will take the scissors and cut it off."

The very next day, I was passing through a door in front of him, when he accidentally stepped upon my train, which was a very long one. Of course I expected my dress to be sacrificed to the Prophet's promise, but to my great surprise, he not only refrained from the threatened application of the scissors, but from any comment, even so much as an apology for his awkwardness.

One of his favorite amusements has been imitating the Grecian bend for the benefit of the congregation, and it pleased him so much, and seemed so highly entertaining, that he kept up the practice long after "the bend" was out of fashion. He indulges in the coarsest witticisms, and is not above positive vulgarity and profanity, both in language and manner, often making himself very offensive to the more refined portion of his audience.

His own practice is entirely at variance with his teachings, since he wears the finest broadcloth of the most fashionable cut, drives the fastest horses, and rides in the most elegant carriages in the Territory, and his favorite wife is indulged in all the extravagances of the age. And yet a large portion of the Saints seem to take no notice of these inconsistencies, but receive all that he says as the strictest law and the most unimpeachable gospel.

In place of a distinctive costume, which he hoped to make the women adopt, the daughters of Zion fairly rival their Babylonian sisters in gaiety and fineness of attire, and the remotest allusion to the "Deseret Costume" is never heard now in the City of the Saints. It was the last attempt at dress reform in Utah.

Immediately on the arrival of the church in Utah, polygamy was urged upon the people. Having no fear of the outside world, since they were so far removed from it, they laid aside all caution, and preached and practiced it openly. The plural-wives taken in Nauvoo were acknowledged for

the first time, and others were added. The men were constantly urged to "build up the kingdom," and in order to do
that they were counselled to "take advantage of their privileges." If they did not hasten to obey counsel, they drew
down Prophetic and Apostolic wrath onto their heads, and
were accused of not "living up to the privileges." It soon
became very unpopular for a man to have but one wife, and
he quickly found himself looking out for another. In fact,
the somewhat coarse song, which was much affected by the
Mormon men, described the state of affairs at the introduction of polygamy : —

> " Some men have a dozen wives,
>   And some men have a score ;
> The man that has but one wife
>   Is looking out for more."

Of course dancing-parties were frequent then, even when
there was nothing but the "Bowery" for a ball-room, with
the earth for a floor. Joseph Smith had told them that it
was the will of the Lord that they should "make themselves merry in the dance," and, like the consistent Chris-
tians they were, they determined that the Lord's will, in
this matter at least, should be done. They had danced in
the Temple at Nauvoo, they had danced while crossing the
plains, and now they commenced again, in the only place
of worship which the city boasted, which was an open
space, overarched by boughs of trees. This served as
tabernacle and dancing-room while the weather permitted ;
after which the religious services were held at Brigham's
own house, the dances at the different houses.

Polygamy became so much the fashion, that if a man
attended a party with only one wife, he felt ashamed and
humiliated, and would instantly select some unappropriated
young woman, and commence paying her "particular and
peculiar" attentions. He would dance with her, and in the
intervals of the dance talk matrimony to his, usually, not

uninterested nor unwilling listener; the poor wife sitting
by, watching the progress of the courtship with heavy heart
and a consciousness of what the result would be. A lady-
friend, who had lived that experience, once said to me,
" I could write volumes on the misery I endured that first
winter in Utah." Another one, referring to the same
period, said, "I have divided my last crust with polygamy."

THE BALL IN THE BOWERY.

It was horrible, the makeshifts that were obliged to be
resorted to, in order to start the system. A neighbor of
ours had four wives, and only one room to live in during
the entire winter. It was used for sitting-room, kitchen,
bedroom and parlor, and the interior arrangements defy all
description. No pen can portray the many ingenious ex-
pedients adopted to preserve appearances. Modesty and
decency forbid my throwing too strong a light on that habi-
tation.

This was only one of many, and was by no means exceptional. The command had gone forth to take more wives,
and it did not matter at all whether there was a place to put
them in; they must be taken into polygamy. It was kept
quiet from the outside world, and the elders who were sent
out on missions were commanded to keep utter silence on

the subject. Rumors did get out after a while, especially after the California miners began to pass through Utah. There were no hotels at Salt Lake City at that time, and the emigrants who stopped there to rest, before finishing their journey, were compelled to become temporary inmates of Mormon families, where they found polygamous wives and children as a matter of course. Naturally they would grow curious after a time concerning these extra women and children, and as the inquiries were sometimes quite embarrassing, every subterfuge had to be resorted to to keep the guests in ignorance of the system.

But, try the best they might, they could not prevent suspicions of the truth; and it was not long before the missionaries, both in the States and in Europe, found themselves terribly perplexed by all sorts of questions concerning the truth of the reports that were coming thicker and faster from Utah. They were ordered to deny the rumors, and they all did so in the most emphatic manner, up to the very time of the publication of Joseph's "Revelation," in 1852.

In Nauvoo it had been represented to those who had been told of the new doctrine that it was optional; that no one need enter the relation unless he chose; and, consequently, although they felt it was a cruel doctrine, yet most of the women flattered themselves that *their* husbands, while they might receive it as a religious truth, would never practice it. But when the church was located in Utah, away from everybody, where help could never reach the oppressed and miserable, and from whence there was no possibility of escape, then polygamy was no longer optional, but every man was compelled to enter it, under pain of Brigham's displeasure, and its results.

That was a miserable winter for the Mormon women; they felt that they had in some way been the victims of false pretenses, but they did not dare to blame anyone, for fear of displeasing "the Lord." It was represented to them that this was God's will, and they must submit, else they would

never see salvation. Many of them were exceedingly rebellious, and would have returned to the States had it been
possible; but they had no means, and no prospect of getting
any, and they could only stay on and endure in sullen
silence and inward rebellion, which, after a while, when
they found there was no escape, became a sort of hopeless
apathy, which was by no means resignation.

Others, actuated by true religious fervor, — like my
mother, — accepted the situation because they really believed it was commanded by God; and while they were
always unhappy in it, and considered it the greatest cross
that could possibly be put upon them to bear, still made the
best of it, and made it a matter of conscience to be as patient, forbearing, and charitable as it was possible for human
nature to be under such circumstances.

Most of the men took kindly to the new state of affairs,
and did not seem at all backward about availing themselves
of their privileges. They had a good example set them by
their Prophet and his counsellors, and the Apostles fulfilled
their duty to the utmost by setting an example to their people in this respect.

The few Saints who had practiced polygamy in Nauvoo
had done so very secretly; consequently, when we came to
Utah, and were beyond the reach of the government, and,
as the leaders taught us, no longer amenable to the laws of
the United States, there were some very strange family revelations made. I will instance one, in the case of Lorenzo
Young — an elder in the church and a brother of Brigham
— and Mrs. Decker. Mr. Young, who had a wife and six
children all living, met Mrs. Decker, a very charming and
fascinating woman, who did not seem to think that the fact
of her having one husband, in the person of Mr. Decker,
prevented her from taking Mr. Young for another; and he
seemed to find Mrs. Young no obstacle to his union with his
new love. Each of them had children married, yet both
declared they had never before met their affinity.

Mr. Young laid the case before Joseph Smith, and the Prophet informed him that no doubt they were kindred spirits, intended for each other from the beginning of the world, and that the day would come when they would be united by the bonds of celestial marriage. This was in 1837, which showed that the idea was in his mind as early as that, although it was not reduced to a form and shown to anyone until 1843.

Joseph having given them this much consolation, they arranged matters to suit themselves, and seemed quite enchanted with one another. The only difficulty in the way was Mr. Decker. It was a puzzle to know how to dispose of him. But he and the world must both be deceived, and appearances must be kept up. So the wife remained with her lawful husband until the Revelation of 1843 cut the perplexing knot for them, and unravelled the intricate affairs.

Mrs. Decker was sealed to Brother Young, and Mrs. Young to Mr. Decker, who by this means had two wives given him in place of the one who was leaving him.

These mixed families were compelled to live in one house until they left the States. They then separated. Their children scattered everywhere, not knowing to whom they belonged; and, altogether disgusted and dissatisfied, felt more at home with strangers than they did with their parents, — especially as they did not know, positively, what name they were entitled to bear. They were by no means the only ones who were perplexed in the same way. There had been a queer and intricate mixing up in Nauvoo; it is not at all strange if the attempt at straightening out was a difficult one.

Joseph Smith's sons contend that he was not a polygamist; yet, with all the facts concerning his own life, and his encouragement of what would be considered in most communities the broadest kind of license, he either must have been a polygamist or something infinitely worse. Certainly the wildest doctrines of promiscuity, as taught by certain socialists of the present day, are no more startling than those taught by Joseph Smith, and have been forced upon the people by his successor, under the guise of polygamy, or, " Celestial Marriage."

CHAPTER VIII.

TROUBLES UNDER THE NEW SYSTEM.

The Sorrows of My Uncle. — "It's a Hopeless Fix." — A Woman's Argument about Polygamy. — My Mother "labors" with a First Wife. — Wife No. 2 "Walks Off." — Marrying a Widow and her Two Daughters. — Mrs. Webb becomes a Wife No. 2. — Wife No. 1 throws Brickbats into the Nuptial Chamber. — She clears the Field of Extra Wives. — "Building up the Kingdom." — The Atrocious Villanies of Orson Pratt. — How he has Seduced Innocent Girls. — Brigham's Nephew Rebels. — Trouble in the Prophet's Family. — Forgetting a Wife's Face. — A Woman who liked Polygamy.

HERE was literally no end to the muddles in which the Mormon people found themselves while trying to adjust their polygamous affairs.

In our own family it was very smooth sailing, as there were no superfluous members to be accounted for, and the two wives made the best of their unfortunate situation. But the same peace did not prevail in all families. I remember one family quite well where affairs were strangely mixed, and in which the wife exhibited a most amusing inconsistency.

A brother of my father, Milo Webb, had married a very pretty and agreeable woman in Illinois, who was perfectly devoted to him, and he returned her love ardently. They were both members of the Mormon Church, and had lived in the greatest harmony, with not the slightest shadow of discord, until 1846, when the " Endowments" were given in Nauvoo Temple.

To those men who were considered worthy to be called to that holy edifice to receive the sacred rite of the Endowments, polygamy was quietly taught as one of the requirements of religion, and these faithful brethren were counselled not to appear with but one wife; and of course after this many felt ashamed to present themselves with only the wife of their first and unbiassed choice, the mother of their children, the sharer of their fortunes, the consoler in trouble, the faithful, loving soul who had made her husband's people her people, his home her home, his God her God; who had considered no sacrifice too great to bear for his sake, no suffering too intense to be endured; who had literally taken him " for better, for worse, for richer, for poorer ; " had clung to him in sickness and health, in poverty and distress, as well as in plenty and comfort, and who fondly believed that only death should part them.

If a man dared be true to his better nature, and present himself for his Endowments with this wife alone, he was ridiculed by the authorities for being so poorly provided for, especially by Brigham and Heber C. Kimball, — who seemed always to supply the buffoonery for the occasions, — and warned that he need never expect to be received into the celestial kingdom until he had entered polygamy, as it was quite impossible for him to do so.

My uncle was a conscientious man and a devoted Mormon, and, like my father, believing the command to be from God, dared not disregard it. He made proposals of marriage to a young girl named Jane Matthews, and she, being taught by the leaders of the church, whom she consulted in the matter, that, except as a polygamous wife, she could not attain to exaltation in the future state, accepted the proposal as the only means within her power of securing salvation ; and the two, together with the wife, received their Endowments, and were united in the "indissoluble" bonds of " Celestial Marriage."

The wife had given only a reluctant consent to the arrangement, impelled to this solely by a sense of religious duty, and not because she approved of or liked it. It was the first bitter experience of her married life, and she did not accept it with the slightest spirit of resignation, but as something inevitable. Neither she nor her husband realized, in any degree, the magnitude of the undertaking, and the young girl was still more ignorant of the situation. Had they known how utterly wretched the future was to be, I believe they would have hesitated a long time before they assumed such relations with each other, even if they thought they were perilling their salvation by the delay.

The new wife was brought to the home where so entire happiness had reigned, and lived there until the church left Nauvoo ; but what a changed home it was ! The spirits of Peace and Love that had brooded over it so long, folded their white wings and fled, leaving the demons of Discord and Hate in their places.

It was not long before the first wife discovered that polygamy was a much more serious matter even than she had supposed it to be, and that it grew constantly worse and more unendurable, instead of better and more easily to be borne, as she had been taught it would become. She grew to cordially hate the young wife, and although they were compelled to live under one roof, she could not even make herself feel like speaking to her ; so they lived without addressing one word to each other. She grew nearly insane under this trouble, and was wrought up to such a frenzy by jealousy and despair that she committed the most flagrant acts of violence.

The poor husband found himself in a dilemma from which he saw no way of extricating himself. He could not understand how such really good women could behave so much like fiends. Neither of them had bad dispositions naturally, yet both were perfect termagants under the new family system. The house was in inextricable confusion, and he saw no way of setting matters right; so he applied to my father for advice, he having taken his second wife but a short time before. I do not know what advice he gave, but I think he must have referred him to my mother, for he came to her, begging her to assist him in bringing order out of the domestic chaos.

"How do you manage these polygamous affairs?" he asked, anxiously : "you do not appear to be very unhappy."

"I cannot tell you how I manage," was my mother's reply. "I am a riddle to myself; but I do assure you that it is no easy matter to live in polygamy. Its ways are not 'ways of pleasantness,' nor are its paths 'peace.' Trials of every description grow constantly more numerous."

"Yet you manage to preserve an outward appearance of serenity, which is more than we do. I wish you would see my wife and reason with her ; I believe she would listen to you. Affairs are horrible with us : my wife hates Jane, and it seems impossible to keep them together, since she will not even try to conceal her aversion towards her. I don't see how I am to keep them together, and yet I cannot afford to build another house. It is a most hopeless fix, and I don't see the way out."

My mother promised him that she would see his wife, and try to induce her to bear her cross more patiently. But what a hypocritical task it seemed to her! While her own heart was breaking with the weight of sorrow and care, she had to counsel patience and resignation to another woman who was suffering from precisely the same cause. It seemed heartless and awry, but it was placed upon her as a duty, and she could not shirk it. She upbraided herself for her reluctance, and prayed for more of the "Spirit." It

10

never occurred to her that the system was false and horrible
in the extreme; she only felt that she was lacking in grace
and the true spirit of the Lord.

Very shortly after my uncle's appeal to her, she visited his
wife, and found her weeping as though her heart would
break. Her first impulse was to put her arms about her
and weep with her. She felt every throb of that poor lacer-
ated heart, for her own was torn with the same anguish;
and for a little while she forgot her mission, and her woman's instinct predominated, while she indulged in a passionate burst of tears.

But horrified at what she feared was a rebellion against
her God, she soon quieted herself, although her heart still
ached with a pain which she could not banish or control,
and as delicately and tenderly as possible introduced the
object of her call. This brought forth a wild outburst of
indignant protest from my aunt; and my mother listened,
not daring to show her sympathy with the passionate utterances. There was quiet between them for a while after
this; then my mother, having regained control of her voice,
said, —

"But can you not see that it is your duty to submit to
the "Order" and be patient. You know very well that when
we cannot cure an ill, the only thing that remains to be
done is to endure it; and we must not rebel against any
doctrine taught by our leaders, no matter how hard it may
be to live it."

"I *don't* believe! I *can't* believe! I *won't* believe! that it is
my duty to submit to anything of the kind," was the quick
answer, made through stormy gusts of weeping. "I cannot live with that woman in the house; I had rather die at
once. O, I wish I could! I wish I could! Do you know,"
continued she, turning round with such suddenness that my
mother was fairly startled, "I shall take measures to rid
myself of that nuisance if somebody doesn't take her away!
I can't endure it! I *won't* endure it any longer!"

Mother tried to reason with her, but she interrupted her:
"If any woman pretends that she is satisfied with polygamy, she is a hypocrite. I don't believe her; and she knows
she is not speaking the truth."

My mother knew that she designed this remark for her,
and that she resented her interference; but she did not let
her see that she understood her, and determined to make
one more effort, though she felt that it was absolutely hopeless.

"We none of us love the doctrine now," she replied; "but
yet we must submit to it as a part of our religion — a duty
which that religion lays upon us; and we may grow to like
it better by and by."

"Well," was the sharp retort, "it will be soon enough for
me to comply with its requirements when I know it to be a
duty. But at present I do not believe it to be such, and I
cannot, nor will not, live in polygamy; on that point I am
determined, and there is no use arguing with me, for I shall
not change my mind, I am sure, and I will not consent to
live in a state against which both conscience and common
sense rebel."

This ended my mother's only attempt as missionary in the
interests of polygamy. She had not been at all successful,
and she was only too glad to drop the subject; for her heart
was not in it, and it must be confessed that in this case she
was a very unskilful special pleader.

There was no help for it; the young wife could not hold out
against all the opposition that was shown her, even though
her husband made some pretence of standing by her, and
she was finally compelled to leave the house. She saw no
prospect of ever being able to live with her husband again,
and she concluded that the best thing for her to do was to
put as great a distance as possible between herself and him;
so she went to Salt Lake with the first body of Saints.

As Brigham had taught the women, if they could not live
happily with a man, to "walk off," and leave him without a

divorce, she, of course, felt freed from her former marriage, and after a year or more she married Mr. Levi Savage, a single man, with whom she lived very happily for about two years, when she died, leaving one child, who is now grown to manhood. Soon after Mrs. Savage's death, Mr. Webb and his wife left the Missouri for Salt Lake. The husband died on the way, and his wife came on into the valley with her children.

Mr. Savage was at that time feeling very much grieved over the death of his wife, and was exceedingly pained because she had never been sealed to him by the proper authorities. He said, "I know she ought to belong to me, and I will contend for her throughout all eternity." He applied to the priesthood to have the sealing in the Temple to my uncle revoked, that she might be sealed to himself. He was told by the man who "holds the keys of life and death," that he must wait until the Temple in Salt Lake was completed.

Mrs. Webb, however, with wonderful inconsistency, considering her former feeling, opposed Mr. Savage's wish by every means in her power, and contended that this woman, whom she could not and would not live with, ought, now she was dead, to belong to her husband; and she said it was very wrong indeed for Mr. Savage to try and rob her dead husband of his rights and privileges. She evidently felt that there was not the slightest doubt of her ability to endure polygamy in a future state, although it was impossible to do so in this life.

After a few years Mr. Savage married a widow and her two daughters, and is still living with them, waiting, meanwhile, for the Temple to be built, when he hopes to have this "spiritual controversy" decided in his favor; for he has not given up his first wife, though he has taken three others to solace him temporarily until she can be given to him spiritually. Judging from present appearances, he will have to wait some time, as there seems no prospect of the Temple being finished during this generation.

Mrs. Webb found it a most difficult task to provide for herself and her children, and becoming discouraged in her attempts, listened with more patience to the doctrines of polygamy than she had done in Illinois. She was instructed that it was her duty to marry someone for time, that she might raise up more children to her dead husband, to swell his " kingdom." She took the instruction with a properly meek spirit, and very shortly accepted the proposal of Bishop McRae, a distinguished and prominent Mormon, and became Mrs. McRae number two.

As may be imagined, Mrs. McRae number one did not take kindly to the interloper, and, having a decided objection to polygamy, emphasized her objection by throwing bricks into Mrs. McRae number two's window, when their mutual husband was her guest. She varied her expressions of opposition and protest by occasionally sending a pistol shot, instead of a brickbat, through the window.

It may not be out of the way to mention, just here, that the heroine of the brickbat and pistol was, and still is, the President of the Female Relief Society in her ward, and that one of her chief duties is to instruct the young sisters in polygamy. I have never heard whether she had a shooting gallery attached to the society rooms.

Her plan of action was quite successful, and she soon had the field again to herself; for Mrs. McRae number two, after adding two children to her husband's kingdom, declined any longer to act as a target for Mrs. McRae number one, and left her husband voluntarily, and has since lived in a state of widowhood. I have often wondered whether she had any sympathy for Jane Matthews while she was herself the object of persecution.

I have known all the actors in this polygamic drama, except the two who died. I was too young to have any but the most indistinct recollection of my uncle, and Mrs. Savage, I, of course, could not remember at all. But the rest I knew very well, all being intimate visitors at my father's house.

"Build up the kingdom, build up the kingdom," has always been the watchword of polygamy. At Nauvoo it was whispered into the ears of those who were considered strong enough in the faith to receive it unquestioningly, but in Utah it is hurled indiscriminately at all alike. "Build up the kingdom, whether you can support it or not," is the almost literal teaching. The pecuniary condition of a man is never taken into consideration. He is expected to take as many wives as he can support, then take a few more to support themselves and their children.

The Apostle Orson Pratt is one of the most persistent polygamists in Utah, and he has nothing to give his wives for their maintenance. They struggle on as best they may, striving in every way to earn a scanty sustenance for themselves and their children. Some of them live in the most wretched squalor and degrading poverty. He, in the mean while, goes on foreign and home missions, and gathers thousands of unsuspecting victims to "Zion." Polygamy is his favorite subject, and he grows very eloquent while discoursing upon it, quoting Scripture freely in support of the glorious system, — which, by the way, is the only support he does give it, or that he feels it his duty to afford. After he has once converted and married a girl, she is left to shift for herself, or to starve and die of neglect. Two, at least, have met this fate, — one a very pretty English girl, who was starved, body and heart, and who, with her little children, died from exposure, while her husband was at Salt Lake, being "entertained" by some of his rich brothers in the church.

THE APOSTLE ORSON PRATT,
"The Champion of Polygamy."

He is still the recognized defender of the gospel of polygamy, and is quoted by every one as an authority ; his numerous and more pressing duties prevent his caring for his family, and nowhere in Utah are the wives more wretched or neglected, or children more ignorant and uncared for, than the wives and children of Orson Pratt, the eloquent expounder of the beauties and glories of a polygamous life, and the best educated and most able man, intellectually, in Utah.

Another polygamist of the same stamp is Joseph Young, brother to Brigham, and President of the Seventies. He has busied himself in "building up his kingdom" ever since Joseph Smith gave him that precious piece of counsel in Nauvoo. When he was a young man, he married a girl, and lived very happily with her until he learned from the Prophet Joseph that it was not only his privilege, but his duty, to enlarge his kingdom more speedily by marrying more wives.

His first acquisition was a young widow, who listened assentingly to his proposals of a "celestial marriage," and soon after entered his family as a second wife. However, the marriage with her did not avail him much, as she could only be his for time. Her former husband died a Mormon, and she and her children would belong to him in eternity.

He was past the prime of life, feeble in health, and compelled to accept the support of his brethren ; yet all this did not deter him from doing what was required of him by his Prophet. About the time that he married the widow, he took a young girl for his third wife, who was supposed to be his, and his

JOSEPH YOUNG, BROTHER OF BRIGHAM, AND PRESIDENT OF THE SEVENTIES.

only, with no former husband "behind the veil" to come up "in the morning of the resurrection" and lay claim to herself and her children. All his wives lived in one house, which had been built for him by the "Seventies," in return for his spiritual ministrations in their behalf.

His first wife did not like the new family arrangement any better than other Mormon women who were first wives; but as a matter of course, her liking or disliking was not of the least consequence. She fretted herself ill over it, however, and was prostrated for months. She had toiled and suffered with her husband for many long years, while they were journeying about with the Mormons, and she could not bear to have the dark shadow of polygamy cast over the hitherto unclouded happiness of their domestic life. It seemed a terrible injustice. Yet, knowing her husband's devotion to the faith, she would not openly rebel, although she complied with his demands, that she should receive his other wives, with a feeling of intense bitterness, and lived in this unnatural relationship with her husband and his other wives.

It is impossible to depict her sufferings; they can never be known or realized outside of Mormonism. It is the very refinement of cruelty, this polygamy, and its hurts are deeper and more poisonous than any other wounds can be. They never heal, but grow constantly more painful, until it makes life unendurable. She was prostrated for months with nervous debility, seeing all the time her family needing her constant care, the care that only a mother can give, and her husband all the while devoting his energies to "building up his kingdom." It is only just to say that he was as kind to her as the circumstances would permit.

After a few years the invalid wife recovered her health, and has been permitted to assist in rearing her children to respectable men and women who do not believe in polygamy. One of her sons has apostatized, and once published a paper in Salt Lake City, called "*The Daily Press.*"

This paper was of course offensive to Brigham, containing, as it did, some unpleasant truths regarding himself and other authorities in the church, and he determined to put a stop to its publication. Accordingly he sent for his brother Joseph, and said, on his arrival, —

" I want that ' *Daily Press* ' suppressed."

Joseph " did not know how it was to be done."

" I want you to use your influence with your son to accomplish my wish," demanded Brigham.

" I cannot do it," said his brother; " my son will do as he likes."

Brother Brigham grew angry. "You must put a stop to the printing of that paper; I will not endure the annoyance from it any longer."

BRIGHAM'S BROTHERLY LOVE.

Joseph's spirit rose to the occasion. If Brigham was his superior in the church, he was also a younger brother, and he didn't like his peremptoriness of manner; so he quietly answered, —

" I shall do nothing more about it than I have done. I have said all to my son that is necessary, and if he does not wish to follow my advice, he can go his own way, and act according to his own judgment; I most certainly shall not interfere."

Brigham was terribly angry, and he raved and stormed, while Joseph listened quietly, and then walked out, making no answer to his threats and railings. The Prophet evidently did not succeed in influencing or terrifying either brother or nephew, as the "*Press*" was still published, and continued to win popularity. I was glad of its success, for the sake of the brave young editor, and the mother who reared him. She, at least, should find comfort and support in her children, although everything else in life has failed her, even her religion proving false and fatal to her happiness.

During his first wife's illness, Joseph added another widow to his establishment. Her husband having been killed at Nauvoo, she wished to assist him to build up a kingdom, and so married Joseph for time. Shortly after another woman applied for " salvation " at his hands, and " conscience " would not allow him to reject her. When he was about seventy years of age he added still another to his family, being united to her the same day that I was married to his brother Brigham, and is still, although over eighty years of age, considered in the matrimonial market.

Joseph had a real romance in his youth, which connects him, in memory and feeling at least, somewhat with my mother's family. His first love, when he was very young, was an aunt of my mother, for whom I was named. He was passionately attached to her, but something occurred to part them, and she died. Her memory has always remained with him, and he has always loved her, in spite of his extensive matrimonial experience. He told my mother that he had had Jane, his first wife, baptized for her, and sealed to him for her; so she is to be his in eternity.

This venerable polygamist has nothing to support his wives upon, or himself, for that matter, except what is given him by the "Seventies." In most respects he is a very good man, much more conscientious and honest than his brother Brigham, of whose conduct towards the people he does not approve; but he has gone mad in his desire to "build up his kingdom," and he considers it a duty to continue to raise up a young family, who must necessarily have to " shift for themselves," both in childhood and later life. They can have no father's care or attention, no matter how much they may need it, and he evidently does not consider how much misery he is entailing on these children.

Besides the wives I have mentioned, I do not know how many he has been sealed to, whom he does not pretend to look after in the flesh, but whom he expects to "resurrect," to swell his heavenly kingdom.

It is possible that, like Heber C. Kimball, he may have " fifty or more scattered over the earth," whom he has not seen for years, and whom he hopes he never may see again in this world.

A very amusing story was told me of Brigham, by a lady who vouches for its truth; and although I cannot, of course, corroborate it, I am quite ready to give it credence enough to publish it. Brigham met a lady in the streets of Salt Lake City, several years since, who recognized him, and addressed him as Brother Young, greeting him quite cordially.

He scrutinized her closely, with a puzzled expression. " I know I have seen you somewhere," he said; " your face is very familiar, but I cannot recall you."

"You are right," replied she; " you have most certainly seen me before; I was married to you ten years ago. I have never seen you since," she continued, " but my memory is more retentive than yours, for I knew you the moment I saw you."

Very few, even of the most enthusiastic Mormon women, were ready to listen with any degree of patience to the first teachings of the doctrine of polygamy. They rebelled against it in their hearts, even if they dared say nothing of their dislike and disgust of the system. Still less were they willing to advise or urge their husbands to introduce it; and never was a woman, with one exception, heard to say she was happy in it, even if they endured it with any degree of patience.

The one exception of which I have spoken was an old neighbor of ours, and quite a friend of my mother's, Mrs. Delia Dorr Curtis. Both she and her husband were faithful Mormons, but he had, for some time after polygamy was taught, continued living "beneath his privileges." He was constantly reminded of his remissness by the priesthood, until at length he felt obliged to yield to their teachings, and "obey counsel." When he mentioned the matter to his wife, she made no objections, but, on the contrary, she encouraged him in his decision, and proposed their niece, Miss Van Orden, for his consideration.

Her husband was exceedingly pleased with her suggestion. "She is the very one I should have chosen," he said in reply. He instantly made proposals for his niece, and she, being quite willing to marry her uncle, accepted the proposals, and was sealed to him at once, Mrs. Curtis giving the bride to her husband with an alacrity and willingness which were rarely seen in similar circumstances.

About three months after the celebration of the nuptials, the first wife of this good elder came to visit my mother, and, as is always the case when two Mormon women meet, and are together for any length of time, the talk turned on to polygamy, and during the conversation Mrs. Curtis remarked, —

"Well, as far as I am concerned, I never have felt any of the stings of polygamy."

"Do you wish me to believe," questioned my mother, in surprise, "that you have seen your husband going through a courtship and marriage with a young wife, have seen him lavish attentions on her that have heretofore belonged alone to you, and have never felt the pangs of jealousy?"

"Yes; I wish you to believe all that."

"Well," said my mother, somewhat incredulously, "I cannot comprehend it, and if I did not know you to be a most truthful woman, I should certainly say I did not believe you."

Mrs. Curtis grew quite eloquent on the subject; she and the other wife lived in one house, not a large one either, and the relation between them was amicable in the extreme. She had always been fond of Sarah; she was fonder than ever of her now.

"Why should there be so much trouble in it?" continued she, waxing earnest; "the Revelation on Celestial Marriage is from the Lord; I know it, and every person might have a testimony for themselves if they would cultivate the Spirit; it is wrong and absurd in us to rebel."

"Yes, to be sure it is," returned my mother, "if one knows it to be true. I do not know it; I merely believe it, and I am not sure that I quite do that even. I try to believe it, and try to practice it, but I must confess to many anxious days and sleepless nights on account of it."

Mrs. Curtis was horrified at my mother's lack of belief. "Why," said she, "if I did not have a perfect knowledge of the truth of polygamy, I should lose all faith in the other principles of Mormonism, I fear."

"Not necessarily so," replied mother. "I still cling to the faith; I must not relinquish that; but polygamy is a hard cross to bear."

"Not at all! not at all!" asseverated Mrs. Curtis; "if you only have the Spirit of the Lord to enlighten your mind, you will find no difficulty."

"Well, you certainly are an exception to the general rule," said mother, "and you are far in advance of me, though I have struggled hard to inure myself to the system."

"Now let me tell you how we manage," persisted the enthusiastic defender of plurality. "When my husband intends going to Sarah's apartment, we first kneel down and have prayers; then he takes me in his arms and blesses me, and after our usual good-night kiss we part, happy in each other's love; and why should there be any trouble?"

"The story you are telling me seems incredible," said my mother; "if it is true, you are really enjoying a very pleasant dream, from which I pray you may never awaken."

"O, no fear of that," was the quick reply. "I love Sarah too well to ever regret giving her to my husband; and you might be just as happy, if you would take the right view of the subject. I am sure, if Sarah had children, I should love them as well as my own, and I really cannot see what there is in polygamy to cause so much annoyance."

"Well," said my mother, as the conversation ended, "let me give you this bit of advice — keep your eyes shut."

My mother did not see her friend again, or even hear from her, for a very long time; but she used often to refer to her, and wonder whether "the stings of polygamy" had reached her in all that time, or whether she was still as enthusiastic a devotee to the system as she was at the time of her memorable visit.

Some years after Mrs. Curtis's visit, the mother of the young wife became our guest. My mother, of course, made instant and interested inquiries regarding the welfare of the family. She was quite surprised when, in answer to them, the lady replied, —

"I do not know what to say or to think about Delia. She behaves in the most peculiar manner; we all think she may be insane, and I am very certain she is, for no woman in her right mind would conduct herself in the way she does."

"Why, what is the matter?"

"You know what a disciple of polygamy she professed to be, and how earnest she was that Sarah should join the family. She has turned completely about; you would not recognize in her the same person she was before we went south to live. She raves wildly about polygamy, and says as many things against it as she used to say for it. I never heard anyone more bitter in my life. She abuses Sarah in every possible way, — you know how fond she used to be of her, — and whips her children shamefully. She has become so violent that Sarah cannot live with her any longer, even if she dared to, and she does not, for Delia absolutely terrifies her in some of her rages; so she is going to move away. I never saw a person so entirely changed in my life. It is terrible."

"What has happened to cause such a change?" asked my mother.

"I do not know, I am sure," was the sad reply; "we none of us know; it is a perfect mystery to us; but of one thing I am quite assured: if she goes on in the way she is going now, she cannot live long; she will literally wear herself out."

It was less than a year from this time that we heard of her death. It was evident she had not been so strong as she imagined, or else the "Spirit" had deserted her. The end of this "happy" woman's life was not so different, after all, from that of hundreds of her "unhappy" sisters. She was another victim to polygamy, that horrible system which crushes women's hearts, kills their bodies, and destroys their souls.

CHAPTER IX.

THE HARDSHIPS AND PERILS OF LIFE IN A NEW COUNTRY.

"Killed by the Indians." — How Apostates Disappeared. — A Suspicious Fact. — How Brigham "took care" of the People's Property. — The Mormon Battalion. — Brigham Pockets the Soldiers' Pay. — How Proselytes were Made. — Scapegraces sent on Mission. — My Father goes to Europe. — How Missionaries' wives are Left. — Collecting funds for the Missionaries. — Brigham Embezzles the Money. — The "Church Train." — Joseph A. Young as a Missionary. — His Misdoings in St. Louis. — What Brother Brown said of Him. — The Perpetual Emigration Fund. — How the Money was Raised. — Cheating the Confiding Saints. — How Brigham Manages the Missionaries' Property. — The "Church" makes Whiskey for the Saints. — The Missionaries bring home new Wives. — How English Girls are Deceived. — My First Baptism.

DISCOURAGING APOSTASY.

HE first years of life in a new country are full of hardships, peril, and adventure, and all these the Mormon people met.

I can remember listening in round-eyed wonder and terror at recitals of Indian atrocities, for we were surrounded by the wandering Southern tribes, and they were constantly thieving from us, and a murder was by no means an uncommon thing. When a man left home and failed to return, the general verdict, as a matter of course, was, "killed by the Indians." Did an exploring party visit the Territory, and fail to leave it again, their fate, if it was ever alluded to at all, was regarded as "massacred by Indians."

It is a significant fact that most of the persons who thus perished were Gentiles, apostates, or people who, for some reason or other, were suspected by, or disagreeable to, Brigham Young; and it came presently to be noticed that if anyone became tired of Mormonism, or impatient of the increasing despotism of the leader, and returned to the East, or started to do so, he invariably was met by the Indians and killed before he had gone very far.

The effect was to discourage apostasy, and there was noone but knew that the moment he announced his intention of leaving Zion and returning to "Babylon," he pronounced his death sentence. He was never discouraged from his plans, nor was any disapprobation of his course expressed. The faces were as friendly that he met every day, the voices just as kind; his hand was shaken at parting, and there was not a touch either of warning or sarcasm in the "God speed" and *bon voyage*. But he knew he was a lucky man if, in less than twenty-four hours after leaving Salt Lake City, he was not lying face downward on the cold earth, shot to death by an unerring rifle ball, while the stars looked sorrowfully down, silent witnesses, on this deed of inhuman butchery, and a man rode swiftly cityward, carrying the news of the midnight murder to his master, who had commanded him in the name of his religion to commit this deed, and send an innocent soul before its Maker. "Ah, poor fellow; killed by the Indians," said all his friends; but Brigham Young and Bill Hickman or "Port" Rockwell knew better.

The Indians have been convenient scapegoats and alternate allies and enemies to Brigham Young. But he has managed to make warfare, even with them, a profitable thing for himself.

The Indians are notoriously thievish; they will steal from

II

each other, and from their very best friends. Civilization, even, doesn't seem to take the taint from their characters; they positively can't keep their hands off what doesn't belong to them.

As a matter of course, the Mormons, being their near neighbors, suffered very much from their depredations. They would often steal an ox, or, indeed, a large number of cattle, when they could do so with comparative safety; the owners would soon be on their trail, and would pursue them until they reached them; and sometimes both Mormons and Indians would be killed.

On occasions like these a proclamation would be issued, by the "authorities," for the brethren to fit themselves out for a campaign of indefinite length for the purpose of quelling the "Indian disturbances," and suppressing the trouble; and Brigham, who always has an eye to the main chance, generally managed in some mysterious manner to make large sums of money out of these "wars," as they were called.

Sometimes the manner of the money-making was not at all mysterious. There is one case in particular which I have often heard spoken of by my mother and other Mormons, who would have disapproved of the proceedings, and even called them dishonest, had they dared; but none of them ventured to connect such an adjective as that to the Prophetic name.

At this particular time he became so very anxious for his people's welfare, and so earnest in his endeavors to "protect" their property, that he sent Captain William Walls, of Provo, with a company, to collect all the surplus stock from the settlements south of Salt Lake, and drive them into the city for safe-keeping, reserving only the necessary teams and the milch cows. The orders were very absolute to "drive every hoof that could be spared."

At Cedar City, Iron County, there were three men who as absolutely refused to give up their stock, as that was all

they had to depend upon; for, being poor men, with large
families, they naturally preferred to keep what property
they had where they could look after it themselves, feeling
certain that they would take quite as careful an interest in
it as a stranger would.

The names of these rebellious men were Hunter, Keer,
and Hadshead. They insisted upon defending their property, and the captain commanded them to be arrested and
put in irons, and then he started with them for Salt Lake
City, having previously secured all their stock.   When they

BRIGHAM "TAKES CARE" OF THE PEOPLE'S CATTLE!

arrived at Parowan, they were chained together and confined
in the school-house, there being no prison or jail in the
place.

They were met by George A. Smith, who at that time
was on a visit to the southern settlements; and he, thinking
the men were treated with unnecessary harshness, ordered their irons taken off, and them set at liberty and
allowed to return to their families — without their stock,
however. These men, after suffering such indignities,
could live among the Mormons no longer, and they left for
California.

Their stock, with a large herd of cattle collected in that vicinity, was driven to Salt Lake City, where they remained until they were in proper order for sale, when Brigham sold every one of them to pay a large debt which he owed to Livingston and Kincade, Salt Lake merchants.

This was his somewhat novel method of "protection." The cattle, to be sure, were out of the reach of the Indians, but they were equally out of the reach of their lawful owners, who neither saw them again nor any money which accrued from the sale of them.

Some of the owners ventured to ask if they might be turned in for tithing, but the inspired Prophet of the Lord replied, "No; if you had kept them, the Indians would have stolen them, and you are as well off as you would have been if I had not taken them." So was he, and several hundred dollars better off, too.

This reminds me of another instance of Brigham's faculty for "turning things to account," or, as a young Mormon quite wittily said, "taking advantage of his opportunities;" although it has nothing to do with the Indians, yet it occurred at an even earlier date, and was among the first of his notoriously dishonest transactions.

At Council Bluffs, as early as 1846, he counselled five hundred of his followers to enlist in the service of the United States; recruits being wanted at that time for the war in Mexico. They went without a question, on being assured that their families should be cared for. The church at that time was camped on the Missouri River, on its way from Nauvoo to Salt Lake.

The Mormon soldiers — commonly called "The Battalion" — sent all their pay to their families, to the care of Brigham Young, and he cared for it so well that the poor families never received it. John D. Lee brought the money which was collected from the soldiers, amounting to several thousand dollars, and gave it to Brigham. The families of these soldiers were, many of them, nearly starving, and all of them were very poor, needing sadly the money that their husbands had sent them; and in the face of all this destitution and suffering Brigham Young bought goods in Missouri to take out to the Valley, and if a soldier's wife ventured to ask him for anything, no matter how trifling it might be, she was rudely repulsed, usually without the slightest excuse for not giving her what was rightfully her own.

The men served in the army two years, receiving pay all the time, which Brigham pocketed, and all the time their families lived on the banks of the Missouri in the most squalid poverty, while Brigham came to Salt Lake in the most comfortable manner possible at that early day, and lived on the provisions that he had brought with him, bought with the money that was not his. He lived in what would be called luxury for the time and the place, by literally taking the bread out of the mouths of hundreds of needy women and children.

When these men came to Utah, after having been honorably discharged, they, of course, expected to find their families there. What was their surprise on learning that they were still at Winter-Quarters, and that no arrangements had been made for bringing them to the Valley! The President of the church would not allow them to go for them until the next spring, and when they did find them in such a wretched, helpless condition, it is no wonder that so many of them apostatized, and refused to believe in a religion whose chief teacher could be capable of such heartless cruelty and mean dishonesty.

It is asserted, by those who have the best means of knowing, that this war put twenty thousand dollars in Brigham Young's pocket; and yet he is very fond of talking about the cruelty and tyranny of the United States government in *forcing* five hundred of the ablest Mormon men into its service at a time when they were the most needed, and leaving the weak and helpless to cross the plains without sufficient protection.

The Mormons have always been very enthusiastic on the subject of missions. Probably no other church has done so much both home and foreign missionary work as the Church of Latter-Day Saints. They began by travelling about the country, making converts wherever they could, in the days when the entire church could easily be numbered : as they increased in numbers they extended their work across the ocean, and now nearly all the work is done in England, Norway, Sweden, and Denmark.

It is a very rare thing nowadays to hear of an American convert, and the southern European nations never did take kindly to the faith.

Brigham Young was among the very earliest of missionaries, and he was very successful at proselyting. He was very different then from the haughty, arrogant blusterer of to-day. He and his brother Joseph were the first Mormons that my mother ever saw, and I have very often heard her describe the peculiar influence they exerted over her, and the manner in which they impressed her.

To her they seemed very humble men, of the most earnest, devoted piety and intense religious zeal, travelling about "without purse or scrip," meeting with ridicule, derision, and persecution, while they preached "the gospel as taught by Christ and his Apostles." They came to a house where she chanced to be visiting, and, after seating themselves, commenced singing one of those earnest, stirring hymns for which the Mormons were at that time celebrated.

> "Hark ! listen to the trumpeters,
>   They call for volunteers.
> On Zion's bright and flowery mount,
>   Behold their officers.
> Their horses white, their armor bright,
>   With courage bold they stand ;
> Enlisting soldiers for their king,
>   To march to Zion's land.

ERASTUS SNOW.

JOSEPH F. SMITH.

LORENZO SNOW.

A. CARRINGTON.

C. C. RICH.

MORMON APOSTLES.

"We want no cowards in our bands,
    That will our colors fly;
We call for valiant-hearted men,
    Who're not afraid to die;
Sinners, enlist with Jesus Christ,
    Th' eternal Son of God,
And march with us to Zion's land,
    Beyond the swelling flood."

They were fine singers, both of them, and they threw so
much fire and fervor into this song that my mother — young,
enthusiastic girl of sixteen — made up her mind on the spot
to enlist and follow this new army to Zion.

She was baptized and confirmed by Brigham Young
almost immediately, and to use her own language, "There
was nothing arrogant, haughty, or tyrannical, either in his
(Brigham Young's) or Heber Kimball's appearance, as they
pronounced, in the most fervent manner, such glorious
blessings upon me, a poor ignorant girl, with no one to
guide me, but who had given up my little all in this world
to follow their teachings, which to me at that time meant
the teachings of Christ."

No sooner had the Saints become fairly settled in Utah
than Brigham Young commenced sending the brethren off
on missions. He had, and still has, a peculiar way of managing, quite original with himself. A few of the leading
members of the church were sent; indeed, at that time one
or more of the apostles was kept in England all the while,
and different elders were sent to relieve each other, and to
assist the apostle in taking charge of the "Branches," and
starting mission churches, which were afterwards held in
charge by some resident brother, who was appointed elder.
In addition to these elders, any one who displeased the
Prophet was "sent on a mission" as a punishment. Did
the polygamous Prophet fancy a man's wife, he was sent to
the farthest possible point from Zion, to "enlist" souls for
the Mormon Church. If any young man is suddenly started

"on a mission" to preach the gospel and win souls to
Christ, it is safe to argue that "he has been a little wild,'
and is accordingly exiled for a while.

My father was sent to England not very long after our
arrival in the Valley, and he had charge while there of the
Sheffield branch of the church. My mother and myself
lived part of the time in Salt Lake City with Elizabeth and
her family, and the remainder of the time in Payson. As
the missionaries are all expected to give their services, and
as they are obliged to go when ordered, whether they wish
to or not, the wives have to take care of themselves as best
they may. They certainly can expect no aid from their
husbands, and they never receive it from the church; so, unless they can do something to support themselves while they
are left in this way, they are pretty sure to suffer discomfort,
and many times actual want. My mother was equal to the
occasion, however, and we got on better than most Mormon
families do whose "head" has gone on a mission. My
mother taught school most of the time, either in the city or in
Payson, and during all the time I studied with her.

Before sending his missionaries to England, Brigham one
Sunday addressed the people in the Tabernacle very much
after this fashion : —

"Brethren and sisters, the time has been when we were
compelled to travel without purse or scrip, and preach the
gospel. We have had to beg our way of an ungodly world,
and have gone, like the Apostles of old, trusting the Lord to
provide for us. And," continued he, waxing excited over
his subject, "I have travelled on foot the length and breadth
of the United States with my shoes full of blood. Foot-sore
and weary, I have often arrived at a house and asked for a
night's lodging. I was hungry and cold; yet I was turned
away; and many a time I have shaken the dust off my feet
as a testimony against those people. But now I want the
elders to travel independent of the Gentile world." Then,
after reading the names of those whom he had selected to
go, he proceeded with his address : —

"Brethren and sisters, the missionaries must be supplied with the necessary funds to defray their expenses. And I want this whole people to come forward and donate freely for this purpose. I do not suppose you are all prepared to-day, but you can call at the office to-morrow and leave the money with my clerk; or we will have another meeting for the purpose of receiving donations, and so give all the opportunity of assisting in the noble work of sending missionaries to a foreign land."

As an answer to this appeal there was a large sum raised, the people responding generously to this call for assistance, and there was sufficient to carry all the laborers to their appointed fields. What was the surprise, then, of these men, when calling on the Prophet previous to their departure, and referring to the subject, they were coolly told by Brother Brigham that there was no money for them — "not one cent"!

"But what are we to do?" said the bewildered and disappointed men, who had relied on this money to assist them.

"You must go to Bishop Hunter; I have nothing for you," was the careless and heartless reply.

Accordingly they went to the Presiding Bishop, and after telling him their errand, and that they had been sent by President Young, he informed them that there was a "church train" of three hundred wagons going East, which would take them to the frontiers for forty dollars apiece; "and after that," said the bishop, "you must get to your fields of labor as best you can."

Now, the Mormon elders in those days were poor, and could barely support their families when they were at home. And to be informed, just at the last moment, when they had supposed they were well provided for, that they must defray their own expenses to England, was really a hard blow for all of them. And yet such was their devotion to their religion, that each one paid his forty dollars to ride to the frontier in the "church" wagons, and then made their way to England at their own expense.

The Saints supposed that these wagons were sent out for the purpose of bringing emigrants from the Missouri River ; but on their return they were loaded with freight, for which Brigham received twenty-five dollars a hundred. Between the amount paid for the passage of the missionaries and the loads of freight on the return, this "church train" certainly paid the head of the church very handsomely for that one trip.

Among the missionaries to England, during my father's residence there, was Joseph A., the Prophet's eldest son, who has recently died. He has always had the reputation among the Saints of being a very "fast" young man. In order, if possible, to cure him of some of his propensities for evil-doing, his father decided to send him on a mission, to carry the light of the everlasting gospel to the benighted nations of the earth. When men of family are sent, it is generally because Brigham wants something belonging to them which he cannot get if they are allowed to stay at home ; and single men are often sent to convert the world, who are not capable of writing their own names in a legible manner.

But Joseph A. was sent because his father did not know what else to do with him ; he had become so dissipated and caused so much trouble at home.

On his way Joseph stopped a few days in St. Louis, after which he went immediately to England. He was appointed in my father's pastorate, he being at that time pastor over several conferences. Everything was moving on harmoniously, when another Mormon elder, named Brown, arrived from America, telling some hard stories about Joseph's conduct while in St. Louis.

Mr. Brown circulated the reports that Joseph had drank immoderately, several times had been beastly drunk, and had constantly and habitually visited most disreputable resorts ; in fact, that his conduct while in that city had been marked by the most profligate excesses, and that it had also been notoriously open, very little attempt being made on his part to hide it.   He seemed to fancy that his personality was sufficient protection from scandal, and that the gossips would not wag their tongues over the misconduct of a son of Brigham Young.

These reports shocked the English Saints very much, and many of them were on the point of apostasy on account of it.   My father did not doubt that there was some foundation for these stories, although he did not think the fellow could

JOSEPH A. YOUNG PREPARING FOR MISSIONARY WORK.

be so bad as he was represented; and he considered it his duty to take immediate steps to suppress the scandal, since it was doing very great injury to the cause of Mormonism. He accordingly represented this view of the case to Mr. Brown, who listened earnestly, and seemed quite convinced of the truth and justice of what my father had said.   He took his leave, agreeing to "make it all right for Joe."

The following Sabbath, at the close of the services, my father said, "Mr. Brown will now have the opportunity to retract the scandal which he has put in circulation concerning Joseph A. Young."

Mr. Brown arose before the thousands of people assembled there, and acknowledged that he had misrepresented the character of the Prophet's "beloved" son, and, in the blandest manner possible, made it appear that Joseph was perfectly pure, upright, and moral, and entirely above reproach.

The chief object of this farce was to prevent apostasy; another was to save the Prophet's son from infamy and disgrace. My father, on his return to America, learned that Mr. Brown's reports were all true, and were not exaggerated in the least. Yet this dissipated libertine was considered sufficiently good to preach the truths of the Mormon religion to "a world lying in darkness."

E. HUNTER, PRESIDING BISHOP.

Brigham Young's sons usually distinguish themselves while on their missions, rather by their aptitude at getting into scrapes than by the number of converts which they make. Brigham Jr. — "the probable successor," or, as he is familiarly called, "Briggy" — succeeded in distinguishing himself in England. The story popularly told among the Saints is, that regarding himself, without doubt, as a "scion of royalty," and with the egotistical assumption and the assurance which characterize his father, and which he honestly inherited, he actually ventured, in spite of the law, to drive the same number of white horses before his carriage that the queen had on her carriage, and that he was arrested and fined a hundred and fifty thousand dollars for the offence.   The true account of the matter is, that when driving in one of the London parks, in a state of inebriety, he committed a trespass, for which he was arrested and mulcted in the ordinary fine — a few shillings, I believe.   Brigham, however, is said to have profited by the exaggerated story, and to have made capital out of it.

The donations that year had been unusually large, for Brigham had announced his intention of " emigrating " a larger number than ever before, and, as a consequence, the " Perpetual Emigration Fund " must be correspondingly increased.

" Brethren and sisters," he commenced one day, in his most delicate and refined style, "you must retrench your expenses.   You have been travelling in a direct line towards eternal damnation for a long time; now you must turn about, and show to the Lord and His holy angels that you still desire to be numbered among His people.   I intend, this year, to bring over every Saint from the Old Country, and you must take hold and help me.   I want the sisters to leave off their ribbons and finery, and stop running to the stores.   I want you, one and all, to stop using tea, coffee, tobacco, and whiskey, and the money you would spend for those things you must donate for the emigration of the poor in Europe.   Now is the time to manifest your faith by your works."

All the Saints in the Territory were personally called upon to assist in the work, and responded generously, if not willingly.   Poor women contributed their mites, and poor men gave of their hardly-won earnings, that could ill be spared, as they could barely support their families at the best.   In England, also, they were made to contribute, and many a working man was compelled to donate an entire week's wages.   The English Saints gave willingly, and suffered the privations caused by their generosity cheerfully, as they confidently expected to be gathered to Zion that year. But their suffering availed them nothing, and their generosity was but ill repaid. It was years before many of these patient, long-enduring Saints saw the Zion of their hopes.

As the Prophet has a most decided objection to seeing any of his followers becoming independent in worldly affairs, either because he is afraid they will be able to act without counsel or advice from him, and so get beyond his power to manage them, or because he is jealous of their pecuniary success, since he has often said that he was the only man in the Territory who knew how to make money or how to use it, he always finds some way to put a stop to their growing prosperity. His usual method of doing this is by sending them on a mission. Of course their business is at a stand-still altogether as soon as the heads of it are away; and it either remains quiet ever after, or, if it is sufficiently lucra-tive to make it worth while, Brigham manages to get it into his own hands, and it is as completely lost to its rightful owners as though they never had possessed it.

For a number of years, two men — named Badley and Hugh Moon — worked a whiskey distillery in Salt Lake City, and appeared to be becoming rapidly wealthy. They were good Mormons, staunch defenders of Brigham Young, ready in every good work with open purses and generous deeds, and they were highly respected by the entire body of Saints.

What was the consternation of the church, when, during the delivery of a temperance sermon on Sunday, the Presi-dent, waxing more personal, more eloquent, and conse-quently more abusive, " cursed, in the name of the Lord," the men that ran the distillery !

They knew very well that these men paid their tithing promptly, — the greatest virtue a Mormon can possess, by the way, — and that they were foremost in all charitable works, and they marvelled very much that the Prophet should deal so hardly with them. His language was so abusive that Badley, who was especially attached to the President Young, shed tears during the denunciation. He finally finished his anathemas by ordering them to take their families and go on a mission to an unsettled portion of the Territory, leaving their homes to "the church," which, of course, meant Brigham Young.

As soon as they had gone, the Prophet removed the apparatus for distilling a few miles from the city, and commenced making whiskey for the church. But, unfortunately, the church whiskey did not prove to be so good as that made by Moon and Badley, and the church distillery was short-lived.

The men who were thus heartlessly ruined and unjustly exiled never returned. Their homes were broken up, their property taken from them, and themselves and their families banished to the wilderness, to gratify the covetousness and grasping of an avaricious tyrant, who committed this outrage, as he has all others, with a "Thus saith the Lord."

Brigham's missions may be considered moral "Botany Bays," where he sends those persons who in any way incur his sovereign displeasure. It is an easy way of punishing offenders; and so common has it become, that lately, whenever a man is sent away on this errand, the spontaneous question which arises to every lip is, "What has he done?" This is specially true of the younger men.

In case of a certain trial which took place some years since, Brigham had given his wishes to a portion of the jury as to how the case should be decided. After retiring, those of the jury who had received instructions from the Prophet came to a decision very readily, while those who had not been "interviewed" by him could see no justice in the way they had decided, and consequently refused to agree with the others.

Brigham was exceedingly angry at this, and took them

very severely to task for their disregard of his known
wishes.

"Well, Brother Brigham," said one of the obstinate jury-
men, "the law will sustain us."

"The law!" said the Prophet. "What do you suppose
I care for the law? My word is law here. I wish you distinctly to understand that; and," he continued, "those men
who decided against my view of the case shall pay the
penalty."

Very soon after that, one of these men, whose only fault
had been that he would not be coerced into committing
what he knew would be a gross injustice, was sent on a
mission to China; another was ordered to Japan, a third to
the Sandwich Islands, and one quite old gentleman was
appointed to Las Vegas. This man having grown gray
in the service of the church, Heber C. Kimball ventured to
propose that, in consideration of his age, he be allowed to
remain at home, and his son sent on the mission in his
stead. The father was actually too feeble to be of any
service in building up a new place, and Las Vegas was
considered an important point to secure; so, after much
deliberation, it was decided that the son should go in his
father's stead. Seventy-five families were ordered to abandon their homes, and take their departure for a new and
almost unknown portion of the Territory.

They expended thousands of dollars in building, fencing,
and every way beautifying and improving their new homes;
and just as they were getting nicely settled, and had made
their new homes habitable and comfortable, the Prophet
pronounced it an utterly unsuitable place for a "Stake of
Zion," and ordered them all back again; so that the years
passed there, and all the expenditures, were a total toss.

After the son of the aged juryman had paid the penalty of
his father's sin, he returned to Salt Lake. He has ever
since fearlessly expressed his opinion of the Las Vegas
mission, in terms not very flattering to its originator, and

Brigham has been obliged to withdraw the hand of fellow-ship from him, very reluctantly indeed, as he had been a faithful servant to the President's interest for several years.

As a comment on his often expressed contempt of the law and of lawyers, I wish to say just here that his son Alphilus Young is at this present time a law student at the University of Michigan, sent there by his father to carry out his own ambitious plans for his son's future, and also to have a lawyer in the family, since he has been forced to have so much to do with the law in late years.

It must not be supposed that none others are sent on missions except those who are to be punished, or got out of the way for a while. Brigham Young is shrewd, and so with these he sends every year prominent members of the church. All the apostles, and most of the leading elders, have been in the mission work, both in the States and in Europe, and it is in response to their efforts that so many converts have been made.

The period of my father's stay in England was one specially marked for success in mission work. Very many of the leaders of the church were there then, and mighty efforts were made to secure converts. They worked day and night with unabated zeal, and so great was their success, the whole world marvelled at the number of converts who came yearly to Zion.

In the mean time, the families of the missionaries were getting on as best they could at home, deprived not only of their husbands' society, but of the support which they gave them when at home, — scanty enough in some cases, I assure you, and yet just as much missed as though it had been larger, since it was the all; and above all, there was the horrible shadow of polygamy hanging over them; for no wife ever knew how much her husband may have been moved to "enlarge his kingdom," and the young English girls were apt to be very much taken with the American

12

elders, and they in turn submitted without much struggle to the fascinations of their youthful converts. Very few of the missionaries failed to bring home an English wife, or at least to induce some young girl to emigrate to Zion, with the prospect of becoming his wife on her arrival.

At first polygamy was not preached. Indeed, so very careful were the elders not to mention the subject, or else to deny polygamy altogether, that many of the girls supposed themselves to be the first and only wives of the men whom they married; and it was not until they reached Utah, and were introduced to their husbands' "other wives," that they were undeceived.

So strong was the feeling in England, that for some time

DOING MISSIONARY WORK.

after polygamy was openly practiced in Utah, the missionaries denied it, and men who had four and five wives living quoted largely from the Book of Mormon, and other church works, to prove the impossibility of the existence of such a system. At length, however, they were obliged to confess to the truth, which they did by causing the "Revelation" to be published in the "*Millennial Star*," the church organ published at Liverpool. For a while it seemed almost as though all the labors of the missionaries would go for nothing, so many apostatized. By strenuous effort and redoubled endeavor, however, many were still held in the church. They were told that polygamy was optional; that while the leaders of the church, many of them, practiced it, "*for conscience' sake*," since the Lord willed it, yet many more had not entered the system, and probably never would, and that no one need enter it, unless they felt themselves especially " called by the Lord."

In England, as in America, the men became much more easily reconciled to the doctrine than the women. The latter had many bitter hours over it; and yet each one, as all their American sisters before them had done, thought her husband would not take a polygamous wife, although he might believe in the theory, and uphold those of his brethren who converted the theory into practice. They had to learn, in the intensest bitterness of suffering, what other women had learned before them — that their husbands were like the majority of men, who had temptation so persistently thrust in their way.

Even now the men who go on missions are very guarded in preaching the doctrine, and advocate it only where they are very certain that it will be received. They admit its existence, but they by no means are willing to confess to what an extent it is practiced; and to this day many of them win wives under false pretences.

It was only a few weeks since, a gentleman living in the British Provinces, on a visit to some friends in New England, spoke of a visit he had received quite recently from a lady friend from England, a relative, I think, who had become converted to Mormonism, and married one of the elders of the church, and was on her way to Utah with him. She was a very lovely person, and in talking of her new religion, concerning which she was very enthusiastic, deplored the existence of polygamy as its only drawback to a perfect faith. Yet she said her husband had told her that it was only a doctrine of the church that was rarely practiced, except by the older Saints, who had received the Revelation directly from Joseph, and had considered the adoption of the system a duty; that in time it would be entirely done away with, except in theory, and that at all events *she* need have no fear.

Great was the surprise of the gentleman on learning that she, who so fondly believed herself the only wife of her husband, made Number 5 or 6 of his plural wives. The poor girl had, without doubt, learned the truth long before, although her pride, no doubt, would prevent her from informing her friends how cruelly she had been duped.

The Mormon mode of managing missions troubled me very little during those early days. I missed my father, and wished President Young would let him come back; beyond that I had little thought or care. I was busy studying with my mother, and I of course was taught the elements of the religion in which she so firmly believed, and on which she so greatly depended; and, like all children of Mormon parents, I was baptized when I was eight years old.

The Mormon people do not baptize or "christen" their infant children. When they are eight days old they are "blessed," and they are baptized at eight years of age. I was baptized by Bishop Taft, my father's second wife's father; and I was exceedingly terrified. I was taken to a pond, and the bishop carried me in his arms, and plunged me into the water; and so great was the nervous shock that I could not think of it without a shudder for years after.

My mother was glad when it was over, for I was made a child of the church, and by this rite she consecrated me to God and the Mormon faith. To God I still hold loving, trustful allegiance; as for the Mormon faith, I can never be too thankful that I have so entirely freed myself from its tyrannical fetters, that held me, soul and body, in such a long and cruel bondage.

CHAPTER X.

THE UTAH "REFORMATION." — "A REIGN OF TERROR." — THE BLOOD-ATONEMENT PREACHED.

The Beginning of the Reformation. — The Payson Saints Stirred Up. — What the Wicked "Saints" had been Doing Secretly. — The Old Lady who stole a Radish. — Confessing the sins of Others. — A System of *Espionnage.* — Brigham bids them "Go Ahead!" — The Story of Brother Jeddy's Mule. — The Saints receive a terrible Drubbing. — Great Excitement in Mormondom. — How the Saints were Catechized. — Indelicate Questions are put to Everybody. — My Mother and Myself Confess. — The Labors of the Home Missionaries. — Making Restitution. — Everybody is Re-baptized. — "Cut off *Below their Ears.*" — The "Blood-Atonement" Preached. — Murder recommended in the Tabernacle. — Cutting their Neighbors' throats for Love. — A "Reign of Terror" in Utah. — Fearful Outrages Committed. — Murdered "*by the Indians*"? — Brigham advises the Assassination of Hatten. — Murder of Almon Babbitt, Dr. Robinson, the Parrishes, and Others. — Bloodshed the Order of the Day.

AWAKENING THE SAINTS.

HILE my father was in England on mission, my mother was urged very strongly to go to Payson, a town about seventy miles south of Salt Lake City, and start a school there.

She had taught in Kirtland, and in Salt Lake City, and was considered a person of superior attainments by the Saints. Her reputation as a teacher was quite extended among them, and since her arrival in Utah she had often been solicited to resume her profession. She had always hith-

erto refused persistently; but now, finding her time somewhat unemployed during my father's absence, and wishing
to add to the family funds, which were running somewhat
low, she decided to accept the situation, which was fairly
thrust upon her. Of course I accompanied her to the
scene of her labors. I had never been separated from her,
and neither she nor I could endure the thought of being
parted.

It was, I think, in January, 1855, that a Mormon, named
Joseph Hovey, came to Payson to preach. He was a man
of an excitable temperament, a fanatic in religion, and he
succeeded in stirring the people up to a state of the most
intense religious enthusiasm. He held a series of meetings, which were very largely attended, and such was his
peculiar magnetism, that he swayed and held the multitudes who thronged to hear him, notwithstanding he was a
man of unprepossessing manner, little education, and no
culture. He commenced by accusing the people of all
sorts of misdeeds and crimes, and he denounced them in
the most scathing and the rudest fashion, and they trembled under his fierce denunciations, and cowered before
him as before the face of an accusing angel. He accused
them of theft, of licentiousness, of blackguardism, of lying,
of swindling and cheating, of hypocrisy and lukewarm-
ness in their religion, and of every other sin, of omission
or commission, of which he could think. He represented
himself as the Lord's messenger, called by Him, and sent
to warn the people of Southern Utah of the horrors of their
situation; their souls were in imminent peril, so weighted
were they with a load of guilt. "Repent, confess, and be
re-baptized," was his urgent call, "and all your sins shall
be forgiven you; yea, verily, for so hath the Lord promised."

The excitement grew daily, and his work of "Reformation," as he styled it, went bravely on. Meetings were
held, lasting all day and late into the night. It was reli-

gious madness run riot. There seemed to be a sort of competition as to who should confess the most and the oftenest. The people of Payson had been considered as good as average communities, but this "Reformation" revealed the most astonishing amount of dishonesty and depravity among them.

I was at one of the meetings, and I remember how shocked I was as one after another arose and confessed the crimes of which they were guilty. It made a very vivid impression on my childish mind, and to this day I can recall the very expression of the faces and tones of the voices as the owners professed their criminality. Many of them confessed to stealing flour from a mill; this, indeed, seemed a common peccadillo; others had stolen lumber for various purposes; and one man said he had stolen a sheep. I remember this man very distinctly; there happened to be a bit of wool sticking to his clothes, on the shoulder, and I know I wondered if that was from the sheep he had stolen.

Some had taken potatoes, some turnips, some others parsnips, others had taken all three; one conscience-stricken old lady, who felt impelled to confess, and could think of nothing that she had done wrong, was immensely relieved when she remembered that she had taken a radish without permission; she seemed, too, to derive much con-solation from the fact that "it had burned in her stomach ever since."

Taking it all in all, it was a time of the wildest confu-sion and the intensest ill-feeling. If there were any persons who did not come forward readily, and acknowledge their faults, some one would do it for them, telling their brothers' and sisters' sins in the public congregation.

My mother did not approve of the state of affairs, and would not countenance them any farther than she was posi-tively compelled to do. It was dangerous to express any disapproval of the proceedings; so she was obliged to keep quiet, although she would not take active part in the excitement. The most fanatical of these blinded enthusiasts did not hesitate to threaten the lives of all who dared dissent from them, and the person who failed to confess was looked upon with suspicion. A close watch was kept upon the actions of these persons, and every word that dropped from their lips was noted. In fact, the entire church, with few exceptions, was converted into a detective force, to keep vigilant watch over those few exceptions who were found to be " cool in the faith."

While the excitement was at its height, Brigham Young was informed of Hovey's movements, and their results in Payson. The few who were not in sympathy with the excitement waited anxiously for the Prophet to speak, expecting, of course, that when he heard the state of affairs, there would be a summary stop put to all these fanatical proceedings. Many of the surrounding settlements were very much exercised over the conduct of the Payson people, thinking they were all going mad together; and they also waited curiously to see what action Brigham would take. He was at Fillmore, attending the legislature, when he was told of the excitement at Payson, and his reply was, " Let them go ahead; they won't confess to more than they are guilty of."

As may be supposed, this cavalier manner of treating the matter surprised the more thoughtful of the Saints, who had counted confidently on his interference; but their surprise increased tenfold, when, the very next winter, 1856, Brigham and his counsellors instituted a similar reform throughout the entire territory. It is said that this latter Reformation was caused by President Jedediah M. Grant losing his temper over a mule.

It seems that Brother Grant was to hold a meeting at Kaysville, and had invited several elders to accompany him. To one of these elders he lent a mule, which should bear him to the appointed place. When he arrived, the sharp eyes of Brother Grant discovered that his mule was heated and somewhat jaded; and although he made no remarks at the time, but, on the contrary, was suavity itself, yet he did not let the brother go unrebuked.   After every one had spoken at the meeting, testifying to the utmost good feeling themselves, and exhorting faithfulness on the part of their hearers, Brother Grant arose for the last word.   He accused the speakers who had preceded him of inconsistency and hypocrisy; charged the bishop with inefficiency,

" SCENE DURING REFORMATION."

and his people with all manner of crimes, and then personally attacked the unfortunate brother for ill-treating his mule.   He called upon everybody to repent, and " do their first works over again," or the judgment of God would speedily overtake them.   This was the beginning of the famous Utah " Reformation," of which the local movement at Payson was the immediate forerunner.   It was the same thing on a much larger scale; confessions were the order of the day, and accusation was as prevalent as confession.

It was a horrible time, and one that never will be forgotten by those who were living in the midst of the excitement. An impressionable twelve-years-old girl, I remember every detail with wonderful distinctness.

This " Reformation " was more systematically conducted than Hovey's revival; a catechism was compiled by the leading spirits of the church, and printed by their order, and elders were appointed to go from house to house with a copy of it, questioning the people. This catechism contained a list of singular questions, many of which I distinctly remember. I *dare* only mention a few. They were after this style : —

" Have you ever committed a murder? "

" Have you ever stolen anything? "

" Have you ever been drunk? "

" Do you believe in polygamy? "

Many were grossly indelicate, others laughably absurd; yet every question was obliged to be answered on pain of expulsion from the church. Men, women, and children alike were catechized; many of the little ones did not know the meaning of some of the questions which were put to them; but they were obliged to answer them; whether understandingly, or not, it made no difference.

It was customary to catechize each member of a family separately; but an exception was made in our case, and my mother and myself were examined together. There was a great part of the catechism that I did not understand, but I always answered as my mother did, feeling sure that what she said must of a necessity be right. When the questioning was over, I was exhorted by the visiting elder to obey my parents, and to marry into polygamy when a little older.

The elders that acted as " Home Missionaries," whose duty it was to catechize the people, were astonished at the grossness of some of the immoralities which were brought to light. The private history and secret acts of all were unfolded. People were accused of sins which they never had committed, and yet they were afraid to deny them. Some of the elders were shocked beyond measure at the sickening details revealed, and begged that a stop be put to this mania for confession; but the poor fanatics were urged forward by their leaders, and they firmly believed that in the fullest and freest confession lay their only hope of salvation. They were goaded to the very verge of frenzy. Every person throughout the Territory was commanded to be re-baptized, even if their sins had not been very grave. It was commanded, too, that every person who had committed a theft should make good what he had taken; and I recollect a man returning some property to my father which he had taken from the family while my father was in England: some others confessed to having stolen the fence from the farm; so, it seems, we had suffered from the dishonesty of our before presumedly honest neighbors. Throughout the whole church there was a general time of accusation, confession, restitution, and re-baptism.

There were many of the Mormon people who did not approve of all this unhealthy excitement, and who foresaw exactly what results would follow, yet not one of them dared venture a protest. It would have been at the risk of their lives, as it was publicly advised, not only by Hovey in Payson, but by men in much more prominent places, to punish such persons as ventured a disapproval by " cutting them off from the church, *below their ears*."

It was during this excitement that the terrible doctrine of the Blood-Atonement was first preached. So high did the feeling run that people who were guilty of certain crimes were counselled to shed their blood to save their souls. Said the arch-fanatic Jedediah M. Grant, in the Tabernacle, speaking of those who had apostatized or were in danger of apostasy, —

" What ought this meek people, who keep the commandments of the Lord, to do unto them? 'Why,' says some one, 'they ought to pray to the Lord to kill them.' I want to know if you would wish the Lord to come down and do all your dirty work? Many of the Latter-Day Saints will pray, and petition, and supplicate the Lord to do a thousand things they themselves would be ashamed to do. When a man prays for a thing, he ought to be willing to perform it himself."

In the same sermon he said, —

"What! do you believe that people would do right and keep the law of God by actually putting to death the transgressors? Putting to death the transgressors would exhibit the law of God, no matter by whom it was done. That is my opinion."

Following the expression of his belief, he uttered the following fervent wish : —

"I wish we were in a situation favorable to our doing that which is justifiable before God, without any contaminating influence of Gentile amalgamation, laws, and traditions, that the people of God might lay the axe to the root of the tree, and that every tree that bringeth not forth good fruit might be hewn down."

He was so in earnest that he would have the atonement by blood commence at once. Listen to his disinterested counsel : —

"I say there are men and women here that I would advise to go to the President immediately, and ask him to appoint a committee to attend to their case ; and then let a place be selected, and let that committee shed their blood."

On another occasion he said, speaking in his wild, fanatical manner, —

"We have been trying long enough with this people ; and I go in for letting the sword of the Almighty to be unsheathed, not only in word, but in deed."

Brigham Young, not to be behind his counsellor, assured the Saints that this doctrine of throat-cutting and bloodshedding was pleasing to the Lord, and that it was a glorious and soul-saving belief. He says, —

"There are sins that can be atoned for by an offering on the altar, as in ancient days; and there are sins that the blood of a lamb or calf, or of turtle-doves, cannot remit, but they must be atoned for *by the blood of the man*."

Another choice bit from one of his Tabernacle discourses is as follows: —

"The time is coming when justice will be laid to the line and righteousness to the plummet: when we shall take the old broadsword, and ask, 'Are you for God?' and if you are not heartily on the Lord's side, you will be hewn down."

In a sermon preached from the text, — the sweetest and tenderest of all the commandments given by Christ, — "Love thy neighbor as thyself," Brigham Young put this peculiarly Christ-like construction on the words: —

"When will we love our neighbor as ourselves? Any of you who understand the principles of eternity, if you have sinned a sin requiring the shedding of blood, except the sin unto death, should not be satisfied or rest until your blood should be spilled, that you might gain that salvation you desire. That is the way to love mankind. Now, brethren and sisters, will you live your religion? How many hundreds of times have I asked that question? Will the Latter-Day Saints live their religion?"

He also asked in the same sermon, —

"Will you love your brothers and sisters when they have a sin that cannot be atoned for without the shedding of their blood? Will you love that man or that woman well enough to shed their blood? *That is what Jesus meant.*

"The time will come when the law of God will be in full force. This is loving our neighbor as ourself: if he needs help, help him; if he wants salvation, and it is necessary to spill his blood upon the earth in order that he may be saved, *spill it.*"

It is no wonder that such language as this, poured into the ears of the already half-crazed Saints, should incite them to deeds of violence. For a while bloodshed and murder were

the order of the day. If any person or family were supposed
to be lacking in the faith, and failing to exhibit the usual
blind submission to the teachings of the priesthood, that
person or family was sure to be visited by some disaster —
whipped, mobbed, or murdered, and their property destroyed or confiscated to the use of the church. Some in-
stances came under my own observation, and I tell the incidents from actual knowledge, and not from mere hearsay.

A merchant of Salt Lake City, an Englishman, named
Jarvis, was suspected of being cool in the faith, and to have
little or no sympathy with the fanatical proceedings which
attended the Reformation and formed its chief feature. His
store was entered one evening by Saints in disguise, he was
pulled over the counter by the hair of his head, dragged
into the street and thrown into the snow, his store plundered,
all the money taken away, his house set on fire, and his two
wives barely given time to escape with their children. As an
excuse for all this he was accused of having "spoken against
the authorities, and had entertained Gentiles at supper."

One of the wives of Mr. Jarvis wrote quite a thrilling
account to some of her English friends respecting their treatment; and as her story is so simply and yet plainly told, I
shall insert it here, as being the best description I can give
of it and similar scenes. It is dated from "Weston, Missouri," the August following the year of the Reformation.

"After Mr. Grimshaw left Salt Lake, Mr. Jarvis made known
to Brigham Young his intention to leave the Territory and return
to the States, with his reasons for so doing; but his letter was
never answered. Brigham made some allusion to it in public,
which seemed to convey the idea that he approved of the course
Mr. Jarvis had taken, rather than try to leave clandestinely. From
that time we began to dispose of our property, and draw everything
into as small a compass as possible. As the winter drew on,
various reports were circulated; such as, that we intended to dispose of our large house to the soldiers, and were buying grain to
store it for them. This is a 'capital' offence in the Salt Lake
Valley, for the Mormons protest that no soldier shall sleep in Salt

Lake City one night. It was also said that Mr. Jarvis had sworn to take the life of President Young; that he was boarding States officers at his house; and many more such stories, as strange and unlikely as they were untrue; for when Mr. Jarvis wrote to President Young, he made the offer of all or any part of his property to him first, if he chose to purchase it, and told him that he would rather sell it to the church than to any one else. Time passed on, and we heard some whispers that something dreadful was going to happen to us; but we thought little about it, and felt perfectly safe, until the 13th of January, 1857, when, at half past six in the evening, a man knocked at the front door, which was locked, and

DEALING WITH A WEAK BROTHER.

asked for some trifling article out of the shop. While Mr. Jarvis was attending to him, two men walked in and hastily stepped up to him. One of them caught him by the hair and by the collar, and pulled him across the counter, saying, 'You are my prisoner.' Mr. Jarvis said, 'For what? If you have any charge against me, I will go where you wish.' To this no answer was returned but oaths and curses. They dragged him on the ground some distance, and then brought him back into the doorway, all the time trying to strangle him, and threatening to shoot him if he made any noise. One of them made a desperate kick at him but missed his aim.

"In the mean time Betsey and I were undressing the children; and hearing sounds of heavy footsteps and muttering undertones of strange voices and persons struggling in the passage, we looked at each other, and rushed to the door, each with a child in our arms. I succeeded in pulling open the room door in the passage, but I had no sooner done so than a man who was holding the door knocked me back into the room, flat upon the floor, with the baby in my arms, and, shutting the door again, held it fast. Instantly I laid the baby on the carpet, and, with all my strength, forced open the door, and found myself surrounded by a number of ruffians, — I believe five or six, — who were all in the dark, for they had extinguished the candle, and I calling aloud for Mr. Jarvis several minutes. In the end he, gasping for breath, answered me.

"When I found where he was, I made a desperate rush at the man who was holding him, and the fellow, lifting up his hand, let go his hold of him, and he darted out of the open door like lightning, across the street, and round the corner to a neighbor's house to obtain assistance. He got to the door almost exhausted, and begged for help; but no one dared come until the master of the house, who was absent, returned. They fetched him, and when he heard the particulars of the attack made upon us, he said, 'Sir, you must leave my house instantly. I have no sympathy for you. I would not protect my own father under the same circumstances.' Mr. Jarvis said, 'What have I done?' The man replied, 'You have done plenty; you covenanted to serve the Lord, and you are serving the devil, and I should not be surprised to see you with your throat cut.'

"After Mr. Jarvis had made his escape from the fiends, I turned to enter the house again, firmly believing that some of them were in pursuit of him, and begged to know of the men on the spot what they wanted. On stepping forward to enter the door, I found it guarded by a man on each side, who pushed me backward into the snow. I rose and again attempted to enter the house, but was prevented in like manner, when I saw Mrs. M. coming out with the babies in their night-gowns, one under each arm, to carry them to a place of safety. When I found I could not, after several such attempts, force an entrance, I ran round to the back door and got in, but no sooner was I in than out again. I was tossed by the same ruthless hands as before. Many a time I was knocked down in the way I have described; and one of my front teeth was loosened, and my limbs most mercilessly bruised.

"Finding I could not enter to ascertain the state of affairs in the house, I determined to let the neighborhood know, and for many minutes stood shouting for help, until I was exhausted. I could hear that the windows were all being broken, and the furniture destroyed; when I was appalled by hearing Mrs. M. shriek out, 'O, Mrs. Jarvis, the house is on fire!' I instantly ran in desperation, and got in at the back part of the shop, — and O, my dear sister, what a scene! Flames and smoke up to the ceiling;

BRUTAL ASSAULT UPON MRS. JARVIS.

the goods in the store, or shop, burning; and two men, almost suffocated, still intent upon the work of destruction — carrying lighted paper, and setting fire to everything that would burn!

"The thoughts of my three boys sleeping up stairs; my husband, I knew not where, — perhaps murdered, — and seeing no hope of saving the house — for three rooms were then burning; the thought that to-morrow I and my children would have no home, no shelter, and be penniless, with the snow two feet deep, and not a friend that dare open the door to us, — they dare not do it, however much disposed they might be; for they were threatened with the same, and were told that if they heard the cry of fire they were to take no notice; all these things rush-

13

ing into my mind at once, I grew desperate, and forced my way
in at the front door, and implored the ruffians to let me fetch my
children down stairs. They muttered, ' There's none of them
there.' I said, ' Yes, they are asleep in bed.' Then he said,
' Go.' On passing up stairs, I saw on one side the shop in
flames, and the room, the furniture and windows broken, and our
clothes scattered about, on fire. I shrieked out, when a man
caught me by the throat, and I had to gasp for breath. I saved
my children in their night-dresses, and the oldest had to run out
with the snow up to his hips.

" When we found that the villains were gone, we put out the fire,
throwing water upon it; and on one shelf was a large canister of
gunpowder, within six inches of the flame, of which I did not
know. I saved the house from being blown up, but I got my
hands severely burned. Four large windows were broken out,
one dozen chairs and a table destroyed; a stove and three tables
broken; carpets, clothes, and goods burned in the store; and
many silver watches and other substantial things stolen, making
the damage sustained amount to nearly eight hundred dollars.
Every day after was a living death, — a dying daily. We were
never safe for an hour. When we appealed to the authorities,
they advised us to be quiet about it, and ' let it slide.' And so
we did; for we could obtain no redress.

" The outrage upon us was never mentioned in the newspaper.
We had to pocket the insult, and bear the loss; and now we are
thankful we are out of it. We exchanged our property for land
in the States, hired conveyances, and left on the 22d of April.
We are now at Weston, eight miles from Leavenworth, where we
arrived without any interruption; but we suffered greatly from
the heat. We shall remain here till Mr. Jarvis makes arrangements for our future abode."

My father knew these people well in England; they
were from Leeds, where they were highly respected. I
have met them quite recently in Burlington, Iowa, where
they are living in very comfortable circumstances. They
have outgrown all tendencies towards Mormonism, and are
now among its bitterest opponents.

This outrage is somewhat remarkable, because it was

unattended by bloodshed, — a most extraordinary circumstance, when so many were killed outright who had sinned
as Mr. Jarvis had.   Innocent people suffered, and at that
time, no Gentile was safe in the Mormon territory.

A cousin of mine, whose parents lived in Utah, married
a man named Hatten, in Illinois. When her mother emigrated with the Saints, she, of course, remained behind
with her husband, to her mother's great distress.   After a
few years, Mr. Hatten decided to remove to California, and
he came by the way of Utah, so as to give his wife an opportunity of visiting her relatives, whom she had not seen
since the exodus from Nauvoo.

At that time it was considered a dishonor to have a
friend married to a Gentile — she was regarded as lost.
And for a girl to be taken to California was a still deeper
disgrace.

My aunt and her husband were devout Mormons, and
they grieved over their daughter as over one dead.   My
aunt prayed and wept for her and over her; and my
uncle — the girl's father — even grew desperate in his despair.   He consulted Brigham as to the best course which
he should pursue, and the Prophet's ready reply was, "Put
Hatten out of the way.   It is a sin and a shame to have so
good a woman dragged around the world by a Gentile."

That was sufficient.   In a few days came the startling
news that Hatten had been "killed by the Indians."   He
had gone to Fillmore on a visit, from which he was destined
never to return.   The young wife was almost heart-broken
at the sudden loss of her husband, but she did not dream
what was his real fate until long afterwards.   She supposed he had fallen a victim to Indian cruelty, as the reports told her; but when, after many years, she learned
the bitter truth, she fairly hated the religion that had made
a martyr of her husband, and brought sorrow and affliction
to her.   She could not get away from it, however; there
was no place to which she could go; she had no friends

elsewhere; all the years that had intervened between her husband's death and her knowledge of his real fate had been passed in Utah, and she had severed herself in that time most effectually from her former friends. There was nothing to do but to endure; and that she did, as patiently as possible. A few years after her husband's death, she married again, but not happily. However, she was speedily released from this unhappy bondage. Heber C. Kimball had seen and fancied her, and he went to Brigham with the story of her unhappiness, and added, as he finished his recital, "She ought never to have married that man. I designed her for myself."

"It is not too late," replied his friend, the Prophet; "you can have her yet." And he made good his word by divorcing her from her uncongenial husband, and bestowing her on Heber. She was too indifferent to care what became of her, and she became a Mrs. Kimball without a protest. She and her two children are living in Utah now.

Another victim to the Blood-Atonement was a young man named Jesse Earl, a musician of rare talent and great promise. He was a very intimate friend of the Prophet's oldest son, Joseph, and had lived a great deal in the Prophet's family. The reason of his death has never been given; it was only said that his sins were past forgiveness, except his blood should atone for them.

Apostates were even more hardly dealt with than the Gentiles. One of the old Mormons, named Almon Babbitt, was "killed by the Indians," on his way to the States. Mr. Babbitt was among the first seventy apostles appointed by Joseph Smith; he had been among those who went up to Missouri, to "Zion's Camp," and was an eloquent preacher and advocate of Mormon doctrines. After Brigham came into power, Babbitt became quite disaffected towards the authorities, and left Utah to return to the States, when he was overtaken by his doom.

Once in a while some person would become so conscience-stricken for some sin he had committed, that he would voluntarily seek to make the "Atonement;" but those were rare cases. I remember hearing of one at the time of its occurrence. A Mormon named John Evan had shot a man in Council Bluffs. He came at once to Salt Lake, visited Brigham, and begged to atone for his crime in the usual way.

Not long after that, he was on his way home one night, when suddenly the report of a pistol was heard; Mr. Evan was found dead, and although it was currently reported that he had committed suicide, it was well known by the better informed that "he had only paid the debt," and given his life for another that he had taken by violence.

The Potter and Parrish murders at Springville, and the assassination of Dr. Robinson at Salt Lake, are notorious. The Parrish brothers were murdered for apostasy, Dr. Robinson because he was a Gentile whose influence was extending in the Territory, so popular was he, and consequently the authorities considered him dangerous.

More vividly stamped upon my memory than any other of the horrible occurrences, is the murder of a woman named Jones, and her son, in Payson. They were suspected of falling away in the faith, and other grave charges were brought against them, for which it was deemed necessary that they should die. One night there was a great commotion in the streets of the town; pistol-shots were heard; there was a sound of hurrying feet, a murmur of voices, and a subdued excitement, lasting all night. No one dared to venture out to learn the cause, lest their curiosity should be summarily punished. In those days it was dangerous to seek to know more than the priesthood chose to tell. In fact, everything but a blind following of fanatical doctrines was dangerous. Free thought was suicidal. The morning following the night of which I have spoken put an end to the suspense. It was proclaimed everywhere that the Joneses had been killed, and their dead bodies, shockingly mutilated, were placed in a wagon, and exposed to the crowd by being driven through the streets, attended by a jeering, taunting mob, who could not cease their insults though their victims were still in death. I did not see the bodies, nor did my mother, although they were driven past our door; we both shunned the fearful sight. But there were plenty of women who did look at them, and who gloried in their death as a deed of service to the Lord. Mrs. Jones was mixing bread at the time she was shot, and the dough still remained clinging to her hands after her death.

BLOOD ATONEMENT. — SCENE DURING REFORMATION.

This was the way that " the Lord" was " worshipped" in Utah in 1856 and 1857. *I have heard men say,* "If I apostatize, I hope some of my brethren will love me well enough to slay me." The Saints are by no means a bloodthirsty people, but these are some of the results of the teachings during the Reformation.

It may be a matter of wonder to many how honest-hearted people could remain in a church that taught and practiced so many and such fearful evils. Concerning the murders, the majority of the people knew nothing, and supposed that the Indians were the assassins, as they were always told so. Yet some were sufficiently fanatical to believe that, if Brigham was the instigator, it was quite right. " The ancient order of things was being restored."

I have heard many Mormons declare that they hoped, some time, light would be thrown on these dark deeds, and the murderers made to pay the penalty of their crimes. But those who suspected that the authorities of the church were implicated felt that their only safeguard was silence. Those living in Utah during the Reformation, and seeing it in all its horrors, as I did, know very well the spirit of the teachings in the Tabernacle; and although many may be slow to impute the commission of crime to Brigham Young, they cannot but admit that his teachings all tended to make crime prevalent. And if they do not acknowledge his direct agency, they must see that his influence all went in the direction of the atonement of sin by blood. As far as I am concerned, I do not hesitate to say that I believe all these murders lie at his door, and that he will have to be personally responsible for them. His hands are red with innocent blood, his garments dyed with it, and no " Atonement" can ever wash out the damning spots.

CHAPTER XI.

"DIVINE EMIGRATION." — THE PROPHET AND THE HAND-CART SCHEME.

Early Emigration to Utah. — The Prophet Meditates Economy. — The "Divine Plan" Invented. — How it was Revealed to the Saints. — They Prepare to "Gather to Zion." — How the Hand-Carts were Built. — The Sufferings of the Emigrants. — On Board Ship. — An Apostolic Quarrel. — Base Conduct of the Apostle Taylor.—The Saints arrive in Iowa City. — How the Summer-time was Wasted. — Beginning a Terrible Journey. — Suffering by the Way. — "Going Cheap." — They reach Council Bluffs. — Levi Savage Behaves Bravely. — Lying Prophecy of the Apostle Richards. — How the Emigrants were Deceived. — Brigham Young sends Help to Them. — Two Apostles are Denounced. — The Prophet in a Fix. — He lays His own Sins on the Backs of Others. — Preparing to Receive the Emigrants.

THE EMIGRANTS' LANDING-PLACE,
Castle Gardens, New York.

N the history of any people there has never been recorded a case of such gross mismanagement as that of gathering the foreign Saints to Zion in the year 1856.

Until this disastrous year the emigrants had always made the journey across the plains with ox-teams, under the charge of some of the returning elders, who were triumphantly bringing the fruits of their labors in foreign vineyards to garner them in Zion. The able-bodied walked, and those who were too young, too old, or too feeble to perform the journey on foot, went in the wagons with the baggage. It was in tne same way that the Saints themselves made their first journey across the plains, and in the proper season of the year was a safe and a pleasant journey. Tedious and wearisome, to be sure, but in no way perilous, as plenty of provisions, bedding, and clothing could be carried, not only for the journey, but sufficient to last some time after the arrival.

The cost of emigration in this way was from £10 to £12, English money, or nominally $50 to $60 in gold — not very expensive, surely, for a journey from Liverpool to Salt Lake City ; but to Brigham, in one of his fits of economy, it seemed altogether too costly, and he set to work to devise some means for retrenchment. During the entire winter of 1855–56, he and his chief supporters were in almost constant consultation on the subject of reducing the expenses of emigration, and they finally hit upon the expedient of having them cross the plains with hand-carts, wheeling their own provisions and baggage, and so saving the expense of teams. The more Brigham thought of his plan, the more in love he grew with it, and he sent detailed instructions concerning it to the Apostle Franklin D. Richards, the Mormon agent at Liverpool, who published it in the "*Millennial Star*," as the new "divine plan" revealed to Brother Brigham by the Lord, whose will it was that the journey should be made in this manner.

My father was in England when the "command of the Lord concerning them" was given to the gathering Saints, and their enthusiastic devotion and instant acceptance of the revelation showed how entirely they entrusted themselves to the leadership of their superiors in the church, implicitly believing them to be inspired of God. They were told by Richards, in the magazine, and by their missionaries in their addresses, that they should meet many difficulties, — that trials would be strewn along their path, and occasional dangers meet them, — but that the Lord's chosen people were to be a tried people, and that they should come out unscathed, and enter Zion with great triumph and rejoicing, coming out from the world as by great tribulation; that

APOSTLE FRANKLIN D. RICHARDS,
Husband of Ten Wives.

the Lord would hold them in special charge, and they need not fear terror by night nor pestilence that walketh at noonday, for they should not so much as hurt a foot against a stone.

It was represented to them that they were specially privileged and honored in thus being called by the Lord to be the means of showing His power and revealing glory to a world lying in darkness and overwhelmed with guilt, deserted by God and given over to destruction. Considering the class of people from whom most of the converts were made, it is not at all strange that all this talk should impress their imaginations and arouse their enthusiasm. Emotion, instead of reason, guided them almost entirely, and they grew almost ecstatic over the new way in which they were called to Zion.

The United States government was beginning to trouble itself a little about Utah; and in order to make the church as strong as possible, in case of an invasion, Brigham was anxious to increase the number of emigrants, and requested Apostle Richards to send as many as he possibly could. To do this, the elders counselled all the emigrants, who had more money than they needed, to deposit it with the Apostle Richards for the purpose of assisting the poor to Zion. The call was instantly and gladly obeyed, and the number of Saints bound Zion-ward was thereby nearly doubled. In the face of the disaster which attended it, it has been the boast of some of the missionaries and elders that this was the largest number that ever was sent over at one time. So much greater, then, is the weight of responsibility which rests upon the souls of those who originated and carried out this selfish design, made more selfish, more cruel, and more terribly culpable for the hypocrisy and deceit which attended it from its conception to its disastrous close.

Great, however, as was the number of emigrants who that year crossed the plains to Utah, as many, if not more, have, during various seasons since then, traversed the same route; although, of course, for obvious reasons, it is difficult to give approximate statistics. During the summer of 1862 — the same year in which Eliza Snow and Geo. A. Smith, the fattest of all fat apostles, together with a select company of Saints, wandered off to the Holy Land in order to bring it within the dominions of Brigham — it was said that more Mormons were landed at Castle Gardens than during any other previous year. I cannot say whether this is true; but it is a fact that only a few weeks ago seven or eight hundred were landed in New York, and every few weeks, all through the summer, other ship-loads will arrive.

On the 14th of March, 1856, my father, who was at Sheffield, England, engaged in missionary work, received a telegram from Richards, telling him to come at once to Liverpool for the purpose of taking passage for America in the mail-packet Canada, which was to sail for Boston on the 15th. He had no time to say good-bye to his friends, but made his preparations hurriedly, and left Sheffield as soon as possible. On arriving at Liverpool and consulting with Richards, he learned that he had been sent for to assist in the proposed hand-cart expedition, and that his part of the work was to be performed in the United States. He, being a practical wagon-maker, was to oversee the building of the carts. In twenty-four hours after the receipt of the telegram — his first intimation that he was to be called home — he was on his way. The passage was unusually rough, and he was glad enough to see the shores of America after tossing about on the ocean for fifteen days. He landed in Boston the 30th of March, and went immediately to Iowa City, the gathering-place of the Saints prior to their departure for Utah, arriving there the 10th of April.

He expected, of course, to go to work at once, and was very impatient to do so, as it was very nearly the season when the emigrants should start to cross the plains, and the first vessel filled with them was already due in New York. He knew that it would be a waste both of time and money to keep them in Iowa City any longer than was absolutely necessary; besides which, after a certain date, every day would increase the perils of crossing the plains. But when he arrived, Daniel Spencer, the principal agent, was east on a visit, and did not make his appearance until an entire month had expired; and there was all that valuable time wasted in order that one man might indulge in a little pleasure. What were a thousand or more human lives in comparison to his enjoyment? Less than nothing, it would seem, in his estimation.

Not only were there no materials provided to work with, but no provision had been made for sheltering the poor Saints, who had already commenced to arrive by ship-loads. Their condition was pitiable in the extreme; they had met nothing but privation from the time they left England. The trials that had been promised them they had already encountered, but so great was their faith, that they bore it all without a word of complaint, and some even rejoicing that it was their lot to suffer for the cause of their religion; they were sure they should all be brought to Zion in safety, for had not God promised that through the mouth of His holy Prophet? Their faith was sublime in its exaltation; and in contrast to it, the cold-blooded, scheming, blasphemous policy of Young and his followers shows out false, and blacker than ever. To have deceived a credulous people by wanton misrepresentation is wicked enough, but to do it "in the name of the Lord" is a sin that can never be atoned for to God or man. It is the height of blasphemy, and I fairly shudder as I endeavor to comprehend, in some slight degree, the magnitude of such an offence.

They had been crowded and huddled together on shipboard more like animals than like human beings; their food had been insufficient and of bad quality; the sleeping accommodations were limited, and there was not the proper amount of bedding for those who were compelled to sleep in the more exposed places. Some of the persons who saw

MORMON EMIGRANTS ON SHIPBOARD.

the emigrants, say that it was like nothing so much as an African slave-ship, filled with its unlawful and ill-gotten freight. The air in the steerage, where most of the emigrants were, was noxious, and yet these people were compelled to breathe it through all the days of the voyage. Many were too ill to leave their beds, and a change of clothing was out of the question. The entire floor was covered with mattresses, and it was impossible to walk about without stepping over some one. Men, women, and children were huddled in together in the most shameless fashion.

Affairs were not much bettered when they arrived at New

York; the Apostle John Taylor, whose duty it was to provide for them there, was too deeply engaged in a quarrel with Apostle Franklin D. Richards, as to which of the two was higher in authority, to attend to these poor creatures, who were thrown on his protection, penniless and helpless, in a strange country. But everyone must understand that his personal dignity must be attended to and his position maintained, if all the poor Saints that were emigrated, or dreamed of emigrating, should die of starvation and exposure. I think the great body of Saints must have learned before this time that it is by no means safe to trust to the tender mercies of a Mormon Apostle. When, after a while, the Apostle Taylor's imperative personal business allowed him a moment in which to think of the unhappy emigrants, he started them for Iowa City, where they arrived only to experience a repetition of their New York sufferings, and see another illustration of apostolic neglect. Nothing had been prepared for them either in the way of shanties or tents, and they were compelled to camp in the open air, their only roof a sky that was not always blue. While in camp, there were several very severe rain-storms, from which, as they had no shelter, there was no escape; they got completely drenched, and this caused a great deal of severe illness among them. They were unprotected alike from burning sun and pitiless, chilling rain, and it is no wonder that fevers and dysentery prevailed, and that hundreds of longing eyes closed in death before they beheld the Zion of their hopes.

It would have been strange if the faith of some had not wavered then; yet none dared complain. There was nothing to do but to go on to the end. They were thousands of miles from home, with no means of returning, and they were taught, too, that it would be a curse upon them to turn their backs on Zion. So there they remained through the long summer days, waiting helplessly until they should be ordered to move onward.

At length my father saw his way clear to commence his

work, and he went to work with a will, pressing everyone who could be of actual assistance into his service. But here the trouble commenced again. He was instructed to make the wagons on as economical a plan as possible, and every step that he took he found himself hedged about by impossibilities. The agents all talked economy, and when one did not raise an objection to a proposal, another did, and difficulties were placed in his way constantly.

They did not wish to furnish iron for the tires, as it was too expensive; raw hide, they were sure, would do just as well. My father argued this point with them until at last the agents decided to give up raw hides, and they furnished him with hoop iron. He was annoyed and angry, all the while he was making the carts, at the extreme parsimony displayed. A thorough workman himself, he wanted good materials to work with; but every time he asked for anything, no matter how absolutely necessary it was to make the work sufficiently durable to stand the strain of so long a journey, the reply invariably was, " O, Brother Webb, the carts must be made cheap. We can't afford this expenditure; you are too extravagant in your outlay; " forgetting, in their zeal to follow their Prophet's instructions, what the consequences would be to the poor Saints, if delayed on their way to the Valley, by having to stop to repair their carts.

As soon as was possible they started companies on the way. My father strongly objected to any of them starting after the last of June; but he was overruled, and the last company left Iowa City the middle of August, for a journey across arid plains and over snow-clad mountains, which it took twelve weeks of the quickest travelling at that time to accomplish; and in the manner in which these emigrants were going it would take much longer. He also opposed their being started with such a scanty allowance of provisions. He insisted they should have at least double the amount; but in this attempt, also, he was unsuccessful, and one of the survivors of the expedition afterwards said that the rations which were given out to each person for a day could easily be eaten at breakfast. They consisted of ten ounces of flour for each adult, and half that amount for each child under eight years of age. At rare intervals, a little rice, coffee, sugar, and bacon were doled out to the hungry travellers, but this was not often done. Many of the people begged of the farmers in Iowa, so famished were they, and so inadequate was their food which was supplied them by the agents. They were limited, too, in the matter of baggage, and again my father tried to use his influence, but all to no purpose; so much might go, but not a pound more.

Almost discouraged, and altogether disgusted with the meanness and heartless carelessness which were exhibited throughout the whole affair, as far, at least, as he had experience with it, he yet made one more attempt to aid the unfortunate travellers, whose trials, great as they had been, had really not fairly begun. His last proposition was, that more teams should be provided, so that the feeble, who were not likely to endure the fatigues of the long march, should have an opportunity of riding; but he was met again with the inevitable reply, "Can't do it, Brother Webb. We tell you we can't afford it; they must go cheap." It was dear enough in the end, if human lives count for anything.

My father never speaks of those days of preparation in Iowa City that he does not grow indignant. It might have been averted had not Brigham Young been so parsimonious, and his followers so eager to curry favor with him, by carrying out his instructions more implicitly than there was any need of doing. They were only quarrelled and found fault with, and reprimanded publicly in the Tabernacle for their faithfulness to him, when it became necessary to shield himself from odium in the matter. Nothing more would have happened if they had obeyed the instincts of humanity, and deferred a little to their consciences, and they

certainly would have been better off, as they would at least
have retained their own self-respect, and the regard of their
unfortunate charges, which, it is needless to say, they lost
most completely.

When some of the last companies reached Council Bluffs,
— better known to most Mormons as "Winter-Quarters," —
there was considerable controversy whether it was best to
try and go any farther before spring. Most of the emigrants knew nothing of the climate and the perils of the
undertaking, and were eager to press on to Zion. Four
men only in the company had crossed the plains; those
were captains of the trains — Willie, Atwood, Savage, and
Woodward; but there were several elders at this place
superintending emigration. Of these, Levi Savage was the
only one to remonstrate against attempting to reach Salt
Lake Valley so late in the season. He declared that it
would be utterly impossible to cross the mountains without
great suffering, and even death.

His remonstrances availed about as much my father's had
done in regard to their starting. He was defeated and reprimanded very sharply for his want of faith. He replied
that there were cases where "common sense" was the best
guide, and he considered this to be one. "However," said
he, "seeing you are to go forward, I will go with you, will
help you all I can, will work with you, suffer with you,
and, if necessary, die with you."

Very soon after the departure of the last company of the
emigrants from Iowa City, my father, with the other elders,
started for the Valley in mule-teams, intending to return,
if they found it necessary, to bring succor to the poor wandering people. In the company with my father were
Apostle Franklin D. Richards, and Elders W. H. Kimball,
G. D. Grant, Joseph A. Young, Brigham's oldest son, and
several others, all of whom were returning to Utah from
foreign missions, and all of whom had been engaged in
the expedition.

14

They overtook the emigrants at their camp on the North Fork of the Platte River, and camped with them over night. Richards was told of the opposition which Savage had made, and he openly rebuked him in the morning. He then informed the Saints that "though it might storm on the right hand and on the left, yet the storms should not reach them. The Lord would keep the way open before them, and they should reach Zion in safety." It may be that he believed all this nonsense himself. It is to be hoped, for charity's sake, that he did. If that were the case, however, it is a pity that he had not been endowed with a little of Levi Savage's common sense. It would have been much better for the Saints than all his vaunted "spirit of prophecy."

It is a significant fact, that in the very face of his prophecy, delivered to the victims of his zeal in the cause of Brigham Young, he was anxious to hasten his arrival in Salt Lake in order to send assistance back to the patient Hand-Cart emigrants, who, he must have seen, would soon be in sore straits for food and clothing. The rations were scanty, and would soon have to be lessened; the nights were chilly, and fast growing cold; and already the seventeen pounds of bedding and clothing allowed to each one were scarcely sufficient protection; and as the season advanced, and they approached the mountains, it would be totally inadequate. It was fortunate that they did not know the climate of the country, and the terrible hardships to which they were to be exposed, else their hearts would have failed them, and they would have had no courage to have recommenced the journey. My father realized it, and so did most of the party with him; yet they had no idea how horrible it was to be, else they would have insisted upon their remaining in camp until spring. Even the usually indifferent heart of Joseph A. was touched, and he hurried on to impress upon his father the urgent need for immediate assistance for those poor, forlorn creatures whom

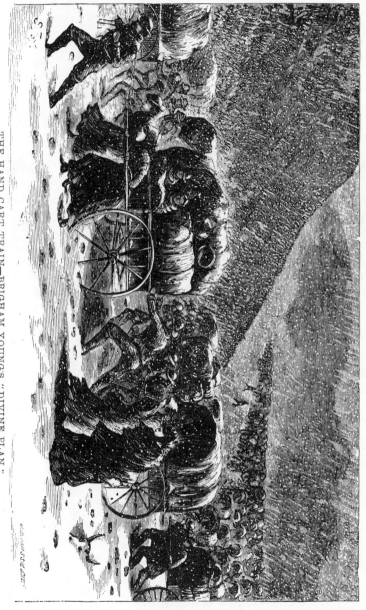

THE HAND CART TRAIN—BRIGHAM YOUNG'S "DIVINE PLAN."

he left preparing to cross the mountains, where they would of a surety meet the late autumn and early winter storms, and where so many of them must of a certainty perish of exposure and hunger. He had no faith in the apostolic prophecy, which seemed a mockery to all those who knew the hardships of the journey which lay before these faithful souls before they could reach the Zion of their hopes.

My father had been four years absent from us, yet such was his concern for the poor people whom he so recently left, and who had been his care for so long, that he could only stay to give us the most hurried greetings. His gladness at his return, and our responsive joy, were marred by the thought of the sufferings and privations of those earnest, simple-hearted Saints, who had literally left all to follow the beck of one whom they supposed to be the Prophet of the Lord. After all these years of absence, he only staid two days with us, — as short a time as it could possibly take to get the relief-train ready with the supplies.

I think Brigham Young's heart and conscience must have been touched, for he really seemed for a while to forget himself in the earnestness with which he pushed forward the preparations for relief. He fairly arose to the occasion, and held back nothing which could contribute to the comfort and welfare of his poor, forlorn followers. Yet he was only acting as both justice and decency commanded that he should act. He was the cause of all this terrible suffering, and he felt that he should be made answerable. Such a transaction as this could by no means remain unknown. It would be spread over America and Europe, and used as a strong weapon against Mormonism and its leader, already unpopular enough. He realized the mistake he had made when too late to rectify it, and, with his usual moral cowardice, he set about hunting for somebody on whose shoulders to shift the blame from his own. Richards and Spencer were the unfortunate victims, and he turned his wrath against them, in private conversation and in public assem-

blies, until they were nearly crushed by the weight of opprobrium which he heaped upon them. He was nearly
beside himself with fear of the consequences which would
follow, when this crowning act of selfish cupidity and egotistical vanity and presumption should be known. Love of
approbation is a striking characteristic of this Latter-Day
Prophet, and he puffs and swells with self-importance at
every word he receives, even of the baldest, most insincere
flattery, and he cringes and crouches in as servile a manner as a whipped cur, when any adverse criticism is passed
upon either his *personnel* or his actions. A moral as well
as a physical coward, he dares not face a just opinion of
himself and his deeds, and he sneaks, and skulks, and
hides behind any one he can find who is broad enough to
shield him.

My father's disgust at a religion which submitted to such
chicanery, and his distrust of Brigham Young, were so
great, that he was very near apostatizing; but my mother
again held him to the church. She argued and explained;
she wept and she entreated, until he said no more about it.
But though, for her sake, he took no steps towards leaving
the church and renouncing the faith, he felt daily his disgust and distrust increasing, and he never again believed
so strongly in the Mormon religion, and ever after regarded
Brigham with much less awe and respect than formerly.

CHAPTER XII.

BRIGHAM'S HAND-CART SCHEME, CONTINUED. — FAILURE OF THE "DIVINE PLAN."

Arrival of the First Train. — Fearful Sufferings of the Emigrants. — Women and Girls toiling at the Carts. — The Prophet's "Experiment." — Burying the Dead. — Greater Mortality among the Men. — Arrival of Assistance. — Hand-Cart Songs. — Scenes in the Camp of the Emigrants. — How every Prophecy of the Elders was Falsified. — How the Tennant Family were Shamelessly Robbed. — One of the Vilest Swindles of the Prophet. — Mr. Tennant's Unhappy Death. — His Wife Views the "Splendid Property" Bought from Brigham. — Brigham Cheats her out of her Last Dollar. — She is Reduced to Abject Poverty. — The Apostle Taylor Hastens to Zion. — Richards and Spencer are made Scapegoats. — Brigham evades all Responsibility. — Utter Failure of the "Divine Plan."

"Some must Push, and Some must Pull."

HE first Hand-Cart Companies, which had left Iowa City early in the season, arrived in the Salt Lake Valley the last of September. They were very much fatigued, and were greatly rejoiced when their journey was ended.

The entire company had waded every river on the route to Salt Lake, and, as a consequence, the health of almost every man and woman was completely broken. The married women suffered the least, as they only had to assist their husbands in pulling the hand-carts. The young girls had to pull theirs unassisted, and they were literally worn out with the exertion. The children were placed on the carts when they became tired, and so added weight to already overburdened wagons. It was when the second of these companies came in that Brigham Young was heard to say, as he rubbed his hands and smiled with overflowing complacency, "This experiment is a success."

Alas for Brother Brigham, this remark was overheard by some of the emigrants, and it is needless to say that their faith in "inspiration," and "revelation," was very much weakened; and the subsequent adventures of their friends and companions, whose arrival had been delayed, by no means tended to reassure them, or restore their waning belief. It was enough to be the victims of a heartless and mercenary experiment; but to be deluded into the belief that it was by the direct revelation of the will of the Lord made it harder to bear, and there was much bitterness of spirit expressed when the people who had endured so much, and gloried in the endurance, because in so doing they were obeying the commands of God, learned that their sufferings were borne merely to help fill the purses of a false prophet and his corrupt followers.

When the relief train reached Captain Willie's company, they were camped on the Sweetwater, near the Rocky Ridges. They had eaten their last provisions, and death was staring them pitilessly in the face. The camp was filled with dead and dying. There was no help for the latter, and the poor souls had lost all desire to live. They were waiting, with almost apathetic indifference, for release, while those dearest to them were doubly agonized because they must see the loved ones perish, and they were helpless even to bring comforts to them, or make life easier while it lasted. Those who were strong enough, dug one large grave in which all the dead were laid together. It was the best they could do; but their hands were no less tender and loving, their hearts no less sore, than if the last rites had been as imposing as those of royalty itself. The only thing they could do to prepare their dear ones for the grave was to close the eyes, the loving eyes that, to the very last, had turned longingly Zion-ward; to fold the pulseless hands over the silent hearts that, through all the hardships and toil, had kept their trust firm and their faith bright; to straighten out the tired feet that, bleeding and

RELIEF IN SIGHT.

sore, had yet toiled joyfully along the rugged path that led to the fair Canaan of their dreams; to smooth the tangled hair away from haggard faces, where the lines of care lay heavily, and yet through which the light of peace divine shone serene and pure; to arrange as decently as possible the tattered garments, which were their only clothing for the tomb, and to lay them, coffinless, in their cold bed in the Rocky Mountains, in their last, long sleep; then to

go away and leave them there, with the relentless winter
storms beating upon them, and no stone to mark their resting-place. The road from Winter-Quarters to Salt Lake
was a *via dolorosa* indeed.

Thirteen had died in Willie's camp the day that succor
reached them; two more died the next day; and all were
buried in one grave. The men succumbed to death before
the women. The cause, no doubt, was the greater weariness on account of their more arduous exertions, and their
wonderful self-denial for the sake of their wives and children. They would work just so long as they could, then
fall dead in front of their carts, their hands still holding
them tight in the tenacious grasp of death. There was no
time for mourning or delay. Hurried graves were dug,
and the bodies placed therein, hastily covered, — then the
survivors must press on again. Wives left their husbands,
husbands their wives, parents their children, and children
their parents, under the frozen earth of the desert and
mountain ridges.

When the poor Saints knew that assistance had really
reached them, that starvation was beaten away and death
held at bay, their joy knew no bounds. They cried like
children, men as well as women, and burst forth into prayer
and songs of praise. They attacked the food like famished
animals, and ate it with a wolfish greed. The scene is one
that can never be adequately described. It was full of a
terrible pathos. It told of a suffering that never can be
comprehended except by those who endured it. The
clothing and bedding were then divided between them, and
they were made comfortable as they could be under the
circumstances. That night, for the first time for many
weeks, the sounds of rejoicing were heard through the
camp. They were not forgotten of the Lord, nor deserted
by his people; and again they found heart to sing their
hand-cart hymns which had been written for them by some
enthusiastic members of the train.

Contrast one of their songs, if you please, with the situation when relief from Salt Lake reached them : —

> " We're going to Zion with our carts,
> And the Spirit of God within our hearts;
> The old, decrepit, feeble dame
> Will lend a hand to pull the same ;
>   For some must push and some must pull,
> As we go marching up the hill,
> Until we reach the Valley, O !

> " Our maidens, they will dance and sing,
> Our young men happier be than kings,
> Our strength increasing every day,
> As we go travelling up the way.
>   Yes, some must push and some must pull,
> As we go marching up the hill,
> Until we reach the Valley, O ! "

Rough in phraseology, and rude in structure, it yet shows the spirit which animated the converts when they first started on their pilgrimage to the promised land. Another favorite song had a stirring chorus, as follows : —

> " Hurrah for the camp of Israel !
> Hurrah for the Hand-Cart scheme !
> Hurrah ! hurrah ! 'tis better far
> Than the wagon and ox-team."

In this song the " divine plan " was extolled with all the enthusiastic fervor with which it was first expounded to them by the elders in England. It is needless to say that these songs were written in the first glow of the furor, before any of the hardships even of the sea-voyage had been encountered. They were not sung after the first encounter with a mountain storm; that took the heart out of them. Even in the rejoicing at their deliverance, they sang only the hymns, making no attempt even to revive the spirit of the hand-cart songs.

After seeing Captain Willie's company made comfortable, the relief train started east again in search of Captain Martin's company. This they found in camp at Grease Wood Creek, twenty miles from Willie's camp. The suffering in this company was quite equal to that of the company just relieved, and precisely the same scenes were enacted. They were wild with joy, and men and women fell on the necks of their deliverers with sobs and kisses, calling them their saviours, and invoking blessings of all kinds on their heads.

The camp was filled with dead and dying, and many had been left behind that day, having fallen exhausted in the way. The storm had been blinding, and their companions could not stop for them; they could only hasten on while daylight lasted, making their slow, painful progress towards the haven of their rest. My father and his comrades spent the night in searching for those that were left behind, and bringing them into camp, where they were tenderly cared for. Many of them died very soon after being brought in; others lived, but they were maimed for life, feet and hands, in many cases, having been literally frozen off. This was the people, "the chosen people of God, for whose benefit the Indians, the seasons, nay, the very elements themselves, should be controlled." Their belief in "prophecy" must have been severely tried by this shock.

Everything had happened to them to make their journey hard. Their carts had broken down repeatedly, as my father had prophesied they would, and a great deal of delay had been caused by the frequent stopping for repairs; their cattle had stampeded, so that their supply of milk and fresh beef was cut off, and only oxen enough left to allow one yoke to a team; some of the men who dropped behind the others, wearied with the journey, were eaten by wolves; very many had died, and others were hopelessly crippled; the winter had set in earlier, and with severer storms than have ever been known in all the Utah experience. It seemed as if the Lord were punishing priest and people, the one for the audacious assumption of power, the other for blind belief in, and dependence on, earthly promises, even when purporting to come from Him. Blasphemous presumption and foolish ignorance were alike hateful in His sight.

Richards had promised the people that they should find supplies at Laramie, but he was unable to reach there with them, and on their arrival the Saints found only a message telling them that the supplies would be at South Pass. It was with heavy hearts that they went on their toilsome way, more discouraged than ever they had been before. The swift-falling winter storms made matters worse, and it is only a wonder that so many survived as did, — that every one did not perish before aid could reach them.

The day after reaching Martin's camp, the party from Salt Lake pushed on about thirty miles farther east, walking most of the way, through a blinding snow, to meet Captain Hunt's wagon train. They found the people connected with this but very little better off than the Hand-Cart companies ; they were suffering severely from the intense cold, and many had their limbs frozen. Captain Hunt might have hastened and reached Salt Lake City earlier, but he had been expressly forbidden to pass the hand-carts, which shows conclusively enough that those very persons who sent the emigrants off at that unfavorable season feared for the results. This was the last company that was to be relieved, and so my father and his companions remained with the train until it overtook the hand-carts at Devil's Gate.

At this point the train was unloaded, and all the goods which were going to Salt Lake City, that could actually be spared, were left there for the winter, and the wagons were filled with the sick and feeble emigrants, who could never have reached the Valley but for this aid. The progress was necessarily slow, but the people were so much more comfortable that the time did not drag so heavily. There were very few deaths after the mountains were well crossed, and a milder climate reached, and those who were ill grew better, although the majority of them have never been well since.

At Fort Bridger, one hundred and thirty miles from Salt Lake City, the emigrants were met by an order from Brigham Young to winter there and at Fort Supply. A general feeling of dismay spread over the camp, in spite of the joy with which the Saints received the added supplies of food and clothing. To be so near their destination, and yet to be kept from it, seemed doubly hard, after all the sorrow and hardships they had met and endured on their way. It did indeed seem as though the way to the land of promise was closed, instead of being opened to them. Were they, like Moses of old, to die in sight of their Canaan? Had they been brought all this way only to perish just outside the walls of their Zion?

The places designated by Brigham were totally unfit to winter in. Should the poor Saints, in their feeble and emaciated condition, attempt it, it was more than likely that they would perish before spring. Seeing the utter impracticability of the plan, and touched by the distress of the poor people, who were again to be made the victims of a prophetic blunder, two or three of the relieving party, among them my father, came at once to the city, travelling day and night, to have arrangements made to bring them to the Valley.

They were successful in their mission, and an express was at once despatched to bring the waiting Saints home. When at length they arrived, they were met with gladness, and given the warmest welcome. The people in Salt Lake City opened their houses to them, and took them gladly in, giving them the best and the kindest care. Those of the Hand-Cart companies, who had come in first, crowded round them, and met them with tears of rejoicing, in which sorrow mingled. It was then that they began to realize their loss. As one after another of their old companions came up, and missing some familiar face, inquired for the friend so dearly beloved, always the same sad answer came — " Died on the Plains." Sixty-seven were left on the way from the Missouri River to the Valley, which was about one sixth of the number which started.

I remember distinctly when these companies came in; their wretched condition impressed me at the time, and I have seen many of them since, poor crippled creatures, stumping about the city, trying to do enough work

ARRIVAL OF "HAND-CART COMPANIES" AT SALT LAKE CITY.

to keep soul and body together; more than that, they were not able to do. I have heard, too, from some of them, the most harrowing stories of their journey, that terrible, fatal journey, which was one of the very worst blunders that the Prince of Blunderers, Brigham Young, ever made.

The recollection is made more vivid because my youngest brother, Edward, who went out with a team to assist the emigrants, got lost in the snow, and for a week we supposed him to be dead. After wandering for some days in the mountains, with both feet badly frozen, he was found by a mountaineer named Battiste, who kept him,

and cared for him most kindly, until the arrival of my
father, who had heard, while with the train, that he was
missing, and had gone at once in search of him. It was a
narrow escape, and the terrible expedition came near proving a tragedy to us as well as to so many others.

Among the emigrants was a very wealthy gentleman of
the name of Tennant. He and his wife were among the
early converts, and were very earnest Mormons. They had
for a long time been resolved to come to Zion, and when
the Hand-Cart scheme was introduced they decided to join
that company. Humble followers of Christ, they thought
they could in no better way show their love for Him and
their devotion to their religion, than by such an act of self-
sacrifice as this. Possessed of ample means to have crossed
the ocean and travelled in the most comfortable and even
luxurious manner, they nevertheless chose to go in this
way, with the poorest of the Saints, and share with them all
the hardships and dangers which should attend this toilsome, perilous journey.

Mr. Tennant gave liberally to the emigration fund, in
order that as many poor Saints as possible might make the
long-anticipated pilgrimage to Zion, and both himself and
his wife provided liberally for the comfort of their poor fellow-travellers. A short time before the emigrant company
left England, the Apostle Richards, in one of his eloquent
dissertations on the "plan" and its divine origin, said that in
order to assist the poor to emigrate, President Young had
given to the Emigration Fund Society an estate in Salt Lake
City, to be sold for its benefit. He dilated largely upon the
disinterested generosity of the Prophet, and his desire that
as many as possible of his faithful followers should be gathered to Zion during that season. Fired by this act of
extreme kindness on the part of his revered leader in the
church, Mr. Tennant at once bought the property, and paid,
it is said, thirty thousand dollars down for it. There is
little need, perhaps, of saying that that was immensely more

than its real value ; but that fact its purchaser was not aware of, as it was glorified by all the apostolic eloquence bestowed upon it, quite beyond recognition.

On the voyage, and during the journey across the States, and the tiresome waiting time at Iowa City, no one was more beloved than Mr. Tennant and his gentle, estimable wife. Sharing alike with the poorer Saints, no word of complaint ever passed their lips. They never for a moment seemed to regret their decision to emigrate at this particular time, but accepted every fresh hardship as a trial to their faith, sent by God Himself to test them, and prove their worthiness to enter His glorious kingdom on earth. They moved among their companions with kindly faces and words of cheer and comfort. They encouraged endurance by their example, and made the forced discomforts of some of the party seem easier to bear by their voluntary assumption of them. As far as they could they alleviated the distress which prevailed, and were always ready to perform any deeds of kindness.

The journey with the hand-carts was doubly hard for them, unused as they were to exertion ; and day after day the wife saw the husband slowly succumbing to fatigue and disease, and she powerless to assist him. But, though his strength waned and his health failed him, yet his courage and his faith remained steadfast and fixed. Whatever came he believed would surely be right, and though he struggled manfully to keep up until he should reach Zion, yet he was overcome, and died at O'Fallon's Bluffs, literally of exhaustion. His last thought was for his sorrowing wife, and his last word was of comfort and consolation to her. He had one thought to make the parting easier — he had provided a home for her in Zion ; Brother Brigham held it in trust for her, and she would find the comforts to which she was used, and rest and peace in the Valley with the chosen people.

The bereaved wife clung wildly to her husband's remains,

with the most heart-broken lamentations. To have him die was a misery in itself; but to see the slow, cruel torture which he underwent, and to watch him slowly dying such a horrible death, was almost unbearable. For a time it seemed almost as though she must be left there with him; that her soul would follow his. Happier would it have been for her had that fate been hers. The cold earth and pitiless winter storms would not be so cold and so pitiless as the world was to her, after this loving protecting arm was taken from her. A woman, unused to toil and hardship, nurtured in luxury, reared in tenderness and love, she was left alone to battle single-handed with the world. And such a world! whose ruling passion was avarice, and whose delight was another's torture; the world of Mormon Sainthood — ruled over by a grasping, lecherous, heartless tyrant, who laughed at a woman's sorrows and flouted at her wrongs. I think if she had known all that was to follow, she would have lain down on the plain by the side of her dead husband, and endured the torture of a horrible, slow death, rather than have gone on to the years of suffering which lay before her.

It is fortunate, indeed, that the future is so closely veiled to us; else we should all lose heart and courage in this unequal struggle called life, and lay down our weapons, convinced that it is of no use to struggle longer. Providence deals wisely with us, after all, and we are forced to admit it at every step of our lives.

The hurried funeral rites were over, and the man who had been so great a benefactor to the people among whom he had cast his lot, was left sleeping his last sleep in a strange land, and the sorrowing party resumed their weary way, saddened by this affliction. On the arrival at Salt Lake Mrs. Tennant at once proceeded to look after her property. The "magnificent estate" for which her husband had paid so fabulous a price, was a small wooden house, inconvenient and out of repair, and worth not a tenth part of what had been paid for it.

She was shocked and troubled at what seemed such a piece of swindling on the part of the President and the church authorities, although at first she was inclined to exonerate Brigham Young and blame Apostle Richards for misrepresentation; but an audience with Brigham soon convinced her that he was at the bottom of the whole affair, and she felt bitterly enough towards the man who, under the guise of religious benevolence, would be guilty of such a piece of trickery. Even this poor shelter was not left her very long. The place, and, indeed, most of the valuable things which her husband had sent to make their home in Zion more comfortable, were taken for tithing and on other pretences, and in a very few months this woman was compelled to go out to daily labor to earn her bread, her rightful property going to fill the already overflowing coffers of the "Prophet of the Lord." Indeed, the entire Hand-Cart expedition was a good speculation for the President, and helped replenish the prophetic pocket.

There is no doubt that Young did repent of this foolish step of his, but it was not at all on account of the suffering and misery which he entailed upon so many innocent persons, but because he knew that an act of that kind, becoming public, would make him and his religion more unpopular than ever, and they were already in sufficiently bad odor with the outside world. He could ill afford to make such a blunder. It would also work against his influence with the Saints themselves, and he was always jealous of his authority over his people.

The Apostle John Taylor arrived home before either Apostle Richards or Elder Spenser, and he, as a matter of course, told his own story, throwing all the blame upon his two co-workers, so that when they arrived they found the full torrent of the Presidential wrath turned against them. They were sadly hurt, for, in their zeal to carry out instructions

15

and gain the approbation of their leader, they had, they affirmed, all through the affair, acted against the dictates of humanity and their own consciences.

He was loud in his denunciations of them; he cursed them "in the name of Israel's God;" he ridiculed them in public until they were compelled to hide their heads in very shame. Their sole fault was, they had been too faithful to him. Spenser never recovered from the disgrace; he always remained a broken-down, helpless man, seeking no favor, expecting none, not even decent treatment, from his master, until, after lingering for ten years under the prophetic ban, he died heart-broken. Richards has, in a degree, overcome the President's feeling towards him, and is gaining favor all the time, but he will never stand as high as he did before this most unfortunate exhibition. The people will never forget his share in it, and those who came to Zion, influenced by his eloquent appeals and encouraged by his prophecies, associate him naturally enough with that unhappy experience. Then, although Brigham Young has partially restored him to favor by certain acts and kindnesses granted to him, yet he has never taken back any of the anathemas which he showered upon him, and they are by no means forgotten by those who heard them, and have a certain influence even now in forming public opinion.

Notwithstanding the terrible consequences of this "divine plan," its originator did not wish to acknowledge that he had in any way been mistaken. The plan, he argued, was all right; it only went wrong through mismanagement, and he would prove its feasibility to the satisfaction of every Saint in the Territory. The plan was "divine," and he would "sanctify it to the glory of the Lord."

So in the April following he sent a company of elders on a mission, compelling them to go with hand-carts. These were properly made, of good material, strongly finished, with iron tires, and everything to make them durable. They had plenty of provisions; so they would not be reduced to the necessity of eating their own shoes nor biting their own flesh in the mad frenzy of starvation, as many a poor fellow did in the expedition whose " divinity " they were sent out to prove. The season was favorable, and there was no danger of their being overtaken by terrible mountain storms, underneath which they would be buried. They were all robust young men, too; better fitted to endure a journey like the one ordained for them by their Prophet, than the feeble old men and women, the young wives, mothers, and maidens, and the tiny, toddling children, who formed a great portion of the other company. Then they started fresh, not wearied already by a rough sea-voyage, a journey thousands of miles across the Continent, to the final starting-point, nor reduced by hunger and exposure. They had the advantage in everything, and yet, although their expedition was by no means fatal, it was very far from being a " success," such as Brigham expected it to be.

On his way to Chicago my father overtook them at Devil's Gate. He found them completely jaded and worn out. In truth, they were almost dead from weariness. They travelled slowly, making long stops to rest, and finally they reached the Missouri River in a perfect state of exhaustion. They left their carts there with the utmost willingness, showing wonderful alacrity at abandoning a " divine " scheme. To this day they all aver they cannot bear to hear the word " Hand-cart " mentioned. It was the last time the " experiment " was tried, and after this but little was said regarding the divine origin of the plan; and it is a significant fact that no one has preserved more utter silence on the subject than the " Revelator," Brigham Young.

CHAPTER XIII.

THE MOUNTAIN MEADOWS' MASSACRE. — "VENGEANCE IS MINE: I WILL REPAY."

The Results of the Reformation. — The Story of a Fiendish Deed. — The People's Mouths Closed. — How the Dreadful Crime was Hushed Up. — Judge Cradlebaugh's Efforts to Unravel the Mystery. — Who were the Guilty Ones ? — The Emigrants on the Way to Utah. — The People Forbidden to sell them Food. — They Arrive at Salt Lake City. — Ordered to Break Camp. — In need of Supplies. — Who was Accountable ? — Why the Mormons hated the Emigrants. — The Story of Parley P. Pratt. — How he Seduced McLean's Wife. — Their Journey to Cedar City. — Hungry and Weary, but still Pressing On. — They Reach the Mountain Meadows. — Attacked by "the Indians." — The Emigrants Besieged. — Dying of Thirst. — Two little Girls shot by the Mormons. — An Appeal for Help. — The Last Hope of the Besieged. — Waiting for Death.

"VENGEANCE IS MINE."

F all the numberless atrocities that succeeded the Utah Reformation, and were the direct outgrowth of the teaching of the revolting doctrine of the "Blood-Atonement," nothing approaches in fiendish barbarity the Massacre at the Mountain Meadows, where, on the 17th of September, 1857, a company of emigrants from Arkansas and Missouri, on their way to California, were assassinated in the most cruel and treacherous manner, by a band of disguised Mormons and Indians, under the leadership of officers of the Mormon militia.

Nearly eighteen years have passed, and until within a

comparatively short time, little has been definitely known
concerning the details of the massacre, either by the Gentile world, or by the mass of the Mormon people, who, to
give them the justice which they deserve, would have
shrunk with horror from the very idea that the commission
of the terrible deed could be laid to the charge of their beloved church.

I was but a child at the time, but I recollect, perfectly,
hearing that an emigrant-train had been attacked by the
Indians, and all members of the band, with the exception
of a few of the smaller children, killed; and I remember,
also, *seeing* these children, who were said to have been
taken from their Indian captors by Mormon officers, and
were to be cared for by the Mormon people. I suppose
the remembrance is the more vivid because, before their
arrival in Utah, the people were forbidden by Brigham
Young and his elders to sell them anything during their
journey through the Territory, and this was so unusual a
command that it was a matter of wondering conjecture to
most of the Mormons, although no one dreamed of questioning the justice of the Prophet's mandate.

Young as I was, I felt the mystery that shrouded the whole
horrible transaction, and I knew instinctively, as did many
others, that something was being hidden from the mass of
the people, by their leaders, which it was not deemed prudent to reveal; but the terrible truth was not then even
suspected by the faithful Saints. I can understand now,
as I could not then, why all wonder concerning this wholesale murder was speedily hushed up; why any definite
mention of it was avoided by the leaders in the church;
why, when it was spoken of at all, it was with cautious
manner, apprehensive glances, and in whispered tones
under the breath. Priests and people alike hesitated to
approach the dreaded subject, and there was an almost superhuman endeavor on the part of the church authorities
to erase all remembrance of it from the minds of their fol-

lowers. But occurrences of this kind are not easily for-gotten, and the memory of that bloody and unprovoked butchery is still fresh in other minds besides my own, re-tained there so distinctly that neither time nor eternity can obliterate it. The very mystery which veiled it made it more awful to me, an imaginative, excitable child; and though I followed the example of my elders, and never spoke of the subject, even to my mother, it haunted me perpetually, and I grew absolutely terrified at the con-stantly recurring fancies which I drew of it.

Although the people were so quiet, since there was a tacit understanding that they must be so, yet their eyes nor ears were never closed, and thought was by no means idle. Indeed, as the years have rolled on, what was at first a vague suspicion, which it seemed a sin to entertain, has grown to a horrible certainty, until to-day it stands forth, stripped of all its first mystery, fearfully vivid in its mon-strosity, the foulest of all the foul blots upon the unclean page of Mormon history. It was a deed unparalleled in its atrocity; unapproachable in the treachery employed by its perpetrators; more horrible in its sickening details than the butcheries by the most barbarous savages; the work of fiends rather than of men; and yet so successful has been the "quiet" policy of the Mormon leaders, that I find the extent of its horrors but dimly understood east of the Rocky Mountains.

Attempts were made by Judge Cradlebaugh to discover the perpetrators, and, above all, the instigators of this deed, and bring them speedily to justice; but with a Mormon jury, blinded by their bigotry, who were taught from the pulpit that allegiance to the church and Brigham Young was paramount to all their duties and obligations to the government of the United States, whose citizens they claimed to be, that perjury to that government would be forgiven by the priesthood, indeed was counselled by it, and that no Mormon was to be delivered over to Gentile justice, no matter what his crime might have been, nor how distinctly it was proved, it followed naturally enough that the efforts, earnest and untiring as they were, were utterly fruitless.

Judge Cradlebaugh's last attempt to ferret out the affair was made in 1859; and since that time no action has been taken by the government until last autumn, when the long-smothered suspicion broke forth into audible accusations, and in this new burst of popular demand for justice, the supposed leaders were arrested. I inadvertently said "supposed" leaders; but it has been shown beyond the possibility of a doubt that John D. Lee, a major in the Mormon militia, and one of the most active and zealous of Brigham Young's devoted adherents, led the attack in person; that many of the victims fell by his hand; and that he, assisted by Bishop Haight and the notorious Dame, acted under instructions from "*a higher authority*." The plans of massacre were fully matured, at a council held at Parowan, by Brigadier-General George A. Smith, first counsellor to Brigham, and a fit servant for such a master, Colonel William C. Dame, Bishop of Fillmore, Lieutenant-Colonel Haight, President of the Cedar City "Stake of Zion," Bishop Higbee, and John D. Lee.

Of all these men, Lee, who is now under arrest, has been the most closely identified with the massacre, in the public mind, until he has grown to be an object of popular aversion, shunned and dreaded. It may seem childish, but so strong a hold had this affair taken on my imagination, that I have never been able to shake off the feeling of terror with which it filled me; and when, last autumn, I was told of his arrest, and knew that he was safe inside prison walls, I positively experienced a feeling of relief and personal safety, as great as though some enemy of my own had been rendered powerless to harm me. I had never even seen the man; but knowing the record of his crimes, and always hearing of him in connection with some deed of bloody brutality, my horror and fear of him never diminished, and he remained, what he had always been, the ogre of my childish fancies.

It is a horrible story, sickening in its every detail; but it cannot be told too often, until it shall be known all over the country by every person who is ignorant of it now.

It was early in September, 1857, when it was first announced in Salt Lake City that a large emigrant party from Missouri and Arkansas had entered the Valley on their way to California. As soon as the announcement was made, a command was issued by the President of the church, that nothing was to be sold to any member of this party, on the pain of death. The command was most arbitrary, and was totally without precedent, showing beyond a doubt the animus of Brigham Young towards this party, and rendering it much easier to believe that the terrible tragedy which followed was approved, if not instigated, by him.

Salt Lake had been for a long time the *depôt* for obtaining fresh supplies prior to crossing the deserts which separated Utah and California. Every emigrant train which had crossed the plains for some years, had made this a resting-place, and taken a fresh start from here for the remainder of the tedious journey. Much money was left in this way in the Mormon country, and, as usual, Brigham Young got his, the "lion's share," of all the profits.

This train, like all that had gone before it, had laid their plans to supply themselves for their journey at Salt Lake City, and had only brought a sufficient quantity of provisions to last them until they reached that point. Greatly to their surprise, they found themselves unable to purchase anything, and, in addition, were peremptorily ordered to break their camp at Salt Lake and move on. All through the country of the Saints they were met with sturdy refusals to sell them anything. Men who would gladly have placed a quantity of provisions at their disposal dared not do it, fearing to disobey their Prophet's mandate. In vain the emigrants offered them money, wagons, personal property of all kinds. Brigham's law was not to be broken, and the person who should venture to disregard it pronounced his own death sentence. Now and then, however, one more humane or more daring than the rest, came to the camp at night with a small amount of provisions — all they could bring without danger of detection; but what was this little to one hundred and fifty hungry men and women, to say nothing of the little children who were to be fed? It might have met a present want, but it did nothing towards providing for future needs. Starvation was staring them in the face while they were journeying in the midst of plenty,—for it is a notorious fact that the harvests never were more plentiful in Utah than they were that year.

Whatever may have been Brigham Young's connection with the massacre itself, — whether it was done at his instigation or merely with his connivance, — he was, to all intents and purposes, the murderer of these people, and should be held responsible for their lives. What right had he, the governor of the Territory of Utah, appointed to office by the United States Government, amenable to its laws as a citizen, much more so as an office-holder, bound by an oath of loyalty to protect every person within the limits of his territory, to refuse food to peaceful, law-abiding citizens of the same government, knowing, as he did, that here was their only opportunity to obtain it, and that certain death was their fate if compelled to cross the desert with the scanty rations which remained to them?

The treatment of these people from the moment of entering Brigham Young's dominions until the final tragedy, was so barbarous, and attended with so many horrors, that the Mormon people, contrary to their usual custom, feel obliged to offer some excuse in extenuation. But all the reasons which they give, when combined, are entirely insufficient to justify the deed. Yet, such as they are, they shall be given.

The "Reformation" was over, and the doctrine of the "Blood-Atonement" was still in full force. Young and his confederates were infuriated because United States troops were ordered to Utah. They considered this act of the government an open insult, and they revenged it on the first Gentiles whom they could reach. The train was one of the largest and richest that had ever crossed the plains. The value of their wagons, horses, and stock alone was said to be $300,000, and the women of the party had rich, full wardrobes and elegant, costly jewelry. Brigham, as you have seen, ignores the tenth commandment, and the sixth is a dead-letter to him; to covet his neighbors' goods is to possess them in some way or other, either honestly or otherwise,—generally otherwise.

A part of the emigrants were from Missouri, and the Mormon people will never regard the Missourians in any other light than that of the bitterest enemies. They had never, in all the years, forgotten the persecution which they received at their hands, and Joseph Smith's death they considered unavenged. It was reported that in the train was a man who had openly boasted of having been present at the assassination of Smith, and that he as openly threatened to take the life of the present prophet. This story is generally believed to be utterly without foundation, circulated by the Mormon leaders to stir up the wrath of the people against the emigrants, and to exonerate themselves, if their share in the slaughter of these people should ever become known. The Arkansas members of the train, also, were objects of Mormon vengeance. Parley P. Pratt, one of the twelve apostles, and also one of the brightest intellectual lights in the Church of the Latter-Day Saints, was sent on a mission to California, where he proselyted with such vigor that many converts were made; among them a Mrs. Eleanor McLean, wife of one Hector McLean, and the mother of three children, who was induced to embrace Mormonism and polygamy as embodied in the person of the seductive apostle. The command to "leave all and follow me" was readily obeyed, especially as she was personally to add to the missionary's present pleasure and future glory, by becoming one of his numerous plural wives.

As there was no authority to marry them in a "legal" manner in this Gentile state, they were obliged to .defer that ceremony until their arrival in "Zion." But in cases like this, which were often occurring to the missionary Saints, it was considered quite

PARLEY P. PRATT.

proper for the pair, who were in haste to wed, to "covenant together," and thereafter to be regarded as man and wife, without ministerial or judicial aid, until such time as they could celebrate their nuptials in the presence of saintly witnesses, and after the true saintly fashion. This covenant the Apostle Pratt and Mrs. McLean were not slow to make.

The news soon reached the husband that his wife was going to Utah with the Mormon Elder, and intended taking the children with her. This last design McLean frustrated by sending them to some relatives in one of the Southern States. He then informed his wife that she was at liberty to go where she chose, but that she must go alone, as he had placed the children beyond her reach.

She came to Utah, and immediately on her arrival was sealed to Parley, after having lived under a covenant with him for months. The mother-heart, however, yearned for her children; neither her new religion nor the fractional part of an apostle could fill the void left by the separation from them, and she determined to gain possession of them and bring them also to Utah. After much entreating, she succeeded in inducing her new husband to go to the States with her for the purpose of finding them. She went alone to the place where her children were at school, leaving Pratt in Arkansas, — which, by the way, was her husband's home. On reaching the town where her children were, she was obliged to assume a disguise, as McLean was there, having followed his children from California. She used every stratagem to obtain them, but only succeeded in carrying away one. She quickly made her way with him to Arkansas, and joined Parley, who was awaiting her there. Together they started to return to Utah, but were overtaken by McLean, who, maddened by the breaking up of his home, the seduction of his wife, and the abduction of his child, determined to wreak summary vengeance on the man who, under the guise of religion, and in the name of the Lord, whom he constantly blasphemed by taking His holy name upon his polluted lips, had wrecked his whole life's happiness.

Being examined before a magistrate, Mrs. McLean Pratt assumed all the responsibility of the abduction of the children, and the Apostle was honorably discharged. His friends, however, apprehended danger, and advised him to escape, if he could, for McLean was a violent man. They also offered him a couple of revolvers for his defence.

The Apostle fled, but McLean was on his trail. At length the wronged husband came within sight of his enemy, and pursued him like the avenger of blood. Pratt left the public road, endeavoring to reach a house not far distant; but McLean was too swift for him. Following him closely, with revolver drawn, he fired at the saintly seducer, but failed to touch him. Furious at Pratt's escape, McLean urged forward his horse, and, as he passed his enemy, made a lunge with his bowie-knife, and gave him a fatal thrust in his side. The wounded man fell from his horse instantly, and McLean fired again at the guilty wretch as he lay bleeding on the ground, and the ball penetrated his breast.

The bloody deed performed, McLean returned to Fort Smith, walked through the town with his friends, and in the evening took the passing steamer for the South. He took his child and left the mother to return to Utah, now

ASSASSINATION OF PARLEY P. PRATT.

doubly widowed and childless. The people of Arkansas upheld McLean, and it was considered that he had only done his duty in ridding the world of such a wolf in sheep's clothing.

But the Mormons were deeply infuriated; they held every Arkansas man personally responsible for the murder of their Apostle, whom they at once canonized as saint, and worshipped as martyr, and whose name, to this day, is spoken with reverence by them; and the fact that any of these emigrants were from that state, gave them, as they thought, an opportunity of revenging Pratt's death, at the same time that they avenged the murder of their Prophet. Many of them, too, were from the immediate neighborhood where McLean resided, and where Pratt was killed; and at least one of the number was said to have been interested in his assassination. The fact that Pratt had brought his death upon himself was not taken into consideration. They found no palliation for McLean's action in his wrecked home and blighted life; though no persons in the world are so quick to resent any, even fancied, interference with their families as the Mormons. Yet this is saintly consistency.

At the Parowan council, of which I have spoken, the mode of action was fully determined upon, and the plan of attack matured to the minutest detail. Meeting with the most inhospitable treatment, and unable to obtain provisions, the emigrants were fairly driven from camp to camp, until they reached Cedar City. They camped here only one day; but during their stay they were allowed to purchase fifty bushels of tithing wheat and have it ground at John D. Lee's mill. But this was an insufficient quantity, and would be exhausted several days before they could reach the nearest point in California where food was obtainable, even if they travelled with the utmost speed, and put themselves on the shortest possible rations.

From Cedar City they proceeded south-west less than forty miles, and camped at the Mountain Meadows, which they reached after a five days' journey, so exhausted were they. It was a most cheerless and dreary spot, and so hemmed in that if attacked they would be completely at the mercy of their assailants. The Meadows are about a mile and a half long and a mile wide, and are shut in on every side by mountains; but at the lower end they converge and form a cañon. Cane Spring is situated just at the mouth of this cañon, and about thirty rods above this spring, a mound, two hundred feet long and one hundred feet wide, shuts out all view. In the midst of this gray desolation of nature, the emigrants settled themselves down for a few days' rest and final preparation before they resumed their perilous journey.

Beyond the annoyance they had experienced by the withholding of provisions, and their enforced march from camp to camp throughout the Mormon territory, they apprehended no ill-treatment from the Saints. I do not think the

JOHN D. LEE, BISHOP IN THE MORMON CHURCH, AND LEADER IN
THE MOUNTAIN MEADOWS MASSACRE.
Has nineteen wives and sixty-four children.

fear of personal danger had entered their minds at all, and they were resting quietly at the Meadows, when, on the morning of the 10th of September, while the women of the party were engaged in preparing breakfast, and the men in caring for their stock, they were suddenly attacked by the Indians. Seven were killed and fifteen wounded at the first fire.

As unexpected as the attack was, they did not lose for one instant their coolness and presence of mind. Had they done so, the massacre would have been general, and the entire party killed on the spot. But with a promptness unparalleled in the history of any border warfare, these emigrants wheeled their wagons into an oblong corral, and with almost lightning-like rapidity threw up the earth from the centre of the corral against the wagon wheels, making an excellent and almost impenetrable barricade.

It had been decided at the Parowan Council to make the attack at Santa Clara Cañon, at the point where it is crossed by the California road, and where the perpendicular walls, which it was impossible to scale, and the blockade of their own wagons, would preclude the possibility of the escape of a single soul. But the Indian allies, "The Battle Axes of the Lord," became impatient, and precipitated the attack. The liberal promises made to them by John D. Lee, the Indian-Agent, of blankets, clothing, rifles, ammunition, and trinkets, excited their cupidity; and so eager were they to obtain the promised·spoils, that they could not wait to carry out the original plan.

As soon as the barricade was finished, the first fire of the Indians was returned, and three of the assailants were wounded. They had crept very close to the train, not dreaming a repulse possible, and lay concealed in the brush along the side of the creek. Two of the Indians died, notwithstanding they were taken to Cedar City, where their wounds were anointed with consecrated oil by Bishop Higbee. For once, at least, the "laying on" of "saintly" hands was not efficacious, and the mortal wounds refused to be healed in spite of persistent priestly prayers.

The leaders of the Mormon militia, at Cedar City, were thrown into a state of excitement by the arrival of an Indian runner, bringing news of the unsuccessful assault, and they at once commenced collecting their forces to go to the Meadows to the assistance of their allies. It is said that Haight told a man that orders had come from headquarters to slay every person in the train. The Cedar City forces being considered inadequate, Lee sent to Washington for re-enforcements. When the troops were within a short distance of the Meadows, they were told that the entire company was to be killed, with the exception of the children who were too young to remember.

The Mormons were disguised as Indians, and so successfully that the unfortuate besieged had no idea that their besiegers were white men. The very knowledge of this would have disheartened them more than all the perils of their situation had power to do, when they supposed they had only a savage foe to meet, whom they hoped speedily to repulse. Safely intrenched behind their barricade, they suffered only for lack of water. The spring was only about forty rods distant, and yet they dared not venture to go to it, and the water was as unattainable as though it had been miles away. Every attempt to obtain a supply was frustrated by the reports of cruel guns, hidden behind mounds of earth. The whole rim of the basin formed by the circling hills was a masked battery sending forth destruction every time a form was seen inside the barricade. At first it was supposed only the men were in danger, and a woman of the party stepped outside the corral to milk a cow. She fell pierced with bullets. At length, their thirst becoming intolerable, they decided to send two of the little girls to the spring for water. Surely, they reasoned, they will be let to go unharmed; their youth and innocence will be their safeguard; the most barbarous savage would certainly be touched, and the hand of destruction stayed.

It might have been, had it been savages with whom they were contending; but no feeling of pity for even the children could enter the hearts of these "civilized" white men who were engaged in the "religious" warfare, and shot down their innocent victims in the name of the Lord.

Hand in hand the little ones advanced towards the spring, dressed in white, — fit robes for such lambs of sacrifice. Suddenly came the crack of scores of rifles, and the tiny

THE MURDER OF TWO LITTLE GIRLS.

bodies fell, fairly riddled with bullets, in the very sight of the frantic parents. It was deeds of this kind which, according to John D. Lee, "glorified the name of Israel's God."

Then the emigrants knew they could not expect mercy; but their courage did not fail them. If aid could only reach them! If there was any way in which they could make their situation known! They might hold out a few days,

16

though starvation and the slow, keen torture of unallayed thirst stared them in the face. After four days of siege, they drew up a prayer for aid, telling how they had been attacked by the Indians, and how they were then surrounded; it contained a list of the emigrants' names, their age, place of birth, and residence at the time of the emigration. The number of clergymen, physicians, and other professional men were given; also the number of Freemasons and Odd-fellows, with the rank of each and the name of the lodge to which they belonged. The letter was addressed to any friend of humanity; and it was a heart-rending cry of distress from souls in mortal straits. Such a cry as that could not go unheeded; it must be answered by speedy relief. It was the only expression of despair that ever came from the brave hearts in the corral; but it told of torture beyond description; of suffering that exceeds imagination.

But how should it find its way outside the barricade? How could the world be made to hear this agonized appeal? No sooner was the petition finished than three men — all honor to their bravery! — volunteered to break through the camp, dash past their enemy, and cross the desert to California. They more than suspected by this time that a portion of their assailants were white men, and they knew they were in more danger from them than from the Indians. It is said that, before these men started on their perilous and almost hopeless undertaking, the entire party knelt down, and an old, white-haired Methodist pastor prayed for their safety. They left the corral in the night under cover of the darkness, and passed their besiegers in safety. But in some way their flight was discovered, the Indian runners were placed on their track, and they were mercilessly murdered. The first one was killed while lying asleep from exhaustion, by an Indian named Jackson, who has since boasted of the deed, and who, in years after, led a person to the spot where he committed the murder; the body had been burned, but the charred remains of the skull and larger bones marked the spot.

The appeal was found near the dead body of the man by Jackson, who gave it to a Mormon gentleman; he kept it for some time without allowing any one to know that it was in his possession; but one day he showed it to one of the men who was nearly concerned in the massacre, and he deliberately tore it in pieces on the spot. Its first possessor has no sympathy with the deed, and expresses himself ready to come forward at any time and testify to the contents of the letter, of which he is perfectly well aware. In speaking of it to a gentleman connected with the western press, he is said to have exclaimed, "I believe that if the Masons and Oddfellows knew how many of their brethren were in the train, they wouldn't let the accursed murderers go unpunished." It must be that in some manner they will be punished.

"The mills of the gods grind slowly,"

to be sure, but they grind with exactness, and retribution is certain to follow crime sooner or later.

The other two men were overtaken at Virgin Hills, stripped of their clothing, and told to run for their lives; a shower of arrows was sent after them, wounding them severely; one could scarcely crawl, and his captors soon overtook him, and, binding him to a stake, piled fagots about him and set fire to them, and exulted with fiendish glee over the death-agonies of their victim.

The last one made his way to the camp of the Vagas Indians, who, pitying his condition, gave him clothing and food. He then tried to make his way to California, but was met by Ira Hatch and his band of Mormons and Indians, and was put to death by slow torture.

In the mean time the condition of the besieged grew worse. Day by day passed, and their sufferings constantly increased; still they kept courageous hearts, and looked for the help that must come. Their food was nearly gone, their increasing thirst was rendered more unendurable, because just beyond they could hear the ripple of the water, as the little brook danced on in merry mockery of their sufferings. And yet not a murmur of complaint was heard; men and women looked calmly into each other's eyes, and parched lips spoke words of cheer and hope, to which, alas! the heavy hearts did not respond. On one thing they were determined; they would die, but they would never surrender. Their wives and children should never be given over to such mercy as they would meet at the hands of their brutal enemies.

CHAPTER XIV.

BETRAYED AND MURDERED. — TRIAL OF JOHN D. LEE.

The "White Flag of Peace." — Friends in the Distance. — A Cruel Deception. — Mormon Fiends plan their Destruction. — John D. Lee's Crocodile Tears. — "Lay down your Arms, and Depart in Peace." — A Horrible Suspicion. — The Massacre. — The Scene of Blood. — No Mercy for Women and Children. — Robbed and Outraged. — Murdered by Lee's Own Hand. — The Field of Slaughter. — Dividing the Property of the Murdered Ones. — Taken to the Tithing-House. — Haunted by Spectres. — John D. Lee's Trial. — Instigated by Brigham. — No Justice in Utah. — Lee's *Confession* made to Shield the False Prophet. — Eight Mormon and Four Gentile Jurors. — What was to be Expected.

HE morning of the 17th of September dawned. The hearts of all the doomed party were sick with deferred hope. Suddenly a cry of relief broke from the corral. A wagon, filled with white men, bearing a white flag, was seen coming down the Meadows. Succor was at hand. Their terrible tortures were over. Strong men wept like children at the thought that their beloved ones, for whom they had agonized through all those dreary days and nights of siege, were safe at last.

MURDERED BY LEE'S OWN HAND.

The deliverers were none other than John D. Lee and the officers of the Mormon militia. Immediately upon their appearance the "Indians" ceased firing, and, in their fancied security, the besieged emigrants rushed outside the corral to meet their rescuers. How their hearts warmed towards Brigham Young and the Mormon people. All the wrongs they had suffered at their hands dwindled into insignificance before this last crowning act of humanity. Into the sympathizing ears of their saviors they poured the terrible story of their sufferings. Lee is said to have wept while listening to the recital, and, at the end, assured them of his deep sympathy, and promised all the relief in his power.

How much he would be able to do for them he was unable to say until he had consulted with the Indians, and he went back, and pretended to hold a consultation. The people were sure he could save them, since he was Indian agent, and must necessarily have much influence over them, and their joy was unspeakable. He soon returned with the welcome news that they were free, but on condition that they would lay aside their arms. There was no thought of treachery in their hearts, and, without a moment's hesitation, they complied with the strange conditions. They laid aside their trusty rifles, that had stood them in such good stead during all the days of the siege; they gave up revolvers and bowie-knives, faithful companions on their dreary journey, and came forth from their intrenchments unarmed, and as defenceless as the children themselves.

As they issued from the corral a guard of soldiers was drawn up to escort them to a place of safety. The men were separated from the women and children, and were placed in front, while the latter were in the rear. It seems almost strange that no suspicion of their deliverers entered their minds at this. But why should even curiosity be aroused? The white flag was waving over their heads, and they were under the protection of United States militia. Where that flag waved, they were safe and free.

Notwithstanding their exhaustion, and their weakness

from hunger, they marched joyously along, exulting in
their regained freedom, when suddenly the troops halted,
and the fatal order to fire was given by Lee, and repeated
down the line by all the under officers.   In an instant it
flashed across the helpless victims how cruelly they had
been betrayed, and, with shrieks of the wildest agony,
they fell bleeding to the earth.   Young and old shared the
same fate.   Gray-haired men and beardless boys were
alike cut down.   The Indians, who were ambushed near
by, joined the Mormons in the work of slaughter, until not
one of all the men was left.

And what of the helpless women and children?   All the
womanhood within revolts at the thought of their horrible

MURDERING THE WOMEN AND CHILDREN.

fate, and my woman's soul cries out in agony at the recital
of the sufferings of these helpless ones.   Some of them
were killed by their husbands, fathers, or brothers, —
happy souls, who thus escaped the most cruel torture.
Death was nothing, compared to the fiendish brutalities
which they suffered before they were allowed to die.
Some of the women were too ill to walk.   They were
taken outside the corral, driven up to the scene of the massacre, stripped of their clothing, shot, and their mutilated
bodies thrown down in a pile, with the rest.

To the honor of many of the men be it said, — the
younger ones, especially, — they refused to join in this horrible work, and some of them made efforts to protect these
helpless women from their fiend-like tormentors. I used
often, while living in Payson, to see a man named Jim
Pearce, whose face was deeply scarred by a bullet wound,
made by his own father, while the brave young fellow was
trying to assist a poor girl, who had appealed to him for
succor. Another girl threw herself on her knees before
Lee's son, and clinging to him, begged for mercy. His
heart was touched, and he promised to spare her, but his
father shot her while she knelt. Lee also shot another girl,
who had drawn a dagger to defend herself from him.

Even the children were not spared. They shared the
horrible fate of their parents. In vain they begged for
mercy. The bloodthirsty brutes to whom they knelt had
no feeling of pity or compassion. They laughed at their
entreaties, and mocked their terrified cries. Their little
throats were cut, and their bodies thrown carelessly in a
heap. Only seventeen of those supposed to be too young
to remember any of the occurrences of this fearful day
were saved; and of these seventeen, two were disposed of
after reaching Salt Lake City, for making some remarks
concerning the massacre, which showed an intelligence
beyond their years. It is said — on how good authority I
do not know — that Daniel H. Wells, mayor of Salt Lake
City, one of the First Presidency, Second Counsellor to
Brigham, Lieutenant-General of the Nauvoo Legion, killed
one of these babes with his own official hand. As I said
before, I cannot vouch for the authenticity of this rumor,
but those who know the man best are the most ready to
believe it. He is certainly capable of an act like this.

The whole affair lasted but about half an hour, when the
assassins rode away, carrying all the clothing and baggage
of the emigrants, leaving the bodies to the wolves and
ravens. But they were past hurt now, and wolves' fangs

THE MOUNTAIN MEADOWS MASSACRE.—MURDERED BY SUPPOSED FRIENDS.

or ravens' beaks were powerless to harm, although they might lacerate the already mutilated bodies until they should be past all recognition.   A person who visited the field of slaughter eight days after the massacre gave. the following account of it.   He said men, women, and children were strewn over the ground, or were thrown into piles. Some were shot, others stabbed, and others had their throats cut.   They were entirely stripped of clothing, and their bodies were mutilated by the wolves.   There were

SCENE AFTER THE MASSACRE.

one hundred and twenty-seven bodies in all.   These, with the three men who were killed while undertaking to bring assistance, another who was shot outside the corral, but whose body could never be found, and the two children who were murdered at Salt Lake City, made one hundred and thirty-three victims of this fearful and unparalleled assassination.

The spoils were carried to Cedar City, and placed in the tithing-office there, after the Indians had received their share.   It is told by a man, who then was a mere boy, that the night that the spoils were brought into town he and two companions slept in the tithing-office. The cellars were filled with everything that had been taken from the emigrants, and the bloody garments, stripped from the dead bodies, were thrown down on the floor. One of the men connected with the massacre came in, and threw himself down to sleep, without perceiving the boys. Scarcely had the place become quiet with the peculiar, painful silence which night brings, when suddenly the room they were in, and the cellar beneath it, where all the plunder was stored, resounded with cries, groans, sobs, and the most piercing, agonized shrieks. The guilty man jumped from his couch and fled out into the night, locking the doors after him. In vain the terrified boys tried to force the lock. It remained fast and firm, and still the wails and cries pierced the air. They were almost dead with terror, and, clambering up to the roof, managed to escape from the haunted spot. Nothing can induce this man to believe that his imagination played him a trick. "I know," he says, "that the spirits of these foully-murdered men and women were in the tithing-house that night." It is not the first time, by any means, nor the last, that a Mormon public building has been haunted.

The property of the emigrants was sold at public auction, in Cedar City, by Bishop John M. Higbee, and they were readily bought by the eager saints. To this day, jewelry is worn in Salt Lake City, and teams are seen in the streets, that are known to have belonged to the fatal emigrant train. A lady in Salt Lake City was one day showing a silk dress and some jewelry to some friends, in the presence of one of the children who had been saved from the massacre. The little one, on catching sight of the dress, burst out into a frantic fit of weeping, and between the sobs cried out, "O, my dear mamma! That is her dress; she used to wear it. Where is my mamma? Why doesn't she come for me?" It is said that other children identified clothing and trinkets which they had seen worn by members of the party. Indeed, these children remember more than their captors fancy; else they would not have been allowed to have left the Territory, as many of them have done, having for the most part been returned to their friends in the States.

My valued friend and travelling companion, Mrs. Cooke, had two of them under her charge for some time, and she has told me that they recognized John D. Lee, and one of them said one day, very quietly, but very determinedly, "When I get to be a man I will go to the President and ask him for a regiment of soldiers, and I will bring them here to kill the men who murdered my father and mother and brother, but I will kill Lee myself. I saw him shoot my sister, and I shall not die happy unless I kill him." Mrs. Cooke says they used often, in their childish prattle, to tell events of the massacre, which showed that they knew perfectly what part Lee and his confederates had in the affair.

On their return from the scene of the massacre, the leaders determined to conceal the crime, but although they kept quiet a year, after that they were unable to refrain from speaking. Lee himself was the first to disclose the fate of the party. Like the Ancient Mariner, he went up and down compelling every person whom he met to listen to his story of an emigrant train that had been murdered by the Indians. By and by it was faintly rumored that the Indians were not alone in their work of destruction, but that they were assisted by the white men. Then the rumors grew louder, and some of the participants, overcome with remorse, confessed their complicity in the crime.

A short time since a man died in Sevier Valley, who was at the Mountain Meadows. He always imagined that he was followed by spectres, and he grew haggard and worn from constant terror. "Brigham Young," he used to say, "will answer for the murder of one hundred and twenty innocent souls sent to their graves at his command." On his death-bed he besought those watching by him to protect him from the spirits that were hovering near him, waiting to avenge themselves, and he died in the fearful ravings of a horrible terror. Another man, much younger than the one referred to above, was also literally haunted to death. "Would to God," he would cry in the bitterest agony, "that I could roll back the scroll of time, and wipe from it the damning record; the terrible scenes at Mountain Meadows haunt me night and day. I cannot drive them away." He has been known to drive out for a load of hay, and return quickly in terror, leaving his team in the field. He used to say that the cold, calm faces of the dead women and children were never out of his sight.

And what of the mangled bodies, and "the cold, calm faces" that were left upturned to the September sky? They were the prey of wolves and vultures; but the bones were collected by an old Mormon, who had no sympathy with the deed of blood, and buried in the hollow they had dug inside the corral. It was a literal labor of love. Alone he performed the last act of kindness, a task which was disagreeable enough, and one that of necessity was done hurriedly. The wild beasts again dug up the bones, and they were strewn all over the plain; there they remained until 1858, when the government sent General Carlton to bury the bones decently. A large cairn of stones was built by the soldiers to mark the resting-place of the remains, and General Carlton erected a cross of red cedar, on which was inscribed the words, "Vengeance is mine, I will repay, saith the Lord." At the other end of the mound was a stone, with the inscription, "Here, one hundred and twenty men, women, and children were massacred in cold blood, early in September, 1857. They were from Arkansas." The cross was destroyed by the order of Brigham Young, after a visit to the spot. It was the first promise of payment that he ever rejected; and this, in spite of his destruction of it, will yet be forced upon him.

The trial of Lee, which has taken place since the fore-going narrative was written, shows more clearly than any-thing I can say, the ascendency which Brigham Young has over this people, and the utter futility of expecting any-thing like justice in a court where this man's followers are allowed to sit on a jury.

Of what value, think you, do they regard any oaths which they may take to serve with fairness, and to be un-biassed, except by such testimony as may be offered in court? If they are good Mormons, they have received their Endowments; and the oaths which they took when they went through with that rite, are a thousand times more binding than those that they take in court, which they re-gard as a mere form, without meaning, and which they are not only allowed by the church to violate, but which they are bound to break, unless the cause of the church can be furthered by keeping them, in which case nothing can exceed their loyalty.

Unsuccessful as the trial was, it yet has been productive of one good result. It has forced the details of this fiendish massacre upon the attention of the entire community. There is no journal in the country, no matter how small or unob-trusive, which has not had brief but concise reports of the trial, and which has not expressed decided opinions upon the result.

A greater farce was never played before a larger or more disgusted audience than this which has just ended in Utah. It is a sarcasm upon justice, a gross, hideous bur-lesque from beginning to end. I have seen surprise ex-pressed at the termination in some of the eastern journals. That shows how little they understand the autocratic man-ner in which the Territory is ruled by Brigham Young, and how impossible it is, under existing laws, to bring to justice any of his followers. I could have prophesied what the ending would be from the moment in which the jurors were drawn. Eight Mormons and four Gentiles, — what could it be but "disagreement?"

As earnest as the prosecution was, and as determined to sift the matter to the very bottom, and get at the real truth of the case, without regard to whoever might be implicated, it was balked in every endeavor, not to prove the guilt of the prisoner, and others higher in authority than he, but to influence the jury to act according to the evidence. In the face of the most conclusive evidence, which the defence were utterly powerless to refute, and indeed did not even attempt to move, the Mormon jurors voted solid for acquittal, and, to his endless shame be it recorded, induced one Gentile to vote with them. The other three stood firm, and would neither be coaxed nor bribed. They saw the right, and refused to desert it. Their companion, as many another has done, sold his principle for Mormon favor. He was in love with a Mormon girl, and hoped, by pandering to the Mormon leader's desires, to obtain her. It will be but a step further into the Mormon Church, and when he has taken that step, and gone through the Endowment House, he will be in the place where he properly belongs, and no doubt will make a willing tool for the priesthood to use.

The trial strengthened the accounts which have already been given of the massacre; and, in fact, established the truth of the whole horrible affair, in its most brutal detail, and so fully that the defence did not attempt to overthrow the proof, but spent its time in assailing the witnesses, and trying to prove that the emigrants poisoned an ox, and then attempted to sell it to the Indians, who found out the treachery, and massacred the party, while Lee and others wept and wrung their hands, and prayed that the lives might not be sacrificed.

The prosecution proved that Brigham Young gave orders regarding the disposal of the property of the murdered party, and ordered the men who brought him the news to say nothing about the matter even to each other. Absolute silence was imposed upon them, and the ones who gave

them the orders, themselves followed the "counsel" which
they gave. The defence failed utterly to prove that Brigham was ignorant of the affair, and even his deposition,
from its very weakness, inconsistency, and contradictory
statements, strengthens the prosecution, and establishes
more firmly in the popular mind the belief in his complicity
in the matter, and his approval at least, if not his actual
instigation.

There was a feeling throughout the trial that Brigham
Young and the Mormon Church were arraigned in the person of John D. Lee, and the defence exhibited their understanding of the case, by endeavoring to clear the authorities, and paying very little heed to the real defendant in
the case, rather allowing the odium to rest on him than to fall
where it more properly belonged. For although Lee merits
well the title which he bears, that of "Butcher Lee," there
is no doubt that he was acting under orders from headquarters, and that his blind and unquestioning obedience
was the effect of religious fanaticism.

It was expected that his confession would reveal beyond
a doubt the truth of the whole matter, and place the blame
where it had belonged. It was well known, that since his
cavalier treatment by the church, he had been impatient
of the odium which he had borne for so long a time, and
had threatened openly to " shift the responsibility from his
own shoulders, and place it on those whose business it was
to bear it." His wives and children, hating the disgrace,
and questioning the President's right to make a scape-goat
of their husband and father, urged him to make a full confession, and take only what of blame belonged to him.
The document was prepared, and was about to be made
public, when consternation seized upon his counsel. They
labored with him, and brought such influence to bear upon
him, that the unsafe paper was destroyed, and another sub-
stituted in its place, in which Lee merely gave the details
of the massacre, but failed to implicate any of the higher
ecclesiasts.

The trial had been appointed for the 12th of July, in the Second District Court, held at Beaver, Southern Utah, before Judge Jacob S. Boreman, who had been trying for some time, ever since the passage of an act of Congress, the 23d of June, 1874, which presented clashing between Federal and Territorial officers, to have some action taken toward punishing those persons who were shown to have been engaged in this Mountain Meadows assassination.

Judge Boreman's attempt to bring the Mountain Meadows' assassins to justice, the first that had been made since the failure of Judge Cradlebaugh's essay to find indictments against any of the persons connected with the massacre, resulted in finding a joint indictment against William H. Dame, John D. Lee, Isaac C. Haight, John M. Higbee, Philip Klingensmith, William C. Stewart, Samuel Jukes, George Adair, Jr., and some others, for conspiracy and murder. Warrants for their apprehension were issued, but after a long search only two were apprehended — Lee and Dame.

Then came another long delay. It was almost impossible to obtain witnesses to testify. This was the same trouble which had sixteen years before beset Judge Cradlebaugh; and District Attorney Carey, who prosecuted the case for the people, was almost discouraged lest he too should fail to sustain his case. "Hold your tongues" has been so long a vital lesson, that the Mormon people find it difficult work to wag them. Over one hundred subpoenas were issued, but it was impossible to collect the witnesses. Some of the least important obeyed the summons, but those who knew the most about the affair, and whose testimony would be of the most vital interest and service, failed to put in an appearance. Among these, and the witness above all others on whom the prosecution relied, was Philip Klingensmith, formerly a bishop in Cedar City, a participant in the massacre, who wished to ease his conscience by a full confession. He had been known to talk very freely to out-

siders on the subject, and it was he who was driven in such
terror from the Cedar City tithing-house the night after the
spoils had been brought thither. Another participant,
named Joel White, was also among the missing, but, fortunately for the prosecution, both were finally found, and
brought to Beaver.

The first week was devoted to legal skirmishing, and the
preparation of Lee's confession. The counsel had agreed
that he should confess fully. It was known that the men
who appeared as actors on this field of carnage were but
instruments in the hands of their authorities who had
planned this deed, and the object of the prosecution was to
obtain a knowledge of the instigators of this "deed of
deathless shame."

Failing in this, and feeling assured that Lee was not acting in good faith, they refused to receive the statement.
His own counsel, Wells Spicer, Judge Hoge, and W. W.
Bishop, were anxious to save their client, no matter what
other guilty parties might suffer. They were true to his
interests, and had they been acting by themselves, there is
little doubt that the confession would have been complete,
and would have implicated the whole of the First Presidency. But fearing this, the church attorneys, Sutherland
and Bates, obtruded their services upon the defence, solici-
tous to shield this precious trio, Brigham Young, George
A. Smith, and Daniel H. Wells, no matter at whose expense. They worked upon Lee's feelings to such an extent
that they evidently induced him to withhold his original
statement, and substitute in its place a partial and pal-
pably incomplete confession. I am certain that this is the
case, and my belief is strengthened by contrasting the
opening of the statement, with its somewhat indignant tone,
and the air of sincerity with which it is invested, with the
cautious, calculating, insincere tone of the latter portion.
The statement opens as follows : —

17

"It now becomes my painful, though imperative duty, to chronicle the circumstances that led to, and fully describe that unfortunate affair, known as the Mountain Meadows Massacre, in Utah history, which has been shrouded in mystery for the last fifteen years, causing much comment, excitement, and vindictive feeling throughout the land. The entire blame has rested upon the Mormon people in Utah. Now, in justice to humanity, I feel it my duty to show up the facts as they exist, according to the best of my ability, though I implicate myself by so doing. I have no vindictive feelings whatever against any man or class of individuals. What I do is done from a sense of duty to myself, my God, and to the people at large, so that the truth may come to light, and the blame rest where it properly belongs.

"I have been arrested on the charge of being engaged in the crime committed at the time and place referred to. I have been in close confinement over eight months since my arrest. I was in irons three months of the time during my confinement. For the last seventeen years — in fact, since the commission of the crime — I have given this subject much thought and reflection. I have made the effort to bear my confinement with fortitude and resignation, well knowing that most of those engaged in this unfortunate affair were led on by religious influences, commonly called fanaticism, and nothing but their devotion to God, and their duty to Him, as taught to them by their religion and their church leaders, would ever have induced them to commit the outrageous and unnatural acts, believing that all who participated in the lamentable transaction, or most of them, *were acting under orders which they considered it their duty, their religious duty, to obey.* I have suffered all kinds of ill-treatment and injury, as well as imprisonment, rather than expose these men, knowing the circumstances as I do, and believing in the sincerity of their motives, as I always have done; but I have a duty to perform, and have, since I was arrested, become convinced that it was not the policy of the government, or the wish of the court, to punish those men, but rather to protect them, and let the blame rest on their leaders, *where it justly and lawfully belongs.*

"After much thought and meditation, I have come to this conclusion: that I would no longer remain silent on this subject, but, so far as I can, bring to light the circumstances connected therewith, and remove the cloud of mystery that has so long obscured the transaction, and seemed to agitate the public mind. Believing it to be my duty as a man, a duty to myself, to my family, to my God, and to humanity, to cast aside the shackles so long holding my conscience, I now submit the facts, so far as I know them, stating nothing from malice, or for the purpose of revenge, *withholding nothing* that I can state of my own knowledge, and willing that the world may know all that was done, and why the acts were committed."

In this introduction, Lee plainly accuses the leaders of the church. The men "were acting under orders." Whose? They could not have emanated from the local officers of the church, since it would have been in no wise a "religious duty" to obey orders from men who were no higher in authority than themselves. Alas for Lee's "conscience," the shackles were more firmly bound than he supposed. His sense of duty to his family, his God, and humanity was blunted by the superior sense of duty to the church, and he failed utterly to do what he had so faithfully promised in the opening sentences of his confession.

After the disappointing delay caused by the preparation of Lee's confession, the trial went steadily on to the end. The prosecution brought forward about twenty witnesses, who corroborated the incidents of the massacre, and testified that the feeling against the party was aroused by George A. Smith, who everywhere preceded the train, and forbade the people selling them anything, under pain of the church's displeasure.

It was shown, too, that when, on being refused food at Cedar City, the last place at which they stopped, they asked where they could obtain it, they were told, at Mountain Meadows; which assists in establishing more fully the fact that the whole affair was premeditated, and that the party were deliberately led to their destruction.

But it remained for Philip Klingensmith to give the most thorough and vivid account of the whole massacre, from its very beginning, when the first plans were laid, until the day when he and Lee, and a man named Charley Hopkins, met in Brigham Young's office. He received them very cordially, took them to his barn to show them his fine horses, and treated them with great hospitality. He told Klingensmith, who had charge of the property, to turn it over to Lee, as he was Indian agent, and the disposal of it more properly belonged to him. He then turned to them, and said, "What you know about this affair do not tell to anybody; do not even talk about it among yourselves."

Klingensmith, with some others, strongly opposed the destruction of the emigrants, and made every effort to prevent it, but to no purpose; for Lee had received instructions from *headquarters*, and their fate was decided. The description of the attack, the steady repulse, the decoy from the corral, and the wholesale assassination, was given exactly as it has been narrated, scarcely varying at all, even in the slightest detail, ending with the interview with President Young.

Five participants in the massacre appeared as witnesses during the trial, but not one of them, with the exception of Klingensmith, admitted that he fired upon the emigrants. In his cross-examination, Judge Sutherland said, "I suppose you fired over the heads of the emigrants?" "I fired at my man," was the reply, "and I suppose I killed him."

I think the transaction has never seemed so horribly real to the outside public, as it has since this man's testimony was published to the world. Given as it was by a remorseful participant, under the solemnity of a judicial investigation, it impressed the people with its reality, and the press of the country has been unanimous in its expressions of horror, and its desire that vengeance should fall speedily on the heads of the guilty instigators.

The pitiful defence only deepened the feeling of indignation, and when, in the face of all the evidence, that was entirely unrefuted, the jury disagreed, I think the eyes of the nation were at last opened to the utter futility of expecting justice to be done, when Mormons are on trial in a Mormon community.

The end is not yet. One of the chief instigators, George A. Smith, has passed on to a higher tribunal, where Justice is not blindfold, and from whose decisions there is no appeal. The other is left, for what fate no one yet can tell. It may be that his punishment will not be given him here; that no earthly judge shall ever pass sentence upon him. But, for all that, retribution is none the less certain, and the measure of suffering which he has meted out to others shall be meted out to him.

In the mean time Justice will not rest. The spirit of the nation, fully aroused, demands a fairer trial, and it will have it. A jury must be found who shall not be bound by the shackles of bigotry, and held by oaths of disloyalty which they dare not break, but who will do their duty honestly, faithfully, and loyally. Then, and then only, shall truth triumph, and hypocrisy and wickedness meet their just reward.

CHAPTER XV.

THE BLOOD-ATONEMENT. — THE DESTROYING AN-GELS. — DANITES AND THEIR DEEDS.

Sweet, Saintly Sentiments. — "He ought to have his Throat cut." — Too many Gentiles About. — The Spirit of "Blood-Atonement" still Cherished. — Present Position of Apostates. — How they used to be "Cut Off." — "*Cutting Men off below the Ears.*" — How "*Accidents*" happened to People who "Knew too Much." — How Mr. Langford expressed his Opinion too Freely. — Mormon Friends kindly advise him to "Shut Up." — "Be on your Guard!" — Poetry among the Saints : a Popular Song. — *Human Sacrifices Proposed!* — How Saints were taught to Atone for their Sins. — "*Somebody*" ready to shed their Blood. — "*The Destroying Angels:*" who they were, and what they Did. — Saints told to do their own "Dirty Work." — People who "ought to be *Used Up.*" — Murdering by Proxy! — Brigham Young *proved* to be the Vilest of Assassins. — Hideous Crimes of Porter Rockwell and Bill Hickman. — How Rockwell tried to Murder Governor Boggs. — Hickman Confesses his Atrocious Crimes. — Six Men Robbed of $25,000, and then "Used Up." — Another Frightful Assassination. — A Council of Mormon Murderers. — The "Church" orders the Assassination of the Aikin Party.

"USING UP" AN APOSTATE.

T is only a very few weeks since two prominent officers of the Mormon Church were overheard in the street, in Salt Lake City, angrily discussing some person who had "broken his covenants." Said one, —

"He ought to have his throat cut."

"It wouldn't do," replied the other; "there are too many Gentiles about."

It is now nearly twenty years since the eventful

"Reformation" and its horrible teachings, and the effects are still felt. The principles that Young, and Grant, and Kimball, and their fellows taught then have not been forgotten in all these years that have intervened, and it is only the presence of a large "Gentile" element that prevents the full exercise of the "Blood-Atonement."

There never has been any real and impartial trial by jury in Utah. No twelve men could be found and sworn in who would dare to render an unbiassed verdict. This has been repeatedly seen in trials which have taken place. So true is it, that hundreds of Gentiles who are conscious of the justice of their several causes, would never think of bringing them into court during the existing state of affairs. They know it would be useless. Prejudice runs high ; in fact, so high that outsiders are perfectly incapable of realizing it. Still, murders have been fewer of late, for President Young knows that the eye of Uncle Sam is fixed with no small degree of sternness upon the City of the Saints ; and, more important still, Deseret has not yet been admitted into the Union as a State !

Yet the spirit of assassination still remains ; and were it unchecked, hundreds would be added to the already appallingly long list of men and women foully dealt with and sent into eternity without a moment's warning, for no crime at all except for daring to differ, if ever so slightly, from those in authority. If any person, deceived by the present peaceful attitude of the Mormon leaders and their constant boast that crime is almost unknown among them, thinks that they have altered in their real views at all since the days when they first advocated the "Blood-Atonement," he is very much mistaken. The feelings that they have been obliged to hide are bitterer because they have not dared to show them.

An apostate nowadays is comparatively safe from any deeds of violence on their part. The most they can do is to abuse him through their newspapers, and curse him in the church, and give him over to the tender mercies of

Satan ; but as " Deseret " newspaper abuse is rarely heard outside of the church which it represents, and as the cursing does not produce physical hurt, and as Satan's mercies are to the full as tender as theirs, the Gentile does not mind anything about the whole of it, but goes on his way quietly enough.

But twenty, fifteen, even ten years ago, an apostate's or Gentile's life was worth absolutely nothing. It was difficult to tell which of the two they hated with the most deadly hatred. The doom of either was irrevocably fixed, and it came, swift and sudden, often before he knew that danger menaced him. It did not need actual knowledge of a man's defection from the church, or that his disapprobation of the course pursued by leaders should be openly expressed ; it was enough that he should be merely suspected, and his fate was just as certain, coming swift and sure, before he had even an opportunity of defending himself.

A strict surveillance was kept over the movements of any stranger in the city, and if his words or actions displeased the Mormon spies, he never got far beyond city limits on his onward journey before some sad accident befell him, which left him lying dead by the road-side. It was well when a stranger had any person to caution him against any expression of his mind against the people or their religion ; above all, against their beloved institution of polygamy, for they are very sensitive on this point, hating and dreading criticism in the very thing, above all others, that provokes and invites it. In this case he might escape with nothing more terrible than the consciousness of a spy dogging his every footstep and listening to every word.

In the autumn of 1863, Mr. N. P. Langford, of St. Paul, Minnesota (the author of the " Yellowstone Articles," published a few years since in *Scribner's Magazine*), in company with several others, started from Montana for Salt Lake City. While on the journey they fell in with a party of Mormons, numbering eight, — all men, and all bound for Salt Lake City. The two parties travelled together the remainder of the way, and became very friendly. As a natural consequence of this companionship, the talk turned upon Mormonism, and the arguments between them were frequent and interesting.

One of the Mormons, named Cunningham, was a very intelligent man, and, while contending that his was the only true faith, would argue with Langford, without showing any ill feeling — a very uncommon thing for a Mormon to do, by the way, since they are usually so very intolerant that they will not listen to an opponent with the least degree of patience, but, at the first sign of opposition, lose temper, and, instead of fairly arguing the question, shower anathemas on the one who has dared to call their religion in question. It must be a weak position that can only be defended by vituperation.

At night, while round the camp-fire, the Mormons would sing of Brigham as "the word of the Lord," and what Langford called a "string of nursery rhymes," in which Cunningham would sing the solo, and the rest the chorus. The idea conveyed in these rhymes was, that only in Mormonism was happiness to be found, and that they were glad that they were Mormons.

After the party arrived in Salt Lake City, Cunningham called Langford on one side, and said to him, "You boys seem to be pretty good fellows, and I do not wish you to come to harm, and will give you a word of advice. Here in Salt Lake, you must not express yourselves about Mormonism as you have when you have talked with me; for, if you do, your lives won't be worth a cent."

"Why so?" asked Langford.

"Because you will be assassinated," was the reply.

Langford thanked him, and followed his advice. Soon afterwards he mentioned the fact to a Gentile with whom he had business, who in reply said, "You must do as he says, or you will never leave the city alive. Do you see

that man with a gray coat? He is a Mormon spy, and is
evidently watching you, and will watch you as long as you
remain in the city. I say, as your Mormon adviser did,
Be on your guard."

During all the time that Langford was in the city he was
followed by this man, and he said he felt sure that if one
word in disparagement, or criticism, of the Mormon people, or their religion, had crossed his lips, he would have
been a dead man. He followed the advice he received,
however, else the readers of *Scribner* would not have been
so charmingly entertained afterwards, as they were by his
readable articles.

It may seem like digressing somewhat, but I cannot refrain from quoting the "nursery rhymes" which the Mormons sang by the camp-fire, and which evidently impressed
Langford with their absurdity. These rhymes are printed
in the Mormon Sunday-school song-book, and are sung in
Sunday-schools and religious meetings to the tune of "The
Bonny Breast Knots." They are a most remarkable piece
of religious composition.

> " What peace and joy pervade the soul,
>   And sweet sensations through me roll,
>   And love and peace my heart console,
>   Since first I met the Mormons!

> " They sing the folly of the wise;
>   Sectarian precepts they despise;
>   A heaven far above the skies
>   Is never sought by Mormons.

> " To Sabbath meetings they repair;
>   Both old and young assemble there,
>   The words of inspiration share:
>   No less can suit the Mormons.

> " At night the Mormons do convene,
>   To chat a while, and sing a hymn;
>   And one, perchance, repeat a rhyme
>   He made about the Mormons.

"The Mormon fathers love to see
Their Mormon families all agree;
The prattling infant on his knee
Cries, 'Daddy, I'm a Mormon!'

"As youth in Israel once decried,
To wed with those that Heaven denied,
So youth among us now have cried,
'We'll marry none but Mormons.'

"High be our heaven, the Mormons cry,
Our place of birth, and when they die,
Celestialize and purify
This earth for perfect Mormons.

"So, while we tread the foeman's ground,
We'll make the trump of freedom sound,
And scatter blessings all around,
Like free and happy Mormons.

[*Chorus to each verse.*]

"Hey, the merry, O, the busy,
Hey, the sturdy Mormons;
I never knew what joy was
Till I became a Mormon."

I have heard women singing this chorus in some meeting, because they dared not be silent, when their faces belied the words of the song, and who I knew hated the life which they were compelled to live, and who had seen nothing but the most abject misery since they had entered it; whose lives were one long, terrible torture, and who would have been perfectly happy had they seen any way of escape from it.

The dangers of non-Mormons in 1863, great as they were, were much less than in days just succeeding the "Reformation," which days have been rightly called "The Reign of Terror." It *was* a terrible time, indeed, and one fairly shudders to recall the blood-curdling atrocities that were committed at that period. All "in the name of the Lord," too, and as an exercise of religious faith. The Spirit of the New Testament, the Christ-like spirit, breathing out "peace on earth, good will to men," seemed entirely lost. The "Church of Jesus Christ of the Latter-Day Saints" forgot the sweet song of good-fellowship and love that the angels sang at the birth of Him whom they professed to follow, and by whose name they were called. The angry denunciations of fanatics and religious tyrants, and their servile followers, demanding blood and calling loudly and openly for the sacrifice of human life, and the destruction of all who dared to differ from them, drowned the angel voices.

The old Mosaic spirit of retribution was abroad in all its most fearful force. "Altars of sacrifice" were loudly recommended, and the victims were advised to place themselves thereon voluntarily; if they would not become willing sacrifices, they became involuntary ones, for "somebody" took the matter in hand, and saw that the "atonement" was made.

Usually this mysterious "somebody" was one of the "Danites," or "Destroying-Angels," a band of men regularly organized for the purpose of putting obnoxious persons out of the way. It is said that the band had its origin in Missouri, in the early days of Mormonism, before the settlement of Nauvoo. But they never became so very notorious until the "Reformation" times, when their peculiar talents were called into play, and their services into constant requisition.

As loudly as the Mormon leaders talked to the people about doing their "dirty work" themselves, they, nevertheless, shrank from soiling their own fingers; so they employed others to do their own share, and contented themselves by saying that such a person ought to be "used up," and thinking no more of it until they received the news of a mysterious death. In this way Brigham Young has "man-

aged" a great many murders, of which he would probably
avow himself entirely guiltless, since his hand did not perform the deed.   But though his hand may have no blood-
stain to haunt him, yet his heart must be terribly weighted
with the load of guilt, which he cannot shake off, let him
try as hard as he may.   To look at the man, rosy and
smiling, comfortable in every particular, you would never
take him to be the hard, cruel despot he is.   He looks
clean enough outwardly, but within he is filled with moral
rottenness to the very core.

Among the men he has employed, the most notorious are
Orrin Porter Rockwell, known familiarily as "Port" Rockwell, and William, or, as he is called, "Bill" Hickman.
"Port" was an old friend and ally of Joseph Smith, holding very much the same relation to him that "Bill Hickman" has held to the present Prophet.   Among other
things of which he was accused, was the murder of Governor Boggs, of Missouri.

Joseph Smith and he were
both accused, the former
of instigating the murder,
the latter for committing
it; but Smith got free
without a trial, through
some quibble of the law,
and Rockwell proved that
he was in another place at
the time of the attempted
assassination.   He was
always near the Prophet

BRIGHAM'S "DESTROYING ANGEL," "PORT"
ROCKWELL.

in the time of danger, and, in return, Joseph promised
"Port" that so long as he wore his hair uncut his life
should be safe.   So he still wears his hair long, in braided
queues down his back, and he says that he shall live until
every enemy of Joseph Smith is killed.

His evil deeds will probably equal, if not outnumber, Bill

Hickman's; but the latter, either touched with remorse at the remembrance of all the crimes which he had committed, or else annoyed because Brigham was so avaricious and parsimonious, and did not give him money enough, or because he thought to save his own neck, turned State's evidence against Brigham and the other Mormon leaders, and made what he calls a " full confession " of his crimes. The list of them is perfectly appalling, and he claims that he did them all at Young's instigation.

Among the most famous of the murders was that of Lobbs, and the massacre of the " Aiken party " — a deed that stands in cold-blooded atrocity and treachery next to the " Mountain Meadow Massacre," and in which Port Rockwell figures also. It was a deed that could be committed by no one except the fanatical Mormons, who were drunk with " Reformation " excitement, and filled with an insane desire for blood-shedding.

A party of six men, on their way from Sacramento, which city they had left in May, 1857, going, as it was supposed, to join Johnston's army. A part of the way they travelled with a party of Mormons who were ordered home from Missouri to assist in the " Mormon war."

The Mormon party took a great liking to them all, and the relations between them were very amicable. John Pendleton, one of the Mormons, said in his testimony, " They were kind, polite, and brave, and always ready to do anything that was needed." Unfortunately for them, they got impatient at the slowness with which the Mormon party travelled, and so they left it, and hurried on. At Raysville, a town about twenty-five miles north of Salt Lake, they were all arrested on the charge of being government spies. A few days after their arrest, the Mormon party came in, and Pendleton, it seems, instantly recognized their horses in the public corral. He at once inquired what it meant, and on being told that the party had been arrested as spies, he replied, with an oath, that it was impossible; that they knew nothing about the army; that, in fact, they had been their companions nearly all the way. "Can't help it; we shall keep them," was the reply. When it is remembered that they had property with them to the amount of twenty-five thousand dollars, I think their detention will be fully explained.

They were tried as spies, and nothing being proved against them, they were promised safe-conduct out of the Territory, but they must be sent by the southern route. Four of them went, leaving the other two of their party in the city, accompanied by Rockwell, John Lot, a man of the name of Watts, and one other man. At Nephi, one hundred miles south of Salt Lake, Rockwell informed Bishop Bryant that the party were to be "used up" there. A council was held, and the Bishop appointed four more men to assist the four who had the men in charge. Among these last appointed was the Bishop's own counsellor, Pitchfor, and a man named Bigbee, who is now a Bishop. This party of four started early in the night, while the Aikens' party did not leave until daylight. When they reached the Sevier River, Rockwell said he thought they had better camp there, for they could find no other camping-place that day; so they stopped. Very soon the other party, who had been lying in wait for them, approached, and asked permission to camp with them, which was readily granted.

The men were tired, and removing their arms, they were soon sound asleep. Their treacherous companions hovered over them like greedy birds of prey. Why didn't something warn those men of the terrible fate that was in store for them? But there came no voice of warning, and still they slept on as peacefully and as trustfully as though in their own homes among those who loved them; and still the assassins hovered over them, waiting for what they did not know. They discussed the manner in which the deed should be done, and decided not to use fire-arms. Armed

with clubs, they crept stealthily up to where their sleeping
companions lay, and dealt furious blows at them while they
slept. Two of the men died without a struggle; John
Aiken was but slightly wounded, and rose to his feet to defend himsef, but received a shot from the pistol of one of the
men which laid him senseless. A man called the "Colonel,"
believing the whole party were attacked by robbers, made
his way into the bush, receiving as he went a shot in the
shoulder from "Port" Rockwell's pistols. He succeeded in

MURDER OF AIKEN PARTY.

evading his pursuers, and made his way to Nephi, twenty-
five miles distant, and arrived, pale and drenched with
blood, at Bishop Foote's, whose guests the party had been
during their stay in Nephi. He told his story, which was
listened to with a surprise and horror that were well
feigned.

The three bodies were thrown into the river; but in some
miraculous manner, in spite of his wounds, John Aiken
managed to get ashore, and, hiding in the bush, he heard
one of the men ask Rockwell "if all the damned Gentiles
were dead;" to which the other replied, that they were, all

but one, but that he ran away. Aiken lay quietly until he heard the assassins leave; then he made his way, as best he could, through the cold November night, drenched with water, sorely wounded, and with very little clothing, back to Nephi. He knew who were his attempted assassins, and he knew that to go to Nephi was to go directly back into the jaws of death; but he did not know what else to do; so he plodded painfully on until he reached the town, where he sank fainting at the door of the very first house which he reached. The woman of the house was surprised at his appearance, and told him that another one was at Bishop Foote's. "It is my brother!" he exclaimed, and moved away from the door. No one attempted to stop him; all were too much shocked at his appearance and manner, and he reached Bishop Foote's in safety, where he found not his brother, but the "Colonel."

The meeting between them was heart-rending. They wept like children, and, falling into each other's arms, embraced one another with all the tenderness of women. And the Mormon men looked on and coolly decided upon the manner of their death.

Bishop Bryant came with condolences and regrets at their own misfortunes and the sad fate of their friends, extracted the balls, dressed the wounds, and advised them to return, as soon as they possibly could, to Salt Lake City. In the mean time the murderers were in Nephi, concocting a new plan of assassination. It is said that the men had saved a watch worth two hundred and fifty dollars, and a pistol. When they got ready to leave, a bill for thirty dollars was presented to them, which, having no money with them, they promised to settle directly on their return to Salt Lake. They were told that such an arrangement could not be made; so Aiken said, "Well, here is my watch and my partner's pistol; you can take which you choose." Without hesitation the Bishop took the pistol; so leaving the men entirely unarmed. As he gave it to Foote, he turned to

18

his friend and said, with the tears rolling down his face, "Prepare for death; we shall never leave this Valley alive."

Previous to their departure, John Aiken had commenced to write an account of the affair; but it moved him so that he was utterly unable to proceed with it, and so he got a son of Bishop Foote, who had proved a good friend to them, to finish it for him. This account, by some mysterious good fortune, has never been destroyed.

They had got but a few miles from Nephi when the driver of their wagon — a Mormon, and in the plot — stopped in front of an old cabin, and saying that he must water his horses, unhitched them and led them away. Instantly, two men stepped from the cabin, and before the doomed men could realize the situation, fired at them, killing them instantly; they were then taken from the wagon, and, loaded with stone, put in a "bottomless spring," — such as is often seen in Utah.

While this atrocious act of villany was going on, Rockwell and his men had returned to Salt Lake, and taking the remaining ones of the party, had started southward with them, plying them with liquor constantly. One of them, named Back, feigned drunkenness; but the other man was absolutely insensible when they reached the "Point of the Mountain," where it had been decided to make away with them; or, in Danite parlance, "use them up." They were suddenly attacked with slung-shot. The drunken man was quickly despatched, without the slightest trouble; but Back, who had been suspicious of his companions, and had been on the lookout for treachery, leaped from the wagon, and succeeded in outrunning his pursuers and in evading their bullets. He swam the Jordan, and came down to the city, where he told the whole story, creating a tremendous excitement. Brigham was terribly exercised, and sent at once for Hickman, telling him, in his usual refined manner, "The boys have made a bad job putting a man out of the way. They all got drunk, bruised up a fellow, and he got away from them at the Point of the Mountain, came back to the city, and is telling all that has happened, which is making a bad stink."

He then told him that he must find that man and use him up; that, first of all, he was to go and find George Grant and William Kimball, both of whom were "generals" in the Utah militia, and consult with them about having him taken care of. Hickman found the "generals" decidedly disgusted at "Rockwell's mismanagement of the affair," as they termed it; that something must be done, and that at once, and asked if Brigham had sent him up. On being told that he had, they informed him that they had arranged everything, and only wished him to carry out their arrangements and follow their instructions.

They had planned with a man with whom Back had stayed a great deal on his first arrival in Utah, and in whom he had implicit confidence, to invite him to visit him. He was to come to town to fetch him to his home, which was about twelve miles from the city, and Hickman was to meet them on the way and despatch Back. He was to go a certain road, which was very quiet, being but little travelled, was to drive white horses, and was to go very fast. Hickman and another man named Meacham started out a little before sundown, and rode to the appointed spot. About dusk, the wagon with the white horses came swiftly along; the two men were talking interestedly, and the poor victim of this treacherous plan was entirely off his guard: supposing himself to be with a friend, no thought of harm had entered his mind, and he was entirely unprepared for his cruel fate. Hickman and Meacham stepped suddenly out into the lonely road, and called to the driver to halt, at the same time firing at Back, shooting him through the head, and killing him instantly. The body was put into a ditch, a rag hung on a bush to mark the spot, and the assassins returned to George Grant's house to report their success.

They found Grant, Kimball, and Port Rockwell all there, and after hearing the result of the expedition, all took spades and went out and buried the man. The next day Hickman gave an account of the affair to Young, who expressed himself as delighted that he had been put out of the way.

It was fourteen years before the truth of this affair was known. It was for a while shrouded in deep mystery, and the blood of the innocent victims cried out for retribution unheeded and unnoted for all those years. Now their fate is known beyond a doubt, and foremost in the list of assassins stands the name of Brigham Young.

CHAPTER XVI.

FRIGHTFUL DEEDS OF BLOOD. — MORMONISM IN ITS TRUE LIGHT.

The Yates Murder. — Brigham and the Leading Mormons Arrested for the Crime. — Mr. Yates accused of being a Spy. — He is Arrested and his Goods Seized. — Bill Hickman takes possession of the Prisoner's Body. — Brigham Embezzles his Gold. — Another Saint steals his Watch. — Hickman carries him to Jones's Camp. — He is murdered there while Asleep. — Hickman asks Brigham for a Share of the Spoil. — The Prophet refuses; sticks to every Cent. — Hickman's "faith" in Mormonism is Shaken. — His fellow-murderer Apostatizes Outright. — How Bill was finally "paid in Wives." — He tries a little matter of Seventeen. — Fiendish Outrage at San Pete. — Bishop Snow contrives the Damnable Deed. — The fate of his Victims. — A Mysterious Marriage. — The Feather-beds and the Prophet. — Mrs. Lewis comes to Live with Me.

BRIGHAM YOUNG'S FARM-HOUSE.

BOUT this time, when the Aiken party were cut off, as I have just related, by Brigham Young's express command, another horrible murder was perpetrated under circumstances of equal atrocity, which has since attracted a considerable amount of public attention.

The reason of the Yates murder becoming so notorious, was not because it was so much worse than hundreds of other murders which have been committed in

Mormondom, but because Brigham Young and other Mormon officials were arrested as the murderers. Hickman turned State's evidence, and it is from his own account that I take the leading facts of the assassination.

Yates was a trader on Green River, and was accused by the Mormons of being a government spy. In those days, if no other charge could be brought against a person, he was called a "spy;" and this, of course, gave sufficient reason for putting him out of the way very summarily. The Mormons were also annoyed because, although among his stores he had a large quantity of ammunition, he would not sell it unless the purchasers bought other goods. They then accused him of supplying the army, and arresting him, carried him to Fort Bridger, while they took possession of his store, stock, &c.

Hickman was detailed to take the prisoner to the city, and Yates's money — nine hundred dollars in gold — was given him to carry to Brigham Young. His watch was "taken care of" by some one at Bridger. Hickman was accompanied by a brother of his, a Gentile, who was on a visit to him; Meacham, the one who was connected with him in the murder of Back; and a man of the name of Flack. On their way they were met by Joseph A. Young, who informed them that his father wanted Yates killed, and that he, Hickman, was to take him to Jones's camp, where he would receive further orders. The party arrived at camp that evening about sundown, and that night Yates was murdered as he lay asleep by the camp-fire.

Hickman and Flack carried the news and the money to Brigham. He was very affable until Hickman suggested that, as they had been to much expense, he thought part of the money ought to come to them. His manner changed at once; he reprimanded the men very severely, and told them that the money was needed for the church; it must go towards defraying the expenses of the war. Flack aposta-

tized at once; renounced Mormonism on the spot; it evidently didn't "pay" well enough to suit him, and Hickman
himself was disgusted with the meanness of his master.
He said that Brigham never
gave him one dollar for all the
"dirty work" he had done for
him; he never made him the
slightest present. But he paid
him, it is said, in wives. I
think he had seventeen, and a
large number of children.

It was a class of men like
this that the Reformation
brought to the surface, and
capital tools they made for a
corrupt and bloodthirsty priesthood. They were earnest dis-

BILL HICKMAN, BRIGHAM'S "DESTROYING
ANGEL."

ciples of the "Blood-Atonement," and could slay an apostate or a Gentile with no compunctions of conscience. Yet,
bad as they were, they did not equal in villany the men
who employed them, and then refused to pay them.

Everything, even the most trifling, that a person did,
which was at all offensive to any member of the priesthood,
was accounted apostasy, and punishment administered as
speedily as possible. Hundreds of innocent victims have
been sacrificed in this way, merely to gratify a petty, personal revenge, or to remove some person who chanced to
be distasteful. Fanaticism and bigotry were at that time at
flood tide, and some of the most revolting and heart-sick-
ening crimes were committed. Many of them were unknown outside the places where they occurred, and so
common were they that, beyond an involuntary feeling of
horror, and a vague sort of wonder as to who would be the
next victim, nothing was thought of them; until, after the
excitement began to die away, and the people had time to
recall the scenes of horror, they began to realize, to a cer-

tain extent, what they had been passing through. Some
of the crimes were almost too shocking even to mention;
they could not be given in detail.

Among the victims to priestly hatred and jealousy was a
young man about twenty years of age, in San Pete County,
named Thomas Lewis, a very quiet, inoffensive fellow,
much liked by all who knew him, very retiring in his manners, and not particularly fond of gay society. He lived
with his widowed mother, and the very sweetest, tenderest
relations that can exist between a mother and child existed
between them.

Contrary to his usual habit, he attended a dancing-party
one evening at the urgent and repeated entreaties of his
friends, and during the evening he was quite attentive to a
young lady-friend of his who was present, and with whom
he was on terms of greater intimacy than with any other
in the company. She knew his shy, retiring disposition,
and seemed to take pleasure in assisting him to make the
evening a pleasant one; just as any good-natured, kindly
girl will do for a young fellow whom she likes, and who she
knows is ill at ease and uncomfortable.

It happened that Snow, the Bishop of the ward in which
the Lewis family lived, had cast his patriarchal eye on this
young girl, and designed her for himself; and he did not
relish the idea of seeing another person pay any attention to
his future wife. He had a large family already, but he
wished to add to it, and he did not choose to be interfered
with.

Lewis's doom was sealed at once; the bewitched Bishop
was mad with jealous rage, and he had only to give a hint
of his feelings to some of his chosen followers, who were
always about, and the sequel was sure. He denounced
Lewis in the most emphatic manner, and really succeeded
in arousing quite a strong feeling of indignation against him
for his presumption in daring to pay even the slightest attention to a lady who was destined to grace a Bishop's harem.

The closest *espionage* was kept upon him by the Bishop's band of ruffians, and one evening a favorable opportunity presented itself; he was waylaid, and the Bishop's sentence carried out, which was to inflict on the boy an injury so brutal and barbarous that no woman's pen may write the words that describe it.

He lay in a concealed spot for twenty-four hours, weak and ill, and unable to move. Here his brother found him in an apparently dying state, and took him home to his poor, distracted mother, who nursed him with a breaking heart, until after a long time, when he partially recovered.

He then withdrew himself from all his former friends, and even refused to resume his place at the table with the family. He became a victim of melancholia, and would take no notice of what was occurring around him. He staid with his mother for several years, when he suddenly disappeared, and has never been heard of since; his mother and brother made every effort to find him, but they could not obtain the slightest clew to his whereabouts.

Whether this victim of priestly rule is dead or living must for ever remain a mystery. It is probable that the emissaries of Bishop Snow have put an end to his existence. Yet during the whole of this affair the bishop was sustained by Brigham Young, who knew all about it. He has held his sacred office as securely as though the stain of human blood was not on his conscience; he has been sent on a mission to preach "the everlasting gospel of Jesus Christ to the poor benighted nations of Christendom," and he has also taken more wives, which were sealed to him by Brigham Young in the Endowment House.

But a still greater marvel is, that the mother of Bishop Snow's poor victim still retains her faith in Mormonism, and since the cruel and disgraceful tragedy which deprived her of her son, has been sealed to Brigham Young as one of his wives. It was not pity that moved him to marry her, nor a desire to comfort her and lighten her burdens; but it was because he saw by so doing that he could advance his own interests.

Mrs. Lewis is never mentioned among his wives, yet he was
sealed to her about two years after his marriage to me.
Brigham's matrimonial experiences hardly find a place here,
but as Mrs. Lewis's alliance with the Prophet came about in
a way through this tragedy, it may not be out of place even
in this chapter on " Blood-Atonement."

San Pete was filled with so many sad memories to Mrs.
Lewis, after the terrible fate of her son, that she could not
remain there, reminded as she constantly was of the affair ;
so she removed to Provo, where she bought herself a very
pleasant home, and, being a woman of considerable wealth,
was living very comfortably, when Brigham commenced
building a factory so near to her that it spoiled the beauty
of the place and made it quite unpleasant.   The agents then
proposed to bring the water-course through her front yard —
an arrangement to which she objected most emphatically.
The agents, shocked at her unwillingness to have her property spoiled for the sake of Brother Brigham's factory,
rushed in breathless haste to the Prophet, and told him of
Mrs. Lewis's rebellion.   He instantly formed a plan of inducing her to surrender.   He went at once to Provo, and
presented himself to Mrs. Lewis with an offer of marriage,
saying at the same time, " I know you have had a great
deal of trouble, Sister Lewis ; you have suffered much for
the sake of the gospel, and I pity you.   I desire to do something for you ; I wish in some way to comfort you ; so I
think you had better become a member of my family."

She was an old lady, with children all grown, and was
perfectly independent of them or any one, and certainly had
no need to marry for support.   As the Mormons believe
that no woman can enter heaven except some man go
through the ordinances with her, very many are sealed in
their old age to secure salvation ; but as her husband had
been a good Mormon, and they had attended to all the important matters, she was saved without prophetic intervention.   She had no need to marry for a husband who should

look out for her welfare, as her children were ready and
willing to do anything she needed done in the way of business. So she informed Brother Brigham that she didn't see
why she should marry at all.

But Brother Brigham assured her that he wanted to marry
as well for his own happiness as hers. He wanted her
always near him, and it should be his first pleasure and
business to look out for a nice place of residence for her,
where he might look after her constantly. In fact he played
the devoted and anxious lover with all the earnestness of a
youth who is wooing his first *innamorata*, and in a fashion
that would have made some of his family stare had they
overheard it.

The Prophet's earnestness was not without effect, and
Mrs. Lewis took her lover's proposal into serious consideration, while he waited anxiously for an answer, with one eye
on the coveted front yard, the other leering at the widow,
who actually concluded to accept his proposals, and, absurd
as it may seem, became one of his wives.

He was ashamed of himself after it was all over, and
requested his bride to say nothing about " the transaction
between them," as it was better that, for the present at
least, no one but themselves should know anything about it.
" They would not understand, you know," murmured he in
his most drivellingly sweet accents. The trouble was,
" they " would understand too well, especially when they
saw the water-course running through the once pretty front
yard of the last Mrs. Young's home.

In a very short time he began to talk about his farm-house,
and extolling it as a most desirable residence. I was living
there at the time, yet he said " it was plenty large enough
for two families, and everything was arranged with such
perfect convenience ; " so he begged that she would move
there at once. He grew eloquent over the beauties of the
situation, and said, " It is a perfectly splendid place, the
nicest farm-place I ever saw in my life. I would give any-

thing if my duties would permit me to live there; but I am kept away by circumstances, and cannot even think of it as a permanent residence, ardently as I long to do so." He continued, "You can raise all the fowls there that you desire; it is a beautiful place for raising ducks and geese, and you may make as many feather-beds as you wish."

What greater inducements could he hold out to her? Dear to every old housekeeper's heart are her plump, soft, billowy feather-beds. We moderns are stifled by them; they are oppressive, and suggestive of dust; but she pats their rotundity with loving hands; gives them many punches

BRIGHAM WOOING WIDOW LEWIS.

of affection, and builds a structure that is wonderful to behold — in which she hospitably smothers her chance visitor, and, while he is sweltering in its embraces, tells him proudly that "that bed is *live* geese!" The pride of Mrs. Lewis's heart was her feather-beds — she wavered.

Her sons were very reluctant to have her leave her own home, and expressed themselves quite strongly on the subject when she mentioned it to them and asked their advice. Yet, in spite of their disapprobation, she concluded to go. Her husband was also her Prophet, and it might be that he spoke from inspiration. At all events, she would give heed

to his words, and regard his wishes; else what punishment
and disgrace might she not bring upon herself? So,
deaf to her children's protestations, — who, by the way, did
not regard the call to the farm as a divine bidding, — she
removed thither, and came into the same house with me.
We neither of us liked this arrangement, as we were both
firm believers in the theory that no one house was ever
yet built large enough for two families. Yet we knew
that it would not be wise to say anything to Brigham; so
we were as quiet as we could be, and awaited his own time
for our separation, Mrs. Lewis was a very kind, patient
woman, and I got very fond of her, and we got on admirably together in our forced companionship, and managed to
live together until my house in the city was finished, which
was about four months after she arrived at the farm.

She said that she told Brother Brigham, most decidedly,
that she had strong objections to moving into a house with
another family, and he told me that he was intending to
have me go to the city immediately, and that I would probably be gone before she arrived at the farm. She post-
poned her removal for some weeks after that, hoping
that I would have gone by that time, and the coast entirely
clear. She found on her arrival that Brigham had grossly
misrepresented affairs at the farm. Nothing at all was as
he had described it to her. This hoary old Claude Mel-
notte deceived his ancient Pauline most cruelly in the vivid
pictures which he drew of the elegance of her future residence.

She made it her first business to visit the Prophet and
ask for some repairs to be made, — which, by the way,
were sadly needed, — but he declared that he had no time
to attend to them — the same answer that he had made to my
requests ever since I had lived there. A busier man than
Brigham Young, when he wishes to be particularly engaged, was never seen, I believe; and his business is
always the most pressing when any of his wives ask him
to do anything for their comfort.

When she had lived at the farm a year, she told me that Brigham had never been to see her once during all that time; but that he had got possession of her property, and was using it for factory purposes. The water-course ran through her yard, her house was made an office, and the whole place was so changed and so entirely spoiled as a residence, that she never could go there again to live. She must, whether she would or not, live there until Brigham chose to move her somewhere else, or until her children could find some place for her to go to. She supports herself entirely, independently of the man who has swindled her out of her home and her property; and the only assistance she receives is from her children, who are very kind to her, annoyed as they were at her for giving up her home, and, above all, allowing it to fall into Brigham Young's hands. His duck-and-goose story was all misrepresentation, made use of merely to induce her to go to the farm; and when she got there she very soon found that she would have those lovely feather beds, not, at least, by raising the fowls to supply the feathers. The Prophet's imagination had evidently run away with memory when he ardently painted the glories of the farm to his bride. This poor old lady was made a tool for the gratification of Brigham Young's avarice, as her son had been the victim to one of his followers' jealous anger. She has little to love Mormonism for. Its two leading doctrines, the "Celestial Marriage" and "Blood-Atonement," have pretty thoroughly shut out happiness from her life, and rendered her in her old age lonely and dependent.

A man named Thomas Williams came early to Utah, was a good Mormon, and embraced polygamy. He was a lawyer, and had acquired both wealth and influence in his profession. He was, however, a very independent man, and a man of very decided opinions. He had differed from Brigham on many political questions, and he was a warm friend and staunch adherent of Judge Stiles, who had drawn

upon himself the displeasure of the "boys" by his just and
impartial judgments. Indeed, Williams had his office
with the judge, and that was a crime, when Judge Stiles's
standing was taken into consideration. Williams was also
in possession of knowledge concerning some murders that
had taken place, had spoken very openly of them, and was
becoming actually dangerous to Brigham and the other
leaders, — so dangerous that Brigham went to his parents
and complained of him and his acts, and ended by saying,
"If Tom don't behave himself, and stop making me trouble,
I must have him attended to."

Soon after that Williams apostatized, and expressed himself very openly concerning the Mormon church and its
leaders, although he knew that it must come to their ears,
and that they would try, at least, to punish him for what
they would consider his wickedness and profanity. He
seemed to have lost all fear, as he had previously lost all
belief in or respect for them. He started for California
soon after his apostasy, designing to stay there, and to send
for his family to join him, so soon as he should be fairly
settled. He was waylaid and killed by the "Indians" on
the plains. His body was fearfully mutilated, and left
hanging for the birds of prey. It was very well known,
however, at Salt Lake, that the "Indians" engaged in this
assassination were *white*, and that Williams was murdered
by the express order of the church authorities, who knew
that he would prove a most dangerous enemy.

His fate was a direct contradiction to Brigham's famous
sermon on apostates, preached a few years before. Here
is what he says about "independent apostates."

"When a man comes right out like an independent devil,
and says, 'Damn Mormonism, and all Mormons,' and is off
with himself to California, I say he is a gentleman, by the
side of the nasty, sneaking apostates, who are opposed to
nothing but Christianity. I say to the former, 'Go in
peace.'"

Williams was certainly independent enough, but his independence did not save him.

In this same sermon, which was preached particularly against the "Gladdenites," as the followers of Gladden Bishop were called,—a man who differed from Brigham in certain points of the Mormon belief, and who would not concede that he (Young) was the proper successor of Joseph Smith,—he said,—

"When I went from meeting last Sabbath, my ears were saluted by an apostate preaching in the streets here. I want to know if any one of you who has got the spirit of Mormonism in you, the spirit that Joseph and Hyrum had, or that we have here, would say, 'Let us hear both sides of the question. Let us listen, and prove all things.' What do you want to prove? Do you want to prove that an old apostate, who has been cut off from the church thirteen times for lying, is anything worthy of notice? We want such men to go to California, or anywhere they choose. I say to these persons, 'You must not court persecution here, lest you get so much of it you will not know what to do with it. Do NOT court persecution. We have known Gladden Bishop for more than twenty years, and know him to be a poor, dirty cuss.'

"Now, you Gladdenites, keep your tongues still, lest sudden destruction come upon you. I say, rather than that apostates should flourish here, I will *unsheathe my bowie-knife*, and conquer or die. Now, you nasty apostates, clear out, or judgment will be laid to the line and righteousness to the plummet. If you say it is all right, raise your hands. Let us call upon the Lord to assist us in this and every other good work."

"I will unsheathe my bowie-knife," has been a favorite threat of his, and it has been unsheathed hundreds of times. But some one of his Danite followers is called upon to use it, and when the murders are laid at his door, he stands coolly and boldly up, and his lying tongue says, I did not do these deeds.

For six or seven years, the spirit of slaughter seemed to stalk about in the beautiful Utah valleys, and *human blood was shed* on the slightest provocation. Did one man bear a grudge against another, he died in some mysterious manner, a Mormon court of investigation could never discover how. Was a man obnoxious to any of the church officers, he disappeared, and was never heard of again; or, like John V. Long, a clerk in Brigham's office, who was the only person who heard the conversation between Brigham and the messenger sent from George A. Smith, just before the Mountain Meadow massacre, and who *wrote out the instructions* which the man was to carry back, was found dead in a ditch, "*drowned*" *in three inches of water*, "accidentally," of course, since that was the decision of the Mormon jury. Did a man suspect his wife of infidelity, either she or her suspected lover, or both, fell a victim to his fury. Sometimes the suspicion was without foundation, but would be discovered too late, as in the case of the husband who murdered a Dr. Vaughan in San Pete for supposed intimacy with his wife.

The man was an enthusiastic Mormon; his wife, a lovely woman, whose reputation had always been irreproachable. Dr. Vaughan was a friend of both, until the husband fancied that he was too fond of the wife. He went at once to Salt Lake City, took counsel of the Prophet, returned home, and shot the doctor dead as he was leaving church. He found out afterwards that his suspicion was unfounded, and that he had murdered an innocent man, who had never wronged him, even in thought. He was haunted by remorse until his death. Yet he had only followed the teachings of his religious leader.

Such were the results of the teaching of the Blood-Atonement doctrine in Utah.

19

CHAPTER XVII.

TROUBLES IN OUR OWN FAMILY. — LOUISE COMES UPON THE SCENE.

Increase of Polygamy. — Marrying going on Day and Night. — "Taking a Wife and Buying a Cow." — A Faithful Husband in a Fix. — How Men get "Married on the Sly." — How Wives were Driven Crazy by their Wrongs. — My Father Marries Considerably. — He "Goes in" for the Hand-Cart Girls. — Marries a Couple to Begin with. — Takes a Third the same Month. — Rapid Increase of his "Kingdom." — How the Girls Chose Husbands. — Instructing the New Wives in our Family. — Louise doesn't want to Work. — My Father goes on Mission Again. — Louise Flirts and Rebels. — She is Scolded and Repents. — Goes to Bed and Weeps. — Bestows her Goods on the Family. — "Lizzie" Interviews Her. — She Poisons Herself. — Is a "Long Time Dying." — She gets a Strong Dose of Cayenne. — Is sent on her Travels. — The Last we Heard of Her.

ONLY A WIFE OUT OF THE WAY.

NOTHER immediate effect of the "Reformation" was to increase the practice of polygamy. To alter an old rhyme to suit the occasion, —

"Then were those wed who
    never wed before;
And those who once were wed
    now wed the more."

Marrying and giving in marriage was carried on to such an extent, that, as in the old days of the first "Endowments" in Nauvoo Temple, the ceremony of sealing was literally going on day and night. "The man who refuses to enter polygamy will be eternally damned," announced Brigham Young from the Tabernacle. "Who marries out of the church marries for hell," supplemented Heber C. Kimball. Polygamy was preached from the platform, and taught by the ward-teachers in private. It was not only advised, — it was commanded, and no one dared of disobeying the prophetic mandates.

There was scarcely a family in the Territory at that time which was not increased by a plurality of wives. Men married in the most reckless fashion, with nothing in the world on which to support their families. Girls went to the Endowment House in the morning to take their Endowments, with no idea of marrying, and came away in the afternoon sealed to some brother whose fancy they had taken, or who, being advised by Brigham or Heber to avail himself of his "privileges," had left the matter in apostolic hands, and submitted to everything, even to the choice of a wife.

Wives did not know when their husbands would bring home another woman to share their home and their husband ; for the clause in the "Revelation" that declared that a man should seek his wife's consent to a plural marriage, and that she should herself give the new wife to her husband, "even as Sarah gave Hagar to Abraham," was merely a dead letter, and was not minded in the majority of cases. Indeed, the men many times did not consider it at all necessary to inform the wives of their intentions, and the poor women would know nothing of the new marriage until the husband brought home his latest acquisition, or until she was informed of it by some outsider.

Those were the days when even the most trusting wives lost faith in their husbands ; when solemn, oft-repeated promises were broken, evidently without the slightest qualm of conscience ; when the tender, watchful affection of the husband and father was swallowed up in mad desire of possession of the brute. There were tragedies enacted then that the world never will hear of; women died of broken hearts, and their sad fates brought no pang, or repentance, or remorse to the men who were as much the murderers as though they had deliberately taken their lives with the knife, the bullet, or the poisoned cup.

" Only a wife " out of the way ; and what did that matter? — plenty more were to be had for the asking. " I think no more of taking a wife than I do of buying a cow," was one of Heber Kimball's delicate remarks, made from the stand in the Tabernacle to a congregation of several thousand. Most of his hearers thought even less of it, for they would have had to pay money for the cow; and as for the other, he had only to throw his handkerchief to some girl, and she would pick it up and follow him.

All the finer feelings and sensibilities of man's nature were killed by this horrible system. He regarded women's suffering with utter indifference ; he did not care for their affection ; their tears bored him, and angered rather than touched him. He lost all the respect and chivalrous regard which he once had for the sex, and spoke of his wives as "my women," "my heifers," or, if he, a Heber Kimball, " my cows." He was taught that they were his inferiors, dependent on him for everything, even for their future existence, and he considered that it was sufficient that he gave them his name ; the rest they might get for themselves. He believed that the Mormon Church was to bring about the time " when seven women shall lay hold on one man, begging to be allowed to be called by his name," and should promise to eat their own bread and wear their own apparel. The latter they have been not merely allowed but obliged to do ever since they entered the system, and poor and scanty have been both bread and apparel in the majority of cases. It makes, in short, a brute of what might be a man.

I know a first wife who was driven to such utter despera-

tion by the total neglect of her husband, that she determined
to take her own life, since it had grown such a burden that
it was intolerable to bear.

One night, in the dead of winter, the snow falling thick
and fast, and the wind sweeping down the mountains and
through the cañons, cutting to the very bone, as only a
mountain wind can, she wrapped a tattered shawl about
her, and rushed madly through the night and the snow to
the river, intending to lay down her life and her miseries

LIFE A BURDEN.

together. With a wild prayer for mercy, she was about to
throw herself into the water, when she was restrained by a
strong, imperative hand, and her husband's voice, hissing
angrily in her ear, bade her go home and not make a fool
of herself.

He was on his way home, or, rather, to his first wife's
house, for a change of linen, that he might attend his second
and more favored wife to a party, when he caught sight of
the flying figure, and, suspecting her intentions, followed her
swiftly, and was just in season to prevent her from taking
the fatal step.

He had no word of sympathy for her; on the contrary, he was angered at what he called her obstinacy "and determination to make a fool of herself." Her anguish of heart brought no response of tenderness from him; he made her return home, get the articles of apparel which he wished, and assist him in his preparations for taking her rival out for the evening. In her frenzy, the maternal instinct which is so strong in every woman utterly failed her, and she went away to seek the death she coveted, leaving her little baby wailing piteously in its cradle.

My mother had a friend whose husband had, for a long time, withstood the desires and counsels of the priesthood, and had incurred their marked displeasure by neglecting for so long to "live up to his religion," and "avail himself of his privileges." At the time of the Reformation, however, he did not dare neglect his "duty" any longer, and decided to take a second wife. Neither did he dare tell his first wife of his determination, for he knew how entirely she loved and trusted him, and he knew, too, how bitter an opponent she always had been to polygamy. He knew as well how many times he had assured her that she had nothing to fear; that he would be faithful to her, as he had promised to be in the old days when he married her, and before God had vowed to "cleave to her only until death should them part." And he felt how bitter would be her sorrow, how justly indignant her feelings towards him, how intense her anger, and he did not dare to brave it all; so he stole quietly away to the Endowment House one day, leaving his true and confiding wife ill in her bed, and fresh from her sick room, took the blasphemous vows which claimed to bind him to another woman for time and for eternity.

The first wife knew nothing of what had transpired until she was very delicately told by a kind neighbor, who, knowing that she must find it out sooner or later, thought it her duty to break the news to her as quietly as possible.

She was almost maddened by the intelligence, and at first

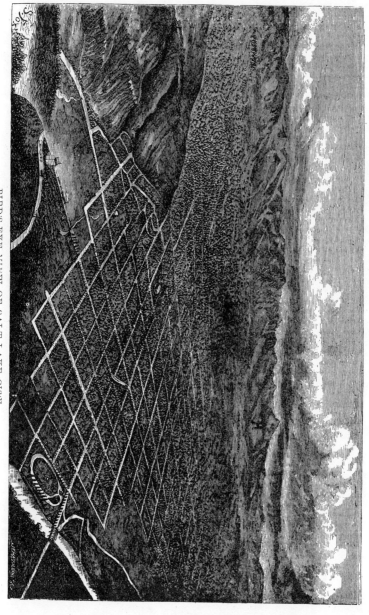

BIRD'S-EYE VIEW OF SALT LAKE CITY

she utterly refused to believe it. It could not be possible that the husband of her youth, the man whom she had so loved and trusted, would betray her thus; would take advantage of her illness to skulk away and take another wife, and that, too, after all his repeated promises to her.

"It can't be true," she cried, wringing her hands, and growing deadly pale. "It *isn't* true! I can't believe it. I won't believe it. O my God, help me if it is true. Tell me that it isn't; that you are mistaken."

But no such assurance could be given her, and her friend tried in the gentlest manner to comfort her; but what consolation could she bring that would heal a shattered faith or bind up a broken heart?

This story has had many, many repetitions since then, until now it has got to be "an old, old story often told."

It was all very well for this man to take this step as a religious duty, if he had been sincere. But would he, or would any true man who believed fully that he was obeying the revealed law of God, and doing what he did for conscience' sake, be afraid to meet any opposition, from whatever quarter it might come? Is not this very lack of courage a tacit acknowledgment that he does not believe in its divinity at all, and that conscience stings, rather than approves him for his cowardly act?

Another wife, whose husband had promised her as faithfully that he would not take another wife, did take one in the same way, and under precisely the same circumstances. On hearing the news she became a raving maniac, and died in the insane hospital. Still another, who was as bitter an opponent of the system of "Celestial Marriage" as either of the other two, was one day invited by her husband to go for a drive. Touched by this unusual act of kindness, — for he had been anything but kind to her, since he could not obtain her consent to his taking another wife, — she quickly made herself ready, and went with him. He drove her to the insane asylum, and left her, and she is still an inmate of the place, although she is as sane as I am at this moment.

I could cite hundreds of such cases that occurred during the first years that directly followed the Reformation, and that have multiplied since, until the recital of them would fill a large volume; but I will, instead, tell a little what the "Reformation," and the subsequent "Celestial Ordinance" fever, did for our own family.

It added several more to our circle in a very short time. My father was counselled, as were most of the Mormon men, to take some of the "Hand-Cart girls," as they must be provided for some way. My mother had already had her burden given her; and after she had been obliged to see another woman taking the love and care that by right belonged to her, and her alone, she grew indifferent on the subject, and declared that a few wives, more or less, would make little difference to her now, and she would be as well satisfied with one fourth of a husband as with one half. That is generally the way first wives argue; if there is to be a plurality of wives, it may as well be half a dozen as one. The hurt comes with the first plural wife; no suffering can ever exceed the pain she feels then.

The second wife was made ill, however, by the new arrangement; it was the first time she had felt the hurt of being superseded; but she bore it very patiently, and made no complaint. After she recovered from her illness, she joined my mother in her efforts to make friends with the other wives, for two had already been added to the family, and placed under the same roof with us.

The Hand-Cart girls, not being disposed of rapidly enough to satisfy the authorities, they urged them to make proposals to the brethren, which, by the way, they were not at all backward in doing. One young lady selected "our" husband, to use my mother's expression; and to quote from her description, "as it was done in obedience to counsel, we extended our arms to receive her, the third one that we had welcomed within the month. Our 'kingdom' was increasing, but each individual share of husband was growing 'small by degrees and beautifully less.'"

This last acquisition proved to be anything but an agreeable one, and she made plenty of trouble for us all. When she offered herself to my father, after having been counselled by the authorities to do so, he received her proposition somewhat coolly and cautiously, for, to tell the truth, he would much have preferred to make his own selection, and Louise (for that was her name) would, most emphatically, have not been his choice. Yet he would have been openly ridiculed, and held up to derision in the Tabernacle, had he ventured to refuse; so there was nothing to do but to take her, and make the best of it.

THE NEW ADDITION.

He had been so long absent that his affairs were by no means in a flourishing condition, and he needed all the assistance he could obtain from his wives. My mother and Elizabeth were both hard-working women, and as hard as they had labored during their husband's absence, they did not relax their exertions in the slightest now that he had returned. My mother took the young wives at once under her protection, and commenced teaching them to be useful. The two first ones proved very nice girls, and worked with a will, showing a great readiness and aptitude at learning, and a genuine desire to do their part.

But the "free-will offering," as Elizabeth and mother always called Louise, did not love work, and she would not do it. She said she was a milliner, and had once been an actress, and declined "to soil her hands with menial labor." That was her speech in refusing to assist about the household work.

There was some little friction in the running of the household machinery on account of this; but Mormon women are expected to exercise patience, and there was very little fault found audibly, although it was quite apparent that the new wife was unhappy, and that all the rest were disgusted with her selfishness and indolence, which amounted to laziness.

My father was appointed to another mission in the States, directly after he was married to Louise, and he left his entire family living all together on a farm about seventy miles west of Salt Lake City.

During his absence Louise made herself disagreeable in every possible way. It actually seemed as though she had made up her mind to annoy us all as much as possible, and that she tried every expedient she could devise to accomplish her intentions.

My mother was particularly annoyed by her familiarity with the men employed on the farm, and remonstrated with her on her undignified behavior. She was very impertinent, although mother had spoken to her in the kindest possible way, and informed her that she should do as she pleased; that she was my father's wife, and her rights in the house were equal to any other person's.

Fortunately, my father remained away but a short time,

and on his return he was speedily made acquainted with the state of affairs. He disapproved of her conduct quite as much as my mother had done, and treated her with such a marked coolness that she demanded the cause. He told her that he was greatly displeased with her, annoyed particularly at her lack of respect for herself, him, or his family, and that he did not feel at all like acknowledging her as his wife unless she would most decidedly behave in a more becoming and dignified manner.

She was very penitent, and promised all sorts of things if he would only allow her to remain in his family; she went about the house the very personification of grief and humility, until my father was called by church business to Salt Lake City. No sooner was he fairly started than she determined to create a sensation in the family.

She shut herself up in her room, after announcing that she wished to be left quiet and not intruded upon by any one. However, one of the younger wives entered her room on some pretext or other, and found Louise in bed.

" Are you ill? " she inquired.

"O, no ; only heart-broken !" was the reply, in the most doleful tone which she could possibly assume, and a great display of grief in the shape of a pocket-handkerchief which she applied to her eyes, then flourished in the air, and then returned to her eyes. After some more conversation, Eliza came out with a pair of valuable ear-rings in her hand. Mother asked her where she got them.

"Louise gave them to me," was the reply.

"Isn't that a sudden freak of generosity? " inquired my mother.

"She says she shall never want them any more, and she cried when she said it," was the answer.

Louise had always seemed to like Eliza better than she did any of the other wives, and my mother at once fancied that there was some trickery going on, and that Louise was trying to win Eliza over to her. I was a little curious my-

self, as girls of thirteen are very apt to be when anything
unusual is going on in the family which they do not fully
understand; so I determined to visit Louise myself, and see
what was the matter with her.

She was very pathetic in her conversation with me, and
made me quite miserable by the recital of her wrongs.
Somehow I felt as though I was personally to blame for all
her misery, and yet I didn't see how that could be. She
gave me her watch and chain, which I had always admired
and coveted, and told me she had done for ever with such
gewgaws. I was so delighted with the jewelry that I quite
neglected to be properly sympathetic, and rushed off to show
my gift to my mother, and tell her what Louise said.

She began to be a little startled by this new development
of affairs, and asked Lizzie, the third wife, to go up to her.
Lizzie was not a great favorite with Louise, and my mother
did not anticipate that she would receive such fine presents,
to say the least. She came back, saying that Louise said
she was going to die, and then she wished her wardrobe
divided among the family. She also wished that my mother
would come to her. She at first felt inclined to refuse, but
upon consideration, and being urged by the different members of the family, she went, and found her groaning with
pain, real or pretended. She couldn't tell which then.

"What is the trouble?" she asked.

"O," said Louise, with a groan, "I am dying. I shall
never cause any more trouble in your family."

"It is not right for you to talk in that manner," replied my
mother; "if you are ill, I will do all I can to relieve you."

"I don't want anything done; I only want to die: my
husband does not love me, and I cannot live; all I desire is
death," wailed the woman.

"It is not always so easy to die when we desire," was my
mother's somewhat crisp reply, as she was a little annoyed
by what she considered Louise's "foolishness."

"But I have made sure," answered she; "I have taken
poison."

"You surely cannot be so wicked as that," was mother's surprised reply. "You are certainly telling me a falsehood." Louise called on all heaven to witness the truth of what she had said, and made so many solemn asseverations to the truth of her having poisoned herself, that my mother began to fear that she had really done so, and that the affair was much more serious than she had supposed, for she had really no idea that Louise would do so desperate a thing as that, for she seemed altogether too fond of the good things of this life to relinquish them voluntarily. We had all considered before this that Louise was giving us a taste of her dramatic powers, and that it was a piece of very poor acting, after all. But if she really had taken her life into her own hands, determined to throw it away so recklessly, she must be looked after at once.

So everything that could be thought of as an antidote to poison was given to her; she all the time groaning and screaming with pain. There was no physician within thirty miles, and our nearest neighbor lived five miles away. My brother was summoned from the hay-field, where he was at work, and sent for our father. There was not a horse to be had, as it happened, and my brother started on foot to try and overtake father, who had set out on horseback some hours before. He would necessarily travel very slowly, however, as he was driving cattle. The boy had to climb high mountains, and consequently made but slow progress; yet, on descending, he ran as fast as possible, and succeeded in overtaking his father when about fifteen miles from home. He was perfectly exhausted by his efforts, and fell fainting at his father's feet, after he had managed to gasp out, "Father, Louise has poisoned herself!"

It was some time before he recovered sufficiently to tell the whole story, which my father instantly pronounced a hoax. "However," he said, "I will go back and settle the difficulty."

During all the time that elapsed between my brother's

departure and his return with his father, Louise was continuing the tragedy in a way that was calculated to frighten the whole family. She reached out her hand and bade us all farewell, at the same time exhorting us to greater piety. She said it had been her desire to do right, but she knew she had failed in her most earnest endeavors; this she regretted, as she was now nearing her end, and had no means of rectifying her past wrong-doing. Yet she wished to die in peace with all, and she forgave the wrongs she had received at the hands of some members of the family.

After talking on in this strain for some time, until, indeed, she had exhausted the topic and could find no more to say, she tried her hand at acting a kind of stupor; from which she soon aroused, however, and recommenced her exhortation, and ended by informing my mother that she had never understood her, and had never sufficiently appreciated her, and that she would rather die than be the cause of contention.

My mother at last was beginning to understand her most thoroughly now; and losing all patience with her, and feeling very indignant at her shallow attempt at deception, which was beginning to be very patent to us all, said, —

"It seems to me you are a long time dying, Louise; I feel quite satisfied that you are deceiving us all, and as I do not care to be duped any longer, we'll call the farce ended — for you can't make a tragedy of it, try hard as you may."

"It is your fault that I am not dead," Louise answered, her eyes flashing suddenly, and a great deal of the old-fashioned spirit in her will; "if you hadn't administered an antidote, against my will, I should be dead now."

We none of us could restrain a smile at her mention of the "antidote," for salt and water, salt and vinegar, and mustard and water, were the only medicines we had given her. With these very simple remedies, — none of which had the slightest effect on the patient, — my mother's "medicine box" was exhausted, and there was nothing else which she could do, except to abandon the case, which she did.

Her friends, the hired men, came in at night anxiously
inquiring after Louise.   We were all totally undeceived by
that time, and one of the wives replied to their questions,
that they need have no fears about her, as she no doubt
would outlive all the rest of the family; and they had all
decided to "leave her for Mr. Webb to deal with."   The
men thought this very heartless, and said they had feared
they should find her dead.

My mother, who had overheard the last remark, replied,
rather sharply, that nothing would kill her unless it was
the mixture she had administered, for she was positive that
she had taken no poison.   Her object had been to frighten
the family, and she had succeeded admirably.   She had
turned the house topsy-turvy, and sent Edward off on a
wild-goose chase, and we were all getting quite angry.

About nine o'clock in the evening my father returned.
My mother met him at the door.

"There's nobody dead!" was her greeting.

"I didn't expect there was," he replied, passing her and
entering Louise's room.

"What are you in bed for?" was his inquiry.

At first she declined to reply to him, but on his repeating
the question, and insisting on an answer, she told the same
story that she had told to the rest of us.   He was as sceptical regarding the truth of it as the rest of us had been,
but said that he would suggest the free use of cayenne pepper, and asked my mother to make her some tea of it.   I am
afraid there was a little malice in her heart, as she asked if
she might make it as strong as she liked.

"Yes," he replied; "give her a strong dose.   She shall
have enough to make her sick of her nonsense."

There was no further assurance needed, and I fancy
there never was a stronger decoction mixed than the one
my mother prepared for the impostor.   At first Louise declared she would not take it; but my father insisted upon
it, telling her that he knew nothing better for people who

had poisoned themselves, and she was compelled to swallow the whole of it.

There was no need, after that, for her to pretend illness, for she was sick enough for one hour to thoroughly frighten her, and to satisfy the rest of the family, who felt that she deserved just the punishment she was getting for the deception she had practiced, and the fright she had caused, which was genuine for a while.

My mother was specially angry because my brother was made very ill by his long run after his father, and he came very near losing his life in consequence. After Louise had recovered somewhat from the paroxysms of pain into which she had been thrown by the cayenne pepper, my father had a serious talk with her, and told her that she must no longer consider herself a member of his family. Her conduct had been such that she had forfeited all right to consideration, and he would not have such a woman as she had proved herself to be in the house with his wives and his young daughter; so she must go away and find a home for herself elsewhere.

She had not expected this, and she suddenly changed her tactics, and begged to be allowed to remain in the family in any capacity whatever. She confessed that she had been trying to frighten us all, and that she had taken no poison, but had got up the scene in order to create sympathy for herself. She professed great sorrow at her actions, and again pleaded to be allowed to remain.

But my father was inexorable; and, in spite of tears, entreaties, and protestations, she was taken to Salt Lake City, and we none of us ever saw her again, although we heard of her several times. She married again in a very short time, and in three weeks was divorced from her second husband, to whom she had been sealed "for time and eternity." After leaving this husband of three weeks, she went to the southern part of the Territory, and married another man, whom she persuaded to take her to St. Louis.

While there she suddenly went away one day, taking her husband's money and leaving him behind. When next heard from, she was on her way to England. Her last husband made no attempt to follow her, but returned to Utah without either money or wife, yet entirely reconciled to the loss of one, since it had been the means of ridding him of the other.

A SCENE IN POLYGAMY—"GREETING THE FAVORITE."

Louise was the only one of all my father's wives who ever made the least trouble. The rest of them were good women, doing their best to make things pleasant. They did not like a polygamous life, and only endured it because they thought they must. They were not happy women, — no women in polygamy are happy, however loudly they may claim to be, — and they made no pretence of being. Neither did they quarrel with each other, or complain of one another to their husband. Whatever difficulties they might have they settled among themselves, and did not trouble any outsiders. In fact, in my father's family the best side of a polygamous life was shown, but the best side was by no means a bright one.

This episode of Louise shows the absurdity of marrying without previous acquaintance, and also the miseries that may be endured by other wives when there is one bad woman in their midst.

20

CHAPTER XVIII.

INCREASE OF POLYGAMY. — MIXED-UP CONDITION OF MATRIMONIAL AFFAIRS.

Christ alleged to be a Polygamist. — The Men to save the Women. — Making "Tabernacles" for little Spirits. — The Story of certain Ladies who were Deceived. — They Discover a Mystery. — Their Fate. — Orson Hyde's False Prophecy. — Throwing Mud at Apostates. — Death preferred to Polygamy. — Frightful Intermarriages. — Married his Mother-in-law. — A Man who Married his Wife's Grandmother, Mother, and All. — Marrying a Half-Sister. — Marrying Nieces and Sisters. — How Emigrant Girls were Married Off. — Frightful Story of a Poor Young Girl. — Polygamy and Madness. — One Woman's Love too Little. — How English Girls were Deceived. — How Claude Spenser committed a Damnable Wrong. — A Girl who was Martyred for her Religion. — How the Bereaved Husband Acted. — A Man with thirty-three Children. — "They never cost him a Cent." — A Many-Wived Saint. — Mixed-up Condition of Marital Affairs.

THE "Reformation" was productive of nothing but evil. The most revolting and blasphemous doctrines were taught, and between Blood-Atonement, Massacres of the Gentiles, and the worst phases of Polygamous Marriage, there was nothing good in the Territory. The whole system of Mormon religion was a mass of revolting crime and wickedness. Bigotry was at flood-tide, and fanaticism ruled reason. The very thought of it brings a shudder. The most horrible things were taught from the pulpit, and decency was outraged every time a Mormon leader opened his mouth to speak.

They were all maniacs on the subject of Celestial Marriage, and the lengths to which they carried their advocacy of it did not stop with mere absurdities; it became the most fearful profanity. There was not a pure character in all the Bible history which their dirty hands did not besmear, and their foul tongues blacken. Not content with bringing up "Abraham, and Isaac, and Jacob," and David and Solomon, as their examples in the practice of polygamy, Brigham Young, in one of his sermons, delivered during the intensest heat of the excitement, declared that "Jesus Christ was a practical polygamist; Mary and Martha, the sisters of Lazarus, were his plural wives, and Mary Magdalen was another. Also, the bridal feast at Cana of Galilee, where Jesus turned the water into wine, was on the occasion of one of his own marriages.

They appealed to women through their maternal as well as through their religious natures. Not only did they teach them that they could never be saved except by the intervention of some man, who should take upon himself the duty of resurrecting them at the last day, but they were also told that floating through space were thousands of infant spirits, who were waiting for bodies; that into every child that was born one of these spirits entered, and was thereby saved; but if they had no bodies given them, their wails of despair would ring through all eternity; and that it was, in order to insure their future happiness, necessary that as many of them as possible should be given bodies by Mormon parents. If a woman refused to marry into polygamy, or, being married, to allow her husband to take other wives, these spirits would rise up in judgment against her, because she had, by her act, kept them in darkness.

No one dared to neglect the counsel of the priesthood. Whoever ventured to do so was charged at once with apostasy. Men and women alike were ruled by the arbitrary will of one man. There is no despotic monarchy in the world where the word of the sovereign is so absolute as in Utah. And never, in the whole history of Mormonism, has the despotic rule been so arbitrary as it was during the period of, and for a short time after, the Reformation. It was a terribly trying time for women — a time that they have never forgotten. More misery was crowded into a few months than they had endured before in a lifetime, and the misery that began then will be life-long. No one outside of Utah and Mormonism can understand it in the least, because nowhere else is there a possibility of such wretchedness to exist. Only women living in a polygamous community, under the rule of a religion whose fundamental principle is the plural-wife system, can fully take in the utter helplessness and hopelessness of the situation — a situation from which escape, at that time at least, was next to impossible.

If they did escape, the tongue of calumny pursued them relentlessly, and the vilest reports that the tongues and hearts of vile men could devise were spread concerning them.

In 1856, during the Reformation, and when converts were pouring into Zion almost from every quarter of the earth, were several lovely and refined ladies, who had been drawn thither by the seeming earnestness and deep religious fervor of the Mormon people whom they had seen. Especial pains had been taken to bring these ladies into the church, for they were a much finer type of women than are generally found among the later converts, and nothing was ever told them of the existence of the plurality system. Among the converts were a Miss Potter, Mrs. Brownhead and three daughters, and Miss Stayner, who were filled with enthusiasm concerning their new faith, and came to Zion most zealous Saints.

But when, on their arrival, they discovered that polygamy was in open practice, they were distressed beyond measure, and sought immediate refuge in the military camp. They were women, all of them, of fine social standing, and had left happy and luxurious homes to come to Zion, impelled by a sense of religious duty. The beastly god which the Mormons so devoutly worshipped had never been even alluded to in their presence.

As a matter of course, their flight enkindled Mormon wrath, and for a while it burned fiercely. They heaped every term of opprobrium upon them that they could think of, and defamed them in every possible way. There was nothing too gross or too indecent for them to say concerning them; and in addition to this wholesale defamation of their characters, they were properly cursed, according to the Mormon liturgy, and all manner of evil was prophesied concerning them. Orson Hyde was inspired one Sunday, in the Tabernacle, to foretell their fate, and he prophesied that they would perish miserably on the way to California, where they had gone under the protection of Colonel Steptoe and his command. It was, no doubt, a great disappointment to the Apostle that, in spite of his prophecies, they arrived safely in California, were married to men of wealth and position, and are now happy wives and mothers, with no thought of Mormondom to mar their happiness, except an occasional burst of thankful feeling that they succeeded in escaping from it. It may be a satisfaction for my readers to know — it is certainly for me to tell — that he not only proved a false prophet, but was publicly punished by one of the officers for the scandalous reports he had put in circulation regarding these ladies.

Calumny and scandal are among the readiest of the Mormon weapons, and its leaders are specially skilled in their use, as every person who has ever thwarted Brigham Young, or one of his satellites, knows to his or her sorrow. They not only lie themselves, but they hire others to do it for them. Occasionally, in this game of mud-throwing, they get bespattered, but not until they have bedaubed their víctim very thoroughly. It is no wonder that suicides have been so common among the Mormon women : if they left "Zion," it must be at the sacrifice either of life or reputation, and in the hopeless apathetic state into which they were sunk, it was easier to die than to struggle.

One woman, who arrived from England during the "Reformation," and who was to be rushed into polygamy, actually killed herself rather than become a plural wife : she had been given to a Mr. Goodsall, and was living in his family, awaiting the time when she was to be sealed; and one morning, but a few days before the time appointed for the ceremony, she was found with her throat cut, a razor lying by her side. She saw nothing but wretchedness before her, and put an end to her life rather than follow priestly "counsels." It was better so than to face the misery life would bring.

Even the laws of consanguinity were not respected at that terrible time, and relatives intermarried in a manner that would shock even the most lax-moralled community. Uncles and nieces were married ; one man would marry several sisters ; and it was a very common thing for a mother and daughter to have the same husband. In one family, at least three generations were represented among the wives — grandmother, mother, and daughter; and a case actually occurred in Salt Lake City where a man married his half sister, and that, too, with the full knowledge and approval of Brigham Young The man stood high in the Mormon Church, and George D. Watt was quoted all through the Territory as a good Saint. He certainly availed himself of his privileges to the fullest extent. He has since apostatized.

Bishop Smith, of Brigham City, married two of his own nieces. Bishop Johnson, of Springville, outdid his brother bishop, and married six. The first one was the daughter of an elder brother ; the other five were sisters, and daughters of Lorenzo Johnson. He first married the eldest one,

Mary, who was only fifteen at the time; then he asked that all the others might be given to him, to be sealed to him when they should grow up. The youngest one was only two years old at the time that her father promised her to her uncle, and she was only about thirteen when she was sealed to him.

All this is sanctioned by the President; else, of course, it would not occur; and he does not hesitate to say that he sees no reason why persons who are nearly related should not marry; they certainly ought to think more of each other than of strangers; and all that he can see that stands in the way of such marriages being of very frequent occurrence is popular prejudice. He has said that he, as far as he is personally concerned, would not enter upon such a relationship, but prejudice alone, and not principle, would restrain him.

There are very many families where two or more sisters are plural wives to one man. This is the case in Brigham's own family. Among his first plural wives were Clara Decker and Lucy Decker; and two of his daughters, Luna and Fanny, are the wives of George Thatcher; two, Mary and Caroline, were married to Mark Croxall, and two, Alice and Emily, to Hiram Clawson.

Among the early emigrants were two Scotch girls, sisters, named McDonald. They had been but a few days in Salt Lake City, when a Mr. Uriah Brower, a would-be patriarch, presented himself before them with an offer of marriage. One of the girls favored the suit, but the other was more capricious, and not so easily suited with the prospect of a polygamous life. She hated the man for proposing marriage, herself for being an object of his patriarchal passion, and was annoyed at her sister for her willingness to accept him. She had yet to learn that women are by no means free agents in Utah, and have very little voice in the settlement of their own affairs; their destinies are in their own hands, but are entirely at the mercy of

some man's caprice, or the commands of the priesthood.

Her lover was determined; and seeing that it was absolutely of no use for her to go on saying "No," since she
must succumb, sooner or later, she gave an indifferent consent, and was sealed to him at the same time with her
sister. She was miserably unhappy, and the very next day
she applied for a divorce from him, saying she could not,
and would not, remain his wife. She obtained the divorce;
but, having no parents and no home, she was forced to live
wherever she could, and she found existence anything but
an easy or pleasant task. In a short time another good
brother, seeking to enlarge his kingdom, offered to take
her; and she, poor girl! not knowing what else to do, and
almost desperate in her loneliness and desolation, consented
to marry a second time in polygamy.

Her new husband already had three wives, and she was
placed in the same house with them. Her situation then was
worse than even before. Being the last comer, all the rest
turned against her, and she had to endure the hatred of
them all. She was ill-treated in every way, but for a long
time bore all the wrongs which were inflicted upon her in
silence. After the birth of her child, she determined to
leave at all hazards; so again applying for a divorce from
her second husband, which was as easily obtained as her
first one had been, she took her child and went away to
earn a living for herself and him. She went out to service; she did washing and cleaning; indeed, she left no
stone unturned to obtain an honest livelihood, and bring up
her child properly.

After a time her first husband presented himself, and told
her that as he had married her "for time and for eternity,"
he should hold her to the first marriage contract; that he
could do so, since her second husband was no higher in
the priesthood than he. He insisted on her returning to
him; and the poor woman, seeing no way of escape, was

sealed again to him, and was taken to his home, a miserable, comfortless place, where he had five wives already
living in poverty and the most terrible degradation. Huddled together like so many animals, they respected neither
the laws of decency nor morality. Hannah was there but
a short time before she became hopelessly insane. She is
living still, but the light of reason has gone out for ever,
quenched by the horrors of a system which she always

THE HAPPY HOME OF A POLYGAMIST.

loathed. Her sister, Margaret, still drags on a miserable,
hopeless existence, not much better off than the poor, unfortunate maniac. She is a moral and physical wreck, and
owes her depraved condition to the cause that made her
sister a mental ruin.

Life opened brightly enough for these girls in their home
among the Scottish hills, but the curse of Mormonism
found them out, and then there was nothing but wretchedness and despair for them.

Incidents like these have multiplied from the beginning

until now; and yet, in the face of all this misery, the world is assured that Mormon women are comfortable and content; that they find no fault with polygamy; indeed, that they prefer the system rather than dislike it; and the world, against all reason and common sense, believes what it is told.

Elder Orson Spencer, now dead, one of the strong pillars of Mormonism, whose letters and theological works are much quoted among the Saints, while on his first mission to England became the guest of a gentleman of considerable property and good social position, and the father of two interesting daughters, both of whom were recent converts to the Mormon faith. The young ladies were finely educated, possessed of more than ordinary talents, and had always been tenderly attached to each other.

When the young missionary from Zion became an inmate of their father's house, they, with all the zeal of new and enthusiastic converts, vied with each other in showing him every hospitable attention, for the sake of the glorious gospel which they supposed he came to preach, and before very long the elder of the sisters found herself becoming deeply interested in him for his own sake.

The interest was apparently mutual; it ripened into love. Mr. Spencer made a formal proposal to the father for the daughter's hand, and very soon after the lovers were married. The young wife was perfectly happy; she was devoted to her husband, and it seemed to her that life could hereafter hold nothing but happiness for her, she rested so securely in her husband's love, that his care would compass her about, and his strength sustain her, all through her days. She was living her first romance, and sweet enough she found it. Ah, if the hard reality had not been so soon to follow it! But Mormon marriage soon kills all the romance of a woman's nature, and either kills her at the same time, or leaves her hopeless, apathetic, her finer nature crushed within her, bearing life because she must, and not because it holds anything for her of love, or care, or sweet tenderness of any kind. It is oftener this way than the other; alas, for the poor victims that such is the case!

Mr. Spencer had lived among a people who teach and practice the doctrine of a plurality of wives. His own father had brought home eight brides to grace his domestic circle, four of them in one day. The high-priest of his religion, the man to whom he had always listened as the mouthpiece of God, not only preached that it was the privilege and duty of every Saint to wed many wives, but practiced what he preached.

No wonder, then, that the disciple believed he should be living beneath his privileges if he contented himself with the love of one woman. His sister-in-law was a remarkably pretty girl, and fervent in her devotion to the new faith she had espoused. In time, perhaps, if caution was exercised in the manner of teaching, she might be won to a cordial belief in the doctrine of plural marriage — a doctrine which the missionary Saints, with damnable wisdom, had not proclaimed openly in England at that date.

This young brother, imitating the prudent course of his colleagues, preached only those truths which he thought would be received most readily. Such portions of the gospel as might be considered hard doctrine by the new converts he left to be learned by them after their arrival in Zion. His growing admiration for his charming sister-in-law he kept to himself; but when the time arrived for his return home with his wife, he had succeeded in making arrangements for her sister to accompany them. In the mean time, however, another young lady, also a new convert, had attracted his favorable notice, and as she was to form one of a large company who were about to start for America, he kindly, and disinterestedly, of course, offered to take her under his own care.

During the voyage across the ocean, and the hurried journey through the States, nothing worthy of note occurred. True, Mr. Spencer was very attentive to the young ladies who were travelling under his protection; but his young wife loved him too well, and believed in him too implicitly, to have any thought that he was actuated by other motives than brotherly affection and Christian kindness. At the Missouri River, where the emigrants took leave of civilization, and commenced their long journey over the plains, the members of the little party were thrown more closely together than before ; and now even the all-confiding wife could not fail to see that her husband demeaned himself as a lover towards the two girls, — her sister and her friend, — and that they by no means discouraged his attentions.

Her reproachful questioning regarding his conduct brought out an explanation of the doctrines of plurality, and an avowal of his intention to marry the girls as soon as they reached Salt Lake. He said that they had both embraced the great truths of their religion fully, and were willing and anxious to be sealed to him as their savior for time and eternity. The poor wife, with all her faith in her husband, her sister, and her religion, shattered at one blow, — but, alas for her, with a heart throbbing with a love that could not die, — never rallied from the shock she received when her doom was thus pronounced by the lips of the one dearest to her.

Day after day, as they continued their toilsome journey, her strength declined, and it was evident, even to the eyes of strangers, that she was dying. Her husband, however, saw nothing, was troubled with no anxieties. He was too much absorbed in his love for the two girls, whose souls he proposed to save, to have any time or thought to spare for his dying wife. The days lengthened into weeks, and still the lamp of life burned lower, while the love that had outlived faith and hope was yet strong enough to torture her with vain longings to hear again the tender words that were never spoken now, and to lean, in her mortal weakness, on the arm that she, so short a time ago, had fondly hoped would be her support, even down to the brink of death. It is easy to say of love unworthily bestowed, —

> " I would pluck it from my bosom,
> Though my heart were at the root; "

but many a wronged and forsaken wife could tell you that these are only idle words.

BROKEN-HEARTED.

Many may wonder if the dying girl's sister had no compunction, no remorse for the part she was playing in this tragedy. None; for so completely was she carried away by the fanaticism with which she had been inspired, that she actually believed she was doing God service in trampling on the holiest feelings of her own nature, and inflicting upon her sister the most cruel wrong that one woman can suffer at the hands of another.

The weary journey was ended at length, and the wanderers reached the Valley which was henceforth to be their home. The wife lived only just to enter the city, of which she once fondly dreamed as a heaven upon earth. From the Zion of her earthly hopes she passed on to the true Zion, where the mercy and love of a God kinder than the one she had been taught to worship healed every earth-wound, and brought infinite peace to the broken heart. Just two weeks from the day of her death there was a double bridal in Salt Lake City. The bereaved and sorrowing husband was united in marriage to the equally afflicted sister and her friend, the young lady who accompanied them from England. I have often wondered if there was a ghost present at that bridal, and if the white, dead face of the wronged and murdered wife did not look in sad reproach at them all as they took upon themselves the vows that bound them together, not only for time, but for eternity.

In a party from England which followed this other company very shortly, was a family named Right, who had, among other children, two lovely daughters. Such girls as they — bright, refined, and pleasing in manner and disposition — could not remain long without lovers in a place where marriageable men were so plentiful as in the Mormon Zion. They were very intimate with Brigham Young's family, and it was not long before the elder became the plural wife of David Candland, a prominent Mormon elder, and a confidential friend of the Prophet. He had had many wives, but only two were living at the time of his marriage with Miss Right. He had thirty-three children, who, he boasted, had never cost him a cent, and the pretty young wife was installed as " mother " over his not very promising brood. He was, as he was pleased to term himself, an " aristocrat," and would not descend to the performance of menial labor ; but, as the family must live somehow, the wives have to get along as best they can, but they live in the depths of poverty and degradation, while he enjoys prophetic favor, stands high in the church, and is a Beau Brummel in dress. He has recently commenced the study of law, probably at the Prophet's instigation.

The other sister became the fourth wife of Mr. Charles Bassett, at that time a prominent merchant in Salt Lake. The third wife was cast aside to make room for her, and for some time she was the favored one, indulged in every whim, and petted and flattered until her head was nearly turned. But, as has happened with other favorite wives, her reign was short, and she was compelled to stand on one side and see another take her place. Mr. Bassett, when he tired of his fourth victim, married his niece and adopted daughter — a mere girl, only fourteen years old. She is the present favorite, and everything that she can possibly desire is lavished upon her — nothing is too fine or too expensive for her; and, in the mean time, the woman whose place she took — and who was herself the usurper of another woman's kingdom — goes out to work to support herself and her children. Her eldest daughter — a girl just in her teens, not much older than her father's new wife — has been compelled to go out to service.

This is the fate (and not an uncommon one) of two young girls who supposed they were marrying two of the best men in the "kingdom." These men were popular preachers, as regular as the Pharisee in attending to all their religious duties, and loud and earnest in their defence of the glorious institution of polygamy, which "institution" they so brightly adorn.

CHAPTER XIX.

THE MYSTERIES OF POLYGAMY.—WHAT THE WIVES COULD TELL.

Incestuous Intermarriages.—A Widow and her Daughters married to the same Man.—"Marrying my Pa."—The "U. S." Government Conniving at Mormon Iniquities.—Beastly Conduct of Delegate George Q. Cannon.—Polygamists Legislating for Bigamists.—Mother and Daughter fighting for the same Man!—It is Wicked to Live with an Old Wife.—A *Young* lover Ninety Years Old!—A Bride *Eleven* years Old!—Brides of Thirteen and Fourteen Years!—I receive an "Offer" when Twelve Years Old!—Old Ladies at a Discount: Young Women at a Premium.—Respect for the Silver Crown of Age.—Heber gives his Opinion.—"Why is She making such a Fuss?"—Seeing One's Husband Once a Year.—The Rascality of Orson Hyde towards his Wife.—When Rival Wives make Friends.—A Very Funny Story about an Apostle and his Wife.—Rights of the First Wife: Brigham Young in a Fix.—He treats an Early Wife to a Dance.—Amelia in the Shade.—The Prophet becomes Frisky.—Poor, neglected Emmeline. —How Polygamy was once Denied.—A Mistake which a French Lady Made.—Milk for Babes.

ORSON HYDE AND FORGOTTEN WIFE.

HE marriage of mother and daughter to one man was of so common an occurrence that it ceased to be regarded as anything out of the ordinary course of events.

I had some schoolmates, two sisters, whose mother was married to a Mr. McDonald, and when she gave herself to him, it was with the express understanding that the daughters should be sealed to him as soon as they were of a proper age. The little girls knew of the arrangement, and used to talk very openly of "marrying Pa," and in very much the same way they would speak of their intention to take tea with a friend.

That mother must have taken a great deal of comfort with her children! Fancy her feelings; knowing that she was bringing up her daughters as wives for her own husband!

Wives and mothers, living outside of polygamy, can anything be more revolting to your ideas of womanly purity, more thoroughly opposed to all the sweet tenderness of the maternal instinct, than cases like this? And yet, horror-stricken as you are by them, they are by no means exceptional, but are of frequent occurrence. And it is in your own country that these outrages against all womanhood occur, under your own government, upheld by your own chosen legislators — tacitly, at least — since in this time, as in the days of Christ's actual presence on earth, those who are not for are against. And if your government and its rulers refuse to do, or even fail to do without refusing, anything to eradicate this foul blot upon national purity and honor, why, they are in so far encouraging its presence, and rendering it daily more difficult of eradication.

For the tide of evil that set so strongly in those terrible days of 1856 has never been stayed. It still rolls on with all the added filth and abomination which it has gathered in its course, until it is one reeking mass of the foulest impurities.

Incest, murder, suicide, mania and bestiality are the chief "beauties" of this infamous system, which are so glowingly alluded to by its eloquent expounders and defenders.

And George Q. Cannon, one of its ablest apostles, — himself a practical polygamist, being the husband of four living wives, three of whom he grossly neglects, — goes to Washington from Utah as Congressional Delegate from that Territory, and helps to make the laws which send George Smith, of Massachusetts, to State Prison for three years for the crime of having two wives! Is it that bigamy is a punishable offence, and polygamy is not? If so, George Smith

21

has only to take two more wives and he can, perhaps, enjoy
the confidence of the government and the protection of its
laws as fully as the Apostolic George Q.

APOSTLE GEORGE Q. CANNON,
MEMBER OF CONGRESS.
[Has four wives and thirteen children.]

If the gentleman in Memphis, Tennessee, who has
recently been indicted for
marrying his deceased wife's
niece had only married six
of his own nieces, he might
now be enjoying his liberty
and his youthful brides' society, with all the freedom
which is accorded to Bishop
Johnson, of Utah — that is,
if he, too, had lived among
the Saints in Utah.

The relation between
mother and daughter, when
one becomes the rival of the other, is by no means the
pleasantest in the world, and it is usually the case that the
mother has much the worse time. She sees herself neglected for a younger and fairer woman by the man in
whose service she has expended both youth and beauty, and
sees the daughter whom she has so carefully and tenderly
nurtured, and who should now be her stay, and her comfort,
and the pride of her maternal heart, usurping her place in
her husband's affection and in her home, and striking a
blow at her happiness that is fatal. She can turn neither to
husband nor daughter for comfort, and the religion which
should be her stay is but a mockery, since it brings all the
misery and desolation into her wrecked life

The leaders of her religion teach openly that it is not
right for husbands to live with their wives after they are
advanced in years; and they also teach that a man is marriageable until he is a hundred years old. This has always
been a strong point with them, and in urging polygamy, in

the "Reformation" times, they used to advise the young girls
to choose for their husbands men of experience, who would
have the power of resurrecting them, rather than a young
man whose position in the church was not fixed. They
carried the practice of this doctrine to the same extreme that
they carried everything else. One enthusiastic elder secured
for a wife a girl of eleven years, and brides of thirteen and
fourteen were often seen, especially in Southern Utah, where
the excitement was most intense, and rose almost to frenzy.
I was about twelve years of age, and my father had several
offers for me from different church dignitaries; but however
easily he might be beguiled himself into the snares set by
the lecherous leaders of Mormonism and polygamy, he had
no idea of making his little girl a victim; and though I was
duly advised by teachers and catechists to marry into polygamy when I was a little older, I gave very little heed to the
advice, and set about making my own romance, just as girls
everywhere do, in my imagination.

It is painful to one used to the finer courtesies of life to
see how age is neglected in Utah, and the want of respect
that is shown towards it, especially towards women, who
have passed out of the sunshine years of life, and are entering the shadow. When I came East, one of the strangest
things to me was the deference that was paid to age, it
was so unlike anything I had been used to; and when I
saw an old couple clinging together, with no dread shadow
of polygamy between them, with only the prospect of death
to part them, I have been thrilled through and through with
the sweetest, strangest emotion. I could scarcely believe
my own senses; it seemed impossible that in this world such
devotion could exist, and I could only wonder and weep,
and thank God that, in the world that I had been taught to
look upon as so wicked and depraved, there was such a
thing as love, and devotion, and thoughtful care for women,
and that every added wrinkle or silver hair brought more
tender care and tenderer devotion. In the light of affection

like this, well-tried and long-enduring, the hateful form of polygamy would rise up before me more monstrous, more hideous, more revolting than ever.

Think, in contrast to this, of a woman who has lived with her husband during all the years of her fresh and mature womanhood, being left alone, when she becomes deserted by the husband whom she has loved so well and so long, at the command of the priesthood! Heber Kimball used to say, when he knew of a woman grieving over the neglect of her husband, "What is she making such a fuss for? She has no business with a husband." Who can blame the disciples when the leader sets the example? Brigham Young's first living wife, — his only real and legal wife, — a woman of his own age, is entirely neglected by him, and long ago ceased to be his wife but in name.

Sometimes these old and middle-aged ladies do not see their husbands once a year, and yet they may not live half a mile apart. A few years since, at a large party at the Social Hall in Salt Lake City, Orson Hyde, one of the twelve apostles, met the wife of his youth, the mother of many of his children. He had escorted some of his younger wives there, and she came with a friend. It chanced that they were seated near each other at the table, and were compelled to speak; they shook hands, exchanged a very commonplace greeting, and that was all that passed between them. Neither is this an isolated case; it very often occurs that an elderly lady attends a party with friends, and meets her husband there with one or more younger wives; and sometimes both she and they have

APOSTLE ORSON HYDE.

to watch their mutual husband while he plays the agreeable to some young girl who has taken captive his wandering fancy, and whom he intends to make the next addition
to his kingdom.

It is then that wives, who have heretofore been rivals,
join their forces against a common enemy; and the young
woman who is engaging the attentions of the already much-
married but still marriageable *beau*, is sure to suffer at the
hands of the new allies, who have so recently struck hands
in a common cause. She, of course, knows this instinctively, and she revenges herself by "drawing" on her admirer
by every art in her power, until he becomes so marked in
his devotion that the entire company know, as well as the
wives themselves, what his intentions are; and, in addition
to the pique caused by his neglect, they have to endure the
congratulations of friends upon the approaching alliance.
In cases like this, the first wife does not feel so much pain
as the younger one, and the whilom favorite, who, no
matter how she has snubbed her before, comes now to seek
her sympathy. She would be something more than human,
if, with the sadness of her heart was not mingled a little
feeling of pleasure that she was getting her revenge in seeing the jealousy and suffering of her late rival.

To return to the encounter between Hyde and his wife.
There is a little romance attached to their separation which
I have just been reminded of. When Joseph Smith first
taught polygamy, and gave the wives as well as the husbands opportunity to make new choice of life-partners, Mrs.
Hyde, at that time a young and quite prepossessing woman,
became one of the Prophet's numerous fancies, and he took
great pains to teach her most thoroughly the principles of
the new celestial doctrines. It was rumored, at the time,
that she was an apt and willing pupil. Hyde was away on
a mission at the time, and when he returned, he, in turn, im-
bibed the teachings of polygamy also, and prepared to
extend his kingdom indefinitely. In the mean time it was

hinted to him that Smith had had his first wife sealed to himself in his absence, as a wife for eternity. Inconsistent as it may seem, Hyde was in a furious passion. Like many other men, he thought it no harm for him to win the affection of another man's wife, and make her his " celestial " spouse ; but he did not propose having *his* rights interfered with even by the holy Prophet whose teachings he so implicitly followed, and he swore that if this was true he would never live with her again. But he did live with her for several years after the exodus from Nauvoo and the settlement of Utah. Finally, the old affair was revived, and I think Brigham himself informed his apostle that she was his wife only for time, but Joseph's for eternity ; and as she was no longer young, and other wives were plentiful, he left her to care for herself as best she could.

Although the Mormons have from the very commencement been very fond of parties, and of amusements generally, they are much more enjoyed by the men than by the women, although both attend. Occasionally some very curious scenes are witnessed, which, after all, are not at all amusing to the persons most nearly concerned. For instance : a man takes two wives to a ball, and, if he be a lover of peace, he is at his wits' ends how to preserve it. He must treat each one alike, as nearly as possible ; dance with each one an equal number of times, and see that each one is equally well served at supper. The beginning of sorrow comes with the vexed question, which he shall dance with *first*. That, however, is quite easily settled, since custom, or, rather, Mormon etiquette, demands that he shall give the older wife the preference. It may be she is not the favorite ; but that does not matter : on this one point etiquette is rigid, and even the Prophet himself dare not defy it.

He had invited Amelia, the present favorite, and Emmeline, whose place in the priestly heart Amelia had taken, to attend a ball with him. It was a very strange thing to do, for generally, when Amelia went with him, he devoted himself exclusively to her. But on this occasion he had brought Emmeline along, too. Early in the evening, one of the committee of management came bustling up, with a "Brother Brigham, won't you dance?"

"Well, I suppose so," was the reply. Then he hesitated for a moment. There sat both Emmeline and Amelia, the former looking quietly unconscious, yet wondering very much, as she afterwards told me, "what Brother Brigham would do," and enjoying his dilemma immensely, while the

BRIGHAM IN A QUANDARY.

latter looked very stately and dignified, and also threatening. There stood the Prophet, inclination pulling him one way, etiquette and duty the other. He hesitated a moment longer; then, walking up to Emmeline, said, ungraciously and gruffly, "Come along and dance;" and, without offering her his arm, walked on to the floor, leaving her to follow.

As is the custom at balls which Brigham and Amelia grace with their presence, one of his satellites instantly begged for the honor of Amelia's hand in the dance, and led her at once as *vis-à-vis* to her husband. During the entire dance he did not address one word to Emmeline, and was evidently made very wretched by the demeanor of Amelia, who snubbed him most decidedly, and would take no notice of all his attempts to win her back to good humor.

At the end of the dance he led Emmeline to her seat as hastily as possible, left her without a word, and endeavored, with all the art which he possessed, to propitiate his angry favorite. Presently, the ubiquitous manager was at his elbow again : —

"Another cotillon, Brother Brigham; will you dance again?"

"With pleasure," answered the delighted President. Then, turning quickly to Amelia, he offered his arm in the most impressive manner, saying, —

"*Now* I will dance with my wife;" and led her off in triumph, as pleased as any young fellow at the opportunity of showing his devotion to her. He was vivacity itself during the dance, and finally succeeded in coaxing a smile from the capricious tyrant of his heart. As deeply hurt as Emmeline was by his rude boorishness of manner towards herself, and the insult conveyed to her by the remark to Amelia, which she overheard, she could not help being pleased at seeing the punishment he was receiving at the hands of the outraged favorite.

A system that engenders feelings like this can surely not be called, with any degree of propriety, a heavenly system, and religion is outraged every time its name is used in connection with it. It panders to the baser passions of men, and crushes the graces of Christian faith and charity out of every woman's heart. It engenders malice, and strife, and envyings, and hatred, and backbiting, and all that is worst in the masculine or feminine heart. It makes men selfish and mean, and women wretched and degraded. It takes from one the dignity and poise which come from absolute self-control, and from the other the sweet, refined, womanly assurance which comes from self-respect. Talk

of its "celestial" origin! It is the devil's own device for
rendering men and women both less godlike and pure.
And the cunning of his device is shown in the religious
mask which he puts upon its frightful face, and the Christian robes with which he hides its horrible deformity.
It began by deception, it has been fostered by lies.

When the first rumor of its existence as a religious ordinance among the American Saints was first exciting Europe, and the American missionaries were assuring their
converts that the rumor was false, and was started by their
enemies to injure them and their cause, the most eloquent
and remarkable denial of it was made by the Apostle John
Taylor, at *Boulogne-sur-Mer*, where there was at that time
quite a large and successful mission.

The Apostle Taylor was the husband of five wives, all living in Salt Lake; yet that slight matter did not hinder him
from most emphatically repudiating the charge brought
against the church. He quoted from the Book of Mormon, dwelling particularly on the passage that expressly
commands that a man shall have but *one* wife; then mentions
the Bible command that a man shall take a wife and cleave
to her *only;* and made the sermon so strong and so convincing that no further proof was asked by those who
heard him. His manner was impressive. He was sor-
rowful, he was indignant, he was reproachful; he was eloquent, and fervent, and almost inspired, thought those who
heard him. He was logical and convincing in what he
said. In short, he was a consummate hypocrite, lying in
the name of God to a confiding people, with a smooth
tongue and an unblushing face.

He employed a French lady — one of his converts, and
a most charming and cultured person — to translate the
sermon for him into her own language. He then had it
published, and distributed largely through the country.
Very many were kept from apostatizing by this tract, and
a large number announced their intention of at once

gathering to Zion. Among them was the lady who had translated the sermon for Taylor, and who, influenced

APOSTLE JOHN TAYLOR.
[Husband of Six Wives.]

by the spirit of the discourse, and the seeming earnestness of the missionary, had become more zealous than ever in her devotion to her new and ardently beloved faith.

Imagine, if you can, her horror, on reaching Utah, at the social state of affairs which found her there, and discovered that she not only had been grossly deceived, but, in her ignorance, had helped to deceive so many others; for it was through the influence of her translation of Taylor's denial that nearly all the party with whom she emigrated had come.

She apostatized at once, but she was conscience-stricken at the part she had so unwittingly played, and could not be comforted. A more remorseful, grief-stricken woman was never seen, and she felt all the more deeply the harm that had been wrought, when she saw how powerless she was to undo it. No effort of hers could ever bring these unhappy people from the infamous community in which they found themselves, and a part of which they were destined to become. For with them, the men especially, as with all others who remain under the baleful influence long, the end was certain. They first endured, and then embraced; pity was left out altogether, although God knows there is no condition that calls for pity as does that of the polygamous wife. The lady herself left Utah, but her people were forced to remain. I wonder how those poor wives, decoyed into a strange country by priestly promises, and deceived by priestly lying, could bear ever again to look in the face, or listen to the voice, of the man who had so wickedly misled them.

When the missionaries were asked why they denied so stoutly the existence of the system, when it must be sooner or later discovered that they were falsifying, they excused themselves by saying that the people could not then stand such strong doctrine, and they must give them only what they could safely take; that in good time the Lord would open their hearts to receive his truth, — the "good time" which the brethren referred to being after they had left their own country, crossed the United States, and put themselves outside the pale of civilization, and were literally in the power of the church. When they had gone so far that retreat was impossible, then they would tell them the truth, knowing that they could not choose but listen.

As long as they possibly could they denied it in the missions abroad, but, by-and-by, it became so notorious that it must be acknowledged; and in the face of all the denial, all the asseverations that there was no such institution, and, according to the laws of God and man there could be no such institution, the *Millennial Star* suddenly published the "Revelation," having given no warning of what it was about to do.

The excitement among the Mormons through Europe, in England especially, was intense, and it took all the eloquence and sophistry of the entire missionary board to prevent a general apostasy. Hundreds did leave the church, and many more were on the point of doing so. But the ingenuity of the Mormon Elders, which seems never to fail them, came to their rescue. They explained that this "Revelation" forced no one into polygamy; it only established it as a church institution that might be availed of by anyone who chose to enter the "Celestial Kingdom," but that it was entirely optional. In fact, the same arguments that were used to win single and special converts were used to con-

vince the masses; and, strange as it may seem, all this
sophistry had actual weight, and many worthy and sensible
men and women stayed by the church who would have
abandoned it in disgust, had they known the truth as it was
forced upon them afterwards. But, as I said a little while
since, the system begun in deception and fraud fattened on
lies and treachery. May it meet with a speedy death,
brought on by a surfeit of its favorite food.

CHAPTER XX.

BRIGHAM BUILDS WAGONS BY "INSPIRATION." — THE CHURCH SETS UP A WHISKEY-STORE.

Saying "Yes" under Difficulties. — A Woman who Meant to have her Way. — Two Company: Three None. — Building Wagons by Inspiration. — My Father despatched to Chicago. — He gets rid of his New Wives. — My Brother sent to the Sandwich Islands. — My Mother tells her own Story. — She Returns to Salt Lake City to see my Father. — Wifely Considerations. — She finds two other Ladies at her Husband's Bedside. — He likes a good deal of Wives about Him ! — A Heart dead to Love. — Brigham "asks no odds of Uncle Sam or the Devil." — He proclaims Martial Law. — Fiery Speeches in the Tabernacle. — Preparing for War. — Government Troops Arrive. — The Saints quit Salt Lake City. — The Church Distillery. — Brigham shamelessly Robs my Father. — He fills his own Pockets. — My Father, being without Funds, takes his Sixth Wife.

MORMONS BURNING A GOVERNMENT TRAIN.

SOME time before our family bereavement by the loss of Louise, my mother and I went to Skull Valley, about seventy miles from Salt Lake City, where my brothers were keeping a herd-ground.

We had intended to go by ourselves; but one of the young wives, who was very much attached to my mother, begged to be allowed to go. She appealed first to my father, and he, in turn, referred her to my mother.

I shall never forget the look of desperation on my mother's face, the hunted look in her eyes, as she came to me after the request had been made and before she had given her answer. She told me of the new proposal, and added, in a bitterer tone than I had ever heard her use before, —

"Why can't she see and understand that I want to make my escape from this confusion and trouble, and go away alone?"

But she could not see, and as she was kind and affectionate, and my mother was quite well aware of her regard for her, she could do nothing but say "yes," although it was a great cross for her to be obliged to do so.

Here was the end of all her sweet dreaming. She had thought to go quietly away, taking me with her, and we two living with "the boys" at the herd-ground. To be sure, there was only a log-cabin there; but what did that matter? She would rest in her children's love, which at least was her very own; and with them about her, she would forget, as far as possible, the horrible system that had brought so much unhappiness to her. Fond as she was of my father, it was much easier for her to be separated from him in this way, than it was to be under the same roof, and see him bestowing attentions, that used to be hers exclusively, on others. Dear as the husband was, yet she took very little comfort with a fifth part of him; and she longed to get away where she could live in memory the old happy days over again, and, with her children's arms about her, forget the suffering the later years had brought, ignoring all but the very present, and close her eyes to the future, which promised but little better, after all, since what was her greatest cross here was to follow her into the hereafter.

I wonder sometimes, knowing as I do now what she suffered, and realizing it as I could not then, that she did not cry out in the bitterness of her sorrow, as one Mormon

woman whom I know did, "O, if I could only believe
that death was an eternal sleep, I think I should be better
able to endure; but to think that we have got to live on
eternally under this curse of polygamy, almost drives me
mad." Or like another, equally desperate and miserable,
"I would kill myself if I thought death would end my misery; but as long as I must suffer, it might as well be here
as anywhere. O for the anticipation of one hour of peace
and rest!"

Ever since my father's return from his mission my mother
had begged to be allowed to go away, — to have a home by
herself; but somehow my father could not bring himself to
let her go until now. She was the balance-wheel in the
domestic machinery, and things seemed to go smoothly
when she was round about. She was always prepared for
any emergency; and both my father and the other wives
instinctively turned to her when anything was wrong. She
was so strong, so helpful, so self-reliant, and so patient,
that she seemed, some way, the protector of us all. I think,
if my father had not seen her so very much in earnest, and
so determined to go at all hazards, that his consent would
not have been won; but finding it useless to oppose her, he
gave a reluctant consent.

Then there was a little season of quiet joy between us
two; for we did not dare make any very open demonstrations, for fear of hurting the feelings of those whom we were
going to leave behind us. Our joy was short-lived, however, for it was decided to take a third with us; and though
we liked her, yet she would be what the children call a
"spoil-sport;" and we didn't want any one outside of our
very selves.

So we went, we three, leaving the others in Salt Lake
City, where they did not remain long after we left, but, to
my mother's great annoyance, followed soon after to Skull
Valley.

Very soon after our removal, Brigham conceived the idea

of establishing an express company, and called on my father to go to Chicago and superintend the construction of wagons and carriages for this purpose. They were to be built after plans which Brigham himself had drawn from "inspiration," and he insisted that the designs should be closely and faithfully followed ; so he sent my father to see that this was done, he being a practical wagon-builder.

Like the labor he had been engaged in for the four previous years, we expected that this would be called " mission " work, and he was not to receive a penny for his services ; they were to be given for the good of the " kingdom." This would make the fifth year he had spent away from us, working for the " church," we receiving none of the benefits of his labors. He had no time, of course, to devote to his family, or to labor for its support ; he must give his strength, and his time, and his labor to Brigham Young. During the three months that he had been at home, he had added as many wives to the family-circle ; but there were no added means with which to care for them ; so that now, when he was called to go away and leave them for an indefinite length of time, it was considered expedient to send the whole family to us, to remain during his absence.

More log-rooms were added to the cabin, and down came the whole flock, so that we were all together again. My mother has said, since then, that she never, in her whole life, felt so rebellious as she did then. She had become so entirely disgusted with polygamy, that even the fact that it was an important adjunct to the religion to which she was so devoted, did not reconcile her to it one bit. She hated it ; she hated everybody connected with it ; and she did not care if she never saw her husband again in the world. She would not pray for his safe return, for she said she did not desire it, and she would not add heartless prayer to her list of hypocrisies.

She kept all this rebellion within her own heart, and I

am sure that none of the wives knew at all the depth and
intensity of her feelings at that time.   An added sorrow to
my mother came, when, about the same time that my father
went to Chicago, my eldest brother was sent on a mission to
the Sandwich Islands.   She mourned his departure deeply,
and even I could not comfort her.   He was sent for five
years, — that was the time designated in his order, — and
my mother was so broken in health and spirits that she did
not believe she should be alive when he returned.   He was,
however, immediately recalled on account of the opening of
the Mormon War, with all other missionaries away from
home.

In the autumn we heard that my father was coming
home ill; he had got "leave of absence" from the head of
the church, and was coming home to be taken care of.   As
soon as we heard the news, my mother suggested to Elizabeth that she should return to Salt Lake City, and prepare
for his reception at the home there.   She went at once, and
my mother was going on quietly with her many duties, when
a messenger arrived in haste from the city for my mother, to
convey her to the husband who was calling for her.

I think I shall let her give the incident in her own
words : —

"At first I declined going; so rebellious was I, and so
bitter, that I actually felt that I *could* not go.   There was a
momentary feeling of triumph, that, in sickness or in trouble,
my husband turned to me, his one *true* wife, for relief
and comfort; that, however he might regard his younger
wives while well and comparatively prosperous, he had no
thought for them now; yet this feeling failed to move me,
— as instantly, choking it almost before it became a definite thought, came the bitter impulse—'Let him alone; leave
him to suffer : you have not been spared; why should you be
more merciful than he has been?   Let him feel what it is to
need, and long for, and even starve for some one's love and
care, and yet have it denied him in all his longing and his

22

need;' and for a moment I was actually glad that I had the power to inflict this pain.

"'Let one of the other wives go,' I replied to the messenger's repeated and more urgent request. 'I don't see how I can leave.'

"'But you must,' was the imperative reply of the man; 'your husband is very sick, and has sent for you, and I shall take no one else.'

"In a moment I relented. I felt ashamed of my selfish heartlessness; something of the old-time feeling came over me, and, with a sudden revulsion of emotion, such as only women ever feel, I was as anxious now to go to him as I had before been indifferent. After all, he was *my* husband, — mine as he could never be anyone's else. I had a claim on him that none of the rest had, and he had a claim on me too. It seemed now as though I could not get to him quickly enough. I made my preparations in feverish haste, with fingers that trembled with nervous impatience, and in a short time was on my way.

"The journey seemed so long and tedious! and yet we made it very quickly; but to me, whose heart outran the very swiftest conveyance, it was inexpressibly tiresome. I expect I wearied the patience of my driver by requesting him constantly to 'go faster,' and perpetually asking if we were not almost there. I pictured to myself the pleasure of having my husband, for a little while even, all my own again. I would make the most of it. I would forget, by his sick bed, that there had ever been the slightest shadow between us. Polygamy should, in that sick chamber, be as though it never had existed. He had sent for me; he had chosen me out of all the rest to be the companion of his sick hours. In his sick-room, at least, my sway should be absolute, and I would not give up one bit of my authority to anyone else. There, at least, as in the days of long ago, he should be 'mine, — mine only;' but, alas! he could never again be 'for ever mine.' In spite of my impatience, I was more really happy than I had been for years. I felt more like myself than I had since that fatal day in Nauvoo, when, after long and prayerful consultation, we decided that duty and right demanded that we should enter polygamy, and made the choice of the first plural wife. I was coming to my own again, and my life was positively glorified by the thought. His illness, rather than distressing, gladdened me. I should have, of course, the exclusive care of him, and he should miss nothing of the old love and tenderness in my regard for him. For the time, at least, we should be all in all to each other.

A GOOD DEAL OF WIVES: — TOO MUCH ATTENTION.

"We arrived at last, and I hurried to the sick-room of my husband, with my heart full of tenderness for him, my eyes brimming over with loving tears. But, in my dreamings, I had forgotten, or had ignored the fact, that others had the same right to minister to him, to care for him, to remain with and watch over him, that I had; and when I entered the room, the tenderness was driven from my heart, the tears from my eyes, and I stood there a polygamic wife, in presence of three of my husband's other wives, who had the *same* privileges of his room that I had, and who were doing their utmost to make the invalid comfortable.

"I was a good nurse, and, on account of my experience, the others deferred to my opinions and advice, but insisted upon sharing my labors. My husband made no objections; indeed, I daresay he would have been contented had the whole five of us been dancing attendance on him. I worked faithfully and hard in the sick-room, but very mechanically, and, in a dazed, bewildered sort of way. All the heart had gone out of my work. Feeling seemed entirely dead. I hadn't the slightest emotion for the man who lay before me there, and I was as indifferent to his fate as though he had been an entire stranger.

"I don't think it was heartlessness; I know it was not. It was because my heart had been tortured into numbness, and I no longer had any power to feel. If he had died, I do not think I should have shed a tear. The fountain of tears was absolutely frozen, and not one would have flowed had he lain before me cold, and mute, and motionless. I should have been as rigid as the white face set in death, on which my dry eyes would have looked vacantly and wonderingly, as on some strange, unaccustomed features.

"I did not wish that he might die; I was simply indifferent. With the last flickering light that burned up so brightly for a little while, until it entered the sick-chamber and was met by the chilling breath of the ghostly presence of polygamy, my life's romance went out for ever. The life or death of one man could not change the face of the world to me. Where I had thought I was strong, I was weak; my dream was broken; life was henceforth a dead level of mere existence. My only thought was to get away. I took my daughter, as soon as I could with decency leave, and went on a visit to some relatives in Southern Utah, saying farewell to my domestic circle, without one regret."

Yet even this separation was of short duration, for just about that time came the famous "move to the South," which every Salt Lake City resident will remember — many of them to their sorrow.

In 1857 there was a prospect of United States troops being sent to the Territory, and Brigham determined to resist them. In a public speech on the 24th of July, the day celebrated by the Mormon Church as the anniversary of their first entrance into the Valley, he said, "God is with us, and I ask no odds of Uncle Sam or the devil."

When it was ascertained beyond a doubt that the United States troops were on the way, he counselled every warlike preparation to be be made. Business was suspended; an adobe wall was built back of the city for protection against

REMAINS OF ADOBE DEFENCES.

Johnson's army; the elders on missions were ordered home at once, and all the people turned their attention to the task of repelling the invasion. "For," said Brigham, "they SHALL NOT enter the Valley." He issued a proclamation, forbidding all armed forces from entering the Territory, and martial law was also proclaimed.

The latter part of the winter the Mormons received a visit from Colonel Thomas S. Kane, of Philadelphia. He had before this proved his friendship for the Saints, and was respected and listened to accordingly. It is supposed the colonel convinced Brigham that he was not yet strong enough to conquer the United States, and advised a change of tactics.

At all events, directly after his departure, Brigham began
to talk of going south; he said he did not know where he
should go; perhaps to the desert — "wherever the Lord
should direct."

Satisfied that it would be better not to fight, I suppose he
thought when the snow melted it would be impossible to keep
the army out; therefore he issued orders to the Saints to
pack up and take their flight. They obeyed the command,
some going only thirty miles, others going three hundred;
in fact, they were scattered along all through the southern
settlements. In direct contradiction to his assertions made
in the Tabernacle, everything was left standing — not even
a tree or a stack of hay being burned. This move south
brought our family together again under one roof, and we
remained together until the church was recalled.

After the departure of the Saints from Salt Lake, the
troops passed through; but they interfered with nothing:
no spirit of retaliation was shown for all they had endured
through the past winter.

Nearly the entire summer was spent in the move south,
and in August, Brigham notified the people that he was
going back, but that "others might do as they pleased."
All that could do so returned to their homes at once; others
went when circumstances would permit; having been living
from March until August in tents, wagons, or in the open
air, they were glad to return. The people were poor, and
dependent on their labor for sustenance, and could not well
afford the time for this flitting; yet they obeyed Brigham
implicitly, asking no questions and hazarding no objections.

With the return to the city our family was again divided.
My mother was urged to go to Payson, and re-open her
school, which she had relinquished on my father's return
from Europe. She decided to do so, and the people furnished a dwelling-house for her, and she and I commenced
living our old cosy life again. We had occasional visits
from different members of our family, and the first summer

that we were there, one of the younger wives, while on a visit, increased our already somewhat numerous family by giving birth to a daughter, and, in addition to her school duties, my mother performed the several offices of cook, housekeeper, and nurse, until she was able to return home.

In the mean time, affairs in Salt Lake City had assumed their usual quiet. The troops were camped about forty miles from Salt Lake, in Cedar Valley. They called the station Camp Floyd. While they remained in the Territory, some of the Saints, wishing to dispose of their produce, sold a large quantity to the troops, and were well paid for

MORMONS SELLING PROVISIONS TO UNITED STATES TROOPS.

it. Brigham heard of it, and the very next Sunday forbade their selling any more, and cursed all those who had had dealings with our enemies, as he called those men who had respected the honor of their government and spared the people who had so injured them.

It was not long before it was whispered that Brigham had agents in Camp Floyd selling tithing flour and lumber; taking large contracts, and obtaining large prices. But in the meanwhile he did not relax his severity towards his people. The bishops were ordered to withdraw the hand of fellowship from every person in their wards who traded at Camp Floyd. It was a sure sign of apostasy to be seen there at all, on any errand whatever; yet the church teams started from the tithing-office, loaded with flour, in the night, and it was known that Brigham received large sums of money from the government in payment.

In this, as in everything else, he was determined to have the monopoly. If there was any money to be made, he must make it. He could not endure to see a dollar go into another man's pocket. I believe the sight was positive pain to him. This incarnation of selfish greed is made absolutely miserable by the prosperity of another, and he takes speedy measures to put a stop to it, as he did in the case of Moon and Badly, the distillers, whom he sent to the south on missions, and also in the affair with Mr. Howard, whose distillery he took possession of in the same manner, after having declared that it ought to be burned down, and the machinery destroyed.

After Howard was well out of the way (in England, I think), Brigham started the distillery again in the "church's" interest, which, as he represents the church, meant himself. And over the door he placed as a sign the All-seeing eye, with the inscription, "HOLINESS TO THE LORD. ZION'S CO-OPERATIVE MERCANTILE INSTITUTION. WHOLESALE LIQUOR-DEALERS AND RECTIFIERS." His whiskey was not nearly so good as Howard's, but he got as much money for it; so what did he care about the quality?

More fortunate than either Mr. Moon or Mr. Badly, Mr. Howard returned from his mission; but he has ever since been an enemy to the Prophet, who, by the way, still runs the distillery.

Mention having been made of the President's "Improved Carriages," I think they deserve a more extended notice, coming, as they do, under the head of Brigham's sublime failures. He had purchased the contract for carrying the mails from Independence, Missouri, to Salt Lake City; so he decided to run an express between these two points, to be called "B. Young's Express," for the purpose of carry-

ing passengers, freight, and the mails. He wanted the
assistance of my father in preparing the train, and although
the latter was very much averse to leaving his family again
so soon after his return to them from his four years in England, yet he was, of course, overcome by the pressing eloquence of his leader.

It was very necessary that he should enter at once into
some lucrative business, as his family was large, increased
recently by the Prophet's orders; and when he informed
Brigham of the necessity of instant and remunerative labor,
he was informed that this would be the most profitable undertaking in which he could engage, and gave him to
understand that he would be well remunerated for his services.

It is by this time a well-established fact among the
Saints — taking his word for it merely — that Brigham
Young knows how to do everything. Therefore no one
will be surprised to learn that he understood all about
wagon and carriage building, and nothing could be more
natural than that he should produce plans representing the
manner in which the carriages should be built. These designs, with the most minute instructions, covering several
sheets of foolscap, were laid before my father, and he ventured to suggest that there might be some slight alterations
which would be for the better; but he was met with the
sharp and abusive reply, that "there must not, on any consideration, be the least variation from this plan." Brigham
insisted that it should be adhered to in every particular.
He became very much elated, and made use of all his
magniloquence in describing the ease and comfort with
which passengers might cross the plains in one of his carriages, saying, "They will be just as comfortable as though
they were at home in their own parlors."

Father said no more, but pocketed the plans, and started
East with them, quite certain what the result would be.
When he arrived in Chicago he presented the Prophet's

model to every carriage-maker in the city, and they only laughed very heartily over it. They said they had never seen anything like it, which was true enough, as it bore not the slightest resemblance to anything on the earth, or in the heavens above, or the waters beneath. It was most decidedly "unique and only." They all declined to undertake the work, knowing that it must prove a failure. Finally, however, a Mr. Schuttler, being anxious to secure the Utah trade, consented to try two of them, on condition that my father should render constant assistance, not feeling exactly safe to proceed in so important an undertaking without the aid of a Mormon who was supposed to know more about it than himself. The orders were to build fourteen carriages, besides a train of wagons. Schuttler's wagons being ordered by the Prophet, of course there was no difficulty about them.

When the two carriages were ready for transportation, they entirely filled a railway car. If my father had followed directions, and had the entire fourteen made, he must have chartered seven cars to convey them to the frontiers. These nondescript affairs were the amusement of all the passengers on the train. As they found no passengers at the frontiers, except "Uncle Sam's troops," the carriages were filled with freight; and I believe the wreck of one of them reached Salt Lake City the following year, after peace had been made with the government. The Prophet was satisfied with the two, and ordered no more built; his "revelation" had proved a great failure, and owing to the rebellion, the mail contract was taken from him. He laid the entire failure to the United States troops, although it would puzzle a person of less acute perceptions than he to discover how the one had anything to do with the other. When a "revelation" fails, there must be some excuse, some reason for it, and President Young is never at fault for one; whether a valid one or not, it seems to make little difference.

Those who were so fortunate as to see one of those carriages in its entirety, say that no one could form any idea
of them without seeing them, and that the only way to
get an adequate idea of the size would be to take the di-
mensions of a "Prairie Schooner," and multiply them by
five.

The wagons proved a success, as they were loaded with
freight for Salt Lake merchants, for which they paid twenty-five cents a pound; and those wagons that came through
with my father brought no less than five thousand two
hundred and fifty dollars' worth of freight for the Prophet.

BRIGHAM'S FOLLY. — "THE PRAIRIE SCHOONER."

It is a poor plan that does not enrich him; he seems,
in some way or other, to make money out of his very
failures.

After my father's recovery from his illness he presented
his accounts for the Prophet's inspection, and expected an
immediate settlement, and his promised pay; instead of
which, he was quietly informed that his services were to
be a gratuity to the church, and at the same time he was
presented by the Prophet with a bill from the express company for bringing his trunk of clothing through.

While in Chicago, he had sent two hundred and fifty
pounds of freight home for the family's use, and they
would not let my mother have it until she had paid the full

freight-charges. The clerks told her that "this was President Young's order, and they dared not disobey." Mother afterwards said that she believed the clerks saw the injustice of the whole proceeding, yet were powerless to do otherwise than according to their orders.

A man that had literally worn himself out in the service of Brigham Young could not be permitted to send a few of the necessaries of life to his family, nor even a trunk of linen, used on a journey for this man, without paying freight, and that when they came in wagons which he had helped to build, and that gratuitously, for the aggrandizement of the church, or, to be more exact, of the man who was constantly crying, " Give, give," and was yet never satisfied. A man of our acquaintance, who had been simlarly swindled, said, in referring to the subject, " Brigham Young would rob the King of heaven of His crown-jewels if he had the opportunity."

It was the unfortunate termination of this " business arrangement " with the Prophet that decided my mother to resume teaching again ; but when my father was again in business, he was so urgent that my mother should return to Salt Lake, that, a little while before my sixteenth birthday, we went there again to live.

CHAPTER XXI.

GOING THROUGH THE "ENDOWMENT–HOUSE."—I TAKE THE MYSTERIOUS BATHS.

No Physic among the Saints. — I am taken Sick. — Heber C. Kimball recommends "Endowments." — How Brigham Murdered his little Grand-
daughter. — The Prophet wants a Doctor. — Being "administered"
To. — I am Re-baptized. — Receive my Endowments. — How Saintly
Sins are Washed Away. — Undignified Conduct of Elders. — The Order of Melchisedec. — How I was "Confirmed." — To become a Celestial Queen. — I go down to the Endowment-House. — The Mysterious
Ceremonies Described. — The Veil at last Lifted. — The Secrets of the
Endowment-House Exposed. — I enter the Bath. — Miss Snow Washes
Me. — She Anoints Me All Over. — I dress in a Bed-gown. — The
"Peculiar Garment" of the Saints. — What the Mormon Girls do
about It — "Going through" without a Husband. — "A Great Shouting for *Sarah !* "

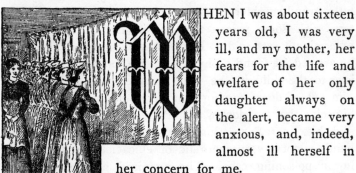

TAKING MY ENDOWMENTS
BEHIND THE CURTAIN.

HEN I was about sixteen years old, I was very ill, and my mother, her fears for the life and welfare of her only daughter always on the alert, became very anxious, and, indeed, almost ill herself in her concern for me.

According to Mormon custom, I was "administered to" by the anointing and laying on of hands, but all to no avail. Bishop Taft, the one who had baptized me in my childhood, Isaac Groo, the Bishop's counsellor, and Elder Samuel Hardy labored earnestly and long, and "wrestled in

prayer" over me, all to no avail. I grew worse, rather
than better, and my family feared I should fall into pul-
monary consumption.

The idea of employing a regular physician seemed never
to occur to any of them. Indeed, at that time it was considered the surest sign of a weakening of faith to resort to
medical aid, and no Mormon in good standing would ever
entertain the suggestion for a moment. Latterly, however,
a great deal of this nonsense has been done away with,
under the subtle Gentile influence that is working throughout Utah, in Salt Lake City more especially, and some of
the young'Saints are actually studying for the medical profession. Brigham used to denounce physicians in the most
wholesale manner in the Tabernacle, and declare that they
should never enter heaven, but that he would himself close
the doors against them.

He was so bitter at that time that he would allow none
of his family to employ medical aid in any emergency. A
little granddaughter of his, a child of one of his daughters, took some poison that her mother had prepared to
exterminate rats with. Brigham was sent for, and when
he arrived he found a physician there, preparing to administer to the child in the usual manner. He rudely turned
him out of doors, saying that he would care for the child
himself; that no doctor should be allowed to worry her;
and his "care," as usual, consisted of the laying on of
hands — not a very energetic or efficacious mode of treating a poisoning case. The agonized parents dared not
interfere, and in a few moments their child died before their
very eyes, in the most terrible agony and distress, an innocent victim to the Prophet's egotism and bigotry.

That was Brigham Young well. Brigham Young ill is
another person. In his variableness of opinion he reminds
one very forcibly of the dignitary treated of in the somewhat profane epigram, —

" The devil was sick ;
   The devil a monk would be :
   The devil got well ;
   The devil a monk was he."

Whenever he has any ailment, a doctor is summoned at once; and during his illness, a little over a year since, he employed at least half a dozen, keeping them in constant consultation, so great was his terror, and so absolute his horror of fatal consequences.

But when I was so ill, the Prophet was in the best of health, and was indulging in the bitterest invectives against physicians and all who employed them; and my mother, great and all-pervading as her affection was for me, and anxiously troubled as she was concerning my restoration to health, would have been shocked and grieved beyond measure, had any one proposed to her to seek medical advice concerning my condition. I was " in the hands of the Lord," and I was to be left there, for Him to do with me as He would.

When it was found that being " administered to " did no good in my case, Heber C. Kimball advised that I receive my " Endowments," promising that then I should surely be fully restored to health. This was considered as a very great favor, since, outside of Brigham Young's and one or two other official families, no young persons are given their Endowments. My mother was overjoyed, and considered the bestowal of this honor a special interposition of Providence on my behalf. As a matter of course, I shared her feelings most fully. I had always been taught to anticipate the time when I should receive my Endowments as the most important epoch of my religious life, when I should be taken fully into the bosom of the church.

It was necessary, in order to receive these rites, that I should be re-baptized. Remembering my childish experience, and the terror which I suffered, I must confess that I

dreaded, in my weakened state of health, that portion of
the ceremony, and I grew quite nervous over it before the
day arrived on which that rite was to be performed. I was
reassured on one point, however. The pond experience
was not to be repeated, but I was to be baptized in the
Twelfth Ward font, which made it seem much less formi-
dable, and divested it of half its terror.

On the day appointed I was taken to the Twelfth Ward
meeting-house by my mother, where we met Isaac Groo,
who was to baptize me. I was half frightened, and wholly
awed, and very nervous; but my ardent desire for the re-
establishment of my health gave me a sort of bravery and

MORMON BAPTISM.

endurance, so that I was quite calm, and behaved myself
very well, considering the unnaturally excited state which
I was in.

The ordinance of baptism, as administered by the Mormons, does not differ very materially from that of the Baptist churches. It is always by immersion. Nothing else is
ever considered efficacious. It must be a literal "watery
burial," and a resurrection therefrom. The officiating elder,
with his candidate for the rite, repairs to some place which
has been previously appointed, and where there is a sufficient quantity of water to immerse the entire person. Not

the least portion of the body must be left above the purifying fluid, else it could not be termed a "perfect burial with Christ." In the early days it was necessary to perform this ordinance in the open air, in some river or pond; but lately fonts have been built in most ward meeting-houses, so that it can all be done under cover, and there is less danger of suffering ill results from exposure.

The elder officiating takes the candidate by the hand and leads him — or her, as the case may be — down into the water, until a sufficient depth is attained; he then raises his hand, and, calling the person by name, commences the ceremony as follows: "Having authority given me of Jesus Christ, I baptize you in the name of the Father, and the Son, and the Holy Ghost. Amen." He then plunges the candidate under the water, bringing him forth into the newness of life, and fully prepared to enter upon a series of ordinances, all of which are attended with covenants calculated to bind the person more strongly to the church.

Following the baptism comes the confirmation, or the laying on of hands for the reception of the Holy Ghost. It is usually administered directly after the first rite, and at the same place; but I was so ill and weak that I was taken directly home, and the elders came there to confirm me. They were Bishop Taft and Isaac Groo, and they certainly gave me every cause to be thankful to them for the prodigality of their promises. I certainly never have had occasion to be grateful on account of their fulfilment.

In the Church of Latter-Day Saints the "Melchisedec" and "Aaronic" priesthood are authorized to perform the ordinance of baptism, but the latter has no power to administer in spiritual things. Hence only a priest after the holy order of the Son of God, or the order of Melchisedec, can perform the ordinance of confirmation, or laying on of hands for imparting the Holy Ghost, which is to lead the newborn Saint into all truth, and teach him the things to come; thus protect him from all falsehood and imposition,

23

and placing him in the most perfect state of progression which, if real, would be a state of the highest felicity and most assured salvation.

Two or three elders lay their hands upon the head of the person to be confirmed, one of whom acts as a mouthpiece for the rest, and pronounces the blessings and promises, generally exhausting his full list of mercies upon him whom they are receiving into full Sainthood. There are two essentials in this ordinance which are never omitted — "I confirm you a member of the Church of Jesus Christ of

MORMON CONFIRMATION.

Latter-Day Saints," and, "I also confer upon you the Gift of the Holy Ghost."

Oftentimes the elder becomes so thoroughly filled with inspiration that he cannot cease his blessing until he has sealed the young Saint up to eternal life, with a perfect assurance that he shall "inherit all the blessings of Abraham, Isaac, and Jacob, with a fulness of the holy priesthood after the order of an endless life;" thus placing him beyond the possibility of falling from grace or missing the celestial gate: though he may wander from the fold and become bewildered in fogs and darkness, yet in the consummation of his mission to earth he will find his way back to the fold of Christ; and as it is supposed that the Word of God, spoken by the mouth of His servant, cannot fail, will inherit thrones, principalities, and dominions, be made King and Priest unto God and His Christ, and reign upon the earth.

The person, having reached this high plane in the kingdom of God on the earth, is considered properly prepared to receive the higher and holier ordinances, which are to be kept entirely secret, and are accompanied by the strongest and most binding covenants, which cannot be broken without incurring the severest penalties.

I was promised everything that I could wish; indeed, I was quite overcome by the magnitude and number of special blessings that was promised me. First of all, as that was my most earnest desire, I was to have perfect health bestowed upon me at once. I was to go on "from grace to glory," in full saintship, and my last days were to be better than my first. I am glad to say that this portion of the blessing promises to be fulfilled, although by no means in the manner that was intended when the blessing was bestowed. I, of course, could not be a King or Priest, but I should be a "Celestial Queen," with all the glory, emoluments, and perquisites which attend that very exalted, but somewhat mythical, position. Having thus settled my future to their evident satisfaction, they left me fully prepared to receive my Endowments.

I was now all eagerness to receive my Endowments. If the first step could have so sudden and marked an effect on me, what would not the greatest, the most important step of all, do for me! My faith in it and its virtues was almost sublime. I could scarcely wait for the next day to come — the day that had been appointed for me to enter into the full fellowship of the church, the full glory of the Lord, and the eternal heirship to heavenly things.

The morning came, however, and, with a heart filled with hopeful anticipation, I took my way to the Endowment-House [carrying a lunch and my Temple-robes, which had to be specially prepared for this occasion], where, in the absence of a regular Temple, the rites were performed. I expected something solemn and awful; something elevating to the spirit, and ennobling to the mind. How I was disappointed, everyone who has entered the Endowment-House with feelings similar to my own will understand. In place of the awe which I expected to find the rites endowed with, they were ridiculous and farcical in the extreme.

I have heard persons speak of the solemnity of their feelings on the occasion of taking their Endowments, but, with all respect to their truthfulness, I am always incredulous in

THE ENDOWMENT-HOUSE.

the extreme. I think either their imagination must have got the better of their common sense, or they could have had very little of the latter commodity to begin with, else they would have seen through the very thin tissue of absurdities which they are obliged to witness with unmoved features, for to laugh in the Endowment-House would be the most fearful sacrilege. For my own part, I was in a most uncomfortable frame of mind. I wanted to laugh; everything seemed so ridiculous; and yet all the while I was conscience-stricken at my own levity. I thought it must be my own wicked heart, and not the rites themselves, and I was constantly upbraiding myself for lack of spiritual grace; and yet I could not alter my feelings in the least. The only thing that in any degree overcame my disposition to laugh, was the horror at the oaths which I was obliged to take. They were fairly blood-curdling, they were so awful; and even now a shudder runs through my whole frame as I recall them.

The Endowment rites are nothing more nor less than a drama, founded partially upon the Bible, but more upon Milton's Paradise Lost. It represents the Creation, the Fall, and the final Restoration of Man to his first glory. To speak in stage parlance, the "different lines of business" are taken by the leaders of the church, who always sustain the same characters. The following is a list of the *dramatis personæ* at the time that I took my Endowments:—

ELOHIM, *or Head God,*	Brigham Young.
JEHOVAH,	Heber C. Kimball.
JESUS,	Daniel H. Wells.
MICHAEL, *or Adam,*	W. C. Staines.
SATAN,	W. W. Phelps.
APOSTLE PETER,	Orson Pratt.
APOSTLE JAMES,	John Taylor.
APOSTLE JOHN,	Erastus Snow.
WASHER,	Dr. Sprague.
CLERK,	David O. Calder.
EVE,	Miss Eliza R. Snow.
TIMOTHY BROADBRIM, *a Quaker,*	Wilfred Woodruff.
DEACON SMITH, *a Methodist,*	Orson Hyde.
PARSON PEABODY, *a Presbyterian,*	Franklin D. Richards.
ELDER SMOOTH-TONGUE, *a Baptist,*	Phineas H. Young.
FATHER BONIFACE, *a Catholic,*	George A. Smith.

When I entered the Endowment-House, I was made, first of all, to take off my shoes, for the place was too holy to be desecrated by outside dust. Having done this, I gave my name and age, the names of my parents, and date of baptism and confirmation, to the officiating clerk, who entered them all in a large book. Several other persons of both

sexes were present, and after all had been similarly catechized, and their answers noted, we were asked to produce
our bottles of oil, — for we had been instructed, among other
things, to bring with us a bottle of the best olive-oil : these
were taken from us ; our bundles of clothing were handed
to us again, and we were told to " pass on."

We entered a large bath-room, which was separated in
the middle by a heavy curtain, for the purpose of dividing
the men from the women. The men passed to one side of
the curtain, the women to the other. In our room were
several large tubs filled with water, and Miss Eliza R. Snow
and two or three other women were in attendance. I was
received by Miss Snow, who placed me in one of the tubs,
and washed me from my head to my feet, repeating certain
formulæ to the effect that I was washed clean from the blood
of this generation, and if I remained firm in the faith, should
never be harmed by any of the ills that beset the world, and
which soon were to be showered in terrible profusion upon
the earth. Plagues, pestilence and famine should cover
the earth, and be let loose in its every corner, but I should
be passed by unscathed, if I was true to my religion — the
only revealed religion of God. After I had been wiped dry,
she proceeded to anoint me with olive-oil. As she did so,
she repeated, solemnly, —

" *Sister*, I anoint your head, that it may be prepared for
that crown of glory awaiting you as a faithful Saint, and the
fruitful wife of a priest of the Lord ; your forehead, that your
brain may be quick of discernment ; your eyes, that they may
be quick to perceive the truth, and to avoid the snares of the
enemy ; your ears, that they may be quick to hear the word
of the Lord ; your mouth, that you may with wisdom speak
the words of eternal life, and show forth the praise of the
immortal gods ; your tongue, to pronounce the true name
which will admit you hereafter behind the veil, and by which
you will be known in the celestial kingdom. I anoint your
arms to labor in the cause of righteousness, and your hands

to be strong in building up the kingdom of God by all manner of profitable works. I anoint your breasts, that you may prove a fruitful vine to nourish a strong race of swift witnesses, earnest in the defence of Zion; your body, to present it an acceptable tabernacle when you come to pass behind the veil; your loins, that you may bring forth a numerous race to crown you with eternal glory, and strengthen the heavenly kingdom of your husband, your master, and crown in the Lord. I anoint your knees, on which to prostrate yourself, and humbly receive the truth from God's holy priesthood; your feet, to run swiftly in the ways of righteousness, and stand firm upon the appointed places. And now I pronounce your body an acceptable temple for the indwelling of the Holy Spirit."

As may be imagined, I was literally besmeared with oil from my head to my feet. I breathed it, smelled it, tasted it; it ran into my eyes, and made them smart fearfully, and dripped in any but an agreeable manner from my hair. I was fairly saturated with it; was cognizant of nothing else; and I was so nauseated from it that I could scarcely go on with the ceremonies. I got a distaste for it then that I have never got over, and to this day even the sight of it makes me ill.

After the washing and anointing, I was given a garment which I was told to put on, and charged, after once assuming it, that I must never leave it off. When it became necessary to change, I must take off one side, then put the fresh one in its place; then I could drop the soiled one altogether, and get the fresh one on as soon as possible. So long as I wore it, I was free from danger, and even from death. Disease should not assail me, and neither shot nor the assassin's knife should have power to harm me; all should be turned one side. Every good Mormon wears this garment, and is very superstitious about allowing it off. It is said that Smith never would have been killed had it not been that he left off this charmed garment when he went to

Carthage. Had he allowed it to remain on, the balls of the murderers would have been utterly powerless to harm him.

There is nothing elegant about this garment; on the contrary, it is quite ugly, and the young Saints who assume it dislike it terribly for its plainness and awkwardness. In shape, it is like a child's sleeping-robe, with the waist and drawers combined, and reaches from the neck to the feet. It is of white, bleached muslin, and untrimmed. Latterly, some of the younger daughters of Brigham Young, and other young ladies of the Mormon *bon ton*, have instituted a reform, and, to the horror of the older ones, — who are not given over to the "pomps and vanities," &c., — have had their garments cut shorter, low in the neck, and short-sleeved, and elaborately trimmed. Of course the majority of the people, who have known of this innovation, have been terribly scandalized; but all to no avail. Mormon girls, like girls of the world, object to making guys of themselves; and neither "counsel" nor ridicule can affect them when once their minds are made up on the subject of dress. They will suffer for that what they will not for their religion.

Mine, of course, was made after the true orthodox fashion. Over it I wore a white night-gown and skirt, and on my feet white stockings and white linen shoes. My Temple robe was the last to be donned. It is a long, loose, flowing robe of homespun linen, falling to the ankle, and at the top plaited into a band, which passes over the right shoulder, and is fastened under the left arm; it was girdled by a white linen belt: the cap, which accompanies it, is a simple square of linen, or muslin, gathered in one corner to fit the head; the remainder falls down over the back of the head, like a veil.

While all this washing and robing was going on on one side of the curtain, the same things were being done on the opposite side. I suppose we could hear the murmur of voices and the splash of water; but everything was quiet and subdued, and the most perfect order reigned.

When we were all ready, a name was secretly given to each one of us, which was the name by which we were to be known in the celestial world, and which was to be told only to the man who should take us through the veil. If a woman was married, her husband took her through; if not, some brother kindly performed the office for her, and he was rewarded for his kindness by having the young Saint's celestial name whispered confidingly in his ear. I was not married; so Elder Samuel Richards took me through, and I told him my name, — and, by the way, he was the only person who ever knew it until after my apostasy, as I never told it to either of my husbands.

It is believed that as the husband has to "resurrect" his wife by her Endowment name, so it is rather necessary that he should know it. Consequently, when he is sealed to her, she is permitted to whisper her name to him through the veil, and after that it must be spoken no more between them until he shall call her by it on the morning of the final resurrection. If the Mormon doctrine were true, there would be a mighty shouting for "Sarah" at that time, as every person whose name I have heard was always called the same. It was the name that was given me, and I have known many others who received it. It certainly will make the husband's work at that time much lighter, since he need call but once to summon his entire family.

CHAPTER XXII.

WE CARRY ON THE ENDOWMENT DRAMA. — I AM FULLY INITIATED.

In the Endowment-House. — How the "Kings and Priests" appeared in their Shirts. — The poor Fellows "feel Bad!" — The "Gods" hold a *Conversazione.* — Michael is sent down to Earth. — The "Tree of Life." — How Raisins grew instead of Apples. — Not good to be Alone. — The Rib abstracted and little Eve made. — The Devil dressed in "Tights." — John D. Lee once a Devil. — Eve's Flirtation. — She eats Forbidden Fruit. — Tempts her Husband. — Fig-leaves come into Fashion. — We hide in Holes and Corners — The Devil is Cursed and we are Lectured. — The Second Degree. — Story of a Pugnacious Woman. — The Terrible Oaths of the Endowment-House. — Pains and Penalties. — Signs and Grips. — "Good-bye!" — Brother Heber gives me Advice.

THE DEVIL OF THE ENDOWMENT-HOUSE.

AFTER our names had been given us, Miss Snow announced that we were ready, in answer to a question from the other side of the curtain. We were arranged in a row facing it, when it was suddenly withdrawn, and we were standing face to face with the men. The sight that met our eyes was very funny, and I had all I could do to keep my features decently straight. I looked out from under my eyelids, for I did not dare give a good, square, honest look; it would have been altogether too much for my gravity; but from my stolen looks I found that the men, over their new gar-

ment of protection, wore a shirt only.   On their feet were
white socks and white linen shoes.   The cap was of white
linen, in shape exactly like those worn by stonemasons,
and tied by a knot in front.   They were certainly no more
beautiful in appearance than we women, and, as is generally the case in embarrassing circumstances, were much
less at their ease.

We were all conducted into another room, where we
were seated opposite each other.   We remained quiet for a
few moments, getting used to the situation and our clothes,
I suppose.   Suddenly the silence was broken by voices in
conversation.   The persons who were carrying it on were
concealed ; but by listening intently we discovered that it
was Elohim in conversation with Jehovah, and he was describing the creation of the world.   His description was
taken mainly from the first chapter of Genesis.   The Gods
then decide to visit the earth and see the works of their
hands.   This they do, and seem quite satisfied with the
results of their labors ; but they decide that it is necessary
to place a ruler over the brute creation, since they must be
governed and brought under the control of a superior order
of intelligence.

The Gods continue their discussions, and Michael the
Archangel is called and given control of "the earth and
all that therein is."   The brute creation is to be subject to
him ; the fruits of the earth shall yield abundantly for his
sustenance.   Of all these he is free to partake, with one
single exception : he shall not eat of the fruit of a tree
which stands in the middle of the garden.

This tree is represented by a small evergreen, on the
branches of which are tied apples, raisins, oranges, or
bunches of grapes, as may happen.   The fruit on the occasion of my passing through was raisins.

Michael — or Adam, as he is now called — finds his new
abode rather a lonesome place, in spite of its beauty ; and
even the knowledge of his power over all about him does not

prevent him from longing for companionship. The Gods, too, decide that it is not good for him to be alone; and as there is nothing on earth that is sufficiently near an equality with him to be admitted to an intimate friendship, it is determined to give him a companion created specially for him. A profound slumber falls upon him, and we were all told at that time to feign sleep also, which we did. Elohim and Jehovah then make their first visible appearance, and go through the form of taking a rib from Adam's side, and on the instant appears Eve, in the person of Miss Eliza R. Snow.

At this point we were told to wake up, and instantly

APOSTLE WILLARD WOODRUFF.
["Timothy Broadbrim."]

every Adam present appropriated to himself an Eve, and, led by the chief Adam and his bride, we all marched about, looking at our new kingdom and marking all its beauties. It was then that Adam became separated from Eve, and wandered off by himself, very much after the fashion of husbands of the present day; and while he was away, Satan entered and commenced a desperate flirtation with the coy and guileless Eve. The Garden of Eden is represented by painted scenery and furnishings.

It requires some imagination to invest this place with all the beauty that is supposed to have belonged to the original garden; but as it is the best Eden that can be provided, we, like all the rest of the Saints, were obliged to be content with it. Satan was for many years represented by W. W. Phelps, who has recently died. Much to his own surprise and great chagrin, he saw his end approaching; for he had always claimed to be immortal, and on a seal-ring which he wore while in the Endowment-House was inscribed the blasphemous legend, —

"The Lord and I
Shall never die."

I do not know who has succeeded him; but I know that in the Temple at Nauvoo, John D. Lee used frequently to assume the character, and I have heard old Mormons say that "he made a first-rate devil." I think no one who has watched his career will doubt that. Since, however, Brigham has recently cut him off from the church, it is hardly probable that he will ever again be able to make his appearance in his old character at the Endowment-House.

Satan was dressed in a tight-fitting suit of black, slashed with pink, pointed shoes, helmet, and a hideous mask. His costume, with the exception of the mask, resembled very closely the dress always worn by the stage Mephistopheles. I think he must have had different costumes, since it has been described several times, and the descriptions have varied in every case.

Eve seemed decidedly pleased with his attentions, and prattled on to him in artless gaiety. He, in turn, showed her the tree of the forbidden fruit, and tempted her to taste it. She did taste it, and finding it pleasant, offered it to Adam, who, by the time the mischief was done, returned to look after his wife. It required but little coaxing on her part to induce him to take the fruit, and he also found it agreeable. At this juncture they seemed to discover their condition of supposed nudity, and instantly they produced white linen aprons, with fig-leaves stitched upon them, and proceeded to put them on. All the rest of us did the same.

The pattern of this apron, by the way, was said to have been given to Joseph Smith by revelation. It was a square of white linen, measuring about eighteen inches, on which were to be sewn nine fig-leaves cut from green silk. Those who first took their Endowments had their aprons made after this model; but there were afterwards many inventions sought out for improving the Lord's pattern, one of which was to paint them. Over these painted aprons fancy fairly ran riot. The borders would be whatever color the person making them might choose, and were red, yellow, or blue, as the caprice dictated, with white centres filled with green leaves. The shape of these leaves was as varied as the people who wore the aprons. Some resembled the oak leaf, some the fig, a part the burdock, and others were like nothing else that ever was seen under the sun. A company going through their Endowments thirty years since, presented, it is said, a decidedly fantastic appearance. Aiter trying every conceivable mode of making the aprons, they have settled down to the "revealed pattern" as the best every way.

After the aprons were on, the voice of Elohim was heard calling Adam; but he was afraid, and hid himself with Eve. All the rest of us were supposed to follow their example, and there was a most undignified scurrying behind sofas, chairs, or any other article of furniture that was convenient. It was like nothing so much as the old game of "hide-and-seek," and it was a rare piece of fun to see men and women scudding in every direction about the room. It was like a good old-fashioned frolic to me, and I actually laughed aloud, much to my discomfiture and Heber Kimball's horror, who reproved me afterwards, and told me it was very wrong. "For," said he, "these things are sacred, and make me feel as solemn as the grave, and I can scarce refrain from shedding tears every time I see them."

I was properly penitent, but I know I thought at the time how very easily Brother Heber was moved.

The devil was then cursed, and he fell upon his hands and knees, and wriggled and hissed in as snake-like a manner as possible; we were all brought out from our several

THE ENDOWMENT CEREMONIES:

1. Listening to Elohim and Jehovah.   2. Appropriating an Eve.   3. Satan tempting Eve.   4. Tasting the forbidden fruit.   5. In the Garden of Eden.   6. Putting on the fig leaf.
7. Hiding from Elohim.   8. Satan before Elohim.   9. Cursed and driven from the Garden of Eden.

hiding-places, the curse was pronounced upon us, which doomed us to leave the beautiful garden, and earn our bread by the sweat of our brows. We were then driven into another room, which was called the world; and then we had taken our "First Degree."

We found the world a very bewildering place. We were drawn hither and thither, and tossed about by every conflicting wave of circumstance. Our friend, the devil, did not leave, but was our constant visitor, urging us to new deeds of sin. We were waited upon by representatives of the different sects, each descanting upon his peculiar plan of salvation, and its advantage over all the rest. The Quaker advocated his non-resistance doctrine. The Methodist gave a graphic, but not very refined description of the future torments of those who did not take his road to heaven. The Presbyterian gave his belief in foreordination and election in the very terse lines, —

> " You can if you can't;
> If you will you won't;
> You'll be damned if you do;
> You'll be damned if you don't."

The Baptist expatiated upon the virtues of immersion and close communion, and insisted upon predestination as the principal basis of religion; the Catholic called for observances of fasts and prayers to the Virgin Mary. Each grew more clamorous in recommending his special creed, and the discussion waxed fast and furious, even the peaceful Quaker shouting his "good will to men" with a red face, an angry voice, and excited manner, when Satan entered, filled with delight at the disturbance, and urging them on to renewed contention.

Then the apostles began to visit the earth, and comfort its afflicted tenants with plans of the true, revealed religion that was to be their salvation. They put the devil to flight, and the representatives of the "false religions" cowered and shrank away before the truth which they brought.

We were then given certain signs, pass-words, and grips, arranged in a circle, and told to kneel; the women were also required to cover their faces with their veils; then we were bidden to raise our right hands heavenward, and take the oath of implicit obedience and inviolable secrecy. The women promised entire subjection to their husbands' will; the men that they would take no woman as a wife without the express permission of the priesthood. We all promised that we would never question the commands of our authorities in the church, but would grant them instant obedience; we swore also to entertain an everlasting enmity to the United States government, and to disregard its laws so far as possible; we swore that we would use every exertion to avenge the death of our Prophet Joseph Smith and his brother Hyrum upon the Gentile race, by whose means they were brought to their unhappy fate, and to teach our children to foster this spirit of revenge also; and last of all, we swore never to reveal the mysteries of the Endowment House.

The breaking of this latter oath was to be followed by the most horrible penalties; torture of the most excruciating kind was to be inflicted upon anyone who should disregard this oath — his bowels should be torn from him while he was yet alive; his throat should then be cut from ear to ear; his heart and his tongue cut out; and in the world to come he should inherit eternal damnation. There should be, nor could be, no chance of salvation for him.

These promised penalties are by no means mere forms of words, given merely to add impressiveness to the ceremony. The "Blood-Atonement" shows that they are carried out, and hundreds of cases could be cited in addition to those already given, to prove that the Endowment-House penalties are by no means dead letters in the Mormon Church law. The cutting of every Gentile and apostate throat, and the "sending to hell across lots," that have been so openly and emphatically urged from the stand by Brigham Young and others, is only a public expression of the mysteries of the Endowment oaths.

Brother Heber endeavored to add weight and emphasis to this horrible rite by delivering a discourse to us on the duty of keeping quiet, even to our husbands or wives, on the subject; from the time we left the room we were in, the transactions therein must not be mentioned, or even hinted at, to anyone. He then entered upon a dissertation of the glories of the Celestial Kingdom, and fairly outdid himself in coarseness and vulgarity. It was then announced to us that the talk finished the ceremony of the " Second Degree," and we were told to enter the next room, for the purpose of having the "Third Degree" of the Order of Melchisedec Priesthood conferred upon us.

In this room a portion of the scenes of the last were repeated : the devil encouraged the ministers of the conflicting denominations to visit the new inhabitants of earth, and urge their religions on them once more. The apostles stop the proposed visit, and explain still further the doctrines of the true faith; they organize a new church, which is, of course, the "Church of Jesus Christ of the Latter-Day Saints." Our Temple robes were changed; resting afterwards upon the left shoulder and fastening under the right arm — which was a sign that we were now received into the true church, and subject to the will of its leaders. Another grip was taught to us, and we then received the "Third Degree," and were ready to "pass through the veil."

The men, of course, went through first, and they were permitted then to take us women through.

The room we were in was divided by a muslin partition, in which was a door; in this door was a hole just large enough to pass the hand through, and over this hole was a curtain of muslin. The persons who were behind this muslin partition — which was supposed to represent "the veil" — were invisible to us, although they could see us distinctly.

24

A man approached the door as if seeking admittance, and the Apostle Peter, appearing at the opening, asked who was there and what was wanted. He was told that some one wished to enter. The applicant was told to come near, and, as he approached, hands came through the opening in the door, and cut a mysterious mark on each breast of the man's garment, another over the abdomen, still another over the right knee. The garments of all the applicants were treated in the same mysterious manner, and the women were told to copy them in their own when they went home. It was also commanded them that whenever other garments were made, these marks must be placed on them.

After the garments had been cut, the applicant for admission gave the last grip which had been taught them, through the slit in the partition, and whispered his or her new name to those behind who were waiting to hear it, and was then permitted to go "behind the veil." The women were then taken through, the married ones by their husbands; I, as I have before said, by Elder Samuel Richards, brother of Apostle Franklin D. Richards, of Hand-Cart memory. Several remained to be sealed, but as I had not that ceremony to go through, I was permitted to go away.

I was perfectly exhausted by what I had passed through, and quite dissatisfied. It was so different from what I expected that I was saddened and disappointed by it all. My feelings of the morning had undergone a most radical change. I was no longer buoyed up by the enthusiasm of religious fervor; that had died away, and I was as hopeless and apathetic as I had before been eager and buoyant.

I was too tired to go home at once; so I went to Heber Kimball's to rest. When he returned from the Endowment-House he found me there, and he asked how I felt since I left the House; if I had found peace and help. I told him no; that I felt worse, if possible, than ever. It was then that he reproved me for the levity which he had seen me show, and told me he feared I did not take my Endowments ín the right spirit. I began to think that that might be the case, and that the fault lay with me and my understanding, and possibly the ordinance was not such a farcical proceeding as it had seemed to me ; and I took the reproof so humbly and with such good grace, that Brother Heber grew absolutely hopeful for me.

It is claimed that the mysterious rites were taken from Masonry, and that the Endowments are a direct outgrowth of the secret society. Brigham Young delights, I know, to speak of it as "Celestial Masonry," but I am very sure all good Masons would repudiate it and its teachings.

"Apostle" Heber C. Kimball.

In regard to the oaths of secrecy which I took at that time, I do not consider that I am doing anything wrong in breaking them ; I am sure I shall in no way be held accountable for so doing. I took them because I felt that I must. I did not know what I was promising until after the oath was given me, while I listened with uplifted hand. I was bound to secrecy, but I feel that right and justice demand that I shall break these bonds. I consider it a duty to expose, as far as I possibly can, the wickedness, cruelty, blasphemy, and disloyalty of the leaders of the deluded Mormon people.

All Mormons who have received their Endowments are buried in their robes — caps, shoes, apron, and all. It is held necessary in order to insure their entrance into the Celestial Kingdom. One of the authorities in the church was once asked what would become of the Mormon children who should die before they were old enough to receive their

Endowments, and consequently were buried without the robes.

He replied that their parents, or whoever had the power of resurrecting them, must prepare the clothing, and when their dead came out of their graves they were to clothe them with the sacred robes.

A few years since a man named Baptiste was discovered robbing the dead of their garments, and as a matter of course the greatest excitement prevailed. He was immediately "made away with," his house searched, and a large number of robes discovered. Some said that he was put on a little island in the lake, and left to perish. Others said that Porter Rockwell looked after his interests. But certain it is that he "disappeared," and was never seen again. The garments were identified, and the friends of the dead began taking up the bodies and replacing the robes. Brigham ordered them to desist, telling them that "under the circumstances their friends would be taken care of in the resurrection;" so most of the robes were never restored.

CHAPTER XXIII.

THE PROPHET MAKES LOVE TO ME. — I HAVE OTHER VIEWS.

The Prophet Casts his Eye on Me. — He Objects to My Beaux. — "A Low Set Anyway." — I Didn't Want to Marry the Prophet. — He Considers Himself an Irresistible Lover. — My First Drive with the Prophet. — I Join the Theatrical Corps. — How We "Got Up" our Parts. — How "Fun Hall" was Built. — The Prophet Erects a Theatre out of Temple Funds. — How Julia Deane, the Actress, Fascinated the Prophet. — How Brigham Cheated the Actors in his Theatre. — The Girls Grumble over their Scanty Fare. — They Want Something Good to Eat. — My New Beau. — Love at First Sight. — I am Engaged to My First Husband.

MY FIRST APPEARANCE IN BRIGHAM'S THEATRE.

SOON after I took my Endowments, Brigham Young showed his consciousness of my existence. He had always seen me frequently, but had regarded me and treated me as a child. He seemed suddenly to realize that I had grown to be a young lady, and the first intimation he gave of it was by interfering with my beaux.

Like most girls of my age, I was very fond of gay society; liked honest admiration and attention; and I should like to know what girl of seventeen does not, whether she be Mormon or Gentile?

I was at that time quite intimate with Emmeline Free's children, and I knew nearly all of the rest of Brigham Young's children; but Emmeline's were nearer my own age, and circumstances had thrown us more together. Emmeline had a younger brother, Finley Free, who was at one time a great friend of mine; indeed, as many boys and girls before us have done, I suppose we fancied we were in love with each other. Finley was a jolly fellow, full of fun, and we agreed capitally. Emmeline used to throw us together in every possible way, — for, I suppose, like most women of a somewhat romantic turn of mind, she was fond of match-making, and having no other convenient couple at hand, she amused herself with us.

Brigham saw me often at Emmeline's, and twice at the theatre, always with Finley Free. He was always very pleasant to me, and I quite liked him, until one day he went to my mother, and told her that he wished her to stop my going about with Finley Free; that I ought not to have any-thing to do with "those Frees;" they were "a low set any-way," and didn't amount to anything, either the boys or girls — a rather peculiar remark for him to make, when his favorite wife at that time — for that was before the reign of Amelia opened — was one of those selfsame Frees of whom he spoke so contemptuously to my mother.

Of course I didn't like this interference at all, and I con-sidered myself quite a martyr to the Mormon priestly rule. I expressed my opinion of the Prophet very freely, and, I have no doubt, very foolishly, and I spoke of him in a man-ner that fairly horrified my mother, who considered me nearly as profane and blasphemous as if I had found fault with the overrulings of Providence. The Mormon people bow as humbly, and say as resignedly, "Thy will, not mine, be done," before a fiat of Brigham Young's as they do be-fore a mysterious dispensation of the Lord's; and I honestly believe they would dare question the justice of God sooner than that of Brigham Young. The latter holds them so com-pletely, body and soul, that they shrink before his displeas-ure in absolute terror, and regard religiously his every slightest wish.

All the girls of my acquaintance knew of the trouble, and, naturally enough, all sympathized with me; and a more rebellious set of mortals was never seen. We indulged in the most incendiary talk, and turned the torrent of our wrath especially against polygamy. One girl suggested that, as the old men always interfered with the girls' "fun," it was more than likely that it was because they wanted them for themselves; and ended by turning to me, and saying, "Perhaps Brother Brigham means to marry you himself."

"But he won't," said I, angrily; "I wouldn't have him if he asked me a thousand times, — hateful old thing."

My spirit was warmly applauded by my auditors, and we all entered into a solemn compact, then and there, never, *never*, to enter polygamy. How fortunate it was that our futures were unrevealed to us! I look back now to that time, and then think of the girls as they are to-day, — most of them polygamous wives, — hating the bondage in which they are held, yet wearing their galling fetters with a hopeless sort of patience, that is, after all, only silent endurance; for it would avail nothing if they should cry out in despair and desperation; they would only be treated with greater neglect, insulted oftener and more openly, or else held up to public ridicule by their religious leader, to whom the unhappy husbands of these complaining wives — women who dared to be wretched when Mormonism declared they should not — had related their domestic grievances.

It may seem rather strange that such a simple affair as a school-girl's indignation-meeting should be reported to the Prophet. But it was; and, among other things, my unlucky speech was repeated to him. Most men would have laughed at it as mere girlish nonsense and folly, and never have thought of it again, much less spoken of it; but not so Brigham Young. No affair is too trivial to fail to be of interest to him; and, besides, in this speech of mine — girl as I was — his vanity was sorely hurt. If he has one weakness above all his other weaknesses, it is his vanity regarding the power he possesses over my sex; and to have his fascinations called in question was a sore hurt for his pride.

What cowards we all are, to be sure! I was as brave as you please in making my declaration of independence to my mates, with whom, at that particular period, I was something of a heroine; but when called upon to defend that declaration, I am ashamed to say, I left it to take care of itself, and employed myself in stammering out excuses for its existence.

MY FIRST RIDE WITH BRIGHAM.

I was going home one day, and was walking leisurely along, when the presidential carriage, with the President himself as the sole occupant, stopped at the edge of the sidewalk. Brother Brigham gave me a very kindly greeting, and said, "You are some distance from home; get in and ride with me; I will carry you there."

I knew the invitation was equivalent to a command; so I got reluctantly into the carriage, feeling very small indeed, and hating myself that I did not refuse. As we rode along, he suddenly burst out with, "I heard you said you wouldn't marry me if I wanted you to ever so much."

I was so surprised that it nearly took away my breath. I managed to stammer out a very incoherent, lame reply, and grew every minute more embarrassed. He said no more to me on the subject, but was very pleasant, and took me home to my mother, who was quite surprised to see me appearing in that style. I think Brigham's mind was made up from that time that I should one day be his wife; not, I think, from any particular affection which he cherished for me, but to punish me for my foolish speech, and to show me that his will was stronger than mine, and that he did not choose to be set at defiance even by so insignificant a person as myself.

The autumn in which I was eighteen years of age, he sent for me to come to the theatre as a member of the company, for he wished to make an actress of me. At the same time he told my mother that he thought I had better stay at the "Lion House," which is where the larger part of the family live, as our own house was so far away from the theatre that it would be extremely inconvenient for me to live there, as I would be obliged to be back and forth from the theatre every evening, and often through the day. He wished me to enter upon my new duties at once, and as I had no thought of disobeying him, I went immediately on receiving the summons. I did not see why I should be sent for, as I had no particular talent or taste for the stage, and I knew absolutely nothing about the art of acting. I never had the slightest training or preparation for it, but plunged into it, entirely ignorant of what I was undertaking. I did "juvenile business," with an occasional "soubrette" part as a variation; but in the latter line I was not nearly so successful. Several of Brigham's daughters were acting at the time. The most prominent were Alice, who did "leading" business, and Zina, who was "leading juvenile."

At that time the theatre was a church affair. All the actors and actresses were Mormons, with the exception of an occasional "star," and all of them played without salaries. They were selected from the first families in the city by the owner of the theatre, who, of course, was Brigham Young, and spent literally all their time in studying, rehearsing, and preparing wardrobes, which they furnished themselves. The honor of being selected by Brother Brigham to amuse him and assist him was supposed to be sufficient remuneration.

The theatre, by the way, has been, and still is, a prolific source of revenue to the Prophet. Theatricals have always been largely patronized by the Saints, and rank with dancing as an amusement. They were introduced into Nauvoo by Joseph Smith, and as soon as possible after the arrival in Salt Lake Valley they were commenced. The actors were all amateurs, and the playing, no doubt, was something quite extraordinary; but it was a recreation, and fortunately the audiences were not critical. Dramatic effects are very much liked by this people, and they would reduce everything to a play, if possible. They certainly make it a part of religious service; for what is the "Endowment," if it is not a drama, and a very silly one at that?

The first Utah theatricals were held in a building called "Social Hall," but after a time the Prophet became impressed that another building was required. So, taking "Amusements" as a text, he delivered a sermon on the proposed new building. He said he should christen it "Fun Hall," as he thought that would be the most appropriate name that could be given it. "It is," he said, "to be a place where the Saints can meet together and have all the fun they desire. And no Gentiles shall ever desecrate its sacred stage with their tragedies. It is built exclusively for ourselves and our own holy fun."

This was good news to a people who were already becoming very weary with the exactions of their priesthood. Now, the Prophet said, it was the will of the Lord that we should have a little relaxation from the constant, wearing toil, which was beginning to be almost unendurable. The Prophet further enlightened us how it was to be built. "We can borrow some of the 'Temple fund,' for present use," he explained; "but that will be a matter of but small moment, since we can so soon replace it." So "Fun Hall"

BRIGHAM'S THEATRE.

was built with the tithing, and any Saint could have access to the amusements given there by paying whatever entrance fee Brigham demanded. It did not retain its name after it was finished, but was called "Brigham's Theatre."

As soon as it was completed it was dedicated, after the usual Mormon fashion. The choir sang, and the singing was followed by earnest and lengthy prayer from some good brother, — I have forgotten which one, — after which Brigham rose, and said, —

"Through the help of the Lord, we have been able to

build this theatre. I know that it is as good a building as any of the kind that was ever built, and I am not going to have it defiled like the Gentile theatres. I will not have a Gentile on this stage. Neither will I have tragedies played. I've said that before, and I mean it. I won't have our women and children coming here to be frightened so they can't sleep at night. I'll have a Saints' theatre, for the Saints, and we'll see what we can do ourselves."

Yet, in flat contradiction to all this bombast, it was not three months before tragedies were represented on that stage, and, the very first winter, a Gentile actor was engaged, who played there through the entire season. Gentile players and Gentile plays have been continued up to this day, and let me assure you there is no more appreciative admirer of the actresses who visit Salt Lake than Brigham Young. He has fallen a victim to the charms of several, but he never was so impressed as he was with Julia Deane Hayne. He was madly in love with her, and, for a while, Amelia's position seemed a little precarious. He bestowed every attention upon the lady, had her portrait painted on his sleigh, and made her an actual offer of marriage, which she refused on the spot, without even taking time for consideration. His regard for her never ceased, and I have heard, on what seemed very good authority, — although I cannot vouch for its truth, — that after he heard of her death he had one of his wives baptized for her, and then sealed to him for her; so he is sure, he thinks, of possessing her in the next world, although he could not induce her to look kindly upon him here. No doubt she will be properly grateful when she finds out that he has taken care of her future welfare, and has assured her salvation, and fixed her position in the next world.

Since the theatre was first opened, all or nearly all the "stars" have played there, on their way to California. We have had all the actors and actresses, from Forrest and Le Clerq to Lydia Thompson and Dickie Lingard, and the

entertainments have varied from tragedy to a "variety show."
We have had as musical entertainments everything from
opera to negro minstrelsy. We have had Gentiles in the
stock company; and some of our Mormon girls, who have
made success in their profession, have slipped away to
other places, renounced Mormonism, and are making fine
positions for themselves in the outside world. A Miss
Alexander, especially, who was one of our most promising
actresses, became a very great favorite in California, where
she played for some time.

The theatre has been a source of wealth to Brigham.
Built by money extorted from the people for the avowed
purpose of erecting a Temple to God, it, of course, was no
expense to him, personally; and yet, although built by the
church money, he has appropriated it as private property,
and he pockets every dollar that is made at the theatre, and
devotes it exclusively to his own use. For a long time his
actors, except the Gentile ones, whom he was obliged to
pay, cost him nothing, and as everyone furnished his or
her wardrobe, the owner of the theatre was put to very
little expense in carrying it on.

Now he has to pay even his Mormon players. He tried
a short time ago to return to the old system again, but he
failed utterly, as the actors would not listen to such a proposition for a moment, and he did not dare to press it, lest
he should lose some of the best members of his company.
The younger Mormons are not afraid to leave Utah, and
the church; and, thrown as they constantly are with people
from the outside world, — the "Babylon," which they have
been taught to dread and look upon with fear and horror,
as a place full of all kinds of lying abominations, and wickedness of every sort, — they have many opportunities of
learning of that same world and what it offers. This Gentile intercourse is doing more than anything else to break
the tyrannical yoke of a corrupt priesthood, and liberalize
the minds of the Utah people.

In the days of my own dramatic experiences, the Gentile
element by no means predominated, and we all worked for
the good of the Prophet.   I was never enthusiastic over my
profession, and never made a brilliant success in it, though
I was something of a favorite, and had very pleasant things
said of me, not only in the Salt Lake, but even in the California papers, by some persons who had seen me act.
Whatever it was that kept me from being an absolute failure I never knew.   It certainly was not because I had prepared for my profession, for I had not; and I only went
through the parts assigned to me as I fancied they should
be given, and I never attempted any stage tricks or man-
nerisms.   If I had, my doom would have been sealed.   I
fancy that my adherence to nature, and a constant refrain-
ing from striving for effect, had a great deal to do with my
popularity; for I was liked, even though I was no artist,
and it is not egotism for me to say it.   I was glad to be
liked, and I am glad still, and I knew that the liking was
genuine and honest, and I returned it, too.   My public was
like a party of friends, and I was always on the best of
terms with them, and grateful to them for giving me so
much encouragement.

Then the company were all my friends.   It was almost
like a family; and I do not believe there was ever a theatre
where there was less of envyings, and jealousies, and
strifes, than there was among us.   I look back to those
days as among my pleasantest recollections; for, in addition to my happy theatrical life, I then first realized the
romance of love.

As had been proposed by Brigham when he summoned
me to the theatre, I spent most of the time at the Lion
House with the family.   Most of them I had known from
my earliest childhood; so I was not among strange people,
but rather among good friends.   I went home every Sunday, and once or twice during every week, and called it
living at home; but I visited in the Prophet's family.

They lived there in the most frugal manner. There was enough on the table, but the fare was not so varied as might have been, and the younger ones, especially, used to get very tired of the constant repetition of dishes. We usually knew just what we should find on the table; for, whatever else was absent, bread and butter and dried peachsauce were always there. It got rather monotonous after a while; and I must confess I used to enjoy rushing off to my mother and getting something good to eat, and "the girls" used to enjoy going with me, when I would take them. They grumbled as much as they dared over the home fare; but they did it very quietly among themselves, as they did not dare to have their complaints reach their father's ears, for he would not endure grumbling from them any better than he would endure it from any of his people.

But it was a very funny sight, if one could only have seen it as I did, to watch the girls when the bell rang for tea or for breakfast. They would all jump up from whatever they happened to be doing, and, striking various attitudes, would exclaim, "Bread and butter and peach-sauce." Sometimes the tone assumed would be tragical in the extreme; sometimes it would be pathetic, sometimes despairing, sometimes expostulatory; and the attitudes would all agree with the tone. Then all the way down the long hall that led to the dining-room, as long as they could without being perceived and reproved by any of the elder members of the family, they would march along, and chant, in subdued tones, in a doleful sort of wail, "bread and butter and peach-sauce." I once suggested that it sounded like a dirge.

"Don't we wish it were!" answered one, quickly; "but in that case, my dear, we should put more spirit into our performance."

I little thought, in those days, that I should ever be in a position to "wail" in earnest over the Prophet's parsimony—in those days when I "assisted" his daughters at their daily performances. I think I should have put more heart into my wailing, and sorrowed quite as much for my own sake as for the lack of luxuries on the prophetic table. But the fun that we got out of it, and the knowledge that we should be disapproved of if our grumblings were known, gave a relish even to the monotonous fare, and we endured it as we could not if we had not the memory of the frolic to assist us. Nothing is hard to endure if you can in some way make a jest of it, not even "bread and butter," and the dryest of dried peach-sauce.

It was while I was acting that I met my first husband, Mr. James L. Dee. He was an Englishman, a very handsome fellow, and a very great favorite with all the girls. It was one of those romantic affairs called "love at first sight," and I surrendered at discretion, without attempting to resist the hold which the new fancy took on me. We met accidentally at the house of a mutual friend, and the chance meeting soon ripened into a friendship, and that into a nearer relation. My whole life was brightened by the new, sweet glory that had swept in in such a torrent upon me. It took on a new look, and even the most common things were invested with a strange, novel interest. Nothing seemed natural. Everything in my life had deepened and broadened in the light of my new experience. Commonplace people grew interesting, commonplace events stirring. The whole world was tinted with the rose-color of my romance. I was very happy. My friends did not approve of my lover at all, and they all advised me not to encourage his attentions. They saw that he was in no way my equal; but I was so blinded that I would not see what they pointed out to me. There was disparity in disposition and in temperament, all of which promised, to those who could see and understand the matter, unhappiness if we came into a closer relationship.

But what girl of eighteen ever thinks seriously of these things? I was, I suppose, no more unwise than all

girls of that age are, nor any more unreasonable. I had a
touch of romance in my nature, and I did what so many
women do who are in love. I made an ideal; then I set
myself to find some living person to invest with all the virtues and graces, mental, moral, and physical, of my imaginary hero. I found the person, and straightway set myself
to worship. But he was a very different person from the
one of my creation; the one was brave, gentle, noble,
kind, and steadfast; the other — well, time will show what
he was.

But all the winter, after I went on to the stage, I was
loving this imaginary being, and calling it James Dee. I
grew ambitious, and I acted better all the time. I think,
perhaps, if I had remained on the stage, and had not lost
my ideal, I should have accomplished something in my
profession. Love does make a woman ambitious. If she
never had before, in all her life, a desire to be, to do, to
excel, she has it now. She wants to do something to make
herself the better worth his taking. There is such a sweet
humility about a woman's love! She is always depreciating
herself, always growing shy and timid in the light of the
superior wisdom which she insists that her lover must
possess.

It is very sweet to worship in this way, but it is disastrous. It is bad for both lover and beloved. But girls, in
their first romance, don't take this into account.

My parents did not forbid my engagement, although
they plainly told me they did not approve of it; and after
they found that I was determined, they gave a reluctant
consent, but they counselled silence on the subject, hoping
that I might see something in my lover which should induce
me to change my mind. They were wise enough not to
tell me the reason, but I knew it intuitively, and the very
knowledge that they were hoping that I might give him
up made me only the more determined to cling to my
lover in spite of them all. And I did. I never wavered

25

in my devotion for a moment.   I gave him the truest love
a woman can give a man ; the entire wealth of my affection I lavished on him ; and he repaid it as men of his
class, selfish, overbearing, and domineering, usually repay
it — in neglect and abuse when once I was in his power.
But he showed none of that domineering spirit in the
days of our early acquaintance ; he deferred to me in the
slightest matter ; he professed to love me very tenderly,
and I believe he did love me as well as he was capable of
loving anything, or anybody, outside of himself.   At all
events, I found nothing to miss in his care for me, and affection towards me, and for the few months preceding my
marriage, everything in my life was tinted with the softest
rose glow.

CHAPTER XXIV.

MY FIRST MARRIAGE — A LIFE'S MISTAKE.

My first Marriage. — Wedded to James Dee. — Marriage Rites in the Endowment-House. — The way in which Plural Wives are Taken. — Brigham sends for Me to help in the Theatre. — Repenting of Matrimony. — I get tired of it in a Month. — Cruel Conduct of my Husband. — He flirts considerably with the Young Girls. — I am greatly Disgusted and furiously Jealous. — He threatens to take another Wife. — The Ownership of Women in Utah. — How Newspaper Reporters are humbugged by Brigham. — How Visitors to Salt Lake are Watched. — The Prophet's Spies. — How People are misled about Utah Affairs. — The Miseries of the Women Overlooked.

A LIFE OF UNHAPPINESS.

WAS married in the Endowment-House, on the 4th of April, 1863.

As persons are not allowed to enter the inner rooms of that mysterious place for the purpose of going through any of the rites or ordinances of the church in their customary dress, we, of course, wore our Temple-robes during the ceremony. We carried our robes with us, and dressed there, not appearing outside in our sacred clothing.

I must confess I no longer regarded the Endowment-House with the awe which I had felt previous to my first visit there, and the whole manner in which everything was done was so very stagey, that I failed to be impressed at all on this my second visit, although the object of my present visit naturally made me feel more solemn than I otherwise should.

The marriage service, which is not long, was performed by Brigham Young. We first gave our names, ages, native town, county, state, and country, to the Elder John Lyon, who acts as scribe in the Endowment-House, and he carefully recorded them, as he does those of every couple who come to be sealed. We then went before Brigham Young, who was waiting for us, and the following ceremony made us man and wife: —

"Do you, Brother James Dee, take Sister Ann-Eliza Webb by the right hand, to receive her unto yourself, to be your lawful and wedded wife, and you to be her lawful and wedded husband, for time and for all eternity, with a covenant and promise on your part that you will fulfil all the laws, rites, and ordinances pertaining to this holy matrimony, in the new and everlasting covenant, doing this in the presence of God, angels, and these witnesses, of your own free will and accord?"

"Yes."

"Do you, Sister Ann-Eliza Webb, take Brother James Dee by the right hand, and give yourself to him to be his lawful and wedded wife, for time and for all eternity, with a covenant and promise on your part that you will fulfil all the laws, rites, and ordinances pertaining to this holy matrimony in the new and everlasting covenant, doing this in the presence of God, angels, and these witnesses, of your own free will and accord?"

"Yes."

"In the name of the Lord Jesus Christ, and by the authority of the holy priesthood, I pronounce you legally and lawfully husband and wife, for time and for all eternity. And I seal upon you the blessings of the holy resurrection,

with power to come forth in the morning of the first resurrection, clothed with glory, immortality, and everlasting
lives; and I seal upon you the blessings of thrones, and
dominions, and principalities, and powers, and exaltations,
together with the blessings of Abraham, Isaac, and Jacob.
And I say unto you, Be fruitful and multiply and replenish
the earth, that you may have joy and rejoicing in your
prosperity in the day of the Lord Jesus. All these blessings, together with all other blessings pertaining to the new
and everlasting covenant, I seal upon your heads, through
your faithfulness unto the end, by the authority of the holy
priesthood, in the name of the Father, and of the Son, and
of the Holy Ghost. Amen."

The scribe then entered the date of the marriage,
together with the names of my mother and the one or two
friends who accompanied us.

When the marriage is a polygamous one, the above service is prefaced in the following manner. The wife stands
on the left of her husband, the bride at her left hand. The
President then puts this question to the wife : —

"Are you willing to give this woman to your husband, to
be his lawful and wedded wife for time and for all eternity?
If you are, you will manifest it by placing her right hand
within the right hand of your husband." The right hands
of the bridegroom and bride being thus joined, the wife
takes her husband by the left arm, as if in the attitude for
walking, and the ceremony then proceeds in the manner
which I have quoted.

Mine was not a polygamous marriage. I had married a
man with no wife, and who assured me that I should be
the only one, and I was correspondingly happy. I had
seen so much wretchedness about me, and so much unhappiness in my father's family, where polygamy showed only
its best side, that I was glad to escape it. To be the only
one who had right to my husband's care seemed so blissful!
and I was sure that very many women were envying me

because I was so fortunate. I acted the evening of my marriage, and the news of it having got out, I was greeted, when I made my appearance, with the most tumultuous applause. Cheer after cheer arose, and it was some minutes before I could speak my lines. Every time I appeared, there was a repetition of this scene, and I was fairly embarrassed, so persistent was the applause. There was the more excitement, probably, because I had kept my approaching marriage a secret, and but very few, even of my personal friends, knew anything about it. I had stolen a march on the public, and not having the opportunity for congratulating me on my engagement, they made up for it by congratulations on my marriage. For once I was the central figure on the stage, and all my superiors gave way to me with a graceful good nature.

I remained in the theatre a month after my marriage, during which time I learned that I had made a fatal mistake in my marriage. I was forced to see, what my friends had tried to show me before, and the honeymoon was not over before I bitterly regretted my headstrong wilfulness. I loved my husband, but he made me terribly unhappy. He was accustomed to indulge in furious fits of anger, which fairly frightened me, during which he would talk shamefully to me, and threaten me with all kinds of ill treatment. I learned, too, that though I was bound to him, he still considered himself, and was considered, an unmarried man, as far as his right to marry again was concerned ; and he soon became quite a noted gallant among the young girls, bestowing on them the attentions that he had given me in our unmarried days, and treating me in the indifferent, matter-of-fact manner, tinged with a " help-it-if-you-can " air, which most Mormon men assume towards their helpless wives. Whenever he wished particularly to torture me, he would threaten to take another wife, and name over the girls whom he said he particularly fancied.

I had one friend, of whom I was very fond. He became

jealous of my affection for her, and in order to win me from her, and to break up our friendship, he pretended very great interest in her. He would leave me to go home by myself from the theatre, and would go off with her and remain a long time; then, on his return, would tell me what he said was the conversation between them, in which he would represent her as making the most ardent love to him, until, at last, I fairly came to hate her. I would not see her if I possibly could help it, and I was anything but cordial to her when we did meet. I believe now that my husband lied to me wickedly and deliberately; and yet, such was the effect of all his influence on me, that to this day I cannot see my old friend that a feeling of the most intense bitterness does not rise up in my heart against her. I never could get back the old feeling of affection for her, even though I felt that I was wronging her by my unjust treatment; but polygamy does not tend to make one woman just towards another. Suspicions, jealousies, heart-burnings, strifes of all kinds are engendered by this system, and it serves to lower the moral tone of women as well as of men. Both are sufferers alike in this respect, although possibly in a different degree. The women have all through the more conscience in the matter, though they grow bitter, and spiteful, and revengeful, while " bearing the cross."

I know I did, although I was only threatened by my husband; and I presume I annoyed him greatly by my tears and reproaches. A woman in Mormonism has need enough for tears, but it is little use for her to shed them; they only bring upon her the ridicule of all the Mormon men, from her husband at home to Brigham in the Tabernacle. This is the sympathy the "Head of the Church" gives her in public. Said he, in one of his most famous sermons : —

" It is said that women are tied down and abused; that they are misused, and have not the liberty they ought to have; that many of them are wading through a perfect flood of tears, because of the conduct of some men, together with their own folly.

"I wish my own women to understand that what I am going to say is for them as well as for others, and I want those who are here to tell their sisters, — yes, all the women of this community, — and then write it back to the States, and do as you please with it. I am going to give you from this time to the sixth day of October next for reflection, that you may determine whether you wish to stay with your husbands or not; and then I am going to set every woman at liberty, and say to them, 'Now, go your way — my women with the rest — go your way.' And my wives have got to do one of two things: either round up their shoulders to endure the afflictions of this world, and live their religion, or they may leave, for I will not have them about me. I will go into heaven alone, rather than have scratching and fighting around me. I will set all at liberty. 'What! your first wife, too?' Yes, I will liberate you all. I know what my women will say. They will say, 'You can have as many women as you please, Brigham.' But I want to go somewhere, and do something, to get rid of the whiners."

Following his Prophet's lead comes Jedediah Grant, in this fashion: —

"We have women here who like anything but the Celestial Law of God; and if they could break asunder the cable of the Church of Christ, there is scarcely a mother in Israel but would do it this day."

This in a tone of the sternest reproof, as though to hate a system which makes them the most abject slaves, under a most terrible master, was a crime. When women go to Brigham Young (as now and then one is foolish enough to do, before she gets thoroughly to know her Prophet and his peculiarities of temper and manner), and tell him of their unhappiness, and ask his advice, he whines, and pretends to cry, and mimics them, until they are fairly outraged by his heartless treatment, and their indignation or grief gets the supremacy over their other trouble. Then he tells them to go home, and make the best of things, and not make everlasting fools of themselves; or something else equally refined and consoling. They may consider themselves fortunate, indeed, if he does not refer to the interview in his next Sunday's sermon, and tell the names of the unhappy women, with coarse jests and unfeeling comments, which render them doubly wretched, since their husbands, incensed at them for complaining, and knowing that they are perfectly safe from priestly indignation or rebuke, make them feel the weight of their displeasure by grosser neglect or more brutal treatment.

The entire ownership of women is nowhere more fully assumed by their husbands than it is in Utah. A woman is obliged to submit to every exaction from him, to grant every request, obey every demand. In return, she need expect nothing, not even support. "You are mine, body and soul, but you have no right to claim anything from me more than what I choose to give you," is the attitude of every man in polygamy towards his wives. A "blessed" system, surely! It is no wonder that Brigham talks about the women's "rounding up their shoulders" to bear it, and one certainly fails to feel the surprise which "Jeddy" probably imagined he would arouse when he announced that the "mothers in Israel," unhappy and desolate, would break "the cable of the church" asunder if they could. This fanatical follower of Brigham Young never spoke a truer word in his life, whether he spake by inspiration or not. There was not a woman, then, who would not have broken her chains if she could, let the whole Mormon Church call these fetters what they might, and there is not a woman among them to-day who would not slip her fetters if she knew how. It is all very well for the Mormon leaders and their sympathizers in the Gentile world to say that the women are contented, and even happy, in polygamy; the one knows he speaks what is not true; the other tells the tale as it is told to him, refusing to use his eyes, his ears, or his common sense.

Newspaper correspondents visit Salt Lake City, and when they arrive they are brimming over with disgust and indignation towards this system and the people who follow it; but, by-and-by, a change comes over them; their readers are informed that the Mormons are a thriving, industrious people, their men brave, hospitable, shrewd, and hard-working; the women quiet and peaceful, evidently well reconciled to their peculiar marital relations; that Brigham Young is not such a bad fellow, after all, and his sons are jolly, free-handed, generous men, with plenty of keenness, and a great deal of knowledge of the world; and then the people who read their letters wonder at the changed tone, and find themselves thinking more leniently of this people and its peculiar social system than ever before, and they say, "If all this is true, why need we meddle?" But it is not true, not one word of it, and these same men who are writing these letters know it; but, in some way, they get to working in the Prophet's interests before they leave the Territory. He manages to get hold of them if they are of any ability, and able to influence the public, and if they are easily influenced themselves they soon see things as he intends they shall see them. I suppose his manner of influencing them differs, but I think it will be readily understood.

The truth is simply this: the Mormon people are absolutely afraid to have the outside world come too close to them; they let them see just so much, but not one bit more. The leaders act as showmen, also as mouthpieces, and the mass of the people are but a cunningly manipulated lot of marionettes, who perform certain antics for a curious public, while the shrewd wire-puller sits behind, and orders every movement, and makes every speech. There has been, until very recently, no such thing as getting at the absolute truth concerning these people; but lately, since the Gentile element has been so largely increased in Utah, and in Salt Lake City especially, it has been useless for the Saints to attempt to hide their real condition.

A Mormon wife-beater is as mercilessly exposed through the columns of the Gentile papers as the Gentile offender of the same class, and the nefarious dealings of Mormon officials are publicly reproved in a manner that does not tend to make them comfortable in the least. The miseries caused by this cursed system are fully ventilated, and the true condition of things revealed. When flippant newspaper correspondents, after a visit to the valley of the Saints, go away and write in terms of ridicule of the Mormon women, calling them fearfully ugly in looks, they little know what bitter, hard, cruel experiences have carved the deep lines round the eyes and mouths, and made the faces grow repulsive and grim, and taken from them all the softness, and tenderness, and grace which glorify a happy woman's face, even if she be ever so plain of feature. If these men, who write so carelessly, could only see the interior of the lives that they are touching with such a rough, rude hand, they might be, perhaps, a little more sympathetic in tone. It is no wonder that the women of Utah are not beautiful; there is nothing in all their lives to glorify or beautify their faces, to add at all to their mental or physical charm or grace. They are pretty enough as children; as young girls they can compare favorably with any girls I have seen in the East; but just so soon as they reach womanhood the curse of polygamy is forced upon them, and from that moment their lives are changed, and they grow hard or die — one of the two — in their struggles to become inured to this unnatural life. This system either kills its victims outright, or crushes out every bit of hope and ambition from them, leaving them aimless and apathetic, dragging out existence without the least ray of present happiness or future anticipation to lighten it.

I was taught from my earliest childhood that there was nothing good outside of the Mormon Church; that the Gentile men were bad to the core, possessing neither honor nor manly virtues of any kind, and that every Gentile woman was so vile as to be utterly unworthy of mention; that goodness was unknown among them, and that certain destruction awaited them and those who associated with them. My mother mourned over her friends and relatives outside of Mormonism as lost souls, and she prayed almost literally "without ceasing" that they might be shown the true way before it was too late. She could not govern her natural affection. She must love them; they were her very own, and were very dear to her; but I really think, especially in the days of the intense religious excitement, that she almost hated herself for loving them so truly and so well. She wrote them the most pathetic letters of entreaty, filled with alternate pleadings and arguments, begging them to come to Zion, and "make sure of their souls' salvation." They, in turn, pitied her delusion, but had no hope that she would ever escape from it; they little knew that the child, whose future they were deploring, would one day be the means of leading that mother out of the bondage in which she was held, through many tears and much tribulation, to the light of a brighter, more comforting faith.

Conscience and an almost superstitious belief in her religious leaders made her cling to her religion long after reason taught her that it was a delusion, and made her accept as a sole means of salvation a practice which her whole soul revolted against. It is well that the Mormon leaders call it a "cross." It is simply that, and the hopelessness of it renders it the more difficult to bear. There is no prospect of laying it down, and, unlike the cross of the old legend, it never becomes flower-wreathed. It grows heavier as the days go on, until it bows its bearer down to the very ground.

I learned the misery of even a monogamic marriage under polygamic laws; and, though I never expressed myself so openly on the subject, I yet felt an intense sympathy with a friend of mine, who, when told that her husband thought of taking another wife, replied, with the fire flashing from her black eyes, "If he does, I'll kill him!" It is not at all likely she would have kept her word; she would probably have settled down, as so many women like her have done, into a sullen sort of rebellion, which is not easy to subdue; but she has never been tried; her husband seems as indifferent to the charms of the marriageable young ladies about her as she could desire: yet she never feels entirely safe. How can she, when she knows her husband is constantly admonished that he is not "living up to his privileges." The sword above her head is suspended by a hair; it is a miracle if it does not fall at last. I know every pang of anxiety, every heart-throb of sick expectation, for I had that selfsame torture for two years, without a moment's cessation. I do not know how I bore it; but I suppose I was only being schooled for what came afterwards.

CHAPTER XXV.

MY EARLY MARRIED LIFE. — MY HUSBAND AND MY MOTHER!

My early married Life. — We go to live with my Mother. — Incompatibility of Temper. — How my Mother had opposed our Marriage. — My Husband does not Admire Her. — He goes after the Girls. — I don't like it at All. — I become extremely angry with Him. — He is advised to "increase his Kingdom." — How promises to Wives are broken by Mormon Men. — How Women are Snubbed and Undervalued. — I become Anxious and Watchful. — How Heber comforted his Wives. — My Husband subjects me to personal Violence. — He is afraid of Results. — My first Baby is Born. — Zina Young marries into Polygamy. — Contrast between Mormon and Gentile Husbands. — "The Bull never Cares for the Calves." — My Husband nearly strangles me. — I leave him, and go to my Parents. — Brigham gives me some good Advice. — I obtain a Divorce. — I rejoice at being free Again.

FAMILY JARS.

HEN I was first married, we went to live in the house with my mother, greatly to her delight, as she could not bear a separation from me. We had always been together so closely, more like sisters than like mother and daughter, and both of us dreaded very much to have this sweet relationship broken. I had been her comfort when every other stay had failed her; her hope when she was almost utterly hopeless. She had lived in me and for me, and my happiness and welfare had been her constant thought. She had opposed my marriage as a duty, and because she thought she saw only misery for me in the relation; not for a want of sympathy for me, for it really hurt her more to oppose me than it did me to persist in spite of her opposition. I had been her companion in all her wanderings, and the confidante alike of her sorrows and joys, and it was hard for her to think of parting from me, even though I might be not very far away; still our interests were naturally somewhat divided when I came to give the first place in my heart to another.

My husband owned a house, but it was rented; so until it was vacated we had a part of my mother's house, where we kept house quite cosily, and should have been very happy, had not my husband's temper and desire to torment me made life almost unbearable. I tried, as far as I could, to hide my unhappiness from my mother; but I did not succeed. Her motherly eyes were too keen, her maternal instinct too unerring, to be deceived by my silence, although she respected my reticence, and said nothing to me; but she showed her sympathy in a hundred nameless ways. My husband knew of her opposition to our marriage, and he did not like what he termed her interference; though why a mother cannot look after her daughter's interest without being accused of interfering is even now a mystery to me, especially when, seeing that her advice is not regarded, she withdraws all "interference," and makes the best of the matter that she can. But some persons never forget, and my husband was one of those; and it used sometimes to seem to me as though, in his treatment of me, he was revenging himself for the opposition shown to him by my friends.

I used to hear of his attentions to other girls, and I was furious, while I knew I was powerless. My visitors — many of whom came only when they had anything to tell — used to tell me that they saw James at the theatre with this young lady, or met him going home with that, or that he passed them walking with another, until I was madly jealous of every girl of my acquaintance. I no longer took pleasure in their society, for I saw in each one a probable rival, and a possible addition to our household. It was no consolation to me to remember that my husband had promised me never to take another wife; I had learned what the promise of a man living under polygamic laws amounts to. It is given as a sort of sedative, and if it soothes temporarily, that is all that is required of it. It is considered no sin to break a promise of this kind; indeed, it would rather seem that it is accounted sin for him to keep it; and I knew that my husband was, as well as other men, occasionally reminded that it was his duty to make his kingdom larger as speedily as possible, by taking another wife, or more than one if he liked.

We had many very stormy interviews on this subject; he used to discuss my callers, and especially the pretty girls, as most Mormon men discuss women, with reference to their "points," as jockeys would talk of horses, or importers of fine stock. Polygamy does not tend to enhance the value of womanly dignity and grace, and very little respect for them is either expressed or felt by one brought up under its baneful influence.

It is strange how quickly men, in a polygamous community, lose that chivalrous courtesy which characterizes men elsewhere. It seemed so strange to me to see the deference shown to my sex when I left Utah, and came, for the first time in my life, among people living under monogamic laws. I was particularly struck by the tenderness and consideration which men showed towards their wives and children; and I wondered to see the women, claiming, with a confidence that assured me they were used to it, and considered that it belonged to them, their husbands' attention and care. It was strange, too, to see the deference shown to a woman by the young men and boys; and when once, in a car, I saw a manly little fellow, about twelve or thir-

teen years of age, rise with a rare grace, and give his seat
to an old lady, the tears sprang to my eyes, such an unaccustomed sight was it. I contrasted that boy with the
youth of Utah, and I felt with a new indignation flashing
through all my veins, and a new sorrow tugging at my
heart, the curse that polygamy was to the young men, as
well as to the young girls, who are growing up under the
teachings of that baneful system. It is horrible! It fouls
and poisons the stream at its very source (and it adds mud
and filth as it crawls along its slimy way), sending up its
noxious vapors, until it has bred a most pestilent moral
malaria, which nothing but the cool, clear air of religious
liberty and education shall ever dispel and purify.

Why cannot men and women, outside of this terrible
system, see the horrors of it, and work for its overthrow?
My soul cries out in very agony sometimes, 'Is there no
help for this great evil?' Everywhere the world seems so
dead to it! the enormity does not seem to manifest itself
unto them. They speak lightly of Mormonism, as of
something to ridicule or laugh at, rather than to condemn.
God knows there is nothing laughable or ridiculous in it to
its victims. It is the most pathetic, tragic earnestness and
reality.

I am not imagining situations, and growing pathetic over
creations of my own fancy. I know what I say, for I have
suffered it. There is not a pang, not a throb of anguish
which I have depicted that I have not felt myself.

My health, which was never very good, gave way under
the terrible mental and physical strain to which I was subjected, and I was in danger of becoming a confirmed invalid. My physical condition did not make my husband
more tender or thoughtful, but he seemed to consider it a
wrong towards himself, and took an aggrieved tone because of it. He had worthy examples, to be sure; for Brigham himself grumbles loudly when one of his wives falls
ill, even if it is from overwork for his welfare, and com-

26

plains that "he never marries a woman that she doesn't get sick to shirk work." Heber C. Kimball, on being called once to see one of his wives who had broken her arm, accosted her, on his entrance to her room, with, "Why didn't you break your neck at once, and done with it?" And it is a notorious fact that two of Orson Pratt's wives have died of neglect during illness. Since the men high in authority set the example, what could you expect of the followers?

Although my husband had often threatened me with personal violence, in addition to the insults and persecution he was constantly subjecting me to, he never offered any until about a month before my baby was born. He made some request of me which I was totally unable to grant, and in his fury at what he termed my stubbornness and rebellion, he struck me violently, and I fell insensible before him.

Then he was frightened for once; he raised me up, carried me to my bed, and used every exertion to bring me to myself. He was afraid the blow was fatal, and he was remorseful enough. When, at last, I regained my senses, he begged my forgiveness, poured out a torrent of self-reproaches, and for a little while was more like my old lover, the man whom I had cared for so tenderly, than he had been since our marriage. I very quickly forgave him : it was so sweet to feel the old tenderness again, that I could in a moment forget all that had passed between, and I readily agreed not to let my family know of this last outrage. He knew, as well as I, that my father and brothers would take me from him, and he really did not wish to lose me ; and as for me, he was my husband, and the father of my unborn child, and for the sake of the little life which I held in trust, I could not bear to go away from him. I had hoped, O, so fondly! that the child would bring us nearer, and I could not give up the hope ; and when he stood before me so penitent, and so tender, I was ready to feel that he had always been the same.

But I was doomed to disappointment; after the birth of
my child, it seemed as though the fits of passion were more
frequent and of longer duration. He neglected me, and
was scarcely at home at all. He did not care for my baby,
seeming to consider it a rival, and my love for it seemed to
anger him. But what a comfort the baby was to me! How
I loved it! All the tide of my affection, that had been
so rudely repelled, turned towards it, and I felt that all the
interest of my life was centred therein. Like all Mormon
women, robbed of a husband's love and care, I should live

My Baby-Boy.

in and for my child. I knew very well that as far as re-
gaining my husband's real affection was concerned — if, indeed, I had ever possessed it, — the future was hopeless; so
I expected nothing from it further, and resigned myself to
the inevitable more quietly than I could have believed I
ever should have done; but my child made resignation
more easy.

The little fellow was very bright and winning, and I
used to imagine that he understood my feelings, and sympathized with me in his baby way. The little hands stray-

ing over my face and neck were full of sweet comfort; the blue eyes raised to mine in baby confidence were full of love; the little mouth which I covered with kisses never failed to smile back at me, and I even forgot to cry under the sweet, restful influence which the dimpled, rosy little bit of humanity brought into my heart.

But this exquisite happiness was of short duration; for, after a few months, my baby grew very ill; and God only knows how I suffered then. I watched over him day and night, and my devotion to him angered my husband beyond measure. He had no sympathy with or for me in those days of trial; and in addition to seeing my baby pining away, until it seemed that it must some day drift out of my clinging arms into the great unknown, unexplored sea beyond, I had to endure the constant abuse from the man who should at that time have been my stay and my comfort. But what Mormon mother ever gets the tender care from her baby's father that other happier mothers get? No time or place is so sacred that polygamy does not obtrude its ugly presence. A mother may not mourn for her child without feeling the heartless intrusion, as the following little instance will show.

A man named Thomas Williams emigrated from England with his wife and children, all eager to reach " Zion," the promised land of the Saint's inheritance. He was a very devout Mormon, and was easily induced to accept polygamy. He took for his second wife Zina Young, a daughter of Brigham and Zina Huntington, an enthusiastic, conscientious believer in polygamy, and a genuinely good, generous girl, of the most kindly impulses, but, unfortunately, wrongly trained, as all girls are under this system.

His first wife never had believed in the plural-wife system, and was never reconciled to her husband's second marriage. She mourned bitterly about it; and, very naturally, her feelings towards her rival were not kindly or pleasant. The husband knew this perfectly well; and yet, when her little baby died, and she was almost mad with grief, he insisted on bringing the second wife to the funeral as one of the family. The mother was almost beside herself at what she considered this insult to her dead child, and she declared that Zina should not come. Her husband, of course, overruled her; for when, in polygamy, does a wife ever have her own way? But Mrs. Williams refused to recognize her, and would not allow her to sit in the room with her and the child.

I was spared this torture, for there was no second wife to measure my misery, and God was good, and spared my child. He repaid all my anxious care, and put the child into my arms well and comparatively strong, at the same time that he intrusted another helpless one to my care. I had lost, at that time, much of my faith in my religion. I think I should have lost my belief in God Himself, had my baby been taken from me. But He knew how much I could bear, and he spared me this last bitter sorrow.

I had been at first jealous of the little new-comer for the other baby's sake, who was only a little over a year old when the second one came; but I soon found that I had love enough in my heart for the two. My boys! How fond, and proud, and even happy I was with them!

The measure of my love seemed to be the measure of their father's indifference, and even hate. He used to either take no notice of them at all, which I infinitely preferred, or he would handle them so roughly that the little things would shriek with pain and terror, and I would be almost frantic with fear lest he should kill them in his mad frolics, which usually ended in a fit of temper because they cried at his rude treatment.

As I was on my way East, I witnessed a little scene that called up painfully the contrast between this father's indifference and another father's care. In one car was a lady with two children; one a little girl about eight years old, and a cunning baby boy, who was just beginning to lisp in that wonderful baby prattle that is so sweet to hear. As we stopped at a station, a gentleman came in, his face beaming with pleasure and expectation. The moment the children saw him, the little girl cried out with joy, " O, my dear papa has come ! " and simultaneously mother and child clasped their arms about his neck and kissed him. The baby threw up his arms, and crowed out, "Papa, papa!" and as he took the little fellow in his arms, and fairly rained kisses over the rosy, delighted little face, the tears sprang to my eyes, and I had fairly to hide my face, for my cheeks were moist, and my mouth would quiver, as I thought of the father's love, of which my children were robbed — of which all children in Utah are robbed — by a fiendish system, given by a corrupt priesthood under the guise of a " Revelation " from God.

What a sarcasm on the infinite, tender, all-pervading love of the Divine Father !

Such a scene as this would be simply impossible in Utah, among that community whose religious leader says, in his peculiarly refined style and expression, when his lack of fatherly attention to his children is noticed and commented upon, " Well, the bull never takes any care of his calves," and whose chief apostles allow their children to grow up without support or training from them, since they are too busy in extolling the beauties of polygamy to the new converts, to give even decent attention to the children whom they have summoned into the world under this " glorious institution."

Two weeks before baby was born, I was sitting one morning with the elder boy on my lap, my husband being in the room, when one of my father's wives' children, a little fellow about three years old, came toddling in. Mr. Dee, happening to want something, asked the child to get it for him. The article in question was on a shelf, out of the child's reach, and to get it he would have to stand on a chair, and even then his tiny fingers could but just touch it.

There was a heavy jar on the shelf, which I feared he might pull down upon himself, and I remonstrated against his trying to get it. I offered to reach it myself, but my husband instantly turned and forbade my leaving my chair, saying that the child should bring him what he desired.

"But he must not," I cried, in an agony of terror.

"I tell you he shall," was my husband's answer.

The child stood looking from one to the other, half crying

STRANGLED BY MY HUSBAND.

with fear, and yet scarcely daring to disobey the command that had been given to him.

"Louis, fetch it to me instantly," commanded he again.

"Louis, you shall not," said I, half rising from my chair.

In an instant, my husband, maddened with fury that I should dare to contradict him, seized me by the throat, and threw me back into the chair. The screams of the terrified child brought my mother into the room at once. She snatched the baby from my arms, which I still held clasped convulsively, while my husband's fingers were tightening about my throat. I was dizzy with pain, and almost suffocated from the grip ; but my maternal instinct was stronger than the pain, and I never relaxed my hold on my child.

My mother called my father, and he came and rescued me from the infuriated man who held me, and carried me into my mother's room. Until that time they had known nothing of the treatment which I received from my husband. They knew that I was unhappy, but so was every woman ; so I was by no means isolated in my misery. But I had managed to keep from them all knowledge of the violent treatment I had received at his hands. Their indignation at finding it out was beyond all bounds ; for when once it was known, my tongue was loosened, and I poured into the sympathizing ears of mother and father the whole story of my wrongs. I left nothing untold, and it was such a relief to let loose the torrent of misery that had been so long pent up in my heart !

My parents and brothers decided at once that I must leave him ; and indeed, I was afraid, both for myself and for my children, to return to him again. He tried to see me in every possible way, but was refused admittance to my mother's rooms. The door of communication that led between her rooms and those I had previously occupied was securely locked, and he was bidden by my father to vacate the rooms as speedily as possible. He then demanded to see me ; he tried threats, entreaties, every means that he could devise, but I was carefully guarded, and he could gain access neither to me nor the children.

He was loud in his threats to take the children from me, and I was in terrible fear lest he should in some way gain possession of them. I knew that it would not be love for them which would impel him, but a desire to strike me where it would wound me most ; and he knew that he could reach me in no other way so surely as through my children. Since he had become convinced that I would never return to him, that of my own free will I gave him up for ever, he seemed possessed by a spirit of fury, and vowed all manner of vengeance on me.

In order to get me out of his power, my parents determined that I should be divorced from him without delay, and, like conscientious church people, they consulted President Young. He and George Q. Cannon, who was also in our confidence, both took very active measures in my behalf. There were two ways in which I could procure a divorce — one from Brigham, which was considered valid in the church, but I suppose would not stand the test of law; the other from the Probate Court. Brigham strongly advised the latter, as, in case my husband should ever apostatize, he could not take my children from me. He behaved, all through the affair, in such a kind, friendly manner that my confidence in him was fully secured. I had at that time no thought of what the future would bring, and certainly never dreamed of any closer relationship with him. My whole thought was to get free from my husband, and to have my children so securely that he could not take them from me. They were my only thought, my only care.

I say this because, since I have renounced Mormonism, Brigham Young and his followers have said that I left my first husband on purpose to become his wife — a statement which no one better knows to be false, than Brigham himself. He it was who counselled me to go to the regular courts, rather than depend on his divorcement, which he knew would not stand out of Mormondom, and he and his apostle Cannon rendered me the most valuable and untiring assistance, which I accepted gladly, as I would have accepted aid from any quarter in this extremity.

I was divorced in 1865, and the decree stands to-day in the Court Records of Utah. Since the memory of my Mormon friends seems so treacherous, I will copy the records here as they stand. They may also convince some doubters who seem to place Brigham Young's denial before my complaint, and pin their faith to him, while regarding me doubtfully as a possible adventuress.

"PROBATE COUNTY DOCKET. [*Page* 5.]

"Great Salt Lake County. — Ann Eliza Dee *vs.* James L. Dee. "In Divorce.

"1865. December 9th. — Petition filed; summons and notice issued, returnable on 23d inst., at 10 P. M.

"December 23d. — Case called; returns made and decree made dissolving bonds of matrimony, and giving to plaintiff the custody and control of her children. Costs taxed to defendant.

"1866. March 3d. — Court ordered execution against defendant for costs of suit.

"March 8th. — Execution issued for $20.50, returnable in 20 days.

"March 28th. — Execution returned; no property found; clerk's fees paid by C. G. Webb, in meat.

[*Page* 516.]

"RECORDS OF PROBATE COURT, GREAT SALT LAKE COUNTY.

"1865. Dec. 23d. — Ten o'clock, A. M. Court opened. Records of 16th and 20th insts. read and signed.

"The case of Ann Eliza Dee *vs.* James L. Dee, in divorce, was called up. This case came up for hearing upon the petition of Ann Eliza Dee, formerly Ann Eliza Webb, and upon the investigation thereof *ex parte*, the defendant, James L. Dee, failing to appear, C. G. Webb and Ann Vine being sworn and examined, the allegations in the plaintiff's petition were taken as confessed, and thereupon, after hearing the evidence and being fully advised in the premises, it was ordered and decreed by the court that the bonds of matrimony heretofore existing between the said parties be, and the same are hereby, for ever dissolved. That said Ann Eliza shall have and retain the custody and control of her two infant children, James Edward and Lorenzo Dee, during their minority, and that defendant pay costs of suit.

(Signed,)   "E. SMITH,
                                     "*Judge of Probate Court.*"

If anyone doubts my copy, they can examine the records for themselves.

My Christmas that year was a merrier one than I had seen for several years. My children were mine, — my very, very own; and no one could take them from me. I clasped them in my arms. I kissed them again and again in an ecstasy of affection. Henceforth I was father, mother, all to them; no one would dispute with me for their affection, no one claim their love. I was supremely, selfishly happy. True, my romance had died; my idol, with its feet of clay, was broken; but maternal love took the place of the girl's romance, and the little souls which had been given into my charge were more beautiful than any idol which I had been able to build for myself. I was saddened by all my disappointments, quieted by all my trials, subdued in spirit by the constant exercise of patience. I had lost my girlish gaiety and vivacity, but I had gained the poise and assurance of womanhood, and was, I hoped, better fitted to be a good mother to my children, which, at that time, was the only ambition I had, and my only interest for the entire future was in them. I dreamed for them, I planned for them, lived in them; and I am only regretful that anything ever divided my interest with them.

But after the one shadow was lifted, before the other fell, I was royally happy, — happier than I ever was in my life before, circled about as I was by clinging baby arms, and held by tiny baby hands.

CHAPTER XXVI.

AFTER MY DIVORCE. — AFFAIRS AT HOME.

After my Divorce from Dee. — "Is Polygamy Good to Eat?" — Curious Experiences Among the Saints. — A Man Who Thought His Heart was Broken. — How Two Wives Rebelled. — The Husband in a Fix. — He Runs Away from Home. — Dismisses his Plural Wife. — Being "Sealed" to Old Women for Eternity. — Nancy Chamberlain's Story. — Who is to be Brigham's Queen in Heaven. — An Old Wife Dresses Up as a Ghost. — How Brother Shaw Replenished his Exchequer. — The Battles Between my Father's Wives. — My Mother Enjoys his Troubles. — The Story of a Turkey. — A First Wife Asserts Her Rights. — My Life at South Cottonwood. — I Receive Offers of Marriage.

"GRANDMA, WHAT IS POLYGAMY?"

AFTER my divorce, I went with my mother to live at my father's farm in South Cottonwood.

Here, I think, I was happier than I had ever before been in my life. My health was much improved, and what with the care of my children and the portion of the household duties which I assumed to assist my mother, my days were well filled. My boys were growing healthy, hearty, rollicking fellows, and they returned my care with all the love which the most jealous heart could desire.

How thankful I was that they were not girls! I knew
too well the troubles of my sex in polygamy to wish to bring
one girl into the world, who, under the system, would be
sure to endure such certain suffering. I made up my mind
to teach my boys to shun it, even if it was a vital part of
my religion. I was willing to accept all else that Mormonism taught, and to teach its underlying principles to my
boys; but that I could teach them was right.

Young as they were, they realized something of polygamy from hearing it constantly talked of; for when any
two women meet, it is the chief topic of their conversation, and they knew enough to discover that it was something that was decidedly unpleasant; but what it was, they,
of course, had not the slightest idea. Still, with the curiosity natural to children, they were determined to come to
the truth of it some way or other.

One day, my youngest boy, then a little over three years
old, astonished my mother by asking, very abruptly, —

"Grandma, do you like polygamy?"

"Not at all," was the reply, wondering what would come
next.

"Is polygamy good to eat?" was the next inquiry of this
youthful investigator.

My mother thought that it was not very palatable; at
least she had not found it so, and as far as her observation
went, she had not seen anyone who relished it particularly.

The men had their "crosses" in polygamy as well as the
women, and I must confess that I was wicked enough to
enjoy their small "miseries," they seemed so insignificant
beside their wives'; but as is the case generally, I fancy,
they bore them with much less patience. The chief masculine troubles seem to be, that they cannot, with all their trying, make their plural wives agree and dwell together in
the "sweet unity" which is so delightful and so essential
to entire family happiness, and that they cannot make the
wives, or wife, they already have, welcome with any great

show of cordiality the proposal to add another to the family circle.

Not very long before my apostasy, while visiting at the house of a friend, I was introduced to a man, who, my friend afterwards told me, was almost heart-broken at the dreadful conduct of his wife. My sympathies went out at once to the sufferer, and I inquired what indiscretion, or crime, his wife had been guilty of. "O," said my friend, "she is determined that he shall not take another wife, and fights against it all the time, and he has just buried two children; and, all together, he is completely bowed down by grief."

This was before I had dared to give my honest opinion, and I was silent; but my heart ached for the poor mother whose babies were dead, and whose husband, not content with her love, was denouncing her to his friends because she was unwilling to have polygamy added to her other burdens.

A man in Utah, whom I knew very well, married a young widow for a second wife, his first strongly disapproving of the principles of polygamy. She had by no means a submissive spirit, and she sought revenge by the only means in her power — by tormenting her husband in all possible ways.

He, like all good Mormon brethren, intended to build up a "celestial kingdom" after the "divinely ordained plan," and he wished his wives to live together. There was no use talking, he said; they must agree well enough for that, as he did not intend to build another house. So he commenced this plan; but he found, after a few days, that whatever it might be in the future, it was far from "celestial" here. There was no such thing as peace in the house. His Prophet had often told him that if he could not rule his earthly kingdom, he never would be fit to be a king in the world to come; and as he was very ambitious for royal honors, he was in terrible grief and perplexity. But how to govern two unruly women was quite beyond him. His first wife was a very independent woman, with a habit of speaking her mind quite freely ; and the second had a fiery temper, which she did not hesitate to display when she considered occasion demanded.

In a few weeks he found that he must separate them ; so he divided the house, giving each one her apartments — the first wife receiving the principal share, as she had several children. But he had not bettered matters, it seemed. He had intended dividing his time equally between the two ;

No Peace within Polygamy.

but the first wife was so opposed to this arrangement that he offered to give her two thirds of his time, which, strange as it may seem, did not satisfy her, and made the second wife very angry, until, between them both, the poor man was driven almost to his wits' ends.

They had a peculiar way of finding out each other's secrets ; and when the husband was visiting one, the other would apply her ear to the key-hole of her rival's apartments. On certain occasions, when the first wife was too much engaged to attend to the key-hole herself, she would place her little daughter — a child not more than six years old — there, and bid her tell her what she heard. Imagine the effect on the child. It seems impossible that any woman, however jealous or curious, would take this means to satisfy her curiosity. Of course the child told the mother the most ridiculous things, which she affected to believe, and told to her husband on his next visit to her; in consequence of which some of the bitterest quarrels ensued.

As soon as possible the husband built a second house, a few rods from the other, and removed the last wife thither, hoping then for a little respite. But he was hoping against hope; for the trouble would never be quieted while the cause remained, and the two women could never come within speaking distance without a fearful quarrel, which often ended in personal violence, blows being exchanged, hair pulled, and dresses torn in the struggle.

Every experiment was in vain. After running away from home once himself, and coming back on account of his children, whom he really loved, he found himself obliged to send Number Two away, when quiet was again restored, although it was secured at the expense of his "kingdom."

The fault was not with either of the women; each one was good enough by herself; but it was in the accursed system, which brought, as it always does, the very worst passions to the surface, and made of each woman — who, alone, would have been a comfort to her husband — a fiend, and a constant torment to him.

Some of the Mormon brethren are so anxious to increase their kingdom that they frequently have very old ladies sealed to them. As they are all to be rejuvenated in the resurrection, and as the sealing is done for " eternity " alone, it will be all right in the future, and the discrepancies in age will go for nothing. Even Brigham Young himself has not hesitated to avail himself of his privileges in this peculiar direction, if Nancy Chamberlain's story can be believed.

Nancy Chamberlain is a very old, half-crazed woman, known, I fancy, to every Mormon in the Territory, who solemnly declares that she was sealed to Brigham in Nauvoo, and that she had the promise of being promoted to the place of first wife. She lived in his family for a long time, but she grew old, and infirm, and useless, and he turned her out of the house some years ago; and now she lives as best she may, going about from house to house, and doing light work to pay for her support.

She considers it her duty every little while to go and "free her mind," as she calls it, to Brigham's wives, telling them that they may usurp her place and defraud her of her rights in this world, but she shall be Brigham's queen in heaven. She is an eccentric old woman, but there is no doubt, I think, about her having been sealed to the Prophet. He has a great many old ladies that he expects to resurrect, and assign them to their true position in the eternal world.

These old ladies are sometimes as exacting as their younger sisters, and the husband has all he can do to pacify them and keep them quiet; but not all of them have my mother's experience and that of my old acquaintance, Mr. Ramsay. He was a very devout follower of Brigham's, and, when he was about forty years of age, he was sealed to an old lady eighty years of age, who had no husband, and consequently no hope of salvation, until he very kindly became her savior. He had three wives already, but that was a trifle not worth mentioning to a man expecting to people a world some time in the future; so, as this woman — who was called Catherine — would count one on the list, she was taken, and brought into the house with his other wives.

The first of these women, who had always been a slave to her husband and his wives, was now called upon to take the sole charge of this last selection, which she did willingly enough. But it was a difficult matter to please Catherine. No woman could do more to keep the peace than Mrs.

27

Ramsay, who was one of the sweetest tempered, kindest hearted women in the world, yet in this case it seemed to require superhuman exertions. Catherine complained of her food, her clothing, and her situation generally; but the principal cause of complaint was, that Mr. Ramsay was not sufficiently attentive to her.

"I am your wife," she used to say, in a querulous, piping voice; "I have rights and privileges equal to any other wife, and you must and shall spend one fourth of your time with me."

This not being Mr. Ramsay's view of the case precisely, he would reply, —

"It is true you were sealed to me, but it was not for time, but for eternity; and I cannot give you any part of my time here. I am willing that you should be taken care of in my family, and that should satisfy you."

But that did not satisfy her, and she determined to make him all the trouble she could. One of her first freaks was to personate a ghost; and, robing herself in white, she visited different apartments of the house while the family slept, more particularly where the husband was. Failing to bring him to terms by this mode of action, she tried something more desperate, and actually set the house on fire; it was soon discovered, however, and not much harm was done. Mr. Ramsay had been very patient with her, and viewed all her pranks in as charitable a light as possible, saying, "it was somebody's duty to exert themselves in her behalf, for she was surely worth saving; and as for her queer actions, she was nothing but a child anyway; so the best thing was not to mind them." Yet this last act of hers made him consider her a very dangerous person, and he advised her to seek a home elsewhere, which she was very soon forced to do, as he went to the southern part of the Territory with his other wives, and left her behind.

She consoled herself by thinking that although she had no husband on earth, she was provided for hereafter, and

was very complacent over the reflection, which seemed to
afford her wonderful consolation. Mr. Ramsay must be
acquitted of having married the old lady for money, as she
was very poor, and he gained nothing at all by his marriage. It was really an act of kindness on his part, and
real conscientious regard for her future.

Not so unselfish was Brother Shaw, a Mormon whose
poverty might be estimated by the fact that he had been
twenty years in Brigham's service as a laborer. His impe-
cuniosity was no bar to his entering the Celestial Kingdom,
and setting up a realm of his own, over which he should
be ruler. He had already married two wives, when a very
old lady, possessed of considerable property, arrived in
Zion, and Brother Shaw decided that she needed salvation
at his hands, and proposed marriage to her.

She saw through him at once, but fearing for her salvation, she accepted the proposal, and was "sealed." This
was her first offer in Zion, but she feared, at her time of
life, she might never have another; so she allowed herself
to be installed as third wife in the Shaw family. Her
money was found very useful for the support of the entire
family, and was spent very freely until it was all gone,
when she, like the rest, was obliged to live in great destitution. She certainly has paid handsomely for her "exaltation."

In a family where all were so peacefully inclined as in
our own, "trying" occasions are rare; but they would
occur sometimes, and I think my mother took a little malicious pleasure in seeing my father bothered about something
that had occurred to make "plurality" a trial. He tried as
hard as possible to be just, and had always been very particular in dividing everything equally between his wives.
One must have no more than the other. There must be
the most perfect exactness in everything. I believe he
thinks he has dealt out the most even-handed justice,
although he used occasionally to be accused of a partiality

for his third wife, especially by those comf♦rting persons who liked to talk to the other wives about him.

One year he had a turkey presented to him two or three days before Christmas. He was away from home on receiving it, and he returned quite late at night to my mother's house with his gift. He was in a dilemma. Here he was with a turkey on his hands, and not feeling rich enough to buy the requisite number in addition to give one to each wife. He could not decide at which house to have the fowl roasted. He would have liked to have had the table of each wife graced with just such a bird, but that was out of the question, and it was equally impossible for all to dine together that day. He was unable to solve the problem; so he concluded to leave it for accident to decide.

On arriving home he placed the turkey quite out of sight, as he supposed, and retired.

My mother, in her rounds of morning work, discovered a suspicious-looking bundle, and, although a little curious concerning it, did not open it, but carried it to my father, with the wrapper on, at the same time asking him what it was.

"It is a turkey," was his reply.

As he said nothing else, she hastily returned it to its place, concluding that she had stumbled on positive proof of his partiality for some other member of his family; and remembering all he had said about equal justice, she resolved that she would find out all about the affair, and, if her suspicions were correct, would not submit with patience, but would "speak her mind," if the heavens fell. She opened the battle by saying, —

"I think it very strange indeed that you should purchase a turkey for only one table, and leave the others destitute; and I also think it a very unjust proceeding on your part; if one portion of the family is to have a Christmas turkey, the others should receive the same attention."

"Hold on, my dear," interrupted my father; "not so fast,

if you please. You shouldn't jump at conclusions in such a hasty manner. I didn't buy the turkey; it was given me by a friend."

"O," said my mother, quite mollified, "is that so?" And she was preparing to be quite amiable, when, unfortunately, she happened to recollect that he had asked her at breakfast if she had not better have some chickens killed for Christmas, and she returned to the charge with renewed vigor.

"What are you going to do with it?" demanded she.

"Why, you may have it if you wish," said he; "I am sure I don't know what else to do with it."

Although she was quite prepared to wage warfare for her rights to the very last, my mother really was not prepared for such willing surrender, and, determined not to be outdone in generosity, she replied, —

"O, I really do not care about it. I have chickens, you know, and I like them equally well; in fact, I think I prefer them. But," she continued, with a beautiful stroke of diplomacy, "I would like to decide which of the other wives shall have the turkey, if you will allow me, since you have given me the privilege of refusing it."

My father was glad enough to leave the disposition of the turkey with her, as he did not really know any better what to do with it than before, and if she decided for him, all responsibility would be off his shoulders. So he said, with very great cordiality of tone, —

"All right. I have given it to you, you know. You shall make what disposition you please of it."

"Thank you," said she, with equal graciousness of manner; "I should like Elizabeth to have it. She deserves it, and needs it, too, and would be very grateful for it; and then, too, you see, she, being next to me, would claim it by right of seniority."

"Wisely said," was my father's rejoinder, delighted to have it settled so amicably. So he carried the turkey to

Elizabeth as his Christmas offering, and she received it, as my mother thought she would, gladly and thankfully.

Our Christmas dinner, with the chickens, and my mother's delectable puddings and pies, was a success, and we didn't even miss the turkey, though we did have a good laugh over it, and my mother was jubilant, because she had kept it from gracing the tables of the younger wives, since, according to her ideas of justice, if any partiality was to be shown, it should be given in the order of "senior-

OLD FARM-HOUSE AT COTTONWOOD.

ity." I have no doubt that the other tables were well set, in some way or other, but we none of us saw the bills of fare. "Father's turkey" was for a long time the standing jest at home.

During this time at South Cottonwood, while I was teaching my children, helping my mother, and getting all these peeps into the inside experiences of polygamy, my own life running along in the smoothest channels it had ever known, a great change was preparing for me. I had no thought nor premonition of it, as I went blithely about my daily duties, happy and content in the quiet life which I was leading in my mother's companionship, and in my darling children's love. I dreamed of nothing beyond this peaceful life; I wished for nothing else. Such a sweet restfulness had taken possession of me, and I pictured myself growing old in this quiet spot, with my strong, brave boys near me to make my rough path smooth, and to help my faltering footsteps over the stony places with their strong arms that would encircle and hold me then, as I encircled them now. The improvement of my health was a source of great joy to me. I never was so well in my life. The color had come back to my cheek, the sparkle to my eye, the smile to my lips, the elasticity to my step, and something of the old life to my spirits, although I had suffered too much to have them quite as light as they were in the old frolicsome days when I had gone merry-making with my old companions, had won friends in the theatre, and had wailed "with the girls" over the monotonous fare of the Prophetic table. I was a child with my children, and it would be difficult to tell which of us got the most scoldings and pettings from the fond grandmamma.

She was happy, too, at having me with her again; and though she sorrowed at my sorrow, she could not regret anything that brought me back to her, so long as it did not make me utterly unhappy; and she recognized as well as I the fact, that my life was fuller and freer without my husband than with him, and that my children were better off, and stood far better chances of becoming the men that both she and I wished them to become, under my guidance alone, than under the influence of such a father as theirs. They would never have felt a strong, steady, guiding hand, but would have been, as their mother had been before them, the victim of alternate passion and rough good nature, that was easily shaken.

I had very many offers of marriage. A moderately prepossessing woman in Utah is sure not to be long without them; and I knew that I was that, at least, but I could not be brought to look with favor upon any of my suitors. I did not care to try matrimony again. I had vowed that I would not become a plural wife, and, with my past experience, I was afraid to try even a monogamic alliance again; for I knew that in Utah the step from monogamy to polygamy is very short, and very easily taken. My answer was the same to one and all — " I have my children; I shall live for them alone; they are my only loves."

Some of them appealed to my father and mother to use their influence to make me change my mind; but they refused to interfere, saying that I probably knew my own mind, and, if I did not wish to marry, that was quite enough.

I usually had my own way; and when I knew that any of my persistent suitors had turned to my parents for sympathy and assistance, I laughed to myself to think how little of either they would receive. To tell the truth, they — especially my mother — were no more anxious for me to marry than I myself; and I knew that so long as they had a home, my children and I should share it. I was not allowed to feel that we were in any way a burden, and, to tell the truth, I did honestly try to do all in my power to assist my mother, and make life easier for her to bear.

" I shall never, never leave you," I used to say, as I would nestle at her feet, and lay my head in her lap in the old childish fashion — a habit that I could not bring myself to abandon, even though I was a mother myself, with two bouncing boys to curl down in my own lap in the same loving way, begging for caresses.

" God willing, we will never be parted, my darling."

" Never! never! " cried I, with loving enthusiasm, as I felt her hand on my head, resting in tender benediction there. I kissed the hand that had grown hard with toil for me and for others; and together we sat with no premonition of the future that was so near, and that was to change the whole current of both our after lives.

Brigham Young and some of the apostles were coming to South Cottonwood to hold a meeting. But what was that to me? How did it affect me when he came or went? I had no part nor lot in his movements. Life was nothing to me beyond my mother and children; and all the Prophetic coming and going would not cause a ripple on the surface of my placid life.

So I thought, as I lay cradled in my mother's arms that summer evening in the old farm-house at Cottonwood; and the stars, as they looked down upon me there, revealed nothing more to me.

CHAPTER XXVII.

A WALK WITH THE PROPHET. — HE MAKES LOVE TO ME.

How Brigham Travels Through the Territory. — Triumphant Receptions Everywhere. — Trying to Establish the "Order of Enoch." — How the Prophet Insulted his Faithful Followers. — "Rheumatism" in the Temper. — Grand Doings in the Settlements. — We Go to Meet the Prophet. — How the Saints were Lectured in the Bowery. — How Brigham *gave* Howard a Piece of Land. — Howard Insulted by the Prophet. — Overlooking the Prophet's Lies. — Van Etten Becomes Brigham's "Friend." — He Helps Him to Steal a Hundred Sheep. — He makes a Big Haul, and Escapes to Canada. — The Prophet Ogles Me during Service-Time. — We Take a Walk Home Together. — He Compliments My Good Looks. — Makes Love to Me. — Matrimonial Advice. — Brigham Wishes Me to Become His Wife.

BRIGHAM ON HIS TRAVELS.

O N Brigham Young's arrival at South Cottonwood, he was very warmly welcomed, all the people turning out to join in the demonstrations.

This is the usual custom; consequently his travels through the Territory are a perfect ovation. He is generally accompanied by some members of his family; perhaps one or more of his wives, and one of his sons. It has lately always been Brigham, Jr., his intended successor, who is taken along, to be initiated into the proper method of doing things ; one or more of his counsellors ; some of the apostles, and whoever else he may choose to invite to join his party. They go in carriages, and form in themselves quite a procession.

He is met outside of every settlement which he visits by a company of cavalry ; and a little farther on, just outside the entrance to the town, he is met by another procession, — sometimes of the children alone, but oftener, in the large settlements, where they are ambitious to "do the thing up in shape," of the entire population who are able to turn out, men, women, and children, headed by a brass band, all ranged along to give greeting to the Prophet. They are arranged in different sections, each section having its appropriate banner. The elderly and middle-aged men are all together under the banner "Fathers in Israel." The women of the same ages are ranged under their banner, "Mothers in Israel." The young men are proud enough of the inscription which theirs carries, "Defenders of Zion ; " and the young girls are fresh and lovely under their banner, "The Daughters of Zion, — Virtue ; " while the little wee bits, that are placed last of all, are "The Hope of Israel." Other banners bear the inscriptions, "Hail to the Prophet ; " "Welcome to our President ; " "God bless Brigham Young ; " "The Lion of the Lord ; " and others of a similar nature are seen along the line of the procession.

As the President and his escort pass down the long line, the band plays, the people cheer, men wave their hats, women their handkerchiefs, and the young girls and children toss bunches of flowers ; and their Prophet — if he chances to be in a good humor — bows and smiles to them as he passes ; and everything is gay, and bright, and merry, and the people are very happy because of the success of their Prophet's reception.

Now and then their gaiety has a dash of cold water from the object of all the display, and they see all their preparations go for nothing, and are made to feel that all their labor has been in vain, as happened not long ago in Salt Lake City. Brigham had been on a long trip through Southern Utah, endeavoring to establish the "United Order of Enoch," with but indifferent success, it must be confessed, in consequence of which he was in anything but good humor with his "rebellious people."

On his return he was met at the station by thousands of his people, who had gathered in unusual numbers, and with unusual display, to meet him. As he stepped from the car, cheers arose from the mass of people, the band played, and all eyes were turned on him, anxiously watching for a recognition. What was their surprise and chagrin to see him step from the car to his carriage, enter it, close the door, and drive away without the slightest notice of their presence, seemingly oblivious to everything about him!

The Saints returned to their homes feeling exceedingly hurt and grieved, but the next Sabbath their Prophet endeavored to soothe their outraged feelings and smooth matters over with them, in the following "explanation : " —

"Brethren and sisters, you may have felt hurt at my not recognizing your greeting on my arrival. If so, I am sorry; but I had just had an attack of rheumatiz in my left foot."

The apology was accepted; there was nothing else to be done. The Prophet had made what he considered the proper *amende*, though some of the brethren were so irreverent as to remark afterwards that they "guessed the 'rheumatiz' was in his temper," on account of his failure to gull the people with his last "effort for their spiritual " — and his temporal — "advancement."

Usually he is in high good humor, and beams on his followers with the most patronizing and reassuring of smiles, accepting all the homage as though it were his by "divine right." Royalty itself could assume no more the manner of receiving only what it is entitled to, than this ex-glazier, who used to work for "six bits" a day, and who begged the farmer for whom he had done two half days' work to give him a new coat, since his old one was too "rusty" to go on a preaching tour in, and the "spirit" had suddenly called him from the haying field to a Methodist meeting in the neighboring town.

While on his journeys, he is always taken to the best house in the place, and everything is done for his comfort; his followers are taken by other residents of the town, a dance is given in the evening, which takes the place of the usual "reception" elsewhere; he is serenaded by the bands and parties of singers, and all night the militia keep sentry about his headquarters. Altogether it is quite a gay thing to go visiting the settlements, and no one likes it better than the Prophet himself. It is the grand event of the year to the Saints, and they make such extensive preparations for the occasion, that many of them have to "live very close," as they express it, for months afterwards.

As a matter of course, I helped "welcome the President" to Cottonwood; so did all the family; and, as we were all old friends, we were glad to see him personally, as well as spiritually, my mother especially being overjoyed, for there was always the warmest friendship between them; indeed, their friendship dated back to the days before they went to Kirtland. At Nauvoo they had been next door neighbors, and he used to be very fond of playing with the "baby." Since then he had helped the "baby" to escape from a domestic thraldom which was harder than she could endure, and she was grateful to him accordingly. I think neither mother nor daughter would have joined so heartily in the welcome, had they known what misery the visit was to bring.

The Sunday services are always largely attended, and as no house is sufficiently capacious to hold all who assemble to listen to the Prophet, the meetings are held in the "Bowery," which is a sort of improvised tabernacle, with open sides, and roofed over with branches of trees. He usually makes this the occasion for reprimanding the people for their sins, dwelling particularly on the extravagance of women in dress, and the habit, among some of the men, of whiskey-drinking.   He came out very strong this time, and the poor Cottonwood Saints were exposed to a merciless fusillade from the Prophet's tongue.   He was more than usually denunciatory and scathing, and he made this the occasion for abusing Mr. Howard, the owner of the distillery. After he had got well warmed up, he said Howard had not a cent in the world which he had not given him, and added,

BRIGHAM PREACHING AT SOUTH COTTONWOOD.

"I even gave the poor, mean scapegrace the very land he lives on."

This was more than Howard could bear, even from his Prophet, and he jumped to his feet, excitedly shouting, —

"It isn't so, and you know it isn't.   I bought the land of you, and gave you twelve hundred dollars for it."

"You lie!" roared Brigham; "I gave it to you."

"Yes, for twelve hundred dollars," was Howard's reply.

"I never got a cent for it," screamed Brigham.

"You're the liar, and you know it," retorted Howard.

I don't know how long this Sabbath-day quarrel would

have lasted, had not Brigham happened to think it was a little out of order, and also to discover that Howard, who was in a great rage by this time, was bound to have the last word. He stopped the dispute, and, turning to the congregation, said, —

"Is there no one who will remove that man from this place?"

Instantly ten or fifteen men started to their feet, and rushed towards the offender; but a man named Van Etten, being much nearer to him than any of the others, reached him first, and led him out of meeting; so there was no opportunity for any of the others to exercise their zeal in the Prophet's behalf. At the close of the services, Brigham publicly thanked Brother Van Etten, and called him "the only friend in the congregation."

The following Sabbath, the party were at Willow Creek holding meeting, and as what he was pleased to term "Howard's insult" was rankling in his memory, he could not refrain from referring to it in his sermon, which he did in the following *truthful* manner : —

"I was never so insulted in my life as I was at Cottonwood last Sabbath. I called seven or eight times for some of the brethren to lead Howard out, and not a man responded but Brother Van Etten. I know how it is; you and they are all bought with Howard's whiskey."

Now, the news of the encounter had reached Willow Creek before the Prophet and his party, and nearly every one present knew that Brigham had only called once for his opponent to be taken away, and that his call had been promptly responded to. But they attributed his misstatement to the Prophet's bad memory. They knew, too, that none of them were bought with Howard's whiskey; but perhaps Brigham thought they were, and it was only "one of his slight mistakes;" so they let it go for what it was worth, and the Prophet felt better after venting his ill-temper.

It was soon after this that Howard was sent on the mis-

sion that has been referred to in a previous chapter. Van
Etten's fortune was made from that moment. The Prophet's heart was full of blessings for him, and found vent in
the following benediction : —

"The Lord will bless you, Brother Van Etten, for so nobly coming forward in my defence. You are the only man
out of several thousand that paid any attention to the insults
I received. I want you to understand that from this time I
am your friend."

The Cottonwood Saints were very much surprised at
Brigham's warmth, for Van Etten was well known as a
worthless, dissipated character, and if Brother Brigham
found any good in him, it was more than anyone else had
succeeded in doing.

The Prophet and Van Etten were ever after bosom
friends; let the latter do what he would, Brigham would
shield him from all difficulty. One instance of this protection of his *protégé* came directly under my notice. Van
Etten stole a hundred sheep from my brother, who prosecuted him for it. When the trial came on, the evidence
was as clear as possible against him; yet Brigham controlled the whole affair, and his "friend" was released.
All who knew the facts concerning the case were astonished that even Brigham should do such a very unjust
thing as to clear him; but at that time the Saints did not
dare to criticise the Prophet's actions as they do now, and
all they said was, "There probably is something good
about Van Etten that Brigham has discovered which we
were unable to see."

Finally, the Prophet's intimate friend took several thousand head of sheep to herd for different parties, and a
short time after, the owners heard that he had left the country; they went instantly to look after their sheep, but not a
trace of them could they find. Van Etten, sheep and all,
were gone, and they never returned again to the "Valley
of Ephraim." It was afterwards found that he was in

Canada; he also was in debt nine thousand dollars at the co-operative store—Brigham's pet institution. I never heard Brigham say whether he missed his friend or not; in fact, he never mentioned him after this last escapade.

I had noticed, during the morning service, that memorable Sunday at Cottonwood, that Brigham looked often at me; but I thought nothing more of it than that mine was a very familiar face, and consequently he was drawn towards it for that reason. Still there were others in the congregation that he knew; so mine was not the only face he looked at for recognition. I began to be a little uneasy under his scrutiny. I thought that possibly there was something about my appearance that displeased him. Possibly he did not approve of my dress. I knew he considered himself perfectly at liberty to criticise any sister's dress when he felt so inclined, and I did not know but I was to be the subject of his next outbreak. That he was not looking at me indifferently or carelessly I knew very well, from the bent brows and keen gaze that I felt was making the most complete scrutiny, and I wished he would look somewhere else. I fidgeted about in my seat, I looked at my little boy who was sitting beside me, and pretended to arrange some article of his clothing. I did everything but to jump up and run away, and I even wanted to do that, to get out of the reach of those sharp eyes, and that steady, unflinching gaze. I am sure he saw my discomfort; but he was pitiless, and all the while the speaking was going on he scarcely turned his eyes from me a moment. I tried to be unconscious, to look in every direction except his, but the steady eyes would always bring mine back again in spite of myself. I felt his power then as I never had felt it before, and I began to understand a little how it was that he compelled so many people to do his will, against their own inclinations. I learned the lesson better still subsequently.

After the services he came up to me and greeted me very cordially. I was surprised, for he had been so ruffled over

28

the Howard matter that I did not expect he would regain his spirits so easily.

"Are you well?" said he.

"As you see," I replied, laughing, and looking up at him.

"May I walk home with you?"

"If you wish; I should be much pleased," said I. I was pleased, too, for I knew that in bringing him home with me I should be conferring the greatest happiness on my mother. He took my little boy's hand, and led him along, and as he looked down at him, he said, —

"A pretty child. What are you going to do with him?"

"Make a good man of him, if possible," was my reply.

"A better one than his father proved to be, I trust."

"God grant it, else he will not be much of a comfort to me," said I, the tears starting to my eyes.

"You are very much improved since you left Mr. Dee," said he; "do you know it? You are a very pretty woman."

"Thank you," said I, laughing, yet embarrassed at this wholesale fashion of complimenting; "if you can only tell me I am a good woman, I should like that, too."

"Yes, you are that, I believe, and a good mother; and you were a good wife, only that foolish fellow didn't have the sense to half appreciate you."

"Thank you again. I don't know that I can take all you tell me, since I am not sure that I deserve such high praise."

"You are your mother's girl; there can be but one conclusion to draw from that. But tell me about yourself; are you happy?"

"Very," said I, earnestly. "I never was happier in my life."

"What makes you specially happy just now?"

"O, my children, my mother, my quiet life, after all the trial and weary struggling to make the best out of the very worst."

"Then you don't regret your divorce?"

"Indeed I do not; and now, Brother Young, let me thank you for your kindness in helping me to regain my freedom, and above all to keep my children. You must be content with gratitude, for I can repay you in no other way."

He looked at me a moment; a peculiar smile flitted across his face; he opened his lips as if to say something; closed them again; looked at me more scrutinizingly than ever; turned away, and was silent for a moment. Then he asked me, quite abruptly, —

"I suppose you have had offers of marriage since your separation from Mr. Dee."

"Yes, many," I replied, answering his question very frankly, as I did not suspect that he had any motive in questioning me, except a friendly interest; and I was as honest in my confidences to him as I should have been with my father.

"Do you feel inclined to accept any of them?" was his next question.

"No, not in the slightest degree; none of them move me in the least."

"And you haven't a preference for any of the suitors?"

"I assure you, no."

"Never had the slightest inclination to say 'yes' to any offer that has been made?"

"Not a bit of inclination; all my lovers have had a rival affection to contend with."

"For whom?" was the question, quick and sudden, as if intending to take me by surprise by its abruptness.

I laid my hand on my boy's head. "For him, and for the other dear child that God gave me; I can have no room for other love while I have them to care for. They fill my heart exclusively, and I am so glad and happy because of it, that I should be jealous if I saw the least hint of regard for anyone creeping in. I couldn't love anybody else; I wouldn't."

" Then you think you will never be induced to marry?"

"Never in my life," I said, vehemently.

Brigham laughed a little, and replied, " I have heard a very great many girls talk that way before."

"Yes, but I am not a girl; I am a woman; a woman, too, with hard, bitter experiences; a woman who has lost faith in mankind, and hasn't much faith in matrimony; a mother, too, who will not give her children a rival."

"No, but you might give them a protector."

"They don't need it; my love is sufficient protection. Besides, they are boys, and will be my protectors in a few years. So, you see, I do not need to marry for protection for myself or them."

"But supposing it were shown to be a duty."

"It can't be. I should not recognize a duty of that kind. I consider myself old enough, and sufficiently experienced, to judge of my duties without any assistance."

He bent his eyes on me again with a keen, questioning look, and said, very kindly, " Child, child, I fear you are very headstrong. Don't let your will run away with you."

"No danger," I replied; "it is not crossed often enough to make it very assertive."

"A spoiled child, eh?"

"Possibly. My will seems to be everybody's way at home."

"Well, my child, I want to give you a little advice. I have known you all your life, and have had an interest in you from your birth. Indeed, you seem like one of my own family, you were always in and out so much with my children; and I am going to speak to you as I would to one of my girls. You will probably marry again, some time, though you say now you won't."

"No," I interrupted; "I shall not marry. I mean what I say when I tell you so."

"Yes, I know it; but you will; now mark my words, and see if you don't."

"Well, don't feel so sure that you send somebody after me," said I, slyly hitting him for his known propensity for "counselling" the brethren to take certain sisters as plural wives.

"You needn't be afraid of my sending anybody. I promise you I won't do that," was his answer.

"Good; then I shall not be obliged to say 'no' to them, and so, perhaps, hurt your feelings as well as mortify them," said I.

"Still, I believe that you will marry again some time. It is in the nature of things that you should. Women of your age, and your looks, don't stay single all their lives; not a bit of it. Now, my advice is this: when you do marry, select some man older than yourself. It doesn't make so much difference whether you're in love with him, if you can respect him and look up to him for counsel. Respect is better than romance, any day. You've tried the one, now give the other a chance. You didn't succeed so well with the other experiment that you care to try that over again, I know. You had your own way, too, if I remember rightly. It wasn't such a smooth one as you thought it was going to be. I knew you was doing the wrong thing when I saw the man. I could have told you so, but you didn't ask my advice. Now I'm giving it to you without asking, for I don't want you to make another mistake. So, when you choose again, remember what I say, and get a husband whom you can look to for good advice."

We had reached home by that time, and I thanked him for his interest, and promised to heed his advice if I found it necessary; but I was sure I should not, for I was firm in my determination not to marry.

I had no idea at all of Brigham's real object in thus sounding me, and drawing me out. It never occurred to me that he could want me for himself. I should just as soon have thought of receiving an offer of marriage from my own father, or to have heard that he (Brigham) was going to marry one of his own daughters. Then I knew, too, that there had been a great deal said in the outside world respecting the practice of polygamy among the Saints, and I thought, from conversations I had heard, that the United States Congress had taken some action in the matter, and that he, being the Head of the Church, was watched pretty closely by government officials. Then he was so old, — much older than my father, — that the thought, had it presented itself, would have been scouted as absurd. I repeated the conversation to my mother, who seemed amused by it, but did not give any more serious thought to it than I had done.

Brigham was uncommonly jovial that day, and made himself particularly agreeable. He was unusually gracious to my father, revived old memories, and joked with my mother; petted and praised the children, and was very paternal in his manner to me. He showed himself, altogether, in his very best light, and made his visit very pleasant.

During the afternoon service he studied me in the same way that he had in the morning; and several times, when I caught his eye, he looked quite amused. I supposed he was thinking of our conversation at noon, and was much more at my ease than I had been in the early part of the day during the first service.

After service in the afternoon, Brigham told my father that he wished to see him on important business. They were closeted together for two hours, talking very earnestly. I supposed it had to do with church matters, as my father was one of the leading men in South Cottonwood, and had been so long a prominent member of the Mormon Church that it was by no means strange that Brigham had so much to say to him. I thought, possibly, they might be discussing the Howard affair; but beyond that I thought nothing. I certainly had no idea that I was the subject under discussion; that my future was being planned for me without any regard to my will in the matter. Had I known it, I should by no means have gone about my duties with such a light heart, nor frolicked so gaily with my children.

At the end of the two hours my mother was called into the room, and the discussion was resumed. After a short time all came out. Brigham went away, bidding us all good-bye with much cordiality, and with an added impressiveness in his manner towards me.

When he had gone, my father told me the subject of their long conversation.

Brigham Young had proposed to him for me as a wife.

CHAPTER XXVIII.

HOW BRIGHAM YOUNG FORCED ME TO MARRY HIM.

Brigham's Offer of Marriage. — I Think the Prophet Too Old. — My Parents are Delighted with the Honor. — They Try to Persuade Me. — I am Very Obstinate. — Arguing the Matter. — How Brigham Found Means to Influence Me. — My Brothers get into Trouble. — The Prophet and the Telegraph-Poles. — He Takes a Nice Little Contract. — Then Sells it to His Son. — Bishop Sharp Makes a *Few* Dollars Out of It. — My Brother Engages in the Work. — He Becomes Involved in Debts and Difficulties. — Brigham Threatens to Cut Him Off for Dishonesty. — My Mother Tries to Excuse Him. — Hemmed In on All Sides, I Determine to Make One Last Appeal. — I Fail, and Consent to Marry Him.

A CRUSHING BLOW. — BRIGHAM WISHES TO MARRY ME.

ROSE to my feet shocked beyond expression.

I looked from my father to my mother, hoping that they were merely jesting with me; for I had no idea that what they told me could be true; it was too monstrous an absurdity. But the expression of their faces did not reassure me. I saw that they were in earnest; that it was true; and I burst out into a passionate fit of weeping.

My mother came to me, and took my hand and caressed it in her own, and my father tried to reassure me.

"Why, my dear, what is the matter? Are you crying because the Head of our Church — the most powerful and influential man among us — has made you an offer of marriage? Why, it is nothing to cry about, surely."

But I felt that it *was* something to cry over — something, indeed, over which to shed the bitterest tears that could be wrung from my heart's deepest anguish. I felt outraged, betrayed; to think, after our conversation that very day, — but a very few hours before, — when I had told him frankly my reluctance and abhorrence at the very idea of marrying again, that he should go deliberately and propose for me, showed a lack of delicacy and consideration which greatly surprised me. It was quite evident that he looked upon my assertions as girlish affectation that a good offer would speedily overcome. He was so confident of his success with the women he chose to woo, that he had no idea of meeting any settled opposition. He had, as I afterwards learned, no conception of feminine delicacy or sensitiveness; laughed at it as ridiculous, and called the women who exhibited it "sentimental fools." I had nothing to hope from his mercy, but I did not know it then. When my first passion of grief had spent itself, I turned to my father, still holding my mother's hand, and said, —

"What answer did you make him?"

"I told him that I would lay the proposition before you, and tell him what your decision was. He said that he had talked with you on the subject of marriage, and that you told him no one had proposed for you whom you fancied; that he was glad you were not easily pleased and suited with every new-comer, for he intended to place you in a position where you would be vastly the social superior of all your present lovers."

"Didn't he tell you that I said I never should marry again? that my life was to be devoted to my children?"

"Yes; he said you mentioned something of that sort, but

that he didn't take any stock in it; all girls talked so; it was
their way of playing the coquette; he understood it, and he
liked you better for your coyness."

"I told him decidedly," I replied, "that I was a girl no
longer, but a woman, who knew her own mind, who had
arrived at the ability to make her own decisions through
terrible suffering; that the thought of marriage was distasteful to me. I wonder if he needs to be told more plainly?
If so, you may go to him, since you told him you should
leave the decision with me, and tell him that I say to him,
No, as I have said it to all my other suitors, and that I do
not even thank him for the position he intended to confer
upon me, for he knew I did not want it. Does he think I
have escaped one misery to wish to enter another? 'Position!' I wonder what he thinks there is particularly fine
about being a plural wife even to Brigham Young? I have
not seen so much happiness in the system, even among his
wives, that I care to enter it. And I never, never can."

My father interrupted me. "You are excited, now, my
daughter. Be calm, and think the matter over reasonably.
Don't decide in this hasty manner."

"I might think it over, reasonably, as you call it, for the
rest of my life, and the conclusion I should arrive at would
be the same. I never will, of my free will and accord,
marry Brigham Young; and you might as well tell him so
at once, and have the matter settled."

"But, my dear child," said my mother, stroking my hair
fondly, and looking at me with anxious eyes, "suppose it
was your duty?"

"O, mother, mother! have you turned against me, too?
Am I to fight you all, single-handed, alone? Won't you,
at least, stand by me?"

"I would, gladly, my only, my darling daughter, if I was
sure that it would be right."

"Do you doubt the right of it? Can you doubt it? Or
do you think it would not be wrong to stifle all natural

feelings, all aversion to another union, above all, to him? Would it be right, do you think, to give myself to a man older than my father, from whom I shrink with aversion when I think of him as my husband, who is already the husband of many wives, the father of children older, by many years, than myself?"

"But he is your spiritual leader."

"That is no reason why he should be my earthly husband. I cannot see what claim that gives him to my affection."

"The doctrines of our church teach you to marry."

"Do you want to get rid of me?" I asked, suddenly, raising my head and looking her full in the face. I dared not enter into religious discussion with her, for I felt so bitterly that I should be sure to say something to shock her; and then I knew that, in argument, I should be fairly worsted; so I made my appeal on personal grounds, and touched her heart, as I was sure I should. She threw both arms about me, and sobbed as violently as I had done.

"You know I do not. How can you say that? I was only saying what I did, because I thought it was for your good here and hereafter. Did I consult my own feelings, no one should have you except myself; but I think of your welfare before my selfish desires."

"O, mother, I can't, I can't," I cried in a sudden agony, as the thought of all such a marriage involved, rushed across me.

"Don't fret so, child," said my father, speaking for the first time since my mother had joined in the conversation. "I will tell Brother Brigham how you feel, and perhaps he will give up the idea. But he seemed to have set his heart on it, and I don't know how he'll take it."

"Why, I belong to you, father. Tell him so, and that you can't give me away to anybody."

My father smiled a little at me, grew grave again, and went away.

He told Brigham how averse I was; and he only laughed, and said I should get over it, if I only had time. He would not give me up, but he would not hasten matters; he would leave me in my parents' hands, and he hoped they would induce me to listen favorably to his proposals. The last remark was made with a peculiar emphasis and a sinister smile, which every Saint who had had dealings with him knew very well, and whose meaning they also knew. It meant, "Do as I command you, or suffer the weight of my displeasure." He sent a message to me, which, though seemingly kind, contained a covert threat; and I began to feel the chains tightening around me already. I felt sure that I could not free myself, but I would struggle to the end.

Thus began a year of anguish and torture. I fought against my fate in every possible way. Brigham was equally persistent, and he tried in every way to win me, a willing bride, before he attempted to coerce me. He told my parents, and myself, too, that he had always had great interest in me, and had intended to propose for me so soon

CHAUNCEY G. WEBB.
["My Father."]

as I was old enough; that when he sent for me to the theatre, and proposed my being at the Lion House, it was that I might become familiar with the place and its inmates, and so not feel strange when he should bring me there as a wife. It had been his intention to have proposed for me then; but he had just married Amelia, and it had made such a hue-and-cry among the Gentiles, especially as he had taken her directly in the face of the late congressional law against polygamy, that he did not think it wise to add another to the list just then; so he said nothing of his intentions, and before he knew anything of my engagement, I was ready to be married. It was a great shock to him; but as matters had gone so far, and as he was in such a questionable position before the government, he thought it best not to interfere, as he most assuredly would, had he known my intentions earlier. Now I was free, and he was at liberty to tell me, what he had wanted to tell me long before, that he loved me.

Finding that this declaration of affection failed to move me, he tried another tack. He asked my father if a house and a thousand dollars a year would make me comfortable, as he wished to settle something on me when I married him, taking for granted that I should do so.

My mother and father both favored his suit, and labored with me to induce me to view it in the same light. Brigham was our spiritual guide; it might be that in refusing him I should lose all hopes of future salvation. That was my mother's plea. My father's was, that Brigham was able to hurt him pecuniarily. And then came my oldest brother, who added his influence in Brigham's favor by telling me that Brigham had it in his power to ruin him, and was very angry with him, and had threatened to "cut him off from the church," which was, to a

ELIZA C. WEBB,
[My Mother.]

person in his position, the very worst thing that could happen.

The trouble between them was of Brigham's own making, and I will give it, as briefly as I can, to show how Brigham managed to get everything out of his people without paying for it, and, at the same time, show the amount of honor which he has in business matters.

In 1860 the first telegraph line was extended from the Atlantic States to the Pacific, passing through Salt Lake City. Feramorz Little, a nephew of the President, took a contract to furnish about one hundred and fifty miles of poles, at three dollars each. According to Brigham's statement, Little was unable to fill the contract until the Prophet came to the rescue, and secured three dollars and a quarter each, by furnishing one hundred miles of sawed poles, although, in truth, the sawed timber was not so good as common round poles.

Six years later, a rival company commenced putting up a new line. Brigham negotiated for a contract, and succeeded in securing nearly eight hundred miles, — extending from Denver City westward, — at the very gratifying price of eight dollars a pole. It is very generally believed that Brigham and one of the new company had a previous understanding to divide the profits on this magnificent job.

He then sub-let the whole contract to Bishop John Sharp and Joseph A. Young, — his eldest son, who has recently died, — at three dollars a pole; and my brother Gilbert took about four hundred and fifty miles — from Green River to Denver — at the very reasonable price of two dollars and a half a pole. He was then the owner of ten freight wagons, with six mules to each wagon; but, in order to fill his contract, he found himself compelled to purchase six additional teams, at a cost of seven thousand dollars, which, with tools, provisions, and general outfit, increased the sum to nearly eleven thousand dollars, which he was obliged to borrow, paying a very heavy interest — five per cent. a month; but that, of course, was his own fault, not the Prophet's.

Brigham was anxious to have the work done immediately, — which is not at all strange when one remembers that he would make five dollars on each pole, — and he had sent for my brother, and urged him to take the job, telling him that he knew of no one so suitable, for Gilbert had such a fine business reputation; adding that he was certain that the blessing of God would rest upon him, for it was His will that all the Saints should accumulate riches. After all this, and very much more talk of the same kind, Gilbert was induced to take the contract, my father giving security for the borrowed money.

My brother left Salt Lake City with his outfit as early as the snow would permit him to cross the mountains. When he had got his wagons loaded with poles for the first time, Brigham telegraphed for him to stop work and return to the city. He immediately complied with the order, and found, on his arrival, that there was a prospect of the new company compromising with the old, and putting up no line. They now desired to buy off all contracts. Brigham would clear on the contract one hundred thousand dollars, if the line was put up, and of course could compromise for no less. Sharp and Joseph A. wanted forty thousand dollars, and my brother ten thousand, if they gave up the contract. Brigham said that, in justice, Gilbert ought to have twenty thousand dollars, to pay the expenses of the delay, &c.

Of course it was cheaper to put up the line than to compromise at this cost, and he returned to his work, having lost twelve days. His expenses at this time were about one hundred dollars a day. He had thirty men employed, at sixty dollars a month and their board, and he also had grain to furnish for one hundred mules. Brigham promised to pay for all this delay, but as usual he failed to do so.

My brother then began to furnish the poles, and succeeded in delivering about twenty-five miles a week. For two months he received his pay quite regularly, and everything went on swimmingly. When he was about one hundred miles from Denver, having completed about three hundred and fifty miles, he was sent for to give up his contract on the eastern line, and take a contract on the northern line instead. That was between Utah and Montana. Gilbert was much averse to the change, as he had finished the most difficult portion of his work, and passed through where the timber is the least accessible. But Brigham insisted, and wrote, promising to make it all right with him if he would come back, and go up north, and furnish one hundred miles or more of poles. Finally he sent Joseph A. down to my brother, who succeeded in persuading him to return.

While on his way back, he met Mr. E. Creighton, the superintendent of the line, with a company of men, setting the poles which he had furnished. Being desirous of giving thorough satisfaction, he sent Mr. Lorenzo Ensign, with three teams, loaded with good poles, to exchange for any poor timber which did not satisfy. Those teams continued with the pole-setters until Mr. Creighton sent them back, remarking that he did not find it necessary to change one pole a day, and that he was entirely satisfied with the timber. I mention this because Brigham afterwards said that the contract was not well filled, and made this an excuse for not paying my brother. Those three teams remained with the pole-setters about four weeks, and, as I before said, were dismissed by one of the owners of the line.

Gilbert returned home in August, and, on starting for the north, Joseph A. asked him to set the poles that he should furnish on the Montana line, at the same time agreeing to pay him a dollar apiece for setting, and three dollars for the poles. That was fifty cents more than he received on the eastern line, but it would scarcely pay him for a move of six hundred miles, to a country where timber was in very high mountains and rough cañons.

Removing from the east of course broke the original contract; but as Gilbert had all the confidence in the world in the word of Brigham and of Joseph A., he neglected to make a new written agreement. After he had furnished the poles for about one hundred miles, my younger brother — who was farming at the time — took his team, and, after hiring six men, went to set the poles, paying his men two dollars a day and their board. They worked four weeks, for which they never received one dollar.

When my youngest brother was about leaving for home, Gilbert gave him an order on Sharp and Young for one thousand dollars. While Gilbert was in the East he had sent orders for money every month for my youngest brother to collect and disburse. Those orders were promptly paid, and he had no thought that this one would not be paid as promptly. He called at Brigham's office, and presented the order, and was curtly informed by Brigham that he must "hunt up Sharp and Joseph A."

On inquiring for their office, it could not be found. The day following he chanced to meet Bishop Sharp, who referred him to Joseph A. He called at the latter's residence three times without seeing him; finally, four days after, my brother succeeded in meeting him in his father's office. He was told to sit down in the outer room, where he was left alone for two hours; then he was called into the private office, and told that there was no money for him.

"But," said he to Brigham and Joseph A., "I must have the money; I have ten men who have already been waiting five days for their pay, and I am still paying them, or am under obligation to do so, and their board in the city also; and none of this can be done without money."

After a little more consultation Brigham said, "We can give you a draft on New York, which you can cash with some of the bankers or merchants in the city. "

My brother then asked for time to inquire on what terms he could cash the draft; but was told that merchants would often pay a percentage on such paper, and that it was always as good as money. He then asked, if he was obliged to have it discounted, if Sharp and Young would lose the

29

amount, but was told that he need not be so particular, for he must take the draft or nothing, since they had no money. He took it then, as he saw very plainly that they did not intend to give him anything else, and presented it to every banker and merchant in Salt Lake City, but could find no one who would take it. On a second call at Walker Brothers', he succeeded in cashing it at three per cent discount. Meeting Joseph A. afterwards, he told him he should charge him with the thirty dollars. Joe replied, "All right;" yet neither he nor Gilbert ever received another dollar from them, though they were in the boys' debt two thousand dollars.

When Gilbert returned from the North he found it difficult to pay his men, and also to meet his other expenses. He spent the winter trying to get his pay, during which my younger brother, Edward, took the teams and went to California for freight, hoping by that means to save Gilbert from bankruptcy. The trip not proving successful, the spring of '67 opened very dark for us financially. Gilbert saw no way but to sell his teams. I remember his coming home one night, feeling extremely dejected, and telling us he had sold sixteen of his best mules for less than half the amount he had paid for them, and expected the remainder to go at a still lower price.

In the spring of 1868 he was forced into bankruptcy by Captain Hooper, one of his principal creditors. This same Captain William H. Hooper had the good fortune to be one of the Prophet's favorites, although he was by no means a Mormon at heart, and Brigham knew it; still, as he liked him, and as Hooper made sufficient pretence to pass for one, it was all right.

When Gilbert delivered up his papers to the assignees, they readily discovered a large indebtedness on the part of Sharp and Young. At a meeting of the creditors, Brigham, who took the responsibility of the whole affair, undertook to have everything his own way, and, as my younger brother remarked, "literally rode over the whole company rough-shod." Among other statements, he said, — "Gilbert Webb's poles were many of them condemned," which was utterly false. He then said he had never written to Gilbert while he was East. In face of this the letter was produced and read before the company. He then said he was sure he had no recollection of it, and asked George Q. Cannon — who was his clerk at that time — if he remembered it. Cannon replied that he believed he did. Previous to this, when Gilbert saw that he must lose everything, he considered it his duty to pay off his men, also to pay the notes which my father had signed, and to save him from utter ruin. At this Brigham's rage knew no bounds; he wanted Hooper to have his pay first. One of Gilbert's creditors was a Mr. Kerr, a Gentile banker, whom he paid without consulting the Prophet, which greatly enraged him. In speaking of it to my mother, he manifested all the growling propensities of an old "cur;" saying that Gilbert had paid all the notes due to Gentiles, and left his friend Hooper to take his chance with the rest of the creditors, and he intended to disfellowship him for it.

This was when he was "counselling" my parents to use their influence with me in his behalf.

"If you do that, Brother Young," said my mother, "I shall find it very hard to forgive you; although Gilbert may have erred in judgment, he designed to do right. Would you, President Young, like to have his father ruined in the crash? The notes held by Mr. Kerr were signed by him." He said, "If his father signed the notes, he ought to pay them."

"Well," replied my mother, with considerable spirit, "if Gilbert had been paid for his work, he would have been able to have paid all his debts."

He was very angry at this, and said, "What do you know about business, I'd like to know?"

"I know enough to know when my children are ill-used

and cheated, Brigham Young," said she, quickly. "I wonder how you would like to have one of your sons cut off from the church, and treated in the manner in which you have treated Gilbert."

"I should think it perfectly right if one of my boys had done wrong and needed punishment." Yet it is well known that there are no more unprincipled men in the Territory than his eldest sons; but there never have been the slightest signs of their being disfellowshipped.

BRIGHAM'S STORMY INTERVIEW WITH MY MOTHER.

After a still more spirited contest with my mother, the Prophet took his departure in a great rage, saying he should see if "Gilbert would pay his Gentile debts in preference to paying the brethren."

All this was for the purpose of influencing me, and I saw that I must yield. There was nothing but ruin in store for us if I persisted in my refusal. The loss of property was by no means so dreadful a thing to my brother — brought up to believe that there was no salvation outside of Mormonism

— as being cut off from the church and receiving the Prophet's curse, and he was heart-broken at the prospect.

I made up my mind to make one last appeal myself to Brigham Young, and see if I could not touch his heart and induce him to resign his claims to me, and not to punish my family because I could not bring myself to become his wife. I was sure that I could move him. I would make myself so humble, so pathetic, before him. I would do all I could to serve him. I would never forget his kindness to me; but I could not marry him without bringing great unhappiness upon myself. I should also fail to bring happiness or comfort to him. I would be so eloquent that he could not refuse to listen to me.

I went up to the city to visit a friend, quite determined to make this appeal to him, but my courage failed me. Two or three times I started to call to see him, but I would only get in sight of his office, and turn back faint and trembling. One day I saw him coming towards me in the street, and I determined to screw up my courage and speak to him. But when I reached him my tongue refused to speak the words, and I only faltered out a common-place greeting. All my eloquence was frozen under the chilling glance of the steely-blue eyes, which had not a ray of sympathetic warmth in them. No one who has ever been under his peculiar influence but will understand me when I say that in his presence I was powerless. My will refused to act, and I went away from him, knowing that I never could say to him what I felt.

I returned home, feeling, more than ever, that my doom was fixed. My religion, my parents — everything was urging me on to my unhappy fate, and I had grown so tired with struggling that I felt it was easier to succumb at once than to fight any longer. I began, too, to be super-stitious about it; I did not know but that I was fighting the will of the Lord as well as the will of the Prophet, and that nothing but disaster would come as long as I was so rebellious. The thought struck me, in a sudden terror, "What if God should take my children, to punish my rebellious spirit?" It was agony. "Not my will, but thine," was my heart-broken cry, — more desperate than resigned, however, — and I went to my mother and told her that I had decided. I would become the wife of Brigham Young!

CHAPTER XXIX.

MY MARRIAGE WITH BRIGHAM YOUNG. — HOW THE OTHER WIVES RECEIVED ME.

The Prophet Rejoices at my Yielding. — My Family Restored to Favor. — The Webbs Reconstructed. — My Prophet-Lover Comes to See Me. — He Goes Courting "on the Sly," for Fear of Amelia. — We are Married Secretly in the Endowment-House. — I am Sent Home Again. — Brigham Establishes Me in the City. — Limited Plates and Dishes. — We Want a Little More Food. — The Prophet's "Ration-Day." — How the Other Wives Received Me. — Mrs. Amelia Doesn't Like Me. — How the Wives of the Prophet Worry and Scold Him. — The Prophet Breaks His Word. — My Father Remembers the Thousand Dollars.

AMELIA TRIES TO KEEP ME OUT.

MY acceptance of his suit was carried to him at once, and he was triumphant, although he did not show it, except by an added suavity of manner, and a disposition to make jokes, which, of course, everyone was expected to laugh at as heartily as he did himself.

My family were restored to favor, although my brother did not receive his money; and everything "went merry as a marriage-bell" for everybody, except myself. I had promised to marry him, but I was not resigned. I still fought against it, but the conflict now was all internal. I did not dare admit anyone to my confidence, not even my mother. So I had to struggle alone with my impending fate, all the time suffering the stings of conscience as well; for I thought I must be terribly wicked to fight so hard against what was represented to me as the direct will of God; and, what was worse, I could not pray for forgiveness, for I could not give up my feeling of desperate rebellion.

I had an early visit from my affianced husband, and during that visit he told me his plans. We were to be married very secretly, as, he said, he wished to keep the matter quiet for a while, for fear of the United States' officials. I found out afterwards, however, that it was fear of Amelia, for she had raised a furious storm a few months before; when, as I previously said, he married Mary Van Cott, to whom, by the way, he was paying his addresses while he was wooing me, and he did not dare so soon encounter another such domestic tornado.

He was very anxious to have the affair over as soon as possible; so we were married the 7th of April, 1869, at the Endowment-House. Heber C. Kimball performed the ceremony, and I was the wife of the head of the Mormon Church; the turbulent, passionate, shrewd, illiterate, strangely powerful man, who was the object of interest both in America and Europe; who was regarded with a strange, curious interest by outsiders; who was dreaded by his own people, and who ruled them with an absolute sway. I little thought into what publicity this new relationship would bring me.

After the ceremony was over, Brigham took me back to my mother's house, where I was to remain for the present, until he should deem it prudent to let Amelia and the United States government know that I was his wife. Before our marriage, he had given me some very pretty dresses, and a small sum of money, as a wedding-gift; but I never got such a present again afterwards. After I had been his wife three weeks, he made me his first call; stayed a few

minutes, and then went away.   A few days after, he came
and asked me to go to drive with him.   I went, and he took
me round all the by-ways where he would see few or no
people, and where he thought there would be no danger
that Amelia would hear of it.   He did not enjoy the drive
one bit, for he was in constant terror lest he should be discovered.   He was anxious and *distrait;* while I, on the
contrary, was in the highest spirits.   I laughed and chatted,
and made myself as pleasant as possible.   I could afford to
do it, for he was suffering all those torments for my sake,
and although he had no idea that I discovered his fears, I
did very readily, and was jubilant in proportion to his
misery.   I didn't feel specially complimented, to be sure;
but, as I did not desire his attentions, and was happier without them, I did not allow my pride to receive a very severe
wound, but was exceedingly gracious to him, the more
nervous and absorbed he got.

I remained at home about a month, during which time,
he said, he was having a house prepared for me in the city.
I saw but little of him during that time, and sometimes I
would almost forget that he had any claim upon me.   Then
I was happy indeed; but the thought would force itself
through everything, and I would become saddened again.
During the year of struggle, I had lost my health again,
and I was by no means the light-hearted, bright-eyed
woman he had looked at so intently that memorable Sunday
at Cottonwood.   I had grown thin and languid, and had
lost all interest in life, except in my children.   I should not
have thought that I would have proved sufficiently attractive
to have made him persevere so in his determination to marry
me.   But I believe that, at the last, he was influenced entirely by pique and wilfulness.   He would have his own
way, and, after that, it was little matter what came.

At last he came to me, and told me that he was ready for
me to move into the city, and invited my mother to come and
live with me — an offer which she accepted, because she

did not wish to be separated from me, and not because she had no home of her own, or was at all dependent upon him for support. He had wanted me to go to the Lion House to live; but on that point I was decided. I would stay at my father's house, but I would not go there; so he had made a home for me in the city. Such a home as it was! A little house, the rent of which would have been extremely moderate had it been a hired house, furnished plainly, even meanly, when the position of the man whose wife was to occupy it was considered. It was the very cheapest pine furniture which could be bought in the city, and the crockery was dishes that Brigham had left when he sold the Globe bakery. There were very few of these, and they were in various stages of dilapidation. My carpet was an old one, taken from the Lion House parlor, all worn out in the centre, and, it being a large room, I took the out edges and pieced out enough to cover two rooms, and the other floors were bare. I had no window curtains of any sort, and there being no blinds to the house, I had to hang up sheets to keep people from looking in.

I told him several times that I was insufficiently supplied; but for a long time he made some excuse or other for not giving me more. At last he sent me a very few additional ones; so that, although there was still a lack of what I actually needed, I managed to get along by a great deal of contriving.

We lived very sparely, even poorly, as did most of the wives, except the favorite, and one or two others, who asserted their rights to things, and got them after a great deal of insisting. I could not insist, and so I got very little. As I made little or no fuss, and rarely complained to him, he took advantage of my quiet tongue, and imposed upon me fearfully. He said, up to the very last of my living with him, that I was the least troublesome of any wife he had ever had; and he should have added, the least expensive, for he spent but very little money for me.

I began to find out, very soon, what a position a neglected wife has, and my heart ached and longed for freedom. The thraldom was worse than I had fancied, for I supposed that I should, at least, have had the comforts of life, such as I had been accustomed to; but I was disappointed even in that. Then I felt that I was bound to this kind of existence for life. There was no escape from it. I was shut in by every circumstance, as by a wall of adamant, and the more I struggled to get free, the worse I should be hurt. There was nothing to do but simply to endure; to die if I could, to live if I must. A pleasant state of mind, surely, for a bride of a few months.

The principal meat which he furnished to us was pork; we had it on all occasions. Very rarely, indeed, we had a piece of beef; but months would elapse between his times of sending it, and we got to look upon it as a very great luxury. He had what he called "Ration-Day" once a month, when the different families were given out their allowance for the month. This allowance for each family was five pounds of sugar, a pound of candles, a bar of soap, and a box of matches. I found this entirely inadequate, and so part of the time — unheard-of liberality! — I was allowed to draw sugar twice a month. Our bread we had from the Prophet's bakery. Once in six months his clerk got a few of the commonest necessaries of life, and each of us had a few yards of calico, and a few yards of both bleached and unbleached muslin.

I could not get anything else out of him, except by the hardest labor, and the little that I got was given so grudgingly that I hated myself for accepting it; and many a time I would have thrown the pitiful amount back in his face, but stern necessity would compel me to accept the money and overlook the insult. I can scarcely look back to those times, now that I am so far beyond them, without a lowering of my self-respect; the hot blood tingles to the very ends of my fingers as I recall the insults I received from that man while I was his wife, and the utter power-lessness of my situation, that would not let me resent them.

When my marriage to him was known by the other wives, as it was on my removal to the city, he took me to the Lion House, to visit the family there. I was very kindly received by most of them, Emmeline Free and Zina Huntington being especially my friends. Two of them, however, — Eliza Burgess and Harriet Cook, — would not speak to me.

The latter had been a servant in my mother's family in Nauvoo, and Brigham had, indeed, married her from our house. She used to take care of me when I was a baby, and she was so angry when she heard that Brigham had married me, that she wished with all her heart that she had choked me when she had a good chance; that she certainly would had she known what my future was to be. Eliza Burgess, though not the first, and never a favorite wife, used to be terribly exercised whenever Brigham added another to the family. She would go about, crying bit-terly, for days, and would sometimes shut herself up in her room, refusing to see anyone. Her sorrow was the joke of the family, since no member of it could see what reason she had for indulging in it. She had but just got over mourning his alliance with Mary Van Cott, when she was called upon to grieve over his union with me.

She knew me perfectly well, as she had been an inmate of the Lion House for some years, and used to see me con-stantly the winter I was at the theatre, and spent so much of my time there; but on the occasion of my first visit after my marriage, she utterly ignored my presence, and would neither look at me nor speak to me. Of course I noticed it, and I knew the reason very well. I had no hard feel-ings towards her, for I knew her suffering was genuine. She got no attention from her husband, and her starved heart cried out for the love that was lavished on others.

After I had gone, one of the wives — Aunt Zina, I think it was — asked why she did not speak to Ann-Eliza.

"O," she said, "I will by-and-by, when I feel like it."

I was in and out several times, and yet Eliza preserved the same demeanor towards me, until one morning she astonished me by coming up abruptly and saying, "Good morning."

I answered her greeting, and she went away as suddenly as she came, but evidently quite satisfied with herself. She "felt like it," I presume ; had grown more reconciled to my position in the family ; and was willing to recognize me as a member of it.

My first encounter with Amelia was somewhat amusing. It happened not long after my marriage. She had not got over her anger at her lord for taking Mary Van Cott, — of whom, by the way, she was terribly jealous, — when fuel was added to the fire of her fury by my introduction to the world as another Mrs. Young. She was terribly bitter towards us both, though I think she hated Mary with a more deadly hatred than she felt for me. I think she considered Mary her most dangerous rival, but for all that she was not drawn towards me at all. It was not that she disliked me less, but Mary more.

I was walking one day with a friend, and we were on our way to the gardens which join the Prophet's residence, which are, by the way, the very finest in the city. Amelia was just in front of us, and she evidently judged from our conversation where we were going to. She kept just about so far in front of us, taking no notice of me at all until she reached the garden gate, when she went in, shut it with a slam, and called out, —

"There, madam! I'd like to see you get in now."

I made no answer, but reaching through the gate, I managed, with the assistance of my friend, to open the gate and go in. We passed Amelia as she stood examining a plant, and as we passed her we did not discontinue our

conversation, but kept on laughing merrily over some girlish reminiscences which we had recalled while on the way.
In a few minutes more we heard her scolding the head-
gardener fearfully. As we returned, I stopped where the
old man was, and said, —

"What is the matter, Mr. Leggett?"

"O," said he, "it is Mrs. Amelia. Did you hear her
scolding me just now? Wasn't she just awful? She's that
mad because you came in, that she had to let out on somebody, and I suppose I came the handiest. But ain't she a
master hand to scold, though? Why, you'd ought to hear
her give it to me sometimes. I'm pretty well used to it, and
don't mind very much. It's some consolation to think that
Brother Brigham gets it worse than I do, and when he's
round, I'm safe."

Just once, after that, Amelia spoke to me. It is customary, on Brother Brigham's birthday, for the wives to
have a dinner in his house. It is held at the Lion House,
and all the family assemble to do honor to its head. At
one of these dinners Amelia sat directly opposite me, and
during the dessert she reached the cake-basket to me, and
with as freezing a tone and manner as she could assume,
asked, —

"Will you have some cake?"

I declined, and that ended our conversation — the last,
and indeed the only one I ever had with her, for the first
encounter could scarcely be called a "conversation," since
the talking was all on one side.

She was even ruder to Mary Van Cott than to me. One
day, while Brigham was furnishing Mary's house, he had
taken her up to the family store in his carriage, to select
some articles which she needed for her housekeeping.
They had finished making their selections, and were just
preparing to enter the carriage, when Amelia came sailing
down upon them. She took in the position of affairs at
once, and stepping directly between the Prophet and

Mary, elbowed them out of the way, got into the carriage, slammed the door, and ordered the driver to carry her home. The coachman hesitated a moment, looked at Brother Brigham, who never said a word; then at Mary, who was furious at the insult, but showed it only by her flashing eyes and deepening color; then back to Amelia, who scowled at him, and repeated, "Home, I say," and started off, leaving the two standing together. They walked home, and Brother Brigham had a nice time after it. Amelia treated him to a lecture longer and stronger

AMELIA'S DISPLAY OF TEMPER.

than usual, not sparing her rival in the least, but calling her every sort of name she could think of that was not complimentary in character, and threatening her recreant lord with all sorts of torments if he went out with that "shameless creature" again; while Mary felt so outraged by Amelia's act, and Brigham's cowardice in not resenting it, that he was obliged to use all his *finesse* to appease her wrath.

This carriage episode reminds me of something that

occurred in George Q. Cannon's family. This family is
no more united than many others in Utah, and they have
occasional disputes among themselves, which are not always settled in the most amicable manner. At one time,
two of his wives wanted the carriage at once. They would
not use it together, and neither one would give up to the
other. In the struggle to get possession of it, a sort of free
fight ensued. Blows were exchanged, hair pulled, finger-
nails used indiscriminately, and one of the women lost off her
dress in the contest. I think that the " apostolic " husband
fails to mention these little domestic scenes in Washington,
when he is expatiating there upon the beauties of Mormonism, and the peace and unity of the people in the Territory.

I must say that such scenes of violence do not often occur
in Brigham's family, as most of his wives feel the dignity
of their position too much to allow the world to see any
disagreement between them, even when it exists. There are
some very fine women among the Prophet's wives — women
that, outside of Mormonism, would grace any social circle.
Educated, cultivated women, who by some strange circumstance have been drawn, first into the church, then into the
Prophet's harem. I think nothing better shows the peculiar
power which Brigham Young possesses, than a look at the
women who are and who have been his wives. Ignorant
as he is, coarse and vulgar as he is, he has at least succeeded in winning women of refinement, of delicate sensibilities, as wives; and in many cases it has been done
without the slightest attempt at coercion on his part. He
had the shrewdness to select such women, and the power
to win them, but he has not the ability to appreciate them ;
and I have no hesitation in saying, from my own experience with and knowledge of them, that more unhappy and
wretched women do not exist in the world, than the more
cultured and delicate wives of Brigham Young. These
women are rarely his favorites, and it is a mystery why he
took them, unless it was that he might " add to his glory,"
and swell his kingdom.

I was always treated very kindly by the other wives, with one or two exceptions, and I have the pleasantest and kindest recollections of them all. Most of them I had known from my childhood, and they were old and intimate friends of my mother's; and I have no doubt, had they dared to have done so, they would have expressed open sympathy for me in my trials, and I am sure in their hearts they respect me for the step I have taken, and would like to find a way of retreat for themselves if it were possible.

My husband called to see me at my new residence whenever he could find opportunity, which was not very often, and he repeated the drive, which was no more comfortable for him than the first one had been. I did not care especially about it, and was glad when I got home. With the exception of those drives, I never went anywhere with him alone; for, with the exception of Amelia, and occasionally Emmeline, — which occasions constantly grew rarer, — he never went with only one wife, but took two or more.

The first winter that I was married to him, the Female Relief Society, to which I then belonged, gave a ball, and all the ladies were to invite the gentlemen. I ventured to ask Brother Young. He was my husband, and whom else should I invite? He accepted my invitation, apparently with much pleasure, and arranged to call for me on the appointed evening to take me to the hall. He was punctual to his appointment, but when he arrived he was accompanied by another wife. I suppose he knew the fact of his being at the ball would be reported to Amelia, and that she would be very angry if he went with me alone. I was very much annoyed at the circumstance, and really a little hurt that he could not take me somewhere just once without someone else along. I said nothing, however, and was as cordial to the other wife as I should have been had she accompanied him at my express invitation.

I never learned to hate anything in my life as I did the word "economy," while I was Brigham Young's wife. It

30

was thrown at me constantly. I never asked for the smallest necessary of life that I was not accused of extravagance and a desire to ruin my husband, and advised to be more economical. I had a mind to reply, several times, that I did not see how I could be, without denying myself everything, and literally going without anything to eat or to wear. I held my tongue, however, and "possessed my soul in patience." I was, in fact, a perfect Griselda; and my husband had got so used to such unquestioning obedience and submission from me that I think he never was so surprised in his life as he was when I rebelled. I am sure he would have expected rebellion from any or all of his wives sooner than from me. And I am quite sure that he was no more surprised than I was.

Before our marriage he had professed a great interest in my boys, and had promised to do many things for them. I had counted very much on his assistance in training them, but as soon as I was really married to him he seemed to forget all his promises. He looked upon my children as interlopers, and treated them as such. He scolded me for spending so much time and money on them; he would allow them to wear only clothes of home-spun cloth, and gave them each one hat and one coarse, heavy pair of shoes a year. When they needed more I had to contrive some way to get them myself; the first time I ever asked him for shoes, he said, "They didn't need shoes; children ought always to go barefoot; they were healthier for it;" and yet I noticed that none of his own children were compelled to do so. I did not allow mine to do so, either, and I am indebted to my father for many things to make me and the children comfortable, and the shoes that Brigham "couldn't afford" to buy were among them. Had I been alone, I probably should never have told my parents of my position; but my mother was with me, and she saw these little meannesses of the Prophet with surprise; yet, strange to say, they did not shake her faith in her religion. She admitted that she could not understand his behavior, and yet she counselled patience, thinking that in some way things would come right some time. I had not so much faith about the " coming right," so far as I was concerned, but I had not then begun to doubt my religion. My father had no faith at all ; for he remembered the one thousand dollars a year, not a cent of which had been seen at the end of my first year as his wife. Yet no one of us dared at that time to question the Prophet's action, although we were all indignant at his breach of faith.

We found afterwards that the promise he made my father regarding the " settlement " was the standard promise which he made to all his wives before he married them, and the fulfilment was, in most cases, the same.

CHAPTER XXX.

THE PROPHET'S FAMILY CIRCLE. — HIS WIVES AND CHILDREN.

The Prophet Marries his First and Legal Wife. — How she lives, and how Brigham has treated Her. — The Prophet's Eldest Son. — The Story of his Life. — His Wives and Families. — Mary and Maggie. — The Favorite Wife, Clara. — Young " Briggy " and his Expectations. — What the Saints think of Him. — His Domestic Joys. — How he visited me when Sick, and Scolded the old Gentleman. — Brigham and " Briggy " make love to Lizzie. — Briggy Wins. — " John W." — He neglects his " Kingdom." — " Won by the Third Wife." — The Story of Lucy C. — The Prophet's Daughters. — Alice and Luna. — Miss Alice's Flirtations. — Sweet language between Father and Daughter. — Tragic death of Alice Clawson.

INSULTED BY HER FATHER.

RIGHAM'S very first wife is not living; she died some time before he became a Mormon, and before his marriage to Mary-Ann Angell, his present legal wife.

He was quite young when he married first, and was a sort of preacher among the Methodists, and by preaching, begging, and occasionally working at his trade as glazier, or as a day-laborer at farming, he managed to pick up a very scanty living for himself and his wife, whose name was Miriam Works. My great grandfather, Gilbert Weed, married them in Auburn, Cayuga County, New York, near which place they lived for some years. My grandfather used to assert that Brigham was the laziest man that ever lived, and that he would not do any work so long as he could live without it. As may be imagined, his family were not in the most comfortable circumstances in the world, and poor Mrs. Young had by no means the easiest time. She died quite early, and the gossips' verdict was, "Died of discouragement." She left two daughters, both of whom are still living, and both are in polygamy. Elizabeth, the elder, is the first wife of Edmund Ellsworth; there are three wives besides her. The second daughter, Vilate, is the first wife of Charley Decker, who has two plural wives since he married Vilate. These girls, with their husbands, were among the very first of the Saints to arrive in the Valley.

Brigham was married to his first living and only legal wife, Mary-Ann Angell, in Kirtland, Ohio, in the year 1834. She is a native of New York State, and is still a pleasant, rather good-looking woman, though much saddened by the neglect of her husband, who rarely, if ever, visits her, and lately by the tragic death of her eldest daughter, and the still more recent death of her eldest son, Joseph A. Young, which has broken her very much. She is about the age of her husband, nearly seventy-three, and consequently is counted an old lady, while he is, according to Mormon theory, "a boy." Her mind is somewhat clouded, and this, like her sadness, is caused by the decline of her husband's affections, of whom she is very fond. She has been entirely devoted to him, and gave him as honest love when she married him, long before there was the slightest prospect of his ever occupying the position he holds now, as she has ever felt for him since his elevation to be the leader of the Mormon people; and she is repaid as it might be expected she would be, after listening to one of her husband's sermons to the women of his church.

Said he, on one occasion, when he felt called upon to

reprimand the complaining sisters, "The old women come snivelling around me, saying, 'I have lived with my husband thirty years, and it is hard to give him up now.' If you have had your husbands that length of time, it is long enough, and you ought to be willing to give them to other women, or give other women to them; you have no business with your husbands, and you are disobeying God's commands to live with them when you are old." He certainly sees to it that his wife does not "disobey God's commands," which, from his blasphemous lips, means simply his own inclinations. She has moved about to suit her husband's caprice, just as he has chosen to move. They lived first of all in the old white house on the hill, not very far from where the Prophet's buildings now stand. When the Bee-Hive was finished she lived there, but as the number of plural wives increased, she was moved back again to the old house, to make room in the other building for the new-comers. She lived there until quite recently, when her husband had her removed to the old school-house behind the Bee-Hive, a dilapidated, cheerless place, not nearly so good as the house she has left. It is, indeed, little better than a barn, and is furnished very scantily. There she lives, and there she will probably remain until her death, unless some of her children see that she is better cared for.

She took no more kindly to polygamy than did any other of the Mormon women; but she was among the very earliest sufferers. I have known her all my life; she lived in the next house to where I was born, in Nauvoo, and I used to visit at her house, with Alice Clawson, when I was engaged at the Prophet's theatre. She was always very kind to me, and I have had for her a real regard and sympathy, which increased after I became a member of her husband's family. She is a very reticent woman, neither invites nor gives confidence, has few intimate friends, and visits but little. Her hair is iron-gray; her eyes intensely sad; her face wears an habitually melancholy expression, with a touch of bitterness about the mouth; and she is rather tall in figure. Her husband's wives regard her very differently, but most of them treat her with respect. She has had five children — Joseph A., Brigham, Jr., Alice, Luna, and John W.

Joseph A., commonly called " Joe," who died during the past summer, was well known throughout the Territory, and was by no means particularly respected. He was very dissipated, and indulged in nearly every kind of vice. He has been what is called a " fast young man," and was sent to Europe on a mission to cure him, if possible, of his

JOSEPH A. YOUNG.

bad habits; but it scarcely had the desired effect, for he came home as wild as ever. He'was in my father's " Conference " in England, and behaved himself quite well there, although there was an unpleasant scandal about him while there, which has been before alluded to. In business matters he was as shrewd and as unprincipled as his father, and managed, with the assistance of the latter, to accumulate a large amount of property. Ambitious as his father is for his sons, he never dared to do anything which should advance "Joe" in the church, for he knew very well that the people would not tolerate it for an instant, for his eldest son was by no means a favorite among the Saints. He, of course, held church offices, but he would never have been any higher in authority, and certainly would never have succeeded his father as Head of the Church, even though he was the eldest son.

He was a professed polygamist, although, strictly speaking, he was a monogamist; for although he had three wives, he only lived with one. His first wife, Mary, called, to distinguish her, "Mary Joe," has several children, but neither she nor they were troubled much with Joseph's attention. She is an independent, high-spirited woman, and would not show in the least that she was troubled by his neglect. She goes about her business in a matter-of-fact way, and shows that she is able to take care of herself, as she succeeded in making her husband furnish the means to support herself and her children, whether he was willing to or not. She used to say that she could herself earn a comfortable living for them all, but so long as she had a husband who was able to do it, she would not do it, and she did not.

She is a decided contrast to poor little English Maggie, his second wife, who is in delicate health, unable to take

MAGGIE YOUNG.
[Joseph A.'s Discarded Wife.]

care of herself and her child, and who is fretting herself into her grave for the husband whom she loved so dearly, but who was so utterly unworthy of such devotion. She and her child live in a poor little room, shabbily furnished, and her husband never visited her. She is allowed the merest pittance on which to live, but the sum is so pitifully small that it does not supply even the needs of life, and the little woman suffers for them sometimes. She is a patient creature, never complaining of her lot; used never to reproach her husband; just living on and bearing her burdens as best she might; hoping for nothing in this world, but trusting that somehow the things that are so wrong here may be put straight hereafter.

Dear, patient, gentle, loving "Maggie Joe!" My heart goes out to her with a pitying tenderness, and I only wish it was in my power to put some happiness into her desolate life. I suppose she thinks of me as pityingly as I do of her, thinking that my feet have strayed into dangerous places, and that my soul is lost for ever by my action. She is one of the many martyrs to polygamy and a false religion. The merry-eyed, round-faced, gay-hearted girl, that came among the Saints so few years ago, and was won by the attractive young elder, is little like the sad-eyed, haggard woman, the broken-hearted, deserted wife. I wonder if Joe Young's heart ever smote him as he looked at her, and saw the wreck that he had made. His third wife, Thalia Grant, he neglected so entirely, that she left him in disgust.

His fourth wife, Clara Stenhouse, was so fortunate as to be the favorite. He was devoted to her exclusively, and she was delighted because she had succeeded in inducing "Joe" to renounce polygamy to this extent: he lived with her, to the exclusion of all his other wives, and promised that he would never take another. He said that she was the only one he ever really loved, although he had been much attracted by the other two. Still, her life with him was not always smooth sailing; for when he was intoxicated, — which sometimes happened even to this son of a Prophet, — he was rather abusive, though by no means so much to her as he was to the two others. Once, however, he forgot himself so far as to chase her about the house, and point a pistol at her. She immediately left him, and returned to her father's house. When he recovered, and found she had gone, he was deeply penitent, and he went for her at once. At first she refused to return with him, but he was so full of remorse, and begged so hard, and promised so fairly, that she relented and went. I think he never repeated the occurrence.

Clara had everything that she could desire; a nice house finely furnished, carriage, jewels, elegant clothes, and not a wish that she expressed but was instantly gratified. A contrast, indeed, to poor little Maggie, living in want, dying for lack of care, and starving, body and soul alike, for sufficient food and for the love which another woman won from her, just as she won that same husband's love from Mary.

Just now Brigham, Jr., or "Briggy," as he is familiarly termed among the Saints, is the most conspicuous member of the Prophet's family, as it is well known that Brigham Young intends that he shall be his successor. He is taken

"BRIGGY."
[The Prophet's Successor.]

everywhere by his father, who seems determined that the Saints shall not lose sight of him; and he already "assists" in different meetings, and his weak voice is often heard piping for polygamy, and the "new Reformation," and the "Order of Enoch," and other of the elder Brigham's pet institutions. He apes his father in manner, and, as nearly as he can, in matter, and his parent is quite proud of him. There was some murmuring among the Saints when Brigham's intentions towards him were first known to them, but they say very little now, but he and his father both know they are opposed to him. I think there would have been open rebellion if either of the other sons, especially Joe, had been thought of as the future ruler.

"Briggy" is not so quick and bright as either of the others, nor so well qualified for taking care of himself without the assistance of the tithing-office and other church perquisites; but he is infinitely better-hearted, kindlier in impulse, and is the most popular of them, although that is not according him a very high place in public estimation. He has been "on a mission," and had his "little fling" before he settled down to the dignity of his present position.

As he is such a preacher of polygamy, he also practices it, and is the husband of three wives, of whom the third is the favorite. Their names are Kate Spencer, Jane Carrington, and Lizzie Fenton. He does not abuse his wives as Joseph A. does, and although the first two have occasion to complain of neglect, since he is completely tied to Lizzie's side just now, yet he does not allow them to want, but sees that they have what they need to make life comfortable. I think he has more feeling for the physical suffering, at least, of women, than his father, or either of his brothers has. I know once, while I was Brigham's wife, when I was very ill, he came to see me, and was shocked at the condition in which he found me. I had sent several times to my husband, telling how ill I was, and asking for things which I really needed; and no attention had been paid to my requests, and he had not seen fit to come near me. He resented my illness as a personal wrong done to himself; and when told by a friend of mine, a little before this visit from Briggy, he had remarked, "That's the way with women; the minute I marry 'em they get sick to shirk work." That is the sympathy he always shows to a woman who is ill. When "Briggy" learned how I was neglected, he went at once for his father on my behalf, although I had not the slightest idea of his intention. He found his father breakfasting at the Bee-Hive House; and, before several of the wives, he burst out, —

"Father, I think it is shameful, the way you are treating Ann-Eliza. She is fearfully sick, and if you don't have something done for her, she'll die on your hands. I've been down to see her, and I know."

The old gentleman didn't say anything, and "Briggy" turned on his heel and left the room. That day I received a portion of the things for which I had sent so many days before. I was quite at a loss to know why they had come so suddenly, and it remained a mystery to me until, some time after, Lucy Decker told me about "Briggy's" attack on his father. She said that, although they were frightened at the fellow's temerity, they delighted in his spunk, and had liked him better ever since. I have been grateful to him ever since I knew of that occurrence, and found that he had constituted himself my champion.

Lizzie, Briggy's third wife, is a native of Philadelphia, and she came to Utah with John W. and Libbie, Johnny's third wife. She was a fine-looking girl, tall and rather large, with a bright, intelligent face, and vivacious, fascinating manners. Both old Brigham and young Brigham were smitten with her at once, and commenced paying her the most marked attentions, and for a long time a fierce rivalry existed between the father and son. Lizzie lived with Mrs. Wilkison before her marriage, and her courtship by Brigham and Briggy was very funny, and quite exciting to the lookers-on, who were anxious to see whether youth or experience would win.

First the old gentleman would come, driving down in fine style with his spanking team ; then Briggy would come, rather on the sly, and spend the remainder of the day, after his parent was well out of the way. He always seemed bent on having the last word, and, finally, he won the young lady. This double courtship went on for several months, much to the delight of the spectators, whose sympathies were, for the most part, with Briggy, and who were delighted when the young fellow won.

Lizzie has two children, and is the favorite wife ; but she is very unhappy, as I have often heard her say. She has seen other "favorite" wives neglected for another, and although her husband certainly has as yet given her no reason to doubt his affection for and his fidelity to her, yet even he may be tempted from her side. I have not so much sympathy for her, however, as I have for those poor girls who are educated in Mormonism, and know nothing else, for she was an Eastern born and educated girl, and entered polygamy with her eyes open.

John W. is the third son and the youngest child of Mary
Ann Angell. He is the best looking of the three, has the best
address, and has seen the most of the world; for although
he has never been sent on a mission, he has been East a
great deal, and has been more
in contact with the outside,
Gentile world, than any of the
others. If any Eastern business is to be done, requiring
the presence of some person
from Utah, Johnny is always
the one to go. He is a shrewd
business fellow, with more
finesse than Joe., and a great
deal of tact, which makes him
very successful. He passes
for quite a good fellow among
those who meet him casually,

JOHN W. YOUNG.

and I found him quite well known among the newspaper
fraternity when I came East. One reporter, whom I met,
told me that John W. had offered him money to keep his
name before the public while he was here; and told the
same man that I was a poor, weak creature that would
never amount to anything. It was, probably, a desire that
the "royal blood of Young" should be honored; and as
that blood coursed through his veins, the honor to the sire
would be honor to the son.

Johnny is not an enthusiastic Mormon, by any means,
and I am quite sure if he were anybody's son but Brigham's,
he would be regarded with suspicion as an "apostate;" but
he is "President of the Salt Lake Stake of Zion," and
his belief is never questioned by his father. I think he
holds to the church because he finds it a good thing; but
if Brigham were to die, and Briggy to fail in the succession,
I don't think he would stick by it long. Its emoluments are
convenient; with its doctrines and beliefs he has no sympathy; indeed, I fancy he is totally indifferent to them.

Like all the rest, he has embraced polygamy, but has been for some time a monogamist. Like the other two brothers, also, he has been won by the third wife, who holds him entirely now. He says openly that she is the only woman that he ever loved; that he married the others to please his father, who was quite anxious for him to "build up a kingdom." He does not hesitate to declare the "kingdom business a humbug," and prefers the society of his third, whom he now considers his only lafwul wife, to that of either or both the others. The first wife, Lucy Canfield, has several children, and she is the cousin of his third wife. She is a spirited woman, like Joseph A.'s first wife, and when she found that her husband did not love her, and had said that he did not, she made no fuss about it, but quietly took her children, went away, and as speedily as possible was divorced from Johnny, saying she would not be any man's wife by simple toleration.

The second wife, Clara Jones, cries her eyes out over her husband's defection, but will not be induced to leave him. He supports her, I believe, but never sees her, and says he shall never live with her again. She really loved the graceless, handsome fellow, and will be called by his name, and be his wife, even if she cannot have his attention.

Johnny met his third wife in Philadelphia, while on a visit there to his first wife's relatives. She was a very pleasing woman, and he an attractive fellow, and they fell in love with each other. She knew very well his matrimonial situation, but that did not deter her from accepting his attentions, nor from accompanying him to Utah under promise of becoming his wife upon their arrival. He was to discard his other wives, and be true to her. She did not seem to think that she was betraying her cousin, and bringing misery to her; she only thought of herself, and the gratification of her own ambition; for, apart from her love for Johnny, which I have no doubt was genuine, she knew very well that she should gain wealth, at least, as the wife of one of Brigham Young's sons. She and Lizzie Fenton came, and as soon as possible she was united to Johnny.

It took the latter some time to arrange his matrimonial affairs successfully, and occasionally a "scene" would occur in this somewhat divided family. She had been married but one week when Johnny first met her; but as Gentile marriages are "null and void" under the Saintly rule, her conversion to Mormonism divorced her at once, — at least from the Mormon point of view, and rendered her perfectly at liberty to go to
Utah with Johnny, who
was also, by the Mor-
mon law, justified in
taking her.

After they were mar-
ried, Johnny placed her,
for the time, in the house
with his other wives, and
they submitted to her
presence with all the pa-
tience of good Mormon
women. It required but
a very short time, how-
ever, for them to dis-
cover that the last was
the only wife he cared

LUCY REBELLIOUS.

to recognize; in fact, he nearly ignored the existence of all, except his "dear Libbie," and he felt it an imperative duty to see that she was treated with the utmost deference by the other wives. One night, as he and Libbie were about withdrawing from the family circle to their own room, he insisted that his first and second wives should, on bidding Libbie "good night," kiss her. And when Lucy declined to comply with his request, he became very much exasperated, and threatened to shut her up in some dark closet, as is sometimes done with disobedient children, unless she

KISSING LIBBIE GOOD NIGHT.

would obey him. Johnny felt that he must not compromise his dignity by yielding the point, and such rebellion must not go unpunished. And, as she still remained obstinate, he put his threats into execution. She remained in her prison until she feared to be longer away from her children, and was forced to yield to his wishes, and kiss Libbie good night.

It was not long after that when Lucy left him, and sought a divorce, which Johnny's father readily granted.

The only acknowledged Mrs. John W. Young lives in elegant style, accompanies her husband on all his Eastern trips, and makes herself, by dress and otherwise, as attractive as possible to her husband; for she knows, as well as the others, that she only holds him so long as she shall prove more fascinating than any other woman.

Alice Clawson was the best known of any of Brigham's daughters. She was the elder of Mary-Ann Angell's girls, and was for many years a leading actress at the Salt Lake theatre. She had no special dramatic talent, but she was a good worker, and so succeeded quite well in her profession. Being Brigham's daughter also gave her a decided *prestige*, and she never made her appearance but what she was warmly applauded. She was quite pretty, being rather small and slight, with blue eyes and fair hair, and had all her father's ambition.

She was quite a favorite with gentlemen, and had several little "affairs" before she was safely married to Hiram B.

Clawson, who was, at the time of her marriage with him, her father's confidential clerk, and the stage manager and "leading man" at the theatre where she was engaged.

In 1851 a Mr. Tobin visited Salt Lake, and fell a victim to Miss Alice's charms, and was engaged to her. Soon after their engagement, he went away, and did not return until 1856. While he was away she flirted quite desperately with another young gentleman, and was reported engaged to him; but her father sent him off to convert the Sandwich Islanders, and took him out of the reach of Miss Alice's charms.

Soon after Mr. Tobin's return, the engagement between them was broken, and her father's ire was so great against him that he was obliged to leave Salt Lake City. He and his party were followed, and while they were in camp on the Santa Clara River, three hundred and seventy miles south of Salt Lake, they were attacked, and narrowly escaped with their lives, leaving all their baggage behind them, and having six horses shot. Some of the party were wounded, but fortunately all escaped. I met Mr. Tobin in Omaha, and he gave me an account of the whole affair.

He broke his engagement because he was displeased with her for flirting. It was not long after this before she married Clawson, who was the husband of two wives, but still aspired to the hand of Alice, which the Prophet was much opposed to; but Alice would have him in spite of her father. Some years after he married one of her half-sisters.

Theoretically she was a polygamist; practically she hated it, and I know that her married life was very unhappy. She had several children, but was not called a very good mother.

The circumstances of her death, which occurred a few months since, are sad in the extreme.

31

She was in the street, one day, and met her father, who

MRS. ALICE YOUNG CLAWSON.

happened to be in one of his ill-humors, and was only waiting for some one to vent it on. Alice, unluckily, was the victim. She was always very fond of dress, and was inclined to be somewhat "loud" in her style. She was dressed, this day, to pay some visits, and was finer than usual. Her father looked at her from head to foot, then said, in the most contemptuous manner which he could assume, —

"Good heavens, Alice! What are you rigged out in that style for? You look like a prostitute."

She faced him with an expression so like his own that it was absolutely startling, and, with terrible intensity, replied, —

"Well, what else am I? And whose teachings have made me so?"

She passed on, leaving him standing gazing after her in surprise. Not long after, she was found dead in her bed, with a bottle, labelled "poison," by her bedside. Tired of life, she had thrown it carelessly aside, for it was of little worth to her. Neither husband nor father was much comfort to her, and, with her mother before her, it is no wonder that she did not wish to live to grow old.

It has been said that at one time she was greatly in her father's confidence, and that she has assisted many a scheme which served to enrich her father, who used her to advance his own interests, without regard to her youth or sex. Of the truth of this I have no means of knowing, but as far as

I had any experience with her, she was an amiable, kind-hearted woman, ambitious and proud, and a strong hater of the polygamic life which she was forced to lead.

Luna Young was a bright, gay girl, the pet and the ruling power of her mother's house. She is very pretty, and extremely imperious. She is blonde, like Alice, but by far the more beautiful and self-willed. She has all her father's strength of purpose, and the two strong wills used often to clash, and it was rarely that hers was subdued. Her father found her the most difficult of all the girls to manage, and yet he seemed more fond of her than of her more yielding and obedient sister.

She is a plural wife of George Thatcher, and endures, although she by no means loves, polygamy.

The children of Mrs. Angell Young are better known to the world than any of the others, and of these five, the ones that the public are most familiar with are John W. and Alice, both of whom seem very widely known by reputation; John W. from his constant contact with the Gentiles, and Alice from the position which she so long held in the theatre, and which brought her so constantly before the public for so many years.

CHAPTER XXXI.

THE WIVES OF THE PROPHET. — BROTHER BRIGHAM'S DOMESTIC TROUBLES.

The Wives of the Prophet. — Lucy Decker. — A Mysterious Disappearance. — Lucy's Boys. — Brigham's Wife Clara. — Her Busy Household Work. — About the Girls. — Harriet Cook. — She Expresses Unpleasant Opinions. — Brigham is frightened of Her. — He Keeps out of the Way. — Amelia and the Sweetmeats. — How one of Brigham's Daughters scandalized the Saints. — How Mrs. Twiss Manages the Prophet's House. — The Work a Woman can Do. — Martha Bowker and her silent Work. — Sweet and saintly doings of the Prophet. — Concerning Harriet Barney. — The Wife who "Served Seven Years" for a Husband. — Another English Wife of the Prophet. — The "Young Widow of Nauvoo."

EMMELINE SERVING BRIGHAM AND AMELIA.

LUCY DECKER was the wife of Isaac Seeley, and had two children before she became a convert to Mormonism, and removed to Nauvoo. The husband had been esteemed a fine young man, and to all appearances they were living quite harmoniously, when Brigham saw her, and fell in love with her. He soon persuaded her that Seeley could never give her an "exaltation" in the eternal world; but that, if she would permit him, he would secure her salvation, and make her a queen in the "first resurrection." She was bewildered by the promises, and consented to become "sealed" to him *secretly.*

In some way or other, Seeley found out the true state of affairs, and was exceedingly indignant, and made some very unpleasant threats of vengeance against Brigham Young for breaking up his family. Brigham at once commenced endeavoring to turn the tide of public opinion against him, by resorting to his always ready weapon, his tongue, and insinuating things against him ; among others, he took care that the impression should get abroad that he had threatened to kill his wife. These reports gained little credence among those who knew him well ; yet Brigham, with Joseph to help him, was sure to succeed in his efforts to ruin the man, or to drive him away, so that he should no longer stand in his light, and Seeley suddenly disappeared.

All sorts of rumors were afloat respecting his disappearance ; some said he was driven from Nauvoo at the point of the knife ; others said he was dead ; others, that he left voluntarily, disgusted with the entire proceedings ; at all events, he has never appeared to interfere with his wife's later domestic arrangements.

Lucy lives in the "Bee Hive," which is supposed to be Brigham's own particular residence, at least his private office and own sleeping-room are there, and he takes his meals there except his dinner. She has always had the charge of this house, and has always been quite highly valued by her husband on account of her numerous domestic virtues, for she is a superior housekeeper, and even Brigham finds great difficulty in getting a good opportunity to find fault with her. It has been Brigham's custom always to keep the "Bee Hive" for his exclusive use, and none of his wives were allowed there, except Lucy Decker, who had the charge. But after he married Amelia, before her house was finished, he brought her to board there with him, contrary to all precedent ; and Lucy Decker was not only obliged to cook for them, but to wait upon them at the table, in the capacity of a servant, and Amelia never recognized her in any other way, never speaking to her as an equal, but ordering her about at her caprice, and the husband allowed it. But then it is no uncommon thing in Utah for a man to marry a woman for a servant; it is more economical than to hire them. It saves the wages.

When Lucy Decker's sons, Brigham's children, grew up, they accepted mercantile situations, as he expects all to work, which is certainly all right; but they were not allowed to stay with their mother without paying him the same amount for board that they would have to pay elsewhere. A married daughter is also allowed to remain with her mother under the same conditions.

She is a short, fleshy woman, with a pleasant, small-featured face, dark eyes and hair, and as practical and matter-of-fact in manner as you please.

She has seven children — Brigham-Heber, Fanny, Ernest, Arthur, Mira, Feramorz, and Clara. Fanny is the plural wife of George Thatcher, who also numbers her half sister, Luna, among his wives. Heber and Ernest are both married, but have, as yet, but one wife each. They do not seem in a hurry to add to their kingdom.

CLARA DECKER.

Clara Decker is the younger sister of Lucy, and was "sealed" to Brigham at the same time. She is a very intelligent, prepossessing woman, and for some time was quite a favorite with her husband. Like her sister, she is short and stout; but she has a very sweet, benevolent face, which truly mirrors her character. She is an indefatigable, but a quiet worker, and the good she does, not only in the Prophet's household, but out of it, cannot be estimated.   In spite of her multitudinous home cares, she finds time to visit the sick and comfort the afflicted, and there is no woman more universally beloved than she.

She has been of great service to her husband in assisting him in the management of his large family, and in addition to her own family of children, she has the care of Margaret Alley's.   She has been as tender and kind to them as to her own, and since their own mother's sad death they have received an untiring and affectionate maternal care from her.   When her husband has taken a new wife, she has often been applied to to assist him in preparing the housekeeping outfit, which she always does willingly and cheerfully, never manifesting the least jealousy, nor making herself disagreeable in any way.   Her griefs she keeps to herself, and gives a kindly, cheery countenance to her family and the world.

She has long since lost all love for her husband, and although she retains her faith in the underlying principles of her religion, is by no means so blinded by bigotry as not to see its faults.   She expresses her opinions rarely, but when she does, they are given decisively, and her husband is not at a loss to understand her meaning.   He has a high regard for her services, and I really believe accords her more respect than he does most women.   She never appears in public with him, being always too much " engaged " at home.

No one can know Clara Decker without loving her ; she has a nature that wins affection spontaneously, and that holds it after it is won.   She has three children, all girls — Nettie, Nabbie, and Lulu.   Nettie is married to Henry Snell, and is the only wife.   Clara and her children are inmates of the Lion House.   She has more room than the others, as her family numbers so many members.

The third "wife in plurality " was Harriet Cook, to whom

the Prophet was sealed at Nauvoo before the church left that place for the west. She was at that time rather a good-looking girl, tall and fair, with blue eyes, but with a sharp nose, that so plainly bespoke her disposition that no one was surprised to hear, not very long after her marriage, that her husband had found he had " caught a Tartar." She was in my mother's employ at Nauvoo, and I think there is where the Prophet became enamoured of her. She does not hesitate to say that " Mormonism, polygamy, and the whole of it, is a humbug, and may go to the devil for all her." Her husband never attempts to argue any theological question with her, but gets out of the way as speedily as possible, letting her abuse religion and him as much as she pleases behind his back.

Brigham, finding her so ungovernable, and being quite unable to exact submission or obedience from her, refused to live with her ; and, although she still lives at the "Lion House" with the other wives, avoids her as studiously as possible, and will not even notice her, unless positively compelled to do so.

She has one son, Oscar, whom his father calls a reprobate, and has entirely disowned ; a wild, headstrong, unruly fellow, now nearly thirty years of age. He speaks of his father as "dad," and "the old man," and openly expresses his disgust at his hyprocrisy and meanness, which he sees through very clearly. He is no more afraid to speak his mind than his mother, of whose tongue not only Brigham, but the other wives, stand in dread ; and when she commences battle they act on the principle that "discretion is the better part of valor," and leave the field to her.

The son has been married, but his wife has left him.

A few years ago Brigham bought a house at St. George, quite an important Mormon settlement, four hundred miles south of Salt Lake City, intending to settle some one of his wives there. He asked me if I would go, but I declined. He then proposed to one or two others, but they had no

more of a mind to go than I had. Lucy Bigelow at last
decided to try St. George as a residence, and she has remained there ever since. Lucy was married to him when
she was very young, and she has been one of the " Society "
wives in the past. She was exceedingly pretty, quite entertaining, and a very graceful dancer. She is not very tall,
but has quite a pretty figure, brown hair, blue eyes, and an
exceedingly pretty mouth.

Her position as housekeeper at St. George has been no
sinecure, for Brigham and Amelia have been in the habit
of passing a portion, at least, of the winter there, and Lucy
Bigelow's position there has been very much what Lucy
Decker's was at the Bee Hive, — that of servitor, entirely.
When Brigham comes she receives no more attention than
a housekeeper would ; and no one, ignorant of the fact,
would ever imagine she had held towards him the position
of wife. She does not sit at the table with them, but cooks
for them, and looks after their comfort generally.

She is quite a prudent housekeeper, and every year puts
up a large quantity of preserves, which Amelia and her
party being very fond of, would speedily put out of the way ;
and when the presidential visits were ended, poor Lucy
would have no sweetmeats left for her own use, or to give to
her friends when they came to see her. On the occasion of
a late visit, she was so annoyed at her treatment, both by
Brigham and Amelia, — the former being particularly captious and insolent, — that she spoke her mind with such
sudden and startling plainness, that they left the house in
a hurry. The Southern wife is to be commended for her
spirit. She does not show it often ; and probably, had the
insults come alone from her husband, she would have
borne them quietly, as she has done for nearly thirty years ;
but she could not endure the·same treatment from Amelia,
and she very justly rebelled.

She has three daughters, Dora, Susan, and Toolie.
Dora is the only wife of Morley Dunford. She scanda-

lized the Saints, and aroused the ire of her father, by going quietly off with her lover to the Episcopal clergyman to be married. According to Gentile laws she is legally married, but according to Mormon laws she is not securely tied. Still, she seems satisfied. Susie is married to Almy Dunford, and is also an only wife.

One of the most important wives, although by no means the recipient of any of her husband's attentions, is the housekeeper at the " Lion House," Mrs. Twiss. She was a young widow living in Nauvoo when Brigham discovered

BEE-HIVE HOUSE. — BRIGHAM YOUNG'S RESIDENCE.

her, and recognizing her useful qualities, had her sealed to him as soon as he could arrange for it. She is not very attractive in personal appearance, having a round face, light blue eyes, low forehead, and sandy hair, which is inclined to curl. In figure she is short and stout. But she is an energetic worker, and as a servant Brigham values her.

She never complains of her position, but she is no better content with it than any other neglected wife in polygamy. She is kind to the other wives, and has an amiable, quiet disposition, although she is exceedingly firm and resolute. She has no children of her own, a circumstance which grieves her very much, but she has adopted a son, of whom she is very fond, and who is a very great comfort to this childless, unbeloved wife.

Martha Bowker is another of the Prophet's "sickly wives," of whom he is so fond of sneering; and the fact that she is an invalid is sufficient to preclude her from receiving care or sympathy from her husband. He married her when she was very young, and never has treated her with much consideration. Why he married her, unless it was because he was anxious to "build up his kingdom" as quickly as possible, and so took every available woman he could find, will always remain a mystery. She is plain, but very quiet and sensible. She never interferes with anyone, and worships her husband at a distance. I think it must be true, in his case at least, that "familiarity breeds contempt," for the wives who have been the favorites stand less in awe of him, have less faith in him, and are less easily deceived by his pretensions than those whom he has neglected, and who do not understand him thoroughly. The less attention a wife has paid her, the greater is her veneration for her husband. Her respect for him seems to increase in proportion to the snubs she receives. Mrs. Bowker Young is by no means accomplished, moderately well educated, and is by no means intellectually brilliant. She says but little, but displays considerable hard common sense when she does speak. She is somewhat of a nonentity in the "Lion House," where she lives, keeping very much to herself, and not making her presence felt. She has an adopted daughter, but no children of her own.

Among all the wives that Brigham claims, there is none the superior of Harriet Barney Young, who, in spite of all her personal charms and graces of mind, has never been a favorite with the Prophet. She is too good and noble-minded for him to appreciate. There is too little of the flatterer about her.   She is tall and stout, but very graceful in every movement.   Her eyes are a clear hazel, with a soft, sad expression in them that is almost pathetic.   Her hair is light-brown, and her face wears a peculiarly mild, sweet look.   She is a person that anyone in trouble would be drawn towards, and would involuntarily rely on and confide in.   She is always ready, with the tenderest sympathy, to comfort sorrow and distress ; and her acts of kindness, which are very numerous, are always unostentatiously performed. She was married before she met Brigham, and was the mother of three children ; but becoming convinced that Mormonism was right, and receiving it, polygamy and all, as a divine religion, given direct from God, she considered it her duty to leave her husband, and cast her lot with this people.   She brought her children with her, determined to bring them up in the true faith, and she was, in every regard, an earnest, conscientious, devout Christian, who would never shirk a duty, no matter how painful it might be, and would never do anything which she considered wrong, no matter how much she might suffer for her persistence in the right.

She loves her husband with all the strength of an earnest devotion, and his careless treatment of her seems to make little difference in the depth of her affection.   She knows her love is hopeless, but she cherishes it, nevertheless, and is content to worship with no hope of return.   She is a devout Mormon, and all she has seen, heard, and suffered, has not shaken her faith one whit.   She believes that "this people" is destined to come up "out of great tribulation," and she accepts her own share without a murmur.

She formerly lived at the Lion House with her children, but latterly she has occupied a cottage near the Tabernacle. She likes this new arrangement infinitely better, as her situation in the large family was particularly trying.   Brigham's own children have always been extremely haughty and arrogant to those not of the "royal" blood; and although Harriet's children were good and amiable, they, as well as their mother, were rendered very unhappy. She supports herself and family now by sewing; but is happier in this than in living in dependence, and receiving favors which are grudgingly bestowed. Her husband is by no means a frequent visitor at her cottage, but she never reproaches him with neglect.

She has had one child since her marriage to the Prophet, — a son, whose name is Howe.

LION HOUSE AND BRIGHAM'S OFFICES.

Eliza Burgess, the wife who is said to have "served seven years" for her husband, is an English woman, a native of Manchester, and came to Nauvoo with her parents among the very earliest of the Mormon emigrants. They had not been long in this country before her parents died, and she was left alone. Mrs. Angell Young took her into the family as a servant, and she came to the Valley with her. She was very attentive and faithful to the Prophet, whom she regarded with the greatest veneration; and when he, noticing her devotion, offered to become her "savior," and secure for her "everlasting salvation," the poor girl was completely overcome, and entered her new relation with the most sacred reverence and joy. It is almost painful to see the dumb worship which she accords to her master, and the cavalier manner in which it is received. For a long time she was an inmate of the Lion House, and assisted Mrs. Twiss in the household labors. She has lately been promoted to the position of housekeeper at Provo, where the Prophet has an establishment for the convenience of himself and his party when he is making a tour of the settlements. This wife is faithful to all his interests, and unflagging in her zeal to serve him. The moment she finds that she is in any way necessary to his comfort, she works with a new earnestness. She is honest and upright, and is in every way worthy of the love of a good man. Yet she lives on, starving for the love that is denied her, and "wearying" for a husband who absents himself from her for a year at a time.

She has one son, Alphilus, a bright young fellow, who is at present a student in the law-school of the Michigan University.

Besides Eliza Burgess, the English wife, Brigham has but one other who is not American. This is Susan Snively, who is a German, and who has been one of his useful wives. She is a woman now considerably past middle age, and carries her nationality very decidedly in her face. She is of medium size, has dark hair, bright eyes, dark complexion, and a stolid, expressionless face. She is decidedly the plainest of the wives, and one of the most capable. Her nature is kindly, and she is a genuinely good woman, quiet and unassuming. She is not the slightest bit assertive, and would remain in a corner unnoticed all her life, unless some one discovered her and brought her out. In her busy days, she was a good housewife, — could spin, dye, weave, and knit, and make excellent butter and cheese.

She was married to Brigham in the early days of polygamy, when she was a young girl; indeed, most of his
wives were taken between 1842 and 1847, and she has
proved herself a good wife in every sense of the word. She
has lived at the farm a great deal; for eight years she was
sole mistress there, and a harder worker never lived. She
paid special attention to the dairy, making all the butter and
cheese for the entire family. She has done a great deal for
all the wives and children, and they have not hesitated to
call on her for services, so cordially and freely has she
given them. The farm was very large, and required many
laborers, and these all boarded at the farm-house, and
Susan had them to look after, which she did faithfully.
Everything that she did was done to promote, as far as
possible, the interests of the Prophet and his family.

At last, under such a constant strain of incessant labor,
she broke down completely, unable any longer to endure
the strain. Her strength failed; her health was destroyed;
her once strong constitution undermined, and she was forced
to seek refuge in the " Lion House," and take her chances
with the numerous family. After she had given all her
strength, and the best part of her life, to the service of her
"master," she was of no more use to him, and she might
live or die, as she saw fit. It mattered nothing to him. She
said once to me, " How I should like a drive! and how much
good it would do me! We have plenty of carriages, to be
sure, yet I am never allowed to ride." Tears trembled in
her eyes, and her voice shook as she made her complaint;
and I wished it were in my power to gratify her. I did pity
her lonely and neglected condition with all my heart.

Her only earthly comfort is an adopted daughter, whom
she dearly loves. She never had any children of her own,
and she lavishes all her maternal affection on this attractive
young girl, who returns her love, and calls her "mother."

She still clings to her religious faith with a sort of hopeless despair. If that should fail her, she would be desolate

indeed.   She suffers in the present, hoping for a recompense
in the future.

Young widows seemed to have abounded in Nauvoo,
judging from the number that have been "sealed" to the
Prophet and his followers. So many men died in defence
of the church, that the wives must, of necessity, fall to someone's care, and the protectors were easily found. Margaret
Peirce was another of Brigham's fancies, and was sealed to
him soon after the death of her husband. Her health has
been very delicate for some years ; consequently she is not in
favor with her husband. She has one son, Morris, whom
she absolutely worships. He is now about twenty years
old, but he is still her baby.

CHAPTER XXXII.

THE PROPHET'S FAVORITE WIFE. — HOW HE CONDUCT-
ED HIS LOVE-AFFAIRS.

The Prophet's Favorite Wife, Amelia. — How Brigham made Love in the
Name of the Lord. — How he won an Unwilling Bride. — A Lady with
a Sweet Temper. — How she Kicked a Sewing-Machine down the
Prophet's Stairs. — She has a new House built for Her. — Rather Ex-
pensive Habits. — Her Pleasant chances for the Future. — Mary Van
Cott Cobb. — A Former Love of the Prophet's. — Miss Eliza-Roxy
Snow. — The Mormon Poetess. — Joseph Smith's Poetic Widow. —
Versification of the Saints. — Mrs. Augusta Cobb. — Emily Partridge.

BRIGHAM LOOKS AMAZED.

THE favorite wife of the
Prophet, Amelia Fol-
som, is a woman about
forty years of age, and
was a New England
girl.

She was born at Ports-
mouth, New Hampshire,
and with her parents,
who were converts to
Mormonism, came to Utah. She is tall,
of a good figure, has rather regular features, brown hair, bluish-gray eyes, and
a querulous, discontented expression, with
a very great deal of decision indicated
by the mouth. And, indeed, in spite of
all that is lavished upon her, she is not
happy. She did not wish to marry Brigham, as she had a
lover to whom she was fondly attached; but he wished to

32

marry her, and that settled her fate. Her parents favored his suit, and urged it strongly; but she was bitterly opposed to it, and it was months before she would yield to their united desires.

He was a most arduous and enthusiastic lover, and during all the time that his suit was in progress, his carriage might be seen standing before the door of her parents' house several hours at a time every day. He evidently did not intend that absence should render her forgetful of him. He promised her anything that she might desire, and also agreed to do everything to advance the family interests. Promises had no weight with her. He then had recourse to " Revelation; " he had been specially told from heaven that she was created especially for him, and if she married

AMELIA FOLSOM.
[Brigham's Favorite Wife.]

anyone else she would be for ever damned. The poor girl begged, pleaded, protested, and shed most bitter tears, but all to no purpose. His mind was made up, and he would not allow his will to be crossed. She had been converted to believe in special revelation, and to look upon Brigham as the savior of all the Mormon people, and to think that disobedience to him was disobedience to God, since God's commands came through him. In answer to her pleading, he said, " Amelia, you must be my wife; God has revealed it to me. You cannot be saved by anyone else. If you marry me, I will save you, and exalt you to be a queen in the celestial world; but if you refuse, you will be destroyed, both soul and body."

This is the same argument he used to win me, and the one he has always in reserve, as the last resort, when everything else fails to secure his victim.

VIEW IN SALT LAKE CITY—SHOWING AMELIA'S NEW HOUSE.

Of course she yielded; what else was she to do? It was a foregone conclusion when the courtship commenced. She was married to him the 23d of January, 1863, more than six months after the anti-polygamy law had been passed by Congress, and the marriage was celebrated openly, and in defiance of the law.

Since the marriage, Amelia has ruled with a hand of iron, and she has her lord in pretty good subjection. She has a terrible temper, and he has the benefit of it. On one occasion he sent her a sewing-machine, thinking to please her; it did not happen to be the kind of a one which she wanted; so she kicked it down stairs, saying, "What did you get this old thing for? You knew I wanted a ' Singer.' "

She had a Singer at once.

I was once present when she wanted her husband to do something for her; he objected, and she repeated her demand, threatening to "thrash him," if he did not comply. It is, perhaps, unnecessary to say that she was not obliged to ask him again. I know he is afraid of her, and that she holds him now through fear, rather than love. She accompanies him to the theatre, and occupies the box, while the rest of the wives sit in the parquet. She goes with him on his visits to the settlements, and drives out with him constantly.

She has a beautiful new house, elegantly furnished, and Brigham has very nearly deserted the " Bee-Hive," except during business hours, and spends most of his time at Amelia's residence. She dresses elegantly, has jewels and laces, and has saved ten thousand dollars out of her " pin-money," which she placed in bank. I am delighted at her success in getting so much; the other wives have succeeded in getting nothing but their living from him, some scarcely that; and I, for my part, congratulate Amelia on her good management. It was a hard struggle for her to marry him, and all she gets will never half repay her for the suffering she has endured in the past, even if she has grown contented now.

She is rather careless in her treatment of the other wives, but gets along the best with the "proxies." When she lived at the "Bee Hive," she dined at the "Lion House," with her husband and the other wives. She and Brigham sat at a table by themselves — a small table, standing at the head of the dining-room. The other wives, with their children, sat at a long table, running nearly the entire length of the room. The fare at this table was very plain, while the other was loaded with every delicacy that the season would afford. When strangers dined with Brigham, the difference in the fare was less noticeable, and the long table would be amply provided for, so as to make a good impression upon the visitor. Amelia is not well; indeed, she is at times quite an invalid. She has no children.

About six months before my marriage to the Prophet, he took a pretty young widow, Mary Van Cott, for a wife, much to Amelia's distress, who had considered herself the last for so long, that she was quite unprepared for the intro-duction of a rival. She was very bitter in her denunciations both of Brigham and Mary, and commenced at once to make friends with some of the other wives. She said to Aunt Zina, I believe, that she knew now how Emmeline felt when Brigham took her. Emmeline had been the favorite wife for years, and was really fond of her husband, and it was a terrible blow to her when he deserted her for another.

For some time Brigham's fickle affections hovered about Mary, but Amelia, with a determination which but few Mormon women possess, fought against her rival until she compelled her lord to withdraw his attentions from the new wife, or to bestow them on the sly. Mary felt very much hurt and aggrieved, but she has managed to hold her own sufficiently to get a very pretty cottage house, which is very daintily furnished, and which she makes very attractive.

She has two children, one by a former husband; the other, a pretty little girl, three or four years old, the youngest of Brigham's children, and who is always called

"Baby." After I left it was said she very nearly decided to take the same step. She was very discontented, and the treatment she received from the Prophet and his family was not such as to encourage her to stay with him. Her own people, who are devout Mormons, became aware of her intention, and finally succeeded, by a great amount of persuasion, in inducing her to try a little longer. Brigham, too, found out what step she was contemplating, and knowing that opinion would set strongly against him if two of his wives should leave him so nearly at the same time, added his arguments to theirs, and also agreed to fix her house, and give her more things, among which was a grand piano, if she would not bring another scandal upon him. For the sake of her child she decided to remain, but she is in a state of mental rebellion, which may break out at any time. She is, since my defection, the last added member of the family.

Miss Eliza R. Snow is the first of Brigham's "proxy" wives, and is the most noted of all Mormon women. She was one of Joseph Smith's wives, and, after his death, was sealed to Brigham for time, but is to return to Joseph in eternity. She was the founder of the "Female Relief Society," is the motive power of the "Woman's Exponent," although Miss Green acts as editor, personates "Eve" in the "Endowments," and is a poetess of no inconsiderable merit. She writes hymns for all

MISS ELIZA R. SNOW.
[Mormon Poetess.]

occasions, and most of her poems are full of a strong religious fervor. She is a thorough Mormon, and believes absolutely every portion of the doctrine, and might contend with Orson Pratt for the title of "Defender of Polygamy."

Brigham regards her very highly, because she is of such inestimable service in the church. She lives at the "Lion House," where she has quite a pleasant room, in which she receives most of her company. She is the most intellectual of all the wives.

ZINA D. HUNTINGTON.
[Wife of Brigham.]

Zina D. Huntington was formerly the wife of a man named Henry Jacobs, who was at one time a Mormon. Brigham was attracted towards the wife, sent the husband off on a mission, and had Zina sealed to him. Dr. Jacobs apostatized, not at all fancying this appropriation of his family. She is a very noble woman, and has spent her life in the service of her ungrateful husband and the church. She is firm and unyielding in her religious faith, and as devout a believer in Mormonism to-day as she was at her first conversion. She has been very useful in the family, acting as physician, nurse, and governess, as her services have been required. She is perfectly unselfish, and her whole life is devoted to others.

She is a large, fine-looking woman, with a somewhat weary and sad expression, but her face still shows signs of mental strength and superiority.

She has one daughter, Zina, who was formerly an actress in the theatre, and has since married an Englishman of the name of Thomas Williams. She was his second wife, and her introduction to the family was strongly resented by the first wife, who would never notice her in any way. They lived apart, and the husband divided his time equally between the two. A few months ago he died very suddenly at Zina's, while sitting at the table. When the news was conveyed to the first wife, she had the remains brought to her, arranged for the funeral without consulting Zina, and refused to allow her to ride in the carriage with her to the burial. Poor Zina was almost heart-broken, for she dearly loved the man whom her father's religion taught her to call husband, and she was ready to do anything to conciliate the first wife. She is a noble girl, and as conscientious as her mother. Not very long before I left her father, we were talking about the practice of polygamy. I expressed myself strongly and bitterly against it. She, in turn, defended it. She knew, she said, that it brought great

ZINA WILLIAMS.
[Brigham's Daughter.]

unhappiness, but that was because it was not rightly lived. The theory was correct, but people did not enter it in the right spirit. She has certainly suffered from it since then, although I believe she tried, to the best of her ability, to "live it right." But she, no more than any one else, could make right out of wrong.

When Mr. Williams asked her in marriage, Brigham said he might have her if he'd "take the mother too." So Zina, the mother, went to live with Zina, the daughter. But Brigham grew ashamed of his meanness toward her, and finally gave her a house and lot.

Years ago, when Brigham was on a mission to New England, he met a very charming lady in Boston, Mrs.

Augusta Cobb, and at once his elastic fancy was charmed for a while. She was a woman of fine social position, cultured and elegant, the head of a lovely establishment, with a kind husband, and a family of interesting children; but she became enamored of the Prophet, accepted the Mormon religion, and came to Nauvoo with him, where she was sealed as his wife. She is still a very stylish, elegant woman for her age, but for several years past she has been grossly neglected by the Prophet. Her religious enthusiasm has increased until it is almost mania, and, finding that her husband was wearying of her, and seeking new faces, she begged to be released from him for eternity, and be sealed to Jesus Christ, who, her church told her, was a polygamist.

Brigham, with all his blasphemous audacity, dared not do that; so he quieted her by telling her that he was not at liberty to do that — his authority did not extend so far; but he would do the next best thing, and seal her to Joseph Smith. She consented, and now belongs to Brigham only for time, "having been transferred to Joseph for eternity."

Her family still remember her fondly, and grieve over her delusion. One of her relatives — a granddaughter, I think — sent word to me, a short time since, that she wished to see me, to ask about Mrs. Cobb, for it had been a long time since they had heard from her directly, and it would be such a comfort to meet one who had seen her so recently. I have not yet met the lady, but shall take the first opportunity to see her, though I can, I fear, tell her little that will satisfy her.

Another proxy wife, Emily Partridge, was a young, childless widow, very patient and gentle, and very pretty, too. She belonged to Joseph Smith, and was among those whom Brigham took. For some time she lived at the farm, but not understanding dairy work, she did not suit her husband. She is willing to work, and do whatever she can do, but is no more able than the rest of the world to accomplish impossibilities. He was so angry at her want of success at the farm, that he said, in speaking of her, "When I take another man's wife *and children* to support, I think the least they could do would be to try and help a little." To be sure, he is the *earthly* father of those children, but he makes a decided distinction between them and those he calls *his own*. There are five children, — Emily, Carlie, Don Carlos, Mary, and Josephine. Emily is plural wife of Hiram B. Clawson, her half-sister Alice's husband; Carlie and Mary were both married to Mark Croxall, the Western Union telegraph operator. He was very fond of Mary, who has since died. Carlie he treats with the utmost indifference, and neglects her openly. A while ago he became very much enamored of a Danish girl, and would allow Carlie to go home alone from the theatre or other place of amusement, while he went off with this girl, who was Carlie's inferior in every way. The poor girl is heart-broken at this careless treatment, but what can she do? There is nothing for any Mormon woman to do but to submit, and let her heart break in the mean while. The sooner it is over, and she is out of her misery, the better. Very few care how soon they die. Life is not pleasant enough to be clung to very tenaciously.

Emily Partridge lived at the "Lion House" for several years, enduring every indignity at the hands of the family. Now she has a cottage outside, which Brigham gave her, telling her, when she moved into it, that he should in future expect her to support herself and children.

This woman ends the list of Brigham's living wives, but some that have died have had such a career, and been so well known, that I cannot refrain from mentioning them.

CHAPTER XXXIII.

THE DEAD WIVES OF THE PROPHET. — HE NEVER WAS KNOWN TO SHED A TEAR.

The Discarded Favorite. — The Story of Emmeline Free. — A Stupendous Humbug. — A "Free" Opinion of Mormonism. — Amelia comes upon the Scene. — How Brigham Insulted Emmeline Free. — Brigham is Ashamed of his Cowardice. — I tell him a little of my Mind. — Joseph A. expresses his Opinion. — Apologizes for his Father. — Death of Emmeline Free. — The Story of Clara Chase. — The Prophet's Maniac Wife. — Ellen Rockwood, and the Cause of her Neglect. — A Wife who was visited once in Six Months. — Margaret Alley. — How the Prophet treated his Dead Wife. — He steals her Children's Property. — How he Scandalized another Wife, and sent her Home. — He "Never shed a tear at a Wife's Death.

A LITTLE CONVERSATION WITH BRIGHAM.

OR many years the favored wife, the one who ruled over her husband, and reigned in the family, was Emmeline Free. The Prophet married her when she was quite young, having first to overrule the objections of her parents, who, although Mormons, were much opposed to polygamy. She was a willing convert, for she had been taught that Brigham Young was a near approach to divinity, and she had unbounded reverence for him; and the child, — for she was

little more than that, — was flattered and delighted at the
Prophet's wish to have her for a wife.

Those who knew her at the time of her marriage say
that she was an extremely lovely girl, and I can well
believe it, for she was a very prepossessing woman. She
was tall and graceful, with brown eyes, and fair hair that
waved naturally. Her face was pleasant in expression
and very bright, until it became saddened by her husband's
desertion of her for Amelia.

I used to see a great deal of her. I visited at her house
when I was a girl, was intimate with her children, and saw
more of her while I was a member of the family than of
any other. In virtue, I suppose, of her former position,
Brigham never neglected her as he did some of his other
wives, and she always retained a certain influence over
him. She was not afraid of him, and had long since
ceased to regard him with awe. I once entered the Prophet's office when she was there; she was talking quite
earnestly, and did not stop on my entrance; she concluded
her conversation by saying, —

"Well, I've lost faith in the whole thing. I consider
Mormonism a stupendous humbug, and all the people who
have been made to believe in it, terrible dupes. I've no
patience with it any longer."

Her husband — "our" husband at the time — laughed as
though he considered it a good joke, and turned the conversation, making it general, so that it included me. I
think he did not wish such "heresy" talked before his
young wives, lest it should engender discontent in their
hearts. He needn't have been troubled about me, for the
mischief was already done. I had begun to think things
out for myself, and I had arrived very much at the same
conclusion that Emmeline had, although I had not dared
to express my opinion to any one.

Once during my married life with him, Brigham invited
Emmeline and myself to go with him to Brigham City,

where he was to hold a conference meeting. There was a large party, and we went with the usual pomp which attends such occasions. I enjoyed it better than I did most of the excursions I took with him, because I was very fond of Emmeline, and preferred to have her rather than any of the other wives. I think she felt the same way toward me, because she knew that I was her champion; moreover, she was quite aware of my feeling toward "our" husband, and the difficulty he had had in inducing me to become his wife, and she did not consider me in any degree her rival. We arrived one afternoon, and everything was most amicable. He was unremitting in his attentions to Emmeline, and I was very happy to see her happy, and enjoyed myself very much with some of the younger members of the family. In the evening he told Emmeline that he should expect her to accompany him to church the next day.

The next morning he arose very early, and drove away in a buggy alone; in a little while he returned with Amelia, breakfasted with her, and started away again. In the meantime Emmeline, who had not heard of Amelia's arrival, was preparing to accompany her husband to church; she dressed with unusual care, and made herself look very pretty. She waited impatiently, but he did not come. I knew of the arrival, and when I went up stairs and saw Emmeline waiting with her bonnet on, I asked her if she was not going to start soon, as it was getting late.

"I am waiting for Brother Young," said she.

"He has gone long ago," said I. "I thought you knew it."

"Gone, without me? Why, that's funny, when he made such a point of my going with him."

"Yes; but that was before Amelia came."

Emmeline's face changed expression in a moment. "She here?"

"Yes; she came this morning. Brother Young went to the depot to meet her."

"Then he must have known she was coming. Can I never go any where without having her thrust in my face? I thought for once I should be spared the infliction."

She took off her things, and I laid mine aside, too, and in place of going to the grand conference meeting and listening to "our" husband's eloquence, we had a confer-

WAITING FOR BRIGHAM TO KEEP HIS PROMISE.

ence of our own, and that morning I came nearer to Emmeline's heart than I ever had before. She talked to me unreservedly and unrestrainedly, and told me events in her history that were full of thrilling interest, but which were given me in confidence, and which I cannot give again to the world. I think the dead eyes would haunt me for ever, and the dead lips would move in ghostly reproach if I betrayed her even now. Dear, loving heart, that beat so wearily through all the years, I hope you are meeting your reward now, cradled in the infinite love of a Divine Father! Tears dimmed my eyes and moistened my cheeks, when I read, a few days since, of your death; but they were tears of joy at your glad release, and not such bitter tears of indignant sorrow as I shed that morning over the story of your wrongs.

I think Brigham felt ashamed and a little conscience-stricken. I know he was decidedly uncomfortable when he met his insulted wife again. He tried every means in his power to propitiate her, and I never saw him assume so abject a manner before. Amelia returned that day, and he told Emmeline that he did not know of her intention to come down, that he had not expected her at all. He also told her that the reason he paid so much attention to Amelia was, that he might "save her soul."

Emmeline did not believe him when he told her he did not expect Amelia, and she told him so very plainly. He then came to me, and said, —

"Emmeline's real mad at me — isn't she?"

"Yes," said I, "but no more than you deserve. I think it's too bad in you to take her for a pleasure trip, and then get Amelia here at the first stopping-place."

"I didn't get her here. I didn't know she was coming."

"Well, all I can say is, it looked like it; you certainly went to the station to meet her."

"I just went down to see who had come, that's all. Seems to me you're taking Emmeline's part pretty strong — ain't you?"

"Yes, I am, for I think you've treated her badly."

"Guess a little of the mad is on your own account — isn't it?"

"Not a particle of it. Amelia doesn't interfere with me."

He laughed and went out. Presently Joe made his appearance, probably sent by his father.

"So Emmeline is cutting up rough about Amelia's coming, is she?" he asked of me.

" Not at all; she's indignant, but that's no more than is to be expected; but as for 'cutting up rough,' as you term it, she's too much of a lady to do that."

"Well, it's too bad to have this fuss; but I suppose I'm to blame for the whole affair. I was coming down, and I didn't want to come alone, so I asked Mary, Alice, and Amelia to come along too. I never thought of Emmeline when I asked Amelia."

"Mary" was Joseph A.'s first wife, Alice was his sister, and the two were very intimate with Amelia. This story sounded very well, but I didn't believe it, neither did Emmeline, when she heard it. It was too evident that Joe had been sent by his father to endeavor to make peace. Be that as it may, Amelia did not put in an appearance again during the trip.

Emmeline had been an invalid for years, and I was not surprised to learn of her death. When I heard of it, I felt as I always do when I hear of the death of any Mormon woman. I thank God to think their misery is over. She had eight children, Marinda, Ella, Louise, — nicknamed " Punk " by her father, — Hyrum, Lorenzo, Alonzo, Ruth, and Della.

Marinda is the only wife of Walter Conrad. Ella and Louise are both married out of polygamy, one to Nelson Empy, the other to James Harris. Hyrum, so far, contents himself with one wife.

Clara Chase is usually spoken of as "the maniac." She died mad several years since, leaving a large family of children. She married him when quite young, but she never was a firm believer in Polygamy, indeed, she distrusted the principles of it from the very beginning, and had many struggles of conscience before she could make up her mind to marry the Prophet, and she suffered perpetual remorse ever after. She had a peculiar face, low-browed and dark, and it was rarely lighted up by any pleasurable motive. There was on it an expression of fixed melancholy that seldom varied or changed.

Knowing her aversion to the system, and her distrust of it and of him, Brigham at first treated her with a very great deal of consideration. He gave her an elegant room, nicely furnished, and placed in it a large portrait of himself. He tried to make her surroundings as cheery as possible, and so wean her from the melancholy into which she had fallen. As long as he devoted himself personally to her, she was comparatively cheerful and content, and tried her best to be happy; but when he neglected her she was almost desperate, and wandered about in a half-dazed fashion, weeping and moaning, and calling on God to forgive her.

Just before her last child was born, her fits of remorse were terrible. She endured untold agonies, and accused herself of having committed the unpardonable sin, and she knew salvation was denied. Those who were about her at the time, say that it was heart-rending to hear her.

Just at this time, when her husband should have given her the most love and tenderest of sympathy, he was, more than ever, harsh, cruel, and unfeeling, and treated her with such marked coldness and contempt, that she went insane, and raved constantly. "I am going to hell! I am going to hell!" was her agonized cry. "Brigham has caused it; he has cursed me for ever. Don't any of you go into polygamy; mind what I say; don't do it. It will curse you, and damn your souls eternally." When she saw her husband, she cursed him as the cause of her downfall. "I have committed the unpardonable sin; you have made me do it. O, curse you! curse you! You have sent me to hell, and I am going soon." To her children, as they gathered round her, she cried, "O, don't follow my example! Don't go into polygamy, unless you wish to be cursed! Don't let my children do as I have done," she would say to those about her. No help could avail her. Brigham and his counsellors "laid hands" on her. A doctor was called, but all to no purpose. She died in the midst of her ravings. Her children's names were Mary, Maria, Willard, and Phœbe. Mary is dead. Maria is the wife of William Dougall. Phœbe is the only wife of Walter Batie. Willard, the only son, has just graduated with honors at West Point.

Ellen Rockwood was one of the least regarded of the wives. She was a little woman, in delicate health, and very fond of fancy-work. She was the daughter of the warden of the penitentiary, one of Brigham's faithful officers. Her influence with the Prophet was very small, as she had no children, and was regarded as of little consequence on that account. Still, I do not think that Brigham ever positively ill-treated her. He used to call on her very ceremoniously once in six months.

Margaret Alley, who was never much of a favorite, died in 1853. She was morbid in temperament, and, before her death, became very melancholy, owing to the neglect of her husband. She had two children, Eva and Mahonri-Morianchamer.

One of Brigham's "proxy" wives was Jemima Angell, a relative of Mary Ann Angell, his first living and legal wife. Her husband had died, leaving her with three children; and when she came to Nauvoo, Brigham found them. He wanted a servant, and she wanted salvation. The discoveries were simultaneous, and she was very soon persuaded to be sealed to him. All the while they were in Nauvoo, "Aunt Mima" worked untiringly, and on the arrival at Salt Lake he gave her a lot of land for her children. One of her sons built a house on it, but she did not occupy it, as she could not be spared from Brigham's kitchen. She worked until she became broken down in mind and body, and then Brigham sent her to her daughter, who was married to a poor man, and had a large family of children, yet was willing to take her mother, and do the best he could by her. She died very soon, and the daughter's husband telegraphed the news of the death to Brigham; also the

33

time they should arrive with the body for burial. They lived fifty miles from Salt Lake, in the Weber Valley, and, as they could not obtain a coffin there, they put the body into a box to convey it to her husband, who, when they arrived, was not at home; at least, he could not be found; and what is called the "Eagle Gate," or the entrance to the Prophet's premises, was closed against them. They could not gain admittance for hours; and, in the mean time, all that was left of "Aunt Mima" lay in a pine box in an open wagon, with every avenue to her husband's house closed against her.

Finally, even Brigham grew ashamed, and allowed himself to be found; and when they asked him where they should take her, said, very carelessly, "O, I suppose she might as well go to her sisters', upon the hill!" She was taken there, and decently buried, though Brigham grumbled about the expense.

In the mean time, the land that he had given her had increased in value, and when the children went to take possession of it, he refused to let them have it, although it would have been a God-send to poor Mrs. Frazier, with her large family of children. But his avarice is so inordinate that no amount of suffering stands in the way of his self-enrichment. Once he is bent on obtaining a piece of property, he does not care whom he defrauds to obtain it.

At the time he was sealed to Lucy Biglow, he had her sister sealed at the same time. She was very pretty, and he had seemed very fond of her. But suddenly his fondness cooled, and he treated her in the most shameful manner. He heaped every indignity upon her, and finally sent her back to her parents, saying she had been untrue to him. She protested her innocence; but all in vain. He would not, or professed not, to believe her, and talked harshly and cruelly to her when she attempted to vindicate herself.

Her parents were very much grieved, and were tossed about with conflicting doubts. They wanted to believe their daughter, and, in their hearts, I believe they did; yet they dared not dispute Brigham. They took the poor, heart-broken girl home, and she fairly pined to death under the disgrace that her husband tried to attach to her name.

Besides those wives whom I have already mentioned, there have been very many more who have been married to

THE DISGRACED WIFE.

him "for eternity." I should be sorry even to guess their numbers. There was also one wife, who, during "Reformation" times, was said to have "run away to California" [a thousand miles away through an uninhabited country, and before the era of railways in the West]; but it was whispered among wicked Gentiles that really she paid the full penalty of the Endowment-Oaths, and in the Endowment-House, too, her throat being cut from ear to ear, and the other horrible performances gone through, on account of some indiscretion, or want of faith. Of course, I do not vouch for the truth of this statement. I simply give it in common with much else for what it is worth.

I have heard Brigham say, in speaking of the number of wives and children that he had buried, "that he never shed a tear at anyone's death;" and I believe that, if every friend he had in the world lay before him, cold and still and with frozen pulse, he would look on unmoved and indifferent, and never shed a tear, so utterly heartless is he.

CHAPTER XXXIV.

THE PROPHET AT HOME. — HOW HE LOOKS, LIVES, AND ACTS. — MORMON PHILANTHROPY AND EDUCATION.

Brigham at Forty-five and at Seventy-five. — Slipping the Yoke. — The Salt Lake Tribune. — Books on Mormonism. — Prophetic Philanthropy. — The New Temple. — Paying the Workmen. — The Tabernacle. — Advantages of the Presidency. — Free Schools and Liberal Education. — Sharp Practice. — The Rich and the Poor. — Unconscious Sarcasm. — Looking into the Future. — The Spectacles of Ignorance. — Personal Habits. — The Prophet's Barber. — Dinner at the Lion House. — The Good Provider. — Helping herself. — Prophetic Cunning. — Evening Devotions. — A Gift in Prayer. — Advice to the Deity. — Fatherless Children. — The Bee Hive. — Monogamist *vs.* Polygamist.

DINNER AT THE LION HOUSE.

NLESS I pause and look back almost to my very babyhood, and contrast Brigham Young as he then was with the Brigham Young of to-day, I can scarcely realize the change that has taken place in this man. As I recollect him first, he was a man in the prime of life, with rather a genial face, and a manner which, though abrupt at times, had nothing of the assumption and intolerance which characterize it now. Indeed there was, at that time, a semblance of humility, which served his purpose well, by strengthening the confidence of the people in him.

Had he claimed, at that auspicious point in his career, when accident placed him at the head of this peculiar sect, that he was the peer of Joseph Smith, upon whom had descended the mantle of that martyred saint, his pretensions would have been treated as contemptuously as were Sidney Rigdon's. His shrewdness plainly showed him that, and his cunning and tact pointed out to him the surest way of gaining an ascendency over his followers.

He taught them that Joseph was their Messiah; that he was only acting in his place until he should be restored to them in person; which, strange as it may seem, many still believe will occur, and actually watch for his visible presence among them again. Still, that belief does not obtain so generally as it did during the first years after Joseph's death. The gradual change in the President has not been without its effects, and there is now very much more of the material than of the spiritual in the Mormon belief.

Nearly everything that was done by him in those earlier days was done in the name of the Lord and Joseph, and he was constantly in the habit of expressing his intentions of carrying out "brother Joseph's" plans. Gradually, as he could without its being too closely observed and commented on, he dropped "brother Joseph," and made his own desires the law by which the people were to be ruled. Yet so quietly and subtly was this done, that the Saints never knew when they passed from the rule of Joseph Smith and superstition, to the absolute despotism of Brigham Young, which has been indeed a "reign of terror."

The absolute belief which he used to express in Joseph, and his unquestioning faith in his works and mission, he expected every one to yield to him in turn; and he and his immediate followers and associates have taught and insisted upon this blind subjection so long, that the Mormon people have neglected to use their reasoning powers, until they have become so blunted, that the majority of them are incapable of arriving at any conclusions by their own unaided effort, or of forming any independent opinions.

In the early days, in his intercourse with the people, he was one of them, — a sharer in their adversity, a companion, and a friend. Now, he holds himself apart from them, looks upon himself as above and beyond them, as something better than they, and they partake of his own delusion, and assist him in his self-deception.

Now and then one keener than the rest sees the change, and deplores it. Rough old Heber C. Kimball could never become reconciled to it, and, more honest and more daring than the others, used to express himself very freely.

"Brigham's God is gold," he said one day to the apostle Orson Hyde; "he is changed much since he and I stood by each other, in the old days, defending the faith. He has become a selfish, cold-hearted tyrant, and he doesn't care at all for the old friends who have stood by him and loved him. What do you think of that, Brother Orson?"

"That sort of talk may do for Brother Heber," was the reply, "but it would not do for Brother Orson. He could not express himself in that manner with impunity, so he will say nothing."

At forty-five Brigham Young was a common looking, very ordinary appearing man, in no way the superior of the majority of the church, and decidedly the inferior of some of the members. He was homely in speech, neither easy nor graceful in manner, and dressed very plainly in homespun.

Brigham Young, at seventy-five, has the appearance of a well-preserved Englishman, of the yeoman class. There is less bluster in his manner than formerly, but more insolent assumption. He is still the mental inferior of some of the officers of his church, but in crafty cunning and malicious shrewdness he is far in advance of any of his associates. He is not more finished and elegant in his mode of speech, but he says less, and consequently has won the opinion of having grown more pleasing in his address. He is arrogant to his inferiors, and unpleasantly familiar to the very few whom he desires for any reason to conciliate. He dresses in the finest of broadcloth, fashionably cut, is more finical than an old beau, and vainer and more anxious than a young belle, concerning his *personnel.* He says that this change in his mode of dress has been brought about by his wives. I have no doubt that Amelia may have had some influence in that direction; still his own inclinations probably had just as much to do with it.

Since he has allowed himself to see and be seen by more of the outside world than he formerly did, he has grown to appear more like the Gentiles, concerning whom he sneers so loudly, even while aping their manners and customs. He is impatient of criticism, and as sensitive to public opinion as though he were not constantly defying it. He is at once ambitious and vain, and, like all persons who turn others to ridicule, is very sensitive to anything approaching it when it is directed towards himself. He reads everything that is written against him. I think no book has ever been published, exposing him and his religious system, which he has not perused, from the title page to the conclusion. He loses his temper every morning over the Salt Lake Tribune, — the leading Gentile paper of Utah, — and longs for a return of the days when one word of his would have put a summary and permanent end to the existence of this sheet, by the utter annihilation of everything and everybody connected with it. But the time is forever past when the "unsheathing of his bowie-knife," or the "crooking of his little finger," pronounced sentence upon offenders, and the Gentile paper and its supporters flourish in spite of him.

I remember once going into his office, and finding him examining the advertising circular of a book on Mormonism, written by a lady who had for a time been a resident of Utah. He commenced reading it aloud to me in a whining voice, imitating the tone of a crying woman. Yet, notwithstanding this attempt to make a jest of it, I knew that the publication of this book annoyed him exces-

BRIGHAM YOUNG.

sively, and that he was both curious and anxious concerning the contents, and the effect they would produce; for, with all his professed contempt for Babylon and its Gentile inhabitants, he is very sensitive concerning the opinions which are held concerning him by these unregenerate souls.

Unscrupulous and avaricious, he has made even disasters profitable to himself. After the tragical hand-cart expedition, he sold the hand-carts that remained when the emigrants had all got in for fifteen dollars apiece. This was to go to the "church fund," which virtually means "Brigham's private purse." It has been already related how he made his "improved carriage scheme" more than pay for itself several times over, although they did not survive the first trip.

As "Trustee in Trust" of the Church of Jesus Christ of the Latter-Day Saints, all the money of the church passes through his hands, or, more properly speaking, *into* them, since it is rarely known to leave them again. The tithing-fund, and the subscriptions for various church purposes, are all given into his keeping; and although the sums of money gathered in this way have been very large, none of it has ever been appropriated to the cause for which it was supposed to be intended by those sacrificing souls who denied themselves that the Lord might be served.

He is as inexorable a beggar to-day as he was forty years ago, when he was a humble follower of Joseph Smith, preaching the new gospel to whoever would hear him, and being fed and clothed by whoever would supply his wants. He made no hesitation in letting these wants be known, and he would request that they should be relieved in the name of the Lord.

"Inasmuch as ye have done it unto the least of these my little ones, ye have done it unto me," has been the standard teaching of the Mormon missionaries from the very earliest days; and no one could enlarge on this passage more eloquently than Brother Brigham when he was in need of a new coat, or a small sum of money, or even a supper and a night's lodging.

He is as eloquent now, when talking on the subject of giving, with this exception in his style of address, that he now demands instead of asks, and it is disastrous to refuse him. He begs for the missionaries, and the poor men never get a cent of the thousands of dollars that are raised for them. He begs for the Temple, which is his pet subject, whenever there is nothing else to beg for, and the amount of money which he has raised for the building ought to have erected several very imposing edifices.

Many years ago he levied contributions upon the English Saints for the purchase of glass for the Temple windows. The sum desired must be collected at once. The Lord was soon coming to enter upon his earthly kingdom, and the place must be prepared for him. Missionaries preached, and laymen exhorted; they astonished even themselves by their eloquence, as they dwelt upon the beauty of Zion, the city of the Lord, and the glory that was to descend upon his chosen people. Those who were not moved by their oratory were impelled by their command; but, for the most part, the money was given voluntarily. Working men and women took a few pennies from their scant wages, and gave them with wonderful readiness, and then suffered from cold and absolute hunger for days after. But they suffered with painful joyousness and devotion, since they were giving it to the Lord, who had chosen them out of all the world for his very own people, and who would make their self-denials here redound to their glory and grace when at last they should arrive in his presence.

At that time, the foundation walls of the Temple were barely above the ground, and the work has progressed very slowly since. At any rate, the glass has not been bought, and there seems very little probability of window material being needed at present; and if the Lord is not to visit the Saints until his home is completed, even the younger

members of the present generation will not be likely to
see Him.

The "Tabernacle,"
where the Saints wor-
ship at present, is one of
Brigham's few "inspira-
tions," and is as great a
success as are most of
his inspired ideas. It is
an ugly-looking build-
ing, oval in shape, with
a sort of arched roof,
which shuts down over
it, like the lid of a wick-
er-work basket. It is
very commodious, which
is its chief recommenda-
tion, holding comforta-
bly twelve thousand persons. In this "inspired" edifice,
every law of acoustics is outraged, and only a small portion of the congregation can hear what the speaker is saying. It is two hundred and fifty feet long, one hundred
and fifty feet wide, and eighty feet high, while there is not
a column in it to obstruct the view, and the interior view is
flat and expansive.

MORMON TEMPLE NOW BUILDING.

The organ claims to have been built by a good Mormon
brother, assisted by a large number of mechanics; and is
said to be the largest ever built in the United States. It is
placed at the end of the Tabernacle, directly back of the
speaker's stand, and the seats for the choir are arranged on
each side of it.

This building, in which the Saints are to worship until
the more pretentious Temple is finished, is ugly in the outward appearance, cheerless in the interior, very inconvenient in its arrangements, and practically useless unless the
walls are draped so as to render the voices of the speakers

audible; but when the new building — which is said by Brigham to be of Divine architecture — shall be completed, it is probable that these things will be vastly improved.

In the mean time the begging goes on, but the work moves slowly. Large contributions come flowing in, but the Temple does not advance visibly; while Brigham adds house to house, field to field, increases his bank deposits, and lives as well as any man in his position would wish to live.

The people will take no bonds from him; and as it would

INTERIOR OF TABERNACLE ON SUNDAYS.

seem like questioning the Lord's anointed, he is supposed to administer the financial affairs under the direction of the Lord, no statements are ever required of him. Once in a while, however, he goes through the form of a settlement of accounts, which he simplifies immensely, by a system all his own. It is said that at one time he balanced his account with the church by ordering the clerk to place two hundred thousand dollars to his account for services rendered, which was exactly the sum of his indebtedness to the church. This was in 1852; and in 1867 he repeated this peculiar financial operation; this time making his services liquidate an obligation for nine hundred and sixty-seven thousand dollars.

It is worth while to be President of the Church of Jesus Christ of Latter-Day Saints at a salary like that, and it is no wonder that he desires to keep it in the family, and is so anxious to appoint a successor.

But on the other side, see at what terrible rates the poor people must have been taxed to have paid for the support of this one man and his family, between the years 1847 and 1867 — a period of just twenty years — one million one hundred and sixty-seven thousand dollars, nearly sixty thousand dollars a year. This does not include many grants of land and other property, made to him by the territorial legislature, nor his compensation by the United States government as governor and Indian agent. Although a very ignorant man himself, able neither to read nor write the English language correctly, he has always been a bitter opponent of free schools and liberal education.

"I will not give a dollar," he says, "to educate another man's child. If you school your children, there is great danger of their becoming blacklegs and horse thieves," he announced on one occasion, yet he seems quite willing that his own should take the risk. All of them have received a certain amount of education, enough to make them presentable in society, and some have had quite superior advantages. One son has just graduated at West Point, another is a student at the Michigan University Law School, and a third has just entered Cornell University.

Every attempt that has been made for the establishment of free schools he has fiercely battled against, and the other officers of the church have invariably followed his lead. He assures his people that education is the bitterest foe to labor. If they allow their children to be taught anything they will no longer be of any service to their parents. He dilates largely upon this subject in the Tabernacle.

"I am utterly opposed to the schools," he said, in one address. "They have been introduced into the States in consequence of the tyranny of the rich over the poor. But instead of keeping the people poor, and then providing free schools for them, I would have the rich put out their money to usury by giving the poor employment, that they may be able to sustain themselves and school their own children. It is the duty of the rich to use their means, as I have done myself, in building factories, railroads, and other branches of industry, in order that the laboring people may have a chance to work together, and improve their condition ; the rich taking their portion, and all growing wealthy together."

There is an unconscious sarcasm in this last sentence that is positively sublime. That one expression, "as I have done myself," is the supremest satire. I do not believe there is anywhere a man so suspicious of his workmen, so penurious in his dealings with them, so anxious to cut their wages down to the very lowest penny, as is Brigham Young. I know men who have been in his employ for years, and have never received the least remuneration. They have worked on and on, and when at last they have brought a bill against him for their labor, they have been met with one equally large on his side for house rent, or goods from the co-operative store, or are told that their labor is to go toward paying their tithing.

If all the rich men use their means, "as I have done mine," therefore there will be very little chance of the poor man being able to educate their children at all : which is exactly what Brigham Young wants. Had he spoken the truth he would have said, "I am opposed to free schools. They will rend this dark veil of superstition which envelops you, and let in the light of reason, and this will loosen my hold on you. If you educate your children you make better men and women of them, but they will not be such blind slaves to me as you have been. The day that sees knowledge generally disseminated throughout this community sees my power broken, my 'opportunities' gone, and therefore, with my consent, we will have no free schools."

Unlettered and uncultured as he is, he recognizes the power of education, and that is why he is such a bitter opponent to general culture, and why, at the same time, he takes special care that his own children shall lack no advantages.

His personal habits are quite simple, and he is very regular in his mode of living. He rises usually about seven o'clock, dresses and breakfasts very leisurely, and appears at his private office about nine. He examines his letters, dictates replies to his secretary, reads the morning papers, or has them read to him, and attends to some of his official business. His barber comes to him at ten o'clock, and for the time he is engaged exclusively at his toilet. The presence of visitors never interrupts this important event of the day. The rest of the morning he devotes to callers, and to such business as requires his own personal attention. At three he dines, and it is then that he meets his family for the first time in the day. Dinner is served at the Lion House, and the appearance of Brigham Young's family at dinner is very similar to that at a country boarding-house, when the gentlemen are all away at business in town, and the wives and children are left together. At a short table, running across the head of the long dining-room, Brigham sits with his favorite wife by his side. In the days when I first used to be at the Lion House, as a partial guest and partial resident, Emmeline Free occupied this place of honor; but after Amelia's advent, poor, loving Emeline was thrust aside. When Brigham brings guests to dine with him, they have seats at this table also. At a long table, running lengthwise of the room, all the other wives are seated, each with her children about her. At the sound of the large dinner-bell, they all file in, seat themselves quietly, grace is said by the "presiding patriarch" from his table, and the meal goes on. The family table is plainly spread, and supplied with the very simplest fare, while the smaller one is laden with every delicacy that the markets will afford. These, however, are only for the President and his favorite wife, and the rest of the family must be satisfied merely to look at them, and enjoy the dainties by proxy.

A very amusing incident took place once at this family dinner. One of the wives, — not usually considered among the most spirited ones, — who, like all the rest, had submissively taken the food which had been set before her for years, was one day seized by the spirit of discontent. She had taken a fancy that she should like some of a particular dish which graced her husband's table. She did not express her wish, but quietly rising from her place, went straight to the other table, helped herself to the coveted article, and returning as quietly as she came, took her seat, and resumed her meal, amidst looks of consternation from the other wives, and of indignant amazement from her husband. Surprise made him absolutely speechless for the moment; but I fancy she was properly reproved in due time, for she never attempted a repetition of the act.

When strangers are invited to dine, the tables are more uniform in their appointments. The usual contrast between the one at which the Prophet and his favorite sit, and that around which the other wives and their families are gathered, is not nearly so marked. There is an air of abundance, and even of luxury, on these occasions, which gives the Prophet the reputation, among his guests, of being, what is called in New England parlance, "a good provider."

If only some of these deluded visitors could accidentally happen into the same room at a similar meal, they would see the true state of affairs; but Brigham's family are never visited accidentally. Indeed, it is but a short time since visitors have been allowed in the Lion House at all, for the

Prophet has always maintained the strictest privacy regarding his family.

After dinner they see no more of him until " family prayers." At seven o'clock the bell is rung, and the wives and
children gather in the large Lion House parlor. Not only
are the wives who live in the house expected to be present,
but those who have homes outside are also supposed to
attend evening worship. Not all of them avail themselves
of this privilege, and the outside attendance is somewhat

FAMILY PRAYERS AT " THE LION HOUSE."

irregular. I used to go whenever I felt inclined, which
was very seldom; and the longer I was a member of the
family, the more infrequent became my attendance.

Brigham sits in the centre of the room, at a large table,
on which is an ornamental " astral" lamp. The wives and
their respective families are ranged around the room, in the
order in which they appear at the table. When all are
seated, Brigham reads a few passages of Scripture, all
kneel down, and he makes a long prayer.

34

He was formerly said to have a special "gift" for prayer, and he has not lost it; but somehow his prayers never inspired me with veneration. He prays with great unction, and, I suppose, unconsciously to himself, some of his patronizing manner slips into his appeals to the throne of Divine Grace, until his petitions always seemed to me to be very much like advice to the Deity rather than entreaties for the Divine blessing. If he chances to be in a good humor, he chats a little while before leaving the room; but if not, he goes away directly prayers are over, and that is the last that is seen of him by the household until the next day at dinner.

Some of his children are almost strangers to him. They know nothing of fatherly affection, and while they feel that they have, socially, a sort of prestige, by being so closely related to him, they feel, personally, only a dread and fear of him. He never invites their confidences, nor shows himself interested in their affairs; all this would be quite incompatible with his ideas of prophetic dignity.

The Lion House, where most of the wives live, is a long, three-storied house, at the very left of what is known as the Prophet's Block. It receives its name from the stone figure of a lion crouching over the front portico. There is a stone basement; then the main building, of wood, with peaked gable, narrow pointed Gothic windows, and steep roof. In the basement are the dining-room, kitchen, laundry, and cellar. The parlor is on the principal floor, and the rest of the house is taken up by the apartments of the wives, each wife having a greater or less number of rooms according to the size of her special family.

Next to the Lion House is a low building, which is used as the "Tithing-Office." Here all the clerks have their desks, and receive visits from the Saints who come on church or personal business. Adjoining that is Brigham's private office, where he receives his own visitors. At the extreme right is the Bee-Hive House, a large building, which has always been used as Governor Young's official residence.

Lucy Decker has always had the care of it, and has lived there with her children. No wife was ever permitted to share her husband's apartments there, until the reign of Amelia was opened. She has lived there since her marriage, and has been virtually the recognized "head of the harem." It is extremely probable that when her new house is fully finished, the Bee-Hive House will be the official residence only in name, and the household there will see less of him than ever.

Polygamist, as he professes to be, he is, under the influence of Amelia, rapidly becoming a monogamist, in all except the name.

CHAPTER XXXV.

BRIGHAM AS A FARMER. — MY NEW HOUSE. — TAKING BOARDERS.

One Year after Marriage. — Life at the Farm. — House-keeping Extraordinary. — Bread and Milk Dinners. — Brigham Tries to Catch us Napping. — Hours of Labor. — Dejection. — My New House. — Parlor Stairs. — "Wells Wanted." — My Mother receives Notice to Quit. — My Elder Brother Pays her Board. — Failing Faith. — Taking Boarders. — The Prophet's Contemptible Meanness. — Brigham's Neglect. — Rev. Mr. Stratton. — I open my Heart. — The New Religion. — Woman's Sphere. — First Glimpses of the Outer World. — Forming Resolutions.

TOILING FOR BRIGHAM.

FTER we had been married a year, Brigham decided that I should go to "The Farm" to live. He has several farms among his landed possessions, but this one, which supplies the Salt Lake City family with milk, butter, cheese, and vegetables, is always spoken of as "*The* Farm." It is about four miles from the city, within pleasant driving distance, but is by no means a desirable place of residence.

Every one of the wives who had been compelled to live there had become confirmed invalids before they left the place, broken down by overwork; and the prospect was not a pleasant one to me, never strong, and unused to hard, continuous labor, such as I knew I should be obliged to perform as mistress of the farm-house. But, as it was my husband's will, I went, without a word of protest. I had one bit of comfort — my mother was to accompany me.

Outwardly, my new home had a lovely appearance, and Brigham never tired of descanting on its beauties to any one who would listen to him. These expressions of admiration would have been reasonable enough, had not the eulogistic owner insisted on its comfort and convenience, as well as on its beauty; but he was just as earnest in recommending it for those virtues which it did not possess, as he was in lauding it for its pleasant exterior. And, indeed, with its somewhat irregular architecture, its wide verandas, vine-draped and shaded, its broad, low windows, and beautiful surroundings, it is one of the pleasantest looking places that one would care to see.

It is built after one of the Prophet's own plans, and he says that it cost twenty-five thousand dollars. Possibly it did; but I am certain that, with the same amount of money, I could build a house that should vastly exceed that in external beauty and interior appointments.

The walls are very thin, and the sun and heat penetrated in summer, and the cold in the winter, making it at once the warmest and the coldest house I ever saw. That might have been a recommendation, had the temperature been regulated to suit the seasons; but, unfortunately for our comfort, it was hot when we wished it cool, and *vice versa.* My mother hazarded an opinion to this effect in Brigham's hearing, and he was greatly scandalized by it. He informed her that she had been so long away from civilization that she was not a proper judge of what a house ought to be! They both left "civilization" at the same time.

Housekeepers will understand something of its inconvenience, when I tell them that the stairs leading to the second story went directly from the parlor; that all the sleeping rooms were up stairs, and that, in order to reach them, we had to pass through a dining-room thirty feet, and a parlor forty feet in length; that hired men, family, and visitors were all compelled to use the same staircase. If any member of the family was ill, everything needed for the invalid had to be carried from the kitchen to the sick room, rendering the care of the invalid tiresome in the extreme.

The duties of housekeeper at "the Farm" were neither slight nor easily performed. There were butter and cheese to make from forty cows, all the other dairy work to attend to, besides cooking for twenty-five or thirty men, including the farm laborers and the workmen from the cocoonery. I know at least six women who have been completely broken down under the work at the farm-house, and neither my mother nor myself have ever recovered from the illness contracted there from overwork. My mother made the butter and cheese, and took charge of the cooking. I assisted in the latter, took care of the house, did the washing and ironing, and was allowed the extreme pleasure of carrying the farm supplies to the other wives every week.

We had occasional visits from Brigham. He was very fond of coming unexpectedly, and at all sorts of irregular hours, hoping, evidently, that some time he might catch us napping. He was so addicted to fault-finding, and so easily displeased, that we took no pleasure in his visits, and I grew to be positively unhappy every time his approach was heralded. If his coming had brought any comfort, I should have looked eagerly forward to his visits; as it was, I dreaded them, and grew ill with nervousness and apprehension every time he came to us.

I remember one day, when he visited us, he came about noon, just as mother had placed dinner for the workmen upon the table. He walked up and down the dining-room, surveying every dish with a critical eye, until we began to fear that something must be terribly amiss. He professed to be such a *connoisseur* in all matters relating to the cuisine, and was so frank, to say the least, in the expression of his opinions, and so careless of the terms which he em-

ployed, that we dreaded the remarks which were almost
certain to follow this critical scrutiny.

After the men were seated at the table, Brigham called
my mother into the adjoining room. "You cook too good
food for those men," he said; "it is too rich for their
stomachs."

"I wish to give them something which they can eat, and
I try to do so," replied she. "They work hard, and I
surely can do no less than give them palatable food; yet if
you do not approve of my manner of providing for them, I
will make any change you may suggest, if I can satisfy
the men with the fare."

"It don't make any difference whether they are satisfied
or not," was the answer. "I say it is healthier for them to
have bread and milk, and you must give it to them."

"Shall I give them this, and nothing else, three times a
day?" inquired she.

"Well, once in a while you may set on a little butter,
too," was the generous reply.

"But are they to have no meat?"

"Perhaps I will allow them a little occasionally, but they
are much better off without it."

This is a specimen of the interference to which we were
constantly subjected.

At another time, he told my mother that six o'clock was
too early an hour to give the men their supper in summer.
It was a waste of time, he said; they ought to work in the
fields two or three hours longer, at the least. My mother
reminded him that after supper there were the forty cows
and other stock to be cared for. He said that could as well
be done after dark as before; there was no danger of the
men hurting themselves with work; nobody ever did, that
was in his employ. They all were leagued together, men
and women alike, to swindle him, and his wives were as
bad as the rest.

My mother told the overseer what Brigham had said, and

he replied that, even for the Prophet, he should not ask the
men to do another hour's work a day; they were over-
worked already, and they should leave off work at six
o'clock each day, as they always had done. That ended
the matter, and the tea hour was unchanged.

I lived here for three years and a half, — long, uneventful
years, — and how I hated my life! It was dull, joyless,
oppressed, and I looked longingly back to the dear old days
at Cottonwood, the restful days that never could come again.
Even the love I bore my children was changed. It was no
less tender, no less deep, but it was less hopeful and more
apathetic. I clung to them in a kind of despair, and I
dreaded the days, which must inevitably come, when my
clinging arms could no longer infold them, when my love
alone would cease to satisfy.

I could not tell my feelings to my mother, for, although
she was as sensitive to Brigham's captious fault-finding as I
was, habit was very strong upon her, and she could never
separate him from her religion.

At the end of the three years and a half, he told me one
day that he was building a house for me in town, which he
intended to have me remove to as soon as possible. It was
out of no feeling of regard for me, or care for my comfort,
which influenced him; he simply wished to put some one
else in the farm-house, and it was necessary that I should
move, to make room for the new comer. I knew all this
perfectly well, yet I was so happy at the thought of getting
out of all the drudgery of the past years, that I was perfectly indifferent to the motives which induced him to make
the change for me.

When he told me of the house, I said I had one request
to make of him, which I hoped he would grant.

"What is it?" inquired he.

"Are there to be chambers in my new house?"

"Yes, certainly."

"Then will you please not to build the stairs from the

parlor. Let them go out of any other room in the house, but do not disfigure that one. Besides being ugly," I continued, "it is inconvenient, and excessively annoying to be obliged to pass through the best room at all times, and on every occasion."

" You can have stairs out of every room in the house, if you want them," was the reply.

I was quite satisfied, for I thought that equivalent to a promise that my parlor should be left as I wished it. He told me that he was spending five thousand dollars on my new house, and, from his description, I fancied it must be a very charming place.

Visitors to Salt Lake City are always taken to see " Ann Eliza's house," and much is made of the fact that it was built expressly for my use ; but the following equally important facts are carefully concealed : —

Taking a view of it from the street, it was an exceedingly pretty cottage, with an air of cosiness about it, which frequently called out remarks from passers by, who thought " Sister Ann Eliza very fortunate in her home." Inside it was very inconvenient, and badly arranged, being built after the stereotyped prophetic plan. The rooms were very small, the kitchen being scarcely large enough for a doll's house, measuring ten feet one way, by six feet the other. And yet in this room all the washing, ironing, and cooking for the family were to be done. Then, to my bitter disappointment, the only stairs in the house ascended from the parlor ! That, too, in the face of my expressed wish.

There were no facilities for obtaining water, and we were compelled to depend upon our neighbors' wells. Naturally enough, this annoyed them, and they used frequently to say that Brigham Young was abundantly able to provide a well, and they did not care to furnish water for his family, or any portion of it. Speaking to him concerning these matters was worse than useless, for I never could influence him in the slightest, while every suggestion which I ventured to make irritated him extremely ; so I held my peace, after one or two attempts to change things a little, so that the house should be more convenient.

I had scarcely got settled in my new home, when he told me that my mother must leave me ; he could not afford to support her any longer. This, too, when she had worked herself ill in his service, and had asked no reward for her labors except the privilege of staying with me, her only daughter ; the child from whom she had never been separated for any great length of time.

I cried bitterly after my husband had left me, but I would not tell my mother what he had said. I knew she would be sorely grieved, and that she would go away at once. Her independent spirit would not permit her to remain a pensioner on this selfish man's unwilling bounty.

I could not live without her. I leaned on her in piteous dependence, and looked to her for all the comfort I had outside of my children. In addition to the dread and dislike which had grown up in my heart toward my husband, I was beginning to lose faith in the religion which he represented. His petty meannesses, his deceit, his unscrupulousness, his open disregard for the truth, all were so utterly at variance with the right, that I could no longer look upon him as a spiritual guide and director.

I looked about me, and on every side I saw so much of misery, that I felt it must be a false faith indeed, which brought such unhappiness to its followers. Yet I knew no other religion, and I groped about in a state of spiritual bewilderment, tortured by many conflicting doubts.

I did not dream, then, of trying to get out of it ; my only thought was how to live with the least misery, and my best comfort was to keep my mother.

Finding that I did not tell her, after repeated orders from him to do so, he threatened to send her away himself. In great distress of mind, I went to my elder brother, who offered to pay me five dollars a week for my mother's board,

and on those terms Brigham expressed his willingness that
she should remain with me.

I now began to find it difficult to make him provide even
the commonest necessaries of life for me, and I plainly saw
that I must take things into my own hands, and earn my
own support, and that of my children. I asked permission
of my husband to take boarders, and he granted my request with amazing readiness; so I went to work in good
earnest, and soon succeeded in filling my house. As it
chanced, all my boarders were Gentiles. Brigham knew
this perfectly well, yet he did not seem in the least concerned about it. Indeed, of so little importance was I, or
my actions, that he never troubled himself to come near
me after he had given his consent that I should support
myself in the way I considered the easiest. The last time
that he ever visited me was months before I left my home.

Previous to the time of receiving these new inmates into
my family, I had one acquaintance outside the Mormon
Church. This was Mr. Howard Sawyer, a Gentile gentleman, to whom I was introduced while visiting at Mrs. Ra-
chel Grant's. Some time after I had commenced my work
of self-support, I met him again at the house of Mr. Na-
thaniel V. Felt, a Mormon. The Rev. Mr. Stratton, pastor of the Methodist church in Salt Lake, was with him,
and he introduced us at once. He had previously told Mr.
Stratton that I spoke very freely on the subject of Mormonism, and that he need not hesitate to question me, as he
would find me very frank and honest in the expression of
my opinions.

Mr. Stratton was the first representative of a religion
outside the Mormon belief whom I had ever met, and I listened anxiously to every word he said, hoping to find some
ray of light and cheer. As he talked, I felt very strongly
drawn toward the world which he and Mr. Sawyer represented, and I longed to know more concerning it. I was
much impressed by this interview; and at its close, Mr.

Stratton expressed a wish to see me again, and to have his wife meet me. I was struck by his very manner of speaking of her. I had never heard a woman referred to in so deferential a tone before, and I wondered at it.

As the days went by, I grew more miserable, and longed inexpressibly for the comfort, which neither my people nor their religion — for it had ceased to be mine — could give me. I remembered Mr. Stratton's kindly words, and I ventured to send him a message by Mr. Graham, one of my boarders, asking if I might see him and his wife, and talk with them.

An urgent invitation to visit them came by way of speedy

RELATING MY STORY TO MR. AND MRS. STRATTON.

reply ; and in response, I spent an entire afternoon at their house. They received me so cordially that my heart went out in love toward them at once. I talked to them unreservedly, and opened my soul to them. I told them of my childhood, my religious training, my unhappy domestic experience, and all the occurrences of my marriage to Brigham Young. They listened with earnest sympathy, and when I finished my story were overflowing with words of pity and consolation. I shall never forget them in my life. They were the sweetest words which had ever been spoken to me, for they helped me to see the way out of bondage.

It was the first glimpse I had ever had of domestic life outside of polygamy, and the deference which the husband showed to the wife, the confidence she displayed in him, and her perfect ease in his presence, were very strange to me. The equality on which they seemed to stand puzzled me. I could not understand this religion which regarded woman as an independent soul, with a free will, and capability of judgment. The inferiority of women is so strongly insisted upon by the Mormon doctrine that I supposed it must be the same everywhere, and the first view which I got of this sweet household was a revelation to me.

I carried home a braver and stronger heart than had beat in my bosom for many a long day. I went about my daily duties as quietly as though there were not a resolution forming in my mind which was speedily to overturn my whole life, and bring me into a new and strange existence.

Meanwhile my destiny was working itself out in a way I knew not, turning my feet into unexplored paths; and I did not yet see where I was straying, nor what the near future was holding in store for me.

CHAPTER XXXVI.

BREAKING THE YOKE. — I LEAVE. MY HOME.

The Workings of Destiny. — A Noble Lawyer. — A Small Stove and a Large Family. — Last Interview with Brigham. — A Startling Proposal. — Sickness and Gentile Care. — Brigham's Police. — A Moral Thunderbolt. — My Third Baptism. — A Religious Farce. — I Decide to Escape. — A Memorable Day. — Removing in Forty Minutes. — The Walker House. — Among the Gentiles. — A Perilous Situation. — New Hopes. — Interviewed by Reporters. — Unwelcome Notoriety. — A Touching Letter. — A Visit from my Father. — The Paper War. — Overshooting the Mark. — Sueing for a Divorce. — A Tempting Offer, $15,000 and my Freedom. — The Prophet Astonished.

ALONE AT THE HOTEL.

FTER a person has made up his or her mind to take any step in a new direction, it seems as though every event of the life points the same way. It is almost as if decision had been forced upon him, and the course of action was inevitable.

It was but a very few days after my first memorable visit to Mr. and Mrs. Stratton, when I received in my family a gentleman and his wife by the name of Hagan. Mr. Hagan was a lawyer of considerable repute in Salt Lake City, and I found both himself and his wife very pleasant inmates of my home.

My family had increased so, that it was quite impossible to do the necessary amount of cooking on the very small stove which was in my "toy" kitchen. I made up my mind to ask Brigham for another, since, as I was working hard to support myself, he ought to be willing to assist me to this extent.

I called one day at his office, — the last call I ever made him, by the way, — and preferred my request. He looked at me for a moment in evident surprise.

"I believe you are keeping boarders."

"Yes, I am," was my reply; "and that is why I want the stove. I cannot do the necessary cooking on the one I have."

"If you want a cooking-stove, you'll get it yourself. I've put you into a good house, and you must see to the rest. I cannot afford to have so many people calling on me for every little thing they happen to think they want."

I was much distressed and disturbed after this interview. I had known that I must take care of myself for some time, and I had gone about it bravely and willingly, and I felt that this rebuff was in every sense undeserved. Never, during my whole married life, had I made one unnecessary request; and, however much I might have "cost him," as he used to say in speaking of the very small amount he spent for me, I felt that I had more than repaid in hard, unceasing labor. If he does not wish to support us, why does he place us in the position to expect support from him, was my bitter thought. I did not seek the position of wife to him; it was forced upon me; and I was now compelled to endure the indignities which he chose to heap upon me.

Mrs. Hagan's kindly eyes discovered my distress, and she instantly begged my confidence. I gave it unreservedly and fully. She asked leave to tell her husband, and he, indignant at the treatment I was receiving, consulted with other lawyers, and all agreed in advising me to bring a suit against Brigham for divorce and alimony.

Mr. Hagan assured me that if I did not gain the suit I

should have found a way of getting out of my life in Mormonism ; that it would be a test case, showing how the polygamous wives of Mormons stood in the law, and that I would find ready sympathy from the outside world.

This proposal, although it startled me, came at a time when I was more ready to entertain it than I should have been at any other period. My mother had discovered Brigham's feelings toward her, and had left my house to return to my father's farm at Cottonwood, and I was grieving over her absence ; still, had she been with me, I should have said nothing to her on this subject ; for, although she was losing confidence in Brigham Young, she still clung to her religion, while I had not one spark of faith in it remaining.

In the mean time Mr. Hagan went to California for a short trip, begging me to decide upon the matter before his return. The more I thought upon the subject the more perplexed I grew, until I fairly broke down under the weight of nervous anxiety, and became very ill. My boarders took all the care of me through my sickness. I was entirely dependent on them for every care. Not one member of Brigham's family came near me, and I was as utterly neglected by them as though they had not known of my existence.

Those days of struggle were dark indeed, and oftentimes I did not know which way to turn. Perils and miseries faced me on every side. I was in doubt as to which was the true religion, or whether any were true. The question frequently arose, What would become of me if I apostatized? My church taught me that I should be given over to eternal damnation. And although I had ceased to regard my church and its teachings, yet I had a slight feeling of superstition left, and in my weak state I could but portray to myself the horrors of my situation if what it taught were really true.

At this juncture, I received a visit from the Ward Teachers, whose duty it is to visit each family in the city, and examine the different members as to their spiritual welfare. They are an inferior order of ecclesiastics, who serve the various purposes of religious instructors for the weak and ignorant, revenue officers to gather tithing, and general police to spy out and report irregularities or weakness of faith among the brethren.

The spokesman began by asking, " Sister Young, do you enjoy the spirit of our religion? "

" No, sir, I do *not*," was my reply.

If a thunderbolt had fallen among them they could not have been more surprised. They argued with me, counselled me, prayed with me, and finally I concluded to make one more attempt to cling to Mormonism. They begged me to be rebaptized, and I consented, although I had little faith in the ordinance.

Accompanied by a friend, I went to the Endowment House, where they have a font in which this rite is performed. We waited two hours for those in charge to get the names and ages of a lot of Danes, who were to be baptized for their dead relatives. My patience and very doubtful faith were about exhausted. At last they were ready, and I, as a wife of the President, was honored by being first taken. The men officiating were talking and laughing as if engaged in an every-day affair, while I was trying to feel solemn and to exercise faith, — a signal failure, I assure you. I was led into the water by a great strapping fellow, who mumbled a few words over me and plunged me in. I was taken from the water gasping for breath, and placed in a chair. Some more words were spoken over me, and the farce ended. Everything was done in such a business-like manner, with an utter absence of anything of a devotional nature, that I was thoroughly disgusted, and made no further effort to believe in Mormonism or its ordinances.

Mr. Hagan, on his return, found me fully determined on following his advice. I was ready to renounce my religion and leave my home. I did not know all that was included

35

in my resolution, else I might have faltered in my new determination. My plans were quickly laid, and with the assistance of the friends whom I had found in this hour of trouble, were carried into instant execution, before they could be discovered by Mormon spies.

On the 17th of July, 1873, I sent all my furniture to an auction-room, leaving my house stripped and desolate. It was done so quickly that no one had time even to suspect

CARRYING MY FURNITURE TO THE AUCTION ROOM.

my intenion. Arrangements having been previously made, three furniture vans came at the same time, and in forty minutes my entire household goods were in charge of the auctioneer. They were sold the next day, and I realized three hundred and eighty dollars from the sale. The furniture was worth almost nothing, being old and worn, and of common quality at its best; but my friends bought it at large prices, "to help the young apostate," as the Tribune said.

I had sent the elder of my boys to his grandmother, the younger remained with me, and together we went to Mr. Stratton's house, where we passed the afternoon. In the evening Mr. and Mrs. Stratton took us to the Walker House, the Gentile hotel, which I have ever since claimed as my Salt Lake City home.

Imagine, if you can, my feelings, on being alone with my little child, in a strange place, under such peculiar circumstances. I had abandoned my religion, left father, mother, home, and friends, — deliberately turned away from them all, knowing that the step I was taking could never be retraced. My heart cried out for my mother, who I knew would be more sorely stricken with my action than any one else in the world. I would have spared her if I could, but I was powerless to act in any other manner.

It was the first time in my life that I had been in a hotel; and, as I was among people who I had been taught were my bitterest enemies, I was overwhelmed by a sense of desolate helplessness. I did not know what my fate would be. Every footstep in the halls startled me; for I expected that each would bring some one to summon me to a dreadful death. I fully believed that was to be my last night on earth, so I prepared for death; but the agony of suspense was awful. I had been taught that no deed was too bad, no outrage too dastardly, for the Gentiles to commit upon the Mormons; and here I had allowed myself to be placed so fully in their power that they might do with me as they pleased, and my fate would never be known.

Does any one wonder that I did not seek refuge with some Mormon friend, of whose sympathy I was sure? No Mormon would have dared to give me shelter. I was in open rebellion against their leader, and had I remained one day among them, my doom would have been irrevocably fixed.

Neither did I dare to remain with my friends, the Strattons; for in so doing I should expose them to Mormon fury, and endanger their lives and their home. So I sought the only place of refuge open to me with untold fear and dread.

I laid awake all night wishing for the day to dawn, yet fearing that I should never see it; and when the first ray of light came through my windows I was relieved and hopeful.

With morning came a new excitement. The news of

EXCITEMENT IN SALT LAKE CITY.

my flight from home had gone abroad, and the morning papers were full of it, — the Mormon journals abusing, the Gentile journals praising and congratulating me. This part of the experience had never suggested itself to me. It had never occurred to me that it would be made a public matter, and I shrank from the very thought. I felt myself a marked object. Reporters called on me, seeking interviews for the California, Chicago, and New York papers, and questioned me until I was fairly bewildered. I had gone to bed a poor, defenceless, outraged woman, trying to find my way out of a false life into something truer and better, and I arose to find that my name had gone the length and breadth of the country, and that I was everywhere known as Brigham Young's rebellious wife.

People who were curious to see one of the wives of the Prophet, swarmed into the hotel. I could not leave my room, nor did I dare to do so, nor to allow my children out of my sight for nearly two months. The Mormon papers commenced to assail me in every way, while the Gentile papers came unanimously to my defence. In the midst of it came this most heart-rending letter from my mother : —

"MY DEAR CHILD : You can never know how dear you are to your grief-stricken mother. Your death would have been far preferable to the course you are taking. How gladly would I have laid you in your grave, had I known what was in your heart. I now pray that you may be spared for repentance and atonement ; for, as sure as you are living, a day of repentance will come ; a day of reckoning and of sorrow, such as you have never imagined. Now, let me entreat of you to pause, and retrace your steps before it is too late. The Lord, my Father, grant that you may listen to your mother's last appeal, and flee from your present dictators, as you would from the fiends of darkness.

"You will never know the effort I am making to write this. When I first received the blow, it struck me down like a flash of lightning, and the first I remember, I was praying for your death before you sinned past redemption. My much-loved child, come to your mother, and try to smooth her pathway to the grave. I should pray to be laid there at once, if I did not hope to save you yet. The path you are pursuing leads to the lowest depths of woe, and I pray, every moment of my life, that you may speedily be arrested. Oh, how could you turn against us? How could you break our hearts? Your father's house, and your brother Gilbert's house, are both filled with weeping friends, who are deploring your fate ; and I implore you, in the name of all that is sacred, to come back to us. You seem to be encircled in a cloud of almost impenetrable darkness, but the Lord our God is able to remove the veil, and enlighten you in his own way. I can only pray for you.

"My heart is broken, my dear and much-loved child. I loathe the sight of food, and sleep has forsaken my eyelids. The idol is rudely broken that I have worshiped so long. My fault has been in loving you too well, and having too great anxiety for your welfare.

"I pray you to forgive me for all the wrongs you imagine I have done you in bringing you up as I have done. I have ever been laboring, teaching, and instructing with the best of motives, with an eye to your interests. I shed the bitterest tears I ever did in my life. God grant you may never have cause to shed such tears. If I can ever be the least comfort to you, do not fear to let me know. I close by repeating, come to the arms of your heart-broken but still anxious

"MOTHER."

If she agonized over the writing of that letter, so I did over the reading. I longed to fly to her; but even to make her happy I could not violate my conscience, and go back into the old bondage of darkness again.

My father came at once to see me; and although he at first disapproved of my course, yet when the Mormon press commenced to assail me, he came over to my side at once.

Brigham and his friends commenced their usual method of warfare against a woman who opposes them, by instigating slanders of all sorts for the Gentile papers outside of Utah to publish. They found a ready assistant for their noble and generous attempt in the person of a fellow of low repute, employed as item-gatherer for the Salt Lake Herald, who had recently been converted to Mormonism through the agency of Brigham Young's purse, and was now ready to do any foul work for his master.

His first act was to send a dictated falsehood to the San Francisco Chronicle. He was a telegraph operator, and, through Brigham Young, who, it is alleged, virtually controls the Associated Press and the Western Telegraph Office in Utah, he had access to wires, and sent all the scandalous messages which his employer dictated, until it became so plainly apparent that he was serving Mormon interests, that the papers refused to publish any more of· his misstatements.

As a reward for his labor, he was promised a daughter of Mayor Wells as his wife. The young lady has not yet acquiesced in the arrangement, and he still hangs about Salt Lake, despised alike by Mormons and Gentiles.

The Gentile element in Salt Lake made itself strongly felt in my favor, and the Gentile press combated bravely the scurrility of the Mormon organs. Ladies and gentlemen called on me with offers of sympathy. All the persons connected with the hotel were kindness itself. Mr. and Mrs. Stratton stood by me nobly, and I have never ceased to thank God for raising up such friends in my time of need. I shall always hold them most specially dear, although our paths in life have so diverged that we rarely meet. Through General Maxwell, who was so kind as to come forward with offers of assistance, I brought suit for divorce against Brigham Young.

Surprised, as every one was, by this action, I think no one was more astonished than the Prophet himself. He would have looked for rebellion from almost any other wife sooner than from me, I had been so quiet and acquiescent during all my married life with him. He was annoyed by the publicity of the affair; for, although he likes notoriety, and courts it, he did not care to appear as defendant in a suit for divorce, on the grounds of neglect and non-support. It would not sound well in the Gentile world.

He tried to effect a compromise with me, and through his son-in-law, Hiram B. Clawson, offered me fifteen thousand dollars and my freedom if I would carry the suit no further. I will confess that the offer tempted me. I could take my children and go away quietly with them, and avoid the notoriety which I so hated. If it had been my own individual case alone, I should have eagerly accepted the offer, and made the compromise. But when I thought how much was involved, how many other lives would be affected by the decision which would be given in my case, I put all thought of settlement aside. I would not now be bought by the man who refused to care for me when it was his duty to do so; and I said to my lawyers, and General Maxwell, "Go on." There was no further delay, and the legal fight commenced at once. As so much has been said concerning this trial, and as it seems so generally misunderstood, I will devote a chapter to the legal points, and an epitome of the court proceedings, as far as they have reached, so that the general public may more fully understand what I sought, and what grounds I had to justify my action.

CHAPTER XXXVII.

THE DIVORCE SUIT. — PROCEEDINGS IN COURT. — BRIGHAM'S AFFIDAVIT.

I bring an Action against the Prophet. — My "Complaint" against Him. — What the "Complaint" Stated. — My Birth and Early Life. — My Marriage with the Prophet. — Exile to Brigham's Farm. — Cause of Action for Divorce. — The Question of Alimony. — My own Affidavit. — Corroborative Testimony. — Opinion of Judge McKean. — Brigham Young's Reply and Affidavit. — The Prophet states the Value of his Property. — Wonderful Difference of Opinion. — Proceedings in Court. — Judge McKean Sums Up. — Order for Allowance and Alimony. — Judge McKean Removed. — His Order Quashed by the New Judge. — The Latest Proceedings.

BRIGHAM FINED AND IMPRISONED FOR CONTEMPT OF COURT.

ON the 28th of July, 1873, I commenced an action for divorce against Brigham Young in the District Court of the Third Judicial District of Utah, and the "Complaint" was served upon him by the United States marshal.

This "Complaint" set forth, with the usual prolixity of all legal instruments, the grievances which I had appealed to the law to remedy; but, as it would be utterly impossible, in the circumscribed limits of these pages, to give that document entire, I shall present the reader with as succinct a *resumé* of its contents as I possibly can.

It was addressed " To the Hon. James B. McKean, Judge
of the Third Judicial District Court, in and for the Territory of Utah, and County of Salt Lake, in Chancery sitting," and the following are the several items which it contained : —

It began by stating who and what I was ; that I was born
at Nauvoo, Illinois, but had, since the year 1848, been resident in Utah ; that I was the wife of Brigham Young ; and
that I was married to him on the 6th of April, 1868, when
I was in my twenty-fifth year, and was the mother of two
children by a former marriage, one four and the other
three years of age ; that neither I nor my children had anything to depend upon, — a fact of which Brigham was well
aware, — and also that my children were boys, still living.

That Brigham had lived with me for about a year after
our marriage, treating me with some degree of kindness,
and providing, though inadequately, for my support ; and
that I had always fulfilled my duties as a wife toward him.

That about a year after our marriage he began to neglect and ill-treat me ; that during the year 1869 he sent me,
against my wishes, to a farm, four miles distant from Salt
Lake City, where, for three years and a half I was compelled to labor until I was completely broken down in
health ; that my only companion was my mother ; that,
except the limited fare which the defendant allowed me, he
appropriated all the proceeds of the farm ; and that on the
few occasions when he visited the farm he treated me with
studied contempt, objecting even to my aged mother remaining with me, after her health was destroyed by overwork on his farm.

That toward the end of 1872 Brigham removed me to a
house in Salt Lake City, where, however, he seldom visited
me ; that when I called upon him to ask a supply of the
necessaries of life, he used the most opprobrious language
toward me, and gave me so little that I had to work constantly to support myself and children.

That for five years past my health had been so bad that
I was now altogether unfitted to labor, and was in constant
need of medical advice; that Brigham knew it, but repeatedly refused to furnish me with assistance, medicine, or
food, so that I was obliged to rely upon the charity of
friends; that Brigham had declared he would never do
anything more for me, and said that henceforth I must support myself, notwithstanding that he was the owner of several millions of dollars; that, as President of the Mormon
Church, he occupied a very important position, and I believed that his monthly income could not be less than forty
thousand dollars.

That I had been compelled to sell my furniture, and all
my household goods, in order to obtain the necessaries of
life; and that, for a year previous to that date [1873], Brigham had entirely deserted me.

Further, I stated that it was impossible for our union to
continue; that I prayed for a separation, and also an allowance, as all I possessed consisted of about three hundred
dollars, and my children were dependent upon me for support; I asserted that I had secured the aid of Messrs. F.
M. Smith, A. Hagan, and F. Tilford as my counsel; that
I had been informed that twenty thousand dollars would be
a reasonable compensation for their services; and I therefore prayed the court to direct a subpœna, commanding
the defendant, Brigham Young, to appear to answer to my
suit; that, pending it, he might be ordered to pay me
a thousand dollars a month from the date of filing this
bill, a preliminary fee of six thousand dollars to my counsel, and that after the final decree he should pay them the
remaining fourteen thousand, and all the expenses of the
court.

Furthermore, I prayed, that after our legal separation, he
might be ordered to support myself and children suitably;
and that for that purpose the sum of two hundred thousand
dollars might be set aside from his estate.

This bill, the substance of which I have given above, was signed by my solicitors, Smith, Hagan, and Jilford, and to it the following was appended : —

"TERRITORY OF UTAH,
    County of Salt Lake, } ss.

"Ann Eliza Young, being first duly sworn, deposes and says : That she is the complainant in the above entitled action ; that she has heard read the foregoing bill of complaint, and knows the contents thereof, and that the same is true of her own knowledge, except the matters and things therein stated on information and belief, and as to those she believes them to be true.

"ANN ELIZA YOUNG.

"Subscribed and sworn to before me, this 19th day of July, A. D., 1873.   JOSEPH F. NOUNNAN, *Clerk.*"

A motion for an allowance and counsel fees was noticed for hearing at the same time, and the service was by the same officer. This document was headed with all due form and ceremony. It stated, I, Ann Eliza Young, the plaintiff, being duly sworn, alleged :

That I was the wife of Brigham Young, the defendant ; that while I was living with him, and performing the work mentioned in the bill already filed, he acquired enormous property, of the value of several millions of dollars, and was now the owner of at least eight millions.

That I had no means of knowing his exact income, but was sufficiently informed to allege that it was at least forty thousand dollars a month.

That the facts stated in the bill were true ; that I and my children were penniless ; that knowing the power and influence of Brigham, that he had the disposition to harm me, and that my life would be unsafe in any private house, I had taken refuge in the chief hotel in Salt Lake City, — the Walker House, — about the 15th of July, where I had since resided; that my expenses were very large, but that I had no income, and that my health was too feeble to allow me to work. I therefore prayed the court to grant me the items included in the bill already filed.

This affidavit was signed by me, and countersigned by Joseph F. Nounnan, the clerk of the court.

Attached to it was an affidavit, signed C. M. Turck, making, upon oath, a statement of the destitute condition in which I was previous to the time when I left my private residence and went to the Walker House.

Of this affidavit it is needless for me to speak in detail, further than to say that it more than fully establishes to the utmost all that the previous bill and affidavit affirmed. Other affidavits were made by gentlemen who knew me well, — one by Mr. Malcolm Graham, and another by my medical adviser, J. M. Williamson, both of which fully confirmed my own statements.

James B. McKean, judge of the court, was absent temporarily on account of sickness at that time, and Judge Emerson, of the First District Court, presided for him. Judge McKean had held that, in equity cases, the United States marshal was the proper officer to serve process, but the defendant came into court at the time appointed for the hearing, and moved to quash the service of the process, on the ground that the "territorial marshal," and not the United States marshal, was the proper officer to serve the process in the case. Reversing the rule administered by Judge McKean, the judge temporarily presiding held the motion good, and quashed the service.

Therefore new process was issued, and placed in the hands of the territorial marshal, accompanied by an order to the defendant to appear and answer to the motion for an allowance and alimony. This was regularly served, and at the day appointed the defendant appeared by counsel, and, for cause against the motion, filed his demurrer to the bill, on the ground that the District Court had not jurisdic-

tion of the subject of divorce in Utah Territory. Two days
were occupied in the argument of this question, and it was
taken under advisement for ten days longer. At the end
of that time the presiding judge came into court, and held
that this court had no jurisdiction in matters of divorce, and
denied the motion.

The case then stood over, by an agreement between the
counsel, until the following May, 1874. The Supreme
Court of the Territory, at its term held in that month, in
the case of Cast *vs.* Cast, decided that the district courts of
the territory had jurisdiction in actions for divorce and alimony, thus reversing the opinion of Emerson, justice in
this case. The case being afterwards — in July, 1874 —
called on for hearing on the demurrer to the complaint in
the District Court, McKean, presiding, overruled the demurrer, and gave the defendant leave to answer.

Thereupon my counsel asked and obtained leave to
renew the motion for an allowance and alimony pending
the suit which had been denied. It is proper also here to
state, that on the 24th of June, 1874, Congress enacted a
law expressly conferring authority in divorce cases on the
District Court of the Territory; but this law only affirmed
by legislation what the Supreme Court had already decided
to be the law.

On the 24th of August, 1874, Brigham Young filed
an answer, of which the following is a correct summary : —

He denied that at any time he had been married to me.

That at the time when my affidavit alleged that this marriage to me took place, I was really the wife of James L.
Dee, never having been legally divorced from him, but
that he [Brigham] believed at the time of alleged marriage
in April, 1868, that I had been properly divorced from Dee.

He alleged his previous marriage with Mrs. Mary Ann
Angell Young, at Kirtland, Ohio, on the 10th of January,
1834, and that the said legal wife was still living, of which
fact I, complainant, was aware.

He admitted his marriage with me, after the custom of the Latter-Day Saints, but denied that the marriage was legal, in any sense acknowledged by the laws of the land.

He then proceeded to deny every one of the counts in my complaint, seriatim, winding up with the following statement : —

"Defendant denies that he is or has been the owner of wealth amounting to several millions of dollars, or that he is or has been in the monthly receipt from his property of forty thousand dollars or more. On the contrary, defendant alleges that, according to his best knowledge, information, and belief, all his property, taken together, does not exceed in value the sum of six hundred thousand dollars, and that his gross income from all of his property, and every source, does not exceed six thousand dollars per month.

"Defendant further says, that at the time of the said alleged marriage, this defendant had, and still has, a very large family ; that his said family now consists of sixty-three persons, all of whom are dependent upon this defendant for maintenance and support.

"Whereof the defendant prays judgment of the court that he be hence dismissed with his costs herein.

"WILLIAMS, YOUNG & SHEEKES, and
HEMPSTEAD & KIRKPATRICK,
Defendant's Attorneys."

To the replication of defendant, which was very lengthy, denying or explaining away every point in the bill which I had filed, the following was appended : —

"TERRITORY OF UTAH, ⎫ ss.
County of Salt Lake. ⎭

"Brigham Young, being duly sworn, on his oath says: That he has heard read the foregoing answer, and knows and understands the contents thereof, and that the same is true of his own knowledge, except those matters therein stated on his information and belief, and as to those matters he believes it to be true. Affiant further says that he is the defendant in the above entitled suit.

"BRIGHAM YOUNG.

"Subscribed and sworn to before me this 25th day of August, 1874.

"Jos. F. NOUNNAN, *Clerk.*"

The court then gave me, or my counsel for me, leave to renew the motion for alimony as asked ; and notice having been given, the motion was by agreement fixed for hearing on the 3d day of October following. My counsel also filed a motion to strike out portions of the defendant's answer, and on the hearing of the motion for alimony, insisted upon submitting it to the court. When the motion was called for hearing, I offered to submit a number of affidavits bearing on the question of alimony, which were filed and served with the original complaint. The defendant objected to the reading of them, on the ground that they had not had sufficient notice of them by the notice renewing the motion, and they were withdrawn.

The defendant then offered to read affidavits in support of his answer, but as they had not been served, and their contents not made known prior to the hearing, they were objected to and excluded. It also appeared that the affidavits were addressed to other matters of defence than those set up in the answer.

The hearing was then had upon my complaint and the defendant's answer, my counsel at the same time submitting their motion to strike out certain objectionable portions of the answer, and insisting that such portions should be disregarded by the court, and treated — if the motion were well founded — as out of the answer.

The questions involved were argued, and on the 23d day

of February, 1875, the judge decided the motion for alimony, pending the suit, in an elaborate written opinion, of which the following is an accurate summary: —

The Judge, Jas. B. McKean, laid down nine general axioms tending to demonstrate that the defendant's pleas were invalid; that a marriage solemnized in Utah, after Mormon fashion, would be legally valid, provided the parties married were competent to enter into that engagement; that the court could not grant a divorce if the marriage were proved bigamous or polygamous; that the court had power to grant alimony, and intended to do so to the extent of one twelfth of what the defendant admitted his income to be, or one eighteenth according to my assertion.

He then summed up the statements of both parties to the suit. He gave the substance of my " Complaint," and then took into consideration Brigham Young's reply.

Then he considered the defendant's denial that any marriage had ever taken place between us; his statement that, at the time when I alleged that our marriage took place, I was actually the wife of Jas. L. Dee, never having been properly divorced from him; and also his admission that we had been married polygamously in April, 1868.

The judge gave quotations from various sources to prove that this marriage was legal and binding according to the laws of the Territory and of the United States, notwithstanding that the forms of the Mormon Church were used; providing, always, that we were both competent to enter into the contract.

He discussed the assertion of defendant that he was also incompetent to marry while his lawful wife, Mary Ann Angell, was still living. This, the judge explained, was the admission of felony; as, if admitted, it would prove that the defendant had entered into a bigamous marriage. Such statements he, the judge, said should be admitted as evidence, so far as they were to defendant's prejudice, but must be proved true before they could be admitted as evi-

36

dence against the plaintiff. The defendant must prove that
the plaintiff was the wife of another man, and that he himself was the husband of another woman, on the 6th of April,
1868.

The judge stated, that in order to prove the allegations
made on both sides, it would be necessary to summon witnesses, procure documentary evidence, &c., which would
involve very great expense. He should, therefore, allow
alimony, and a certain amount for costs of prosecution.

He quoted legal precedents to show what amount should
be considered reasonable ; and then he summed up, and decreed that, after considering all circumstances, the court
had concluded to order defendant to pay three thousand
dollars for the prosecution of the suit, and also five hundred
dollars a month for the maintenance of plaintiff and her
children, from the day of the filing of the "Complaint."
The order was accordingly made.

In deciding the question, it will be seen that virtually the
court disregarded portions of the answer, and, to that extent, sustained the motion to strike out those portions, though
it did not formally pass on that motion.

The defendant excepted to the decision, and shortly after-
ward filed a notice of appeal, and bond to stay proceedings
under the order.

The copy of the order directing the payment of the alimony was duly served personally on Brigham Young ; and
demand having been made upon him for the allowance made
for my attorney's fees, and payment refused, he was arrested
in proceedings in contempt, and brought before the court.

His answer to the proceedings consisted of a showing that
he had taken an appeal, and filed a bond for a stay, &c.,
and, therefore, he was not in contempt. The court held it
not to be an appealable order, and adjudged that he pay a
fine of twenty-five dollars, and be committed to custody for
one day, which was complied with.

Thereupon he caused the amount then due under the

order to be paid. My allowance he had been given twenty days to pay, and this portion of the order had not been complied with, and had not become due, except five hundred dollars, which was paid, when Judge McKean was removed by President Grant, and David P. Lowe, an ex-congressman from Kansas, was appointed chief-justice, and succeeded to the position.

Shortly after Judge Lowe entered upon his duties, proceedings were begun by counsel to bring the defendant up again in contempt, for refusing to comply with the order as first stated. On appearing, he again showed cause, by claiming his right of appeal, as in the former hearing; and objected, also, that the district courts had no jurisdiction of matters of divorce at the time of the bringing of the suit; that the order was null and void; that there was no contempt.

The court held, in deciding the matter, that it had jurisdiction; that the order was not appealable. In the course of his summing up, he said, "The complaint and answer are each upon oath, and it appears from the record as well as from the statement of counsel in argument, that the order for alimony and expenses was made upon the complaint and answer alone, *without any other evidence or showing whatever*. It is the general doctrine of the courts in divorce, that before temporary alimony can properly be awarded, the marriage must be admitted by the parties, or established by proofs. In the very recent case of York *vs.* York, 34 Iowa, 530, it is said, 'Alimony is a right that results from the *marital relation*, and *the fact of marriage between the parties must be admitted or proved before there can be a decree for it* even *pendente lite.*'" He then decided that the order was erroneously made, and dismissed the proceedings against the defendant.

The case now stands, therefore, on the motion (not yet formally passed upon) to strike out portions of the defendant's answer. The defendant has also filed a motion to vacate and set aside the original order granting the alimony, and the two will probably be heard together.

My counsel, for me, insist that I am entitled to the alimony upon the following grounds : —

1st. That it is alleged in the complaint that the plaintiff and defendant were married at a time and place designated. The defendant admits that a marriage ceremony did take place, and sets up new facts to show that the marriage which actually occurred was invalid. On this state of facts the plaintiff insists that, pending the question as to the *legality* of the marriage, she is entitled to alimony.

2d. It is denied by the plaintiff that the new matter in the answer ought to be disregarded; first, because it is badly pleaded; and, second, it is an attempt on the part of the defendant to take advantage of his own wrong, to wit, the assertion that he had a lawful wife living, which a court of equity will not permit. The defendant admits that he was married to the plaintiff; that they lived and cohabited together as husband and wife ; that he supported and maintained her as such; avers that he never deserted or illtreated her ; and, in fine, clearly shows that a relation of marriage existed in fact between them.

3d. The plaintiff claims that she will succeed on the merits; first, because the defence on the new matter ought to be disregarded as badly pleaded, and inadmissible under any form of plea; second, because the marriage of the defendant to Mary Ann Angell *cannot be proved*, and never was a *lawful marriage*. There was cohabitation, but no marriage according to law. This will appear if the true state of facts is ever reached in the trial. And the first alleged marriage must be shown to have been a lawful marriage. In Case *vs.* Case, 17 Cal. Rep., 598, the law is well stated on this point.

As to the allegation in the answer, that the plaintiff had a lawful husband living at the time of the alleged union between plaintiff and defendant, it is sufficient to say that she was divorced from James L. Dee by the Probate Court of Utah, and that it was done under the statute, and that the Supreme Court of Utah had previously decided that such court had *exclusive* jurisdiction in divorce matters. While this decision was probably erroneous, it was made by the highest tribunal of the territory, and was not appealable; *hence it was the law.*

More than this: the act of Congress of June 23, 1874, provided that all judgments of the Probate Courts of Utah which had been executed, or which had not been appealed from, should be held good. So that, upon the facts, there is nothing in the allegation that plaintiff had a husband living at the time of the marriage between the plaintiff and defendant.

It is only right to say, that in the opinion of the ablest lawyers of the West, Judge Lowe, in holding that the new matter in an answer is only denied " *at the trial*," has misconceived the California case which he cites, and mistakes the law. In *injunction* cases the pleadings are treated as *affidavits* by express provision of the California statutes; but no case can be found in California or elsewhere, under the code, where a *pleading* is treated as true in one stage of a case, and false in another. Such a doctrine would be absurd under any system of pleading that has ever existed.

The last legal step that has been taken, so far, was taken by me in making an affidavit for the purpose of proving that the defendant perjured himself, and which will furnish the foundation for his prosecution for the crime. With this affidavit, the case is stayed for the present.

CHAPTER XXXVIII.

MY ESCAPE FROM SALT LAKE CITY. — MY PUBLIC CAREER.

Thoughts of the Future. — The Gentile Papers. — A Private Audience at the Walker House. — Hopes and Fears. — I Resolve to Take the Platform. — Sneers and Ridicule. — Brigham is made Acquainted with my Plans. — Packing under Difficulties. — My Perilous Escape from Utah. — A Noble Woman. — Arrival at Laramie. — Denver. — My First Public Lecture. — A Grand Success. — Brigham at Work. — A Scandalous Article in the Chicago Times. — A Mean Lawyer. — Lecture at Boston. — Kindness of the Members of Boston Press. — Opposed by George Q. Cannon. — Washington Lecture a Success. — First Glimpses of the True Faith. — Conversion to Christianity.

MY FLIGHT AT NIGHT.

AS soon as I had fully decided that compromise was impossible, I began to consider my future. I felt able to take care of myself and my children, if I could see the way to do it. I was not afraid to work, and I felt a new impulse stirring within me which made me strong. Life was my own, and I would do the best I could.

The thought of a public career had never occurred to me. I had no ambition to gratify, and I had already gained more notoriety than I cared for. I was keenly sensitive to what was said about me, and many of the newspaper paragraphs, wittily written, by persons who neither knew me nor understood the situation in which I was placed, wounded me deeply.

The Gentile papers in Utah were, without exception, friendly to me, and I am sure kindlier words were never given than they have sent after me, since the very day I came out from under Brigham's control.

During my residence at the Walker House I was requested to give some account of Mormonism to the residents of the hotel and a few of their friends. I consented to do so, and an evening was appointed. I prepared a simple history of my life, and introduced, in the course of it, an epitomized description of the Mormon religion and its rites; and when the evening arrived, and I entered the parlors of the Walker House, I was startled to see the number of persons who had assembled to listen to me. I stood for a moment gazing in sudden bewilderment; the blood rushed to my face, and my first impulse was to run away and hide myself in my own room. But the applause which greeted me, the smiling, reassuring faces which were turned towards me, and the sympathy which I read in them all, gave me courage.

My audience listened with the closest attention, and when, after a while, I grew more accustomed to my strange position, and ventured to look up, I saw tears on more than one cheek, and when the last word was read, and I laid my manuscript down, I was surrounded by my newly made friends, all enthusiastic in their demonstrations of sympathy.

Previous to this involuntary public appearance, it had been suggested to me that I should take the lecture platform against Mormonism. I shrank from the very mention of it, and replied to the friends who proposed it that I could not, and would not, do it. To parade myself and my troubles before the world seemed such an indelicate thing to do! But when it was shown me that I might make of myself a power against Mormonism which should be felt, and which should open people's eyes to the enormity of the religious system which was tolerated by the government, I hesitated no longer.

I wish it to be distinctly understood that I did not undertake this work with a view to self-aggrandizement, or to gratify an inordinate ambition. Nothing has wounded me more, since I commenced my labors, than the oft-repeated accusation, that I was "trying to make capital" out of my position as the wife of Brigham Young. I have seen that accusation within a few months in the Woman's Journal, the leading organ of woman suffrage in Boston, in an article written by one of its editors and part proprietors, who, in the same article, commended Brigham Young to public favor because he gave the suffrage to women.

"Making capital" out of her woes, and, above all, her domestic infelicities, is something no woman of delicacy could do; and had I been governed by no motive except one so unworthy, I should deserve all the contemptuous criticism which I have been treated to by this apostle of "Fair Play for Women."

Does any one think that, for the sake of emolument, I could thus open my heart to the rude gaze of a curious public, bear all the slurs, slights, jeers, and aspersions that are cast at me by malicious Mormon and thoughtless Gentile papers, be made a by-word of, have my name on every vulgar lip? Never. My womanhood revolts at the idea.

As a means of support, I would never have undertaken it. When I saw it was a duty, I adopted it without hesitation, and I shall never cease my labors as long as I have strength to work. While I have a hand or a voice, Mormonism and Polygamy shall find in me a relentless foe. I will never rest, God helping me, until either I, or this hellish system, so fraught with misery, go down in the contest.

When my decision was fully made, I confided it to my father, who was my constant visitor. He gave me the warmest encouragement; but it was a terrible blow to my mother, who considered that I was setting the final seal to my future and eternal misery.

AT THE WALKER HOUSE. MY FIRST AUDIENCE.

I discovered, after my arrangements were made, that my intention had become known to the Mormons, who were threatening me with all sorts of vengeance if I insisted on carrying out my plans. It had been arranged that I should make my first appearance in Denver, and as I was extensively advertised there, the news of my proposed lecture had been telegraphed to Salt Lake, so that the date of my departure was made public.

I did not dare to leave Salt Lake by rail, nor would my friends allow it, and all our final arrangements were forced to be made with the greatest secrecy. I did not venture even to take my own trunk. A new one was bought, carried to a friend's room, my clothing conveyed to the same room, a piece or two at a time, packed as we could find opportunity, and then taken to a carriage, and carried outside the city.

On the evening of the 27th of November, I went with my father, and one or two friends, to the house of Mr. and Mrs. Stratton. We left the hotel by the back door, for the front entrance was closely watched, although it was not expected that I would attempt to leave the city until the next morning. About eleven o'clock we left the Strattons', and started, ostensibly to walk home. A carriage was in waiting at the corner. We got in, called for Mrs. Cooke, who was to be my travelling companion, and were driven rapidly out of the city. I was to take the cars on the Union Pacific road at Uintah, and thus avoid travelling at all on the Utah railroad, where I should be sure to be recognized.

The night was intensely dark; we could not see our hands before our faces, and, as we plunged on through the night and the darkness, we were a gloomy and apprehensive party. We were not sure how closely we had been watched, or whether we had succeeded in eluding Mormon vigilance. Even then, the "Danites," those terrible ministers of Mormon vengeance, might be upon our track, and I could not cast off the feeling that every moment brought us nearer and nearer to some dreadful death.

Twice during the night we were lost. The last time, we missed our way, and went several miles up a cañon, and I felt sure that we were betrayed, and that our driver was carrying us to certain destruction. I spoke to him, without letting him know my suspicions, and told him we were going wrong. He turned about, and drove rapidly back, and we reached the mouth of the cañon just as the day dawned. Confusion vanished with the darkness, our driver found the right road, and by fast driving we reached Uintah just as the train came up. Tickets and checks had been secured at Ogden, and with a hurried "good by" to

MY ESCAPE FROM SALT LAKE CITY.

my father, I jumped on board the train, with Mrs. Cooke, and we were off.

I can never describe my sensations when the train began to move. With the new sense of freedom came a feeling of such utter loneliness that, for a moment, I was bewildered by the situation, and, turning to Mrs. Cooke, I said, helplessly, "What shall I do?"

"Keep up a brave heart, and think of the work before you," said she.

Her experience in Mormonism had been no pleasanter than mine, and she was as glad to get away from it as I

STREET SCENE IN SALT LAKE CITY.

was. For twenty years she had taught Brigham's children, and acted in the Mormon theatre, and had never received a cent of remuneration. Her husband, a member of the special police force, was killed on duty, and after his death the prophet, through his counsellor, Daniel H. Wells, swindled her out of the two thousand dollars which the city had granted her, and tried to get her house from her. She put the matter into a Gentile lawyer's hands, and still re-

VIEW OF SALT LAKE CITY, SHOWING TABERNACLE.

tains her home. She was with me several months, a devoted and faithful companion.

Our first stopping-place was at Laramie, Wyoming Territory, where we were to await the arrival of my agent from Salt Lake. My presence in town was soon discovered, and I received many friendly and congratulatory calls. After my lecture every hospitality was shown me, and I felt fresh courage, so kindly was my reception, and so genuine were all the expressions of interest.

My agent arrived in a day or two, and we set out for Denver. The news of my escape from Utah had been

telegraphed, and on my arrival, I found myself eagerly expected. I was visited by the editors of the different papers,
who assured me of the friendly feeling toward me, and
offered me the use of their columns. The clergymen all
came to see me, and spoke generous words in my behalf
from every pulpit in the city. They all literally "took me
on trust." I shall never forget the earnest, spontaneous
kindness which I met from the professional men of Denver.

The night on which I was to give my first lecture, the
5th of December, 1873, was extremely cold, and the snow
fell heavily. I was discouraged and despondent, for I had
come to consider this first evening as prophetic of my future
career, and I saw failure before me. I did not know
whether I should be able to reach the church, the storm was
so furious ; but as a faithful few had promised to be in attendance, let what might happen, I determined to make the trial.

My forebodings had been utterly useless. Long before
the church doors were opened a large crowd was in waiting, and before the hour for beginning the lecture arrived
the house was full, and hundreds had gone away unable to
gain admission. As I looked into the crowded house, before I came on the platform, my courage almost left me.
But while hesitating, the thought of the poor women whose
cause I was to plead, came vividly into my mind, and with
a firm step, and beating heart, I walked onto the platform,
and stood facing my first audience, who greeted me with
tumultuous applause.

I have never spoken more effectively in my life than I did
that night. It seemed to myself almost as though I was
inspired. I forgot myself in my subject, and new indignation thrilled me as I told my story of bondage, such as my
hearers never dreamed of, and unveiled the horrors of the
Mormon religion. I made no attempts at oratorical effects,
I worked up no dramatic "points." Naturally and simply
as I could, I said what I had to say, without a single
rhetorical flourish.

The lecture was a success. After it was over, my audience crowded around me, with such earnest words of commendation, that I felt my first victory won. Since that memorable evening I have addressed hundreds of audiences, but never have I found one more sympathetic than the one composed of the true-hearted people of Denver.

I was not permitted to be quiet after that evening. Engagements came pouring in, and I worked my way steadily eastward. I was universally well received, but I knew that I should somewhere encounter Mormon opposition. I had seen too many attempts made by Brigham Young to ruin anyone who dared to differ with him, to think that I should escape.

The first blow came through the columns of a Chicago Paper, which devoted considerable space one day to a scandalous article concerning me, giving an air of truth to the statement by mentioning the persons who were authority for the reports. I was overwhelmed by it, for I feared it would put an end to the career of usefulness which I had marked out for myself. After I read the shameful article, my first words were, "Brigham Young's money is at the bottom of this."

And so it proved. The matter was put into the hands of Leonard Swett, Esq., of Chicago, for investigation. Letters came, in most cases unsolicited, from the persons referred to as having started the scandal, each one indignantly denying the whole. Further inquiry revealed that George C. Bates, a Mormon lawyer, of low repute, and twenty thousand dollars, induced the Paper to publish the article which originated in the foul imagination of Bates.

The papers of good standing came at once to my defence, and endeavored in every possible way to heal the wounds which the article had so cruelly inflicted on me.

The scandal was published on the eve of my first appearance in Boston, and I was greatly distressed lest it should injure my prospects in that city. I wanted my visit there to be a success, as I felt that, if I made a favorable impression, I should hold the key to all New England. And it was to the stanch and loyal New Englanders that I looked for assistance in my labors. My new and good friends had taught me to consider Reform and New England synonymous terms, and I really believed my battle would be well begun if I could gain such devoted allies as her brave, inflexible sons and daughters. But after the attack by the Chicago Paper, I regarded failure as certain. How surprised and gratified I was to find, instead of the prejudice I had expected to meet, a feeling of earnest kindliness toward myself personally, and of unfeigned interest in my work.

All the papers sent representatives to visit me, and I found them kind and intelligent gentlemen, and the papers which they represented were as generous as they. Nowhere have I met that courtesy and chivalric consideration which have been uniformly accorded me by the members of the Boston press. They have refrained from sarcasm and indelicate witticisms; they have been ready with sympathy, and quick to encourage; and whatever their politics or principles, they have been unanimous in their generous treatment of me.

My first lecture was given in Tremont Temple, before a large and enthusiastic audience. Mr. James Redpath introduced me, and the short speech he made fairly inspired me, it was so kind, so reassuring, so generous, and above all, so just. He had never heard me speak, but he was so bitter an enemy to this horrible system, as indeed he is to every wrong, that he was willing to take me for my work's sake. After the lecture was over, I felt that my hopes were realized, and that New England was open to me.

In Washington, nearly all the government officials attended my lecture, and expressed themselves enthusiastically in my favor. George Q. Cannon was contesting his seat in Congress, and Mormonism and its rulers were at that juncture prominently before the public. Cannon resented my appearance at the capital, and tried to break me down by ridicule. He made friends with the Washington Chronicle, in Brigham's most approved style of winning allegiance, and the day after my first lecture a burlesque report of it appeared in that paper. It was intended to prejudice the public; but when the lecture was over, and all the papers were unanimous in their commendation, the Chronicle suddenly grew ashamed of its disreputable alliance, and refused to maintain it longer, and, at the same time, grew more respectful toward me.

I have had hundreds of pleasant platform experiences since I commenced my crusade against polygamy; but the three which stand out the most vividly in my memory, are the first evenings at Denver, Boston, and Washington.

All this time I was learning to love my Gentile friends very dearly, and to feel at home in "Babylon." I was comparatively happy, but I was not at rest. There was something lacking in my life, — a void which nothing seemed to fill. Ever since I had found myself the dupe of a false religion, I had drifted blindly on, with no belief in anything, no faith in any system; sometimes, even, doubting the existence of God.

I was in this bitter mood when I spoke, one day, before the Methodist clergymen of Boston and vicinity. Among the persons to whom I was introduced on this occasion, was the Rev. Dr. Daniel Steele, of Auburndale. I had noticed him during my address, and felt quite strongly toward him, on account of the extreme interest which he evinced. One of his first questions was whether I had found any religion to take the place of the superstition I had cast off.

A hopeless "No," was my reply.

Then, for the first time in my life, I heard the principles of the religion of Christ. It was like day-dawn after a night of the blackest darkness, and I cried out eagerly, —

"This is what I want, — this religion of love."

A few weeks after this I was the guest of the Methodist Female College, at Delaware, Ohio, of which Rev. Dr. M'Cabe was president. I was recovering from a severe illness, and was very much depressed. My mother was constantly writing to me, telling me of the struggles through which she was passing in giving up her religion; for Brigham's treatment of me, his utter disregard of the truth, and his malicious attempts to ruin me, opened her eyes, and unbound her reason; and she soon saw the falsity of the whole Mormon plan of salvation. I knew every pang which she was suffering, for I have passed through it all myself. Yet I was powerless to comfort her, for I was not at peace.

Dr. M'Cabe was my frequent visitor, and patiently and kindly he pointed out the way of rest to me, until at last I willingly placed myself and my troubles in the loving, outstretched arms of God. Life opened out to me fuller than ever of possibilities, and my work grew holier. Peace brooded over my tired heart, and in the new experience I found infinite rest. Tossed all my life on a stormy sea of superstition, I was at last anchored in the sheltered haven of Christian belief.

CHAPTER XXXIX.

CHURCH GOVERNMENT. — MORMON APOSTLES. — THE ORDER OF ENOCH.

Mormon Administration. — The Earthly Trinity. — Filling Vacancies. — Mormon Apostles. — Polygamy made Profitable. — The Seventy. — Two-Dollar Blessings. — Astounding Promises. — Bishops and Spies. — The Order of Enoch. — All things in Common. — An Apostolic Row. —How Enoch Works. — A Stupid Telegram. — Logic Extraordinary. — A Gigantic Swindle. — Zion's Co-operative Mercantile Institution. — Brigham's Revelations. — The Saints Laugh in their Sleeves. — "It Pays to be a Mormon." — Beginning to see Through It. — The Apostate President.

THE CO-OPERATIVE STORE.

ALTHOUGH the power wielded by Brigham Young is absolute, he is ostensibly assisted in the administration of church affairs by a large number of officers, whose real business it is to see that the President's plans are carried out, and his commands obeyed. He is the motive power, and they are mere tools in his hands, to be employed as he sees fit.

The "First Presidency," which controls the whole church, is supposed to be the earthly representative of the Trinity, "the Eternal Godhead, Three in One," and consists of the President and the First and Second Counsellors, who are the types on earth of "the Father, the Son, and the Holy Ghost," in heaven. It is needless to say which rank Brigham assigns to himself.

37

GEORGE A. SMITH.
[Counsellor.]

His first counsellor, George A. Smith, has recently died, and it is yet undecided who shall fill his place. If the plan was followed which raised Brigham to his present position, the second counsellor would have it by right of seniority; but the general impression is that "Young Briggy" will be jumped into the position, and the Saints will be obliged to receive him as certain "successor," whether they wish it or not. They will have less difficulty in becoming reconciled to the inevitable, since he has been for so long a time persistently thrust upon the people as the "*probable* successor," that they have grown used to hearing his claims discussed.

The second counsellor is Daniel H. Wells, who is notoriously one of the most cruel, bigoted, and tyrannical men in Utah. He, like Smith and Brigham, has the title of "Prophet, Seer, and Revelator."

The Prophet Wells served for years as general, or commander-in-chief, of the Mormon army; and has ever been Brigham's right-hand man in iniquity, fearlessly disposing of life and property in the name of the Lord, counselling his superior to deeds of blood without number, and then treating with the most consummate cruelty the very men who have assisted him in the carrying out of his atrocious plans. He is Mayor of Salt Lake City, and stands high among the dignitaries of the church, but he rules with an iron hand, and cruelty and oppression predominate in all he does.

The "apostles" rank in church affairs next to the First Presidency. There are twelve of them, and Orson Hyde is their worthy President. This apostle is a practical polygamist, as are all the rest, but he has a convenient way of utilizing the system. He marries a cook, a laundress, a sempstress, a dairy-maid, or any servant he may happen to need. It is so much cheaper to marry domestics than to hire them. Under the latter arrangement he would be compelled to pay them for their services, while by the

DANIEL H. WELLS.
[Second Counsellor.]

former he is only obliged to give them shelter, food, and clothing. His wives represent nearly every nationality, and when visitors come to the house, the first Mrs. Hyde introduces her husband's other wives, as " Mr. Hyde's German wife, Mr. Hyde's English wife, Mr. Hyde's Danish wife," and so on, until all are presented.

He apostatized·in 1833, and made some remarkable revelations concerning Smith's polygamous practices, but he soon found his way back into the church, and has been one of the most stanch allies of the Prophet. He is supposed to have been connected with some of the most atrocious murders which have been committed in Utah. William Hickman implicated him most seriously in his confessions.

Next to him comes Orson Pratt, who has six wives and several children, and is by far the most able man in the church.

The other apostles are John Taylor, the happy husband of six wives ; Willard Woodruff, whose kingdom numbers but four ; Charles C. Rich, who has an indefinite number of wives and fifty children ; Lorenzo Snow ; Erastus Snow, whose kingdom is the size of Woodruff's ; Franklin D. Richards, who has five wives of his own, and in addition has five "proxies," who, before becoming his wives, held the less responsible positions of aunts-in-law. On his uncle's death, Richards assumed the earthly care of them, and promoted them to be members of his own family; George Q. Cannon, the Mormon politician, who repudiates polygamy in Washington, but is one of its most ardent supporters, both theoretically and practically, at home, having four wives and thirteen children; Brigham Young, Jr., whose family has already been described; Joseph F. Smith, who has three wives; and Albert Carrington, who holds the office of Church Historian.

THE OLD MORMON TABERNACLE.

The apostles have a general supervision of the Territory. They also go on missions, edit magazines, or take charge of the newly selected "stakes."

The working body of male Mormons is divided into seventy quorums, each having seventy members. Each quorum has a president, and these constitute the "Seventy." These presidents also have a president, who ranks next to the apostles. This body, the Quorum of Seventies, might with propriety be called the Mormon Missionary Board, as they attend to all matters connected with the propagation of the faith. The present president is Joseph Young, brother to Brigham.

In the year 1834, while the Saints were in Kirtland, Brigham's father expressed a desire to bless his children before he died, as did the patriarchs of old. On mentioning the subject to Joseph Smith, he, as usual, had a revelation that the Lord wished every father to bless his children, and that there should be Patriarchs set apart to bless those who had no father in the church. The first Patriarch was "Old Father Smith," Joseph's father, and his business was to bless all the fatherless who applied to him for blessing. At that time blessings were free for all who sought them; but when the first Patriarch died, and was succeeded by his son Hyrum, the business became so engrossing that it was thought best to charge one dollar for every person blessed. Hyrum was succeeded by "Uncle John Smith," his cousin, and he by William Smith, son of Hyrum. The only necessary qualification for this office is to be a Smith, and in some way a relative or descendant of the Prophet.

These "blessings" are rather wonderful affairs; they promise all sorts of things, in a vague, indefinite way, if only the recipient proves "faithful." Some are assured "they shall never taste death, but live until Christ comes, and be caught up to meet Him in the air;" others are assured that they are to have the privilege of redeeming their dead so far back, that there shall not be a broken link in the chain. Absurd as all this seems, there are hundreds of Saints who believe that "every word *shall* be fulfilled," as they are sometimes promised unconditionally, and the office of Patriarch is quite a profitable one, now that the price of blessings has been advanced to two dollars.

The bishops act at once as ecclesiasts, directors of municipal affairs, and judges of probate. Salt Lake City has twenty-one wards, each of which has a bishop over it. The entire Territory is also divided into wards, each with its governing bishop. Their duty is to settle disputes in the church, and to act as general spies and reporters, alike over Mormons and Gentiles.

In this last duty they are assisted by the Ward Teachers, whose duty it is to visit all the people in their ward, report all suspected persons, catechise every one, and discover all heresies, false doctrines, and schisms among the people, who are obliged to answer every question which is asked them, reserving nothing. Through these spies and informers, and their superiors the bishops, Brigham knows all the most private affairs connected with every individual, and this knowledge serves to render more binding his hold on this people.

Although the Ward Teachers are subordinate to the bishops, indeed, are the agents by which the latter do their work, they do not rank next to them. This position is held by the High Counsel. This body constitutes a sort of court of appeals, when the bishops do not give satisfaction to litigants. Appeal may be made from the High Counsel to the First Presidency.

In the early days of the church, the duty was strongly enjoined of consecrating all the possessions to the Lord; and this was not to be a figurative, but a real consecration; in which all the possessions were to be catalogued and consecrated in legal form, and the transaction authenticated by witnesses. The custodian of this property was to be a "Trustee in Trust," the community into which the faithful Saint thus entered was to be called "The United Order of Enoch," and the property was to be held for the benefit of this community.

The Saints did not take kindly to the Order, and it existed in theory merely. Within a year or two Brigham has been making the most arduous efforts to bring his followers into this community, meeting, however, with very little better success than its founders. When he first proposed its re-establishment, it was decidedly opposed in the

Tabernacle, by the apostles Orson Pratt, John Taylor, and George Q. Cannon, and a regular quarrel took place; the Prophet and his dissenting followers parting, each with a firm determination not to yield to the other side. The next week the four went north on a preaching tour, and labored harmoniously together in the attempt to build up the Order.

Whoever joins this community gives all his earthly possessions into the keeping of Brigham Young. His children, too, are required to sign away all claim or title to the property; if any are too young to write, the pen is given them, and their hands guided by their elders, and they are thus deprived of their rightful patrimony; and in return for all this, the family is to be furnished with what food and clothing the officers think they require.

As Brigham and his co-workers journeyed northward, he telegraphed to the bishops of the various settlements through which he would pass, informing them what time he would visit them, and requesting them to call special meetings of the residents of their wards before his arrival, and read to them the following telegram: "I am coming north, organizing branches of the Order of Enoch; how many of you are willing to join the Order without knowing anything about it?"

In the little town of Fillmore seventy-five men responded to the call for a meeting, and, strange as it may seem, fifty of those men voted to join the "Order." They fully understood that all on becoming members were required to deed their property to the "Trustee in Trust," otherwise, "Brigham Young, his heirs, executors, and assigns," yet they decided, with full knowledge of this, to make a blind investment of all their "worldly gear," and upon the arrival of the religious Autocrat, one half of the remaining twenty-five accepted the situation, and signed their names to an agreement binding themselves to obey "Enoch's" requirements. The following were the unanswerable arguments which Brigham used to secure their conversion : " I want you to understand that the car (meaning Enoch) is rolling on. The set time of the Lord has come, and no man can stay its progress. If you do not want to be run over, jump on, or get out of the way. I do not want a part of your property, I want it all. If there are any of you who cannot abide the requirements of the Lord, I do not want you to come near me, or to speak to me. I feel as far above you as the heavens are above the earth."

Those who became members of this branch of Enoch worked well, determined to make it a success. All labored together for the interest of the Order, and were credited a certain sum, I think fifteen cents an hour. They were economical, hoping to make the books show a balance in their favor, after deducting expenses of sustaining their families. But there were so many sinecures, and so much mismanagement, that after the lapse of one single summer an investigation of affairs became necessary, and the fact became known that their divinely directed labors had not paid the running expenses of the inspiration. Many who had expected that the records would exhibit a balance in their favor, awoke to the disagreeable fact that they, as co-partners in the United Order, the grand scheme that was to reconcile " the irrepressible conflict between capital and labor," must discount the sum stipulated as payment for their services. And they are at present in debt for the commonest necessaries of life consumed during their short-lived experiment.

A similar condition of affairs exists wherever this gigantic swindle has been in operation. And while Brigham has been gloating over his ill-gotten gains, he has bound these poor victims more firmly to himself by the terrible bondage of debt. The wildest dissatisfaction exists, and in nearly every county the Order may be regarded as dead, and beyond even the power of Brigham Young to restore.

The Tithing System is a direct outgrowth of " Enoch."

When Joseph saw that the people did not take kindly to his community plan, he found it necessary to adopt some other means of raising a permanent fund for the church, and Orson Pratt proposed that every member should every year be obliged to pay one tenth of his income, out of which the church should be supported. This plan met with the approval of the officers, and it has been continued ever since.

Every town has its tithing-house, which is in charge of the local bishop. He takes charge of all the goods that are

MORMON TITHING STORE AND OFFICE OF DESERET NEWS.

brought in, usually paying himself a handsome commission, and sees, when any quantity has been gathered, that it is transported to the large tithing-house in Salt Lake City.

This tithing-house is under the direct control of Brigham Young, and he, his counsellors and clerks, have the first choice of all the goods that are brought in; the remaining stores are dealt out as payment to the poor men who are employed by Brigham as laborers. I have seen the tithing-store beseiged by a crowd of tired, care-worn women, wives of these men, waiting for their turn to be served. Sometimes a poor woman will stand all day waiting for a sack of flour, a basket of potatoes, or a quart of molasses. Let the day be ever so cold or stormy, there she must wait, until the clerks see fit to attend to her wants.

Everything is received here in payment for tithing : hay, grain, vegetables, butter, cheese, wool, or any other product. If a man has not money, he must give one tenth of what he has. It matters little whether he can afford it; the church demands it, and "the church" gets it.

The nearest approach to the practical realization of the Order of Enoch was what is called Zion's Co-operative Mercantile Institution. This was a great commercial corporation, engaged in buying and selling the produce of the people, and supplying them with every kind of merchandise needed in a new country. The stock was held by the people of the Territory, and branches of the parent concern were scattered throughout all the leading settlements ; so that all the commercial exchanges of the country might be made through this establishment. It was designed to destroy the business of Gentile merchants in Zion, and accordingly all were commanded to patronize it; but the completion of the Pacific Railroad, and the influx of Gentiles, came to the relief of the proscribed merchants ; their goods, too, were of a better class, and there was a greater opportunity for selection, so that Mormons and Gentiles alike patronized them ; and at the present time, while the Co-operative Institution seems tottering to its fall, in spite of the frantic attempts of Brigham and his assistants to prop it up and make it secure, the Gentile houses are rapidly gaining in wealth and credit.

Most of Brigham's "revelations" have met with about the same degree of success in their attempted carrying out. His project of making silk, and another equally wild scheme of producing sugar from beet-roots, were gigantic failures, although he will not acknowledge it. Two more of his "inspirations" are kept in the minds of the Saints, by being so constantly before their eyes. The unfinished mud wall, which was to protect the city from invasion, and the divinely projected canal, which was to bring the stone for the new Temple from the quarries to Salt Lake City, and which Brigham announced that he had seen just as distinctly in a "vision" as he "ever should with his natural eyes." A large amount of money, and a great deal of hard labor

BRIGHAM'S CANAL.

was expended on these enterprises; all of which is a total loss.

Brigham is shrewd enough to see that "revelation" is not one of his strong points, and he rarely attempts it; less frequently now than formerly, even. The catch-words, "Thus saith the Lord," are not nearly so potent as they were before the Saints came so much in contact with the Gentile world, and unconsciously lost some of their superstition. They do not openly laugh at Brigham's prophecies, but a few of the more honest and far-seeing venture to criticise him very quietly, although they submit to his rule, and are seemingly as good Saints as ever. They are not ready to apostatize; their interests and associations bind them to the church, and they do not wish to leave it. Some cling to it, like George Q. Cannon, through ambition; for that young apostle dares to cast his eyes toward Brigham's position, and has expressed the belief that he might ultimately succeed him. Others, like Orson Pratt, are so closely identified with it, that they cannot and would not cut themselves adrift from it. The church is their life, and they will only leave one when they are compelled to give up the other. Another class, to which Brigham's sons notably belong, stay because their pecuniary interests demand it. It "pays" to be a Mormon. But when once the present ruler is taken, they will have nothing to hold them, and they will do openly what they have long since done in their hearts, — repudiate Mormonism, and all its superstitions and practices. And I am morally certain that the first one to take advantage of his newly-obtained liberty will be John W. Young, who is even now known as "the Prophet's Apostate Son," and who yet, in spite of his apostasy, holds the position of "President of the Salt Lake State of Zion," with the rank of bishop.

CHAPTER XL.

THE CONDITION OF MORMON WOMEN. — HIGH AND LOW LIFE IN POLYGAMY.

Increasing Light. — The Equality of the Sexes. — Exaggeration Impossible. — Likely Saviours. — The Present Condition of Mormon Women. — The Prospects for the Future. — Polygamy Bad for Rich and Poor. — A Happy Family. — The Happiness Marred. — Sealed for Time Only. — Building on Another Man's Foundation. — The New Wife. — How the Old One Fared. — The Husband's Death a Relief. — Asa Calkins's English Mission. — What Came of It. — How to Get Rich. — Two Sermons from One Text. — Dividing the Spoil. — No Woman Happy in Polygamy.

POLYGAMY IN HIGH AND LOW LIFE.

ALL this while I was gaining knowledge of the domestic customs and relations of the "Gentiles." At nearly every place that I visited I was entertained in some private family, and my eyes were constantly being opened to the enormities of the wicked system from which I had escaped.

I had felt its misery; I had known the abject wretchedness of the condition to which it reduced women, but I did not fully realize the extent of its depravity, the depths of the woes in which it plunged

women, until I saw the contrasted lives of monogamic
wives.

I had seen women neglected, or, worse than that, cruelly
wronged, every attribute of womanhood outraged and insulted. I now saw other women, holding the same relation, cared for tenderly, cherished, protected, loved, and
honored. I had been taught to believe that my sex was
inferior to the other; that the curse pronounced upon the
race in the Garden of Eden was woman's curse alone, and
that it was to man that she must look for salvation. No
road lay open for her to the throne of grace; no gate of
eternal life swinging wide to the knockings of her weary
hands; no loving Father listened to the wails of sorrow
and supplication wrung by a worse than death-agony from
her broken heart. Heaven was inaccessible to her, except
as she might win it through some man's will. I found, to
my surprise, that woman was made the companion and not
the subject of man. She was the sharer alike of his joys
and his sorrows. Morally, she was a free agent. Her
husband's God was her God as well, and she could seek
Him for herself, asking no mortal intercession. Mother-
hood took on a new sacredness, and the fatherly care and
tenderness, brooding over a family, strengthening and defending it, seemed sadly sweet to me, used as I was to see
children ignored by their fathers.

Seeing this, I began to comprehend a little why it was so
difficult to make the state of affairs in Utah understood.
The contrast was so very great that, unless it was seen, it
could not be realized, even ever so faintly. I feel sometimes, both in speaking to audiences, and in private conversations, the thrill of shocked surprise which runs through
my listeners' veins as I relate some particular atrocity, or
narrate some fearful wrong, which has been suffered either
by myself or some person known to me; but even then I
know the enormity of the system which permits such things
to be possible is but vaguely understood.

I am accused sometimes of exaggeration. In reply to that accusation I would say, that is simply impossible, I could not exaggerate, since language is inadequate to even half unveil the horrors. There are events of daily occurrence which decency and womanly modesty forbid my even hinting at. No one can, even if they would, quite tear the covering away from the foul, loathsome object, called "Celestial Marriage," reeking as it is with filth and moral poison; rotten to the very core; a leprous spot on the body politic; a defilement to our fair fame as a nation. I am compelled to silence on points that would make what I have already said seem tame in comparison. Not a word of all my story is exaggerated or embellished. The difficulty has been rather to suppress and tone down.

Women are the greatest sufferers. The moral natures of the men must necessarily suffer also; but to them comes no such agony of soul as comes to women. Their sensibilities are blunted; their spiritual natures deadened; their animal natures quickened; they lose manliness, and descend to the level of brutes; and these dull-witted, intellectually-dwarfed moral corpses, the women are told, are their only saviours.

What wonder that they, too, become dull and apathetic? Who wonders at the immovable mouths, expressionless eyes, and gray, hopeless faces, which tourists mark always as the characteristics of the Mormon women? What does life offer to make them otherwise than dull and hopeless? Or what even does eternity promise? A continuation merely of the sufferings which have already crushed the womanhood out of them. A cheering prospect, is it not? Yet it is what every poor Mormon woman has to look forward to. Just that, and nothing more.

Rich or poor alike suffer. Polygamy bears no more lightly on the one than the other. If they are poor, they have to work for themselves and their children, suffer every deprivation, submit to every indignity. If they are in more affluent circumstances, they have more time for brooding over their sorrows, more leisure for the exercise of the natural jealousy which they cannot help feeling for the other wives. Happiness and contentment are utterly unknown to Mormon women; they are impossible conditions, either to dwellers in poverty or plenty.

A few years ago, a man and wife of the name of Painter, decided to cast in their lot with the Saints, and enroll themselves among the Lord's chosen people. The woman had been previously married, and her husband had died shortly after his conversion to the Mormon faith. The elders urged her marrying again, and, after a time, she found her heart adding its persuasions to the "counsel" of the brethren, and she married William Painter, an honest, kind-hearted fellow, who made her a good husband, and with whom she lived very happily.

As soon as possible they came to America, but that was not until their family had been increased by two or three children, who were alike the objects of the mother's care and the father's pride. Although they were poor, hard-working people, I have never known a happier family than this when they first came to Utah.

Like all new arrivals they were anxious to receive their Endowments, and it was shortly arranged for them to go through the rites. When they presented themselves at the Endowment House, Heber C. Kimball told the wife that she could only be sealed to her present husband for time. She must belong to her first husband in eternity, he having died in the faith. She was not at liberty to deprive him of his privileges, or to rob him of his kingdom.

The poor woman felt very badly, for this man was the father of her children, and she felt that her claim on him should be the strongest; but the authorities refused to see the matter as she did, and insisted that the sealing should be only for time. There was no help for it, and the poor woman was obliged to submit. Neither was the husband satisfied. It did not suit him to "build a kingdom on another man's foundation;" he must commence one for himself; and, in obedience to counsel, he looked about diligently for a wife "all his own." He was not long in finding one, and, greatly to his wife's distress, he brought home an ignorant young girl, who turned the house topsyturvy in her endeavors to exercise the authority which she arrogated to herself. The first wife considered that she had some rights still remaining, and that, certainly, she might dictate somewhat concerning household affairs, as she had been so long the ruling power, and understood the manner of regulating and running the domestic machinery; but the new-comer claimed entire supremacy, declaring that she was "the only wife William had," her rival belonging to another man.

Strange as it may seem, the husband took sides instantly with the new-comer against the woman who had been a faithful wife for years, and was the mother of his children. She ruled the household affairs, the first wife, and even the husband and all were compelled to submit to her decision. She heaped every indignity upon the poor wife, even resorting to personal violence, and the victim could obtain neither sympathy nor redress. She was compelled to live under the same roof with her rival, as her husband's means would not admit of two establishments, and for several years she endured the misery silently. We all knew her to be very unhappy, and we pitied her extremely. She was our near neighbor, and the nearest approach to confidences which she ever made was given to my mother. But we did not know for a long time how very much she had to bear.

One cold day, in the midst of a dreary storm, the poor woman came rushing into our house, with her babe in her arms, crying bitterly. She sank into a chair, which my mother placed for her near the fire; and in answer to the anxious inquiries, she sobbed out, "O, sister Webb, I have

38

left my home and my husband. I have been compelled to do it. I can endure no more. If you knew all, I am sure you would not blame me!"

Mother inquired what it was that had occasioned this new rupture, and brought her to this final decision.

The poor, distressed creature replied, that her husband had taken Emma, the second wife, and gone on a visit of several days to some relatives, leaving her and the children utterly unprovided either with food or fire, and they were nearly perishing with cold and hunger. She had sent the

DRIVEN FROM HOME.

other children to another neighbor's to get warm, and she and the younger ones had taken refuge with us.

In two or three days the husband returned, and finding where his wife was, compelled her to come back to him, by threats of taking the children from her unless she did. After a few years he died, and what little property there was the young wife claimed. The first wife appealed to the church authorities, but they upheld the last wife's claims, and she was driven penniless away with her children. She had to support herself and them; but she used frankly to say, that she was happier than she had been for years, and that her husband's death was a positive relief to her. I knew this woman well, and I knew that no more worthy woman lived than she. Polygamy blighted her life, and made a miserable dependent of one who would have been, in other circumstances, a happy wife.

About fifteen years since, a man by the name of Asa Calkins was sent by Brigham Young to preside over the Saints in the British Isles. He left two wives in Salt Lake, but on his arrival in England, he met with a young lady who completely fascinated him, and having obtained the permission of his Prophet to marry while on the mission, began paying her the most devoted attention.

He met with no difficulty in his wooing, and no obstacle was placed in the way of his speedy marriage. After the marriage, he informed his wives in Utah of the event, and they received the news with resignation, as they expected nothing different. But he was not so frank with the new wife. Brigham had told him, when he gave him permission to marry, to say nothing about his other wives, so the young English lady supposed herself to be the only Mrs. Calkins. About two years after the marriage, the first went to some of the Eastern states on a visit to some relatives. While there her health became impaired, and on being advised that a sea-voyage would benefit her, wrote at once to her husband in Liverpool, asking permission to join him in England.

He said, in reply, that she might come, if she was willing to pass as his sister, as he had all the wife there that the English law would allow. As she felt obliged to take the voyage on account of her failing health, she agreed to do as he desired.

On her arrival at Liverpool, she found her husband so

infatuated with his new wife that he scarcely noticed her at all, and she almost regretted having crossed the sea; yet she saw no way of escape from the trial, as she was to remain there until her husband's mission was ended, which would not be for two years at least.

Mr. Calkins almost entirely ignored the existence of his first wife, and, taking Agnes, travelled all over Europe, introducing her everywhere as Mrs. Calkins, while the poor "sister" remained in Liverpool. He lavished every luxury of dress and ornament upon his idol, while the poor, neglected wife was supplied with the merest necessities of life.

In course of time, they all returned to Zion; but Agnes still remained the favorite wife. Calkins had always been one of the most prosperous Saints, but he returned from his mission a rich man. About the time of his return we often heard rumors concerning his manner of obtaining this wealth, which were not altogether creditable to him, and, consequently, no one was surprised to hear brother Brigham apply the lash to the delinquent missionary the Sabbath after his arrival at Salt Lake, for what he was pleased to term a species of highway robbery. The Saints universally believed that the man merited the rebuke. But the surprise came the Sabbath following. Brigham changed his tactics, and put in a warm plea in the missionary's defence. He said that he had not distinctly understood all about Brother Calkins's course in England until some time during the previous week, when he had visited him, and explained matters to his entire satisfaction. He omitted to state that "Brother Calkins" not only visited him, but divided the spoils with him, his own share amounting to several thousand dollars.

Mr. Calkins was restored to favor. The English Mrs. Calkins was recognized as the chosen wife, and the other two were merely tolerated, and were obliged to see their husband's devotion and wealth lavished on her, while they starved for love and lacked for comforts.

These two cases show the workings of the polygamic system in the families of the rich and the poor. It is as hateful in the one case as in the other, and equally productive of misery in both.

I have yet to learn of one woman who is happy in it. Like Zina Young, they say, " The system must be right, I suppose; we are taught that it is. But if that is the case, we must live it wrongly; there is fault somewhere."

There is worse than that. There is positive sin; and in her heart of hearts, no woman of them all believes it to be right, although she may try, with all the sophistry at her command, to convince herself that it is. Her heart and her reason both give her arguments the lie, and she cannot help but heed them, even when she counts herself a sinner for so doing.

CHAPTER XLI.

MY RETURN TO UTAH. — SECRET OF BRIGHAM'S POWER. — UTAH'S FUTURE.

I return to Utah. — Reception at the Walker House. — Greeting old Friends. — My Love for the Place. — Six Lectures in the Territory. — Brigham's Daughters make Faces at me. — My Father and Mother in the Audience. — The Half not told. — Multitudes Pleading for Freedom. — Eastern Newspaper Reports. — Indiscretion. — The Poland Bill. — Increase of Polygamy. — The Secrets of Brigham's Power. — The Pulpit and Press on Mormonism. — The Salt Lake City Tribune. — A Word to the Sufferers. — Calls for Help. — The Future of Utah.

RECEIVING MY FRIENDS AT THE WALKER HOUSE.

N August, 1874, I returned to Salt Lake City; but not in the secret way in which I had left it months before. I was met with every expression of good will, and congratulations and welcomes poured in upon me from every side. A reception was held for me at the Walker House, and I had the opportunity of greeting again the friends who had so nobly assisted me in my struggles for freedom. Foremost of all, Judge McKean, the truest, most upright, and inflexible chief justice who had ever presided over the Utah courts; the man who could neither be bribed nor cajoled; who did right for the right's sake, and who consequently had gained the enmity of Brigham Young and his followers, but who was implicitly trusted by all lovers of justice; General Maxwell, too, who was so kindly acting for me in my suit; Colonel Wickizer, who lent his room for my trunk to be taken to, and otherwise assisted me in my flight from Utah; and Mr. and Mrs. Stratton, the dearly beloved friends who

MY RECEPTION AT SALT LAKE CITY.

had first shown me the possibilities of an escape from bondage and a life outside.

This welcome, hearty and spontaneous, touched me deeply, and I felt then that however much my interests might be drawn away from Salt Lake City, and my work lead me away from there personally, yet it was my home, its people were my people, and my heart would always turn lovingly toward it to the day of my death.

And why should I not love it? I had grown with it, and there is not a building in it that I have not watched as it arose, not an improvement that I have not rejoiced in. I have seen a lovely city spring up in an alkali desert as if by magic. True, I have suffered there. Many of its associations are bitter. But that is the city as it has been — the Salt Lake of the past, not the Salt Lake of the future, as I hope its future will be.

During the summer, I lectured six times in the city, and several times in other towns in the Territory. Brigham did not attend any of my lectures, but he sent his daughters and daughters-in-law, and bade them sit on the front seats, and make faces at me. They filled the two rows nearest the platform, and, as I saw them there, my heart went out in pity toward them. I knew all of them ; many of them had been my dear friends from girlhood, and I had known how unhappy they had been under the cruel system which I was fighting against. I had been in the confidence of several, and more than one had commiserated me upon my unhappy situation while I was their father's wife. Instead of annoying me, and causing me to falter and break down completely, as the prophet hoped, it only lent new strength to my purpose, new fire to my words. I knew that these women sympathized with me in every word I uttered, and that in their hearts they earnestly wished me success.

My father and mother were in my audience, too. It had required a great deal of persuasion to induce the latter to be present, but she finally yielded to us all, and went. Long before this she had lost her faith in Mormonism, and was ranked among the apostates. Brigham's attempts to ruin me had opened her eyes, and she at last saw him as he really was. I think no one rejoiced in my success more than she did, and certainly no one else has had power to imbue me with such fresh courage and strength. And now that she has abandoned Mormonism, when I think of her, away from all the old associations, united in her old age to the friends of her childhood, happy in a home safe from the intrusion of polygamy, every shade of bigotry blotted out, her reason unfettered, her will free, I am happier than I ever can say; and if this result only were reached in the cases of the other women of the Territory, I should feel that my suffering and my labors had not been in vain.

Next to these lectures in Salt Lake, my most successful appearance was made at Provo, where I spoke under the auspices of the Rev. C. P. Lyford, the pastor of the Methodist church in that place, and one of the most inveterate foes of Polygamy and Brigham Young. Three years ago Provo was one of the most powerful of all the Mormon strongholds in Utah. Many deeds of violence had been committed there, and bigotry in its worst form ruled the people. Mr. Lyford, young, brave, and enthusiastic, determined to build a Gentile church there. He went into the work cheerfully and determinedly, although he was warned to leave the county, his life threatened, and every possible insult and indignity offered him. But he could not be intimidated, and flatly refused to leave; and now he has a society fully organized, a church built, and a free school established. He has been one of my strongest allies and warmest defenders, and I owe to no one more gratitude than to him.

I have told my story as simply as I could. I have added nothing, but I have left much untold. Another volume, as large as this, would not contain all I could write on this subject. My life is but the life of one; while thousands are suffering, as I suffered, and are powerless even to plead for themselves, so I plead for them. The voices of twenty thousand women speak in mine, begging for freedom both from social and religious tyranny.

I take up papers, and I read letters from eastern correspondents who have visited Utah; and while I do not wonder at the enthusiasm which they display concerning the outward beauty of this city of the desert, I marvel at the blindness which fails to see the misery of the majority of its people. " Polygamy is on the decrease," they almost unanimously exclaim; "the ballot and education are its foes, and it cannot stand before them; the young people will not enter the system, and while polygamous marriages diminish in number, monogamic ones steadily increase."

This is not so. I have no doubt it is the story which is told to these strangers by Mormons. But that is an old trick. They have been accustomed, in other days, to repudiate polygamy while practising it most extensively. They are only following "Brother Joseph's" example. He denied it, to save the reputation of himself and his followers; and they do it still, when they wish to blind the Gentiles' eyes, and escape their criticism.

Last year, as the records will show, there were more polygamous marriages in Utah than there have been any previous year since the " Reformation." The Order of Enoch and Polygamy are, to-day, Brigham's two strongest holds on the people. By the first, he holds the men through sheer necessity; for all who have entered the Order have given themselves and their possessions so entirely to him, that they cannot, by any possibility, get free. By the other system, he holds the women in a crueller bondage still. He and Cannon may repudiate the "Celestial Marriage" as strongly as they choose, but they cannot change the facts. They are more shrewd, but not so honest as the fellow who was seen reeling through the streets of Salt Lake City, with a bottle under each arm, shouting, " I've taken a new wife to-day, and I'm not afraid of the Poland Bill." They do care for " the Poland Bill," or, rather, they care about public opinion very much, and they like the positions which they might be obliged to resign if they ventured to claim the legality of Polygamy.

There is a strong working-power against it in its very midst, however, and it seems to me that it is a power which must prevail. The pulpit and press combined are dealing some heavy blows upon it, and it cannot always stand under it. Instead of the Mormon church being the only church in Utah, nearly every denomination is represented there now, and the most of these churches have schools connected with them, — such superior schools, some of them, that a few of the more liberal and intelligent Mormons venture to send their children to them.

But the strongest power in the Territory against Polygamy, — the most implacable and relentless foe to Brigham Young and his pet institution, — is the *Salt Lake City Tribune*, the leading Gentile paper in Utah. It is owned

"NOT AFRAID OF THE POLAND BILL."

by a stock company, composed of the leading Gentiles in the Territory; is ably conducted, and is hated and dreaded by the Mormons, although they all read it. It has been my constant friend, and has stood bravely by me ever since I turned my back on my false faith, and sought shelter and friends in "Babylon."

It is a power in politics. When Governor Woods — although a loyal and brave officer of the government — was removed to make place for Axtell, who was a mere tool in the Prophet's hands, the indignant utterances of the paper made themselves felt all over the country; and the supporters of the new governor in Washington grew ashamed, and he was removed to make room for Governor Emory, the present governor, who, as yet, has shown no disposition to assimilate with the saintly portion of his subjects.

Now, as I approach the end of my story, I turn longing eyes toward my old home, and my heart goes out in pitying tenderness to it and the women there. To them I want to say, Your cause is my cause, your wrongs have been my wrongs; and while you are still bearing them patiently, because you know there is no redress; hopelessly, because while your hearts are breaking, you see no avenue of escape, I am trying the best I know to make the way easy and plain to your eyes, dimmed with tears, and your feet, tired of wandering in broken paths. Many of you, I know, think that I am wrong; you believe, as I once did, that to fight against Brigham Young, and his will, is certain damnation. You mourn for me as one lost; you regard me with pity; but yet, in your hearts, you wish to believe that I am right; you would like to be convinced that I am. Some of you are certain of it, but you do not see your own way out. The darkness closes around you thicker and heavier, and, tired of groping about, you fold your hands and sit in an apathy worse than death, waiting until the dawn of eternity shall throw light upon your path. God help you, sisters, one and all, and bring you out of the spiritual bondage in which you are held.

And you, happier women, — you to whom life has given of its best, and has crowned royally, — can you not help me? The cry of my suffering and sorrowing sisters sweeps over the broad prairies, and asks you, as I ask you now, "Can you do nothing for us?" Women's pens, and women's voices pleaded earnestly and pathetically for the abolition of slavery. Thousands of women, some of them your country-women, and your social and intellectual equals, are held in a more revolting slavery to-day. Something must be done for them. This system that blights every woman's life who enters it, ought not to remain a curse and a stain upon this nation any longer. It should be blotted out so completely that even its foul memory would die.

Yet, how is it to be done? I confess myself discouraged when I ask that question. Legislation will do no good, unless the laws can be enforced after they are once made. But if laws are to be framed, and the men who enforce them are to be removed as a punishment for their faithfulness, they are better not made.

But one thing is certain. If one voice, or one pen, can exert any influence, the pen will never be laid aside, the voice never be silenced. I have given myself to this work, and I have promised before God never to withdraw from it. It is my life-mission; and I have faith to believe that my work will not be in vain, and that I shall live to see the foul curse removed, and Utah — my beloved Utah — free from the unholy rule of the religious tyrant, — Brigham Young.

THE END.

American Women: Images and Realities
An Arno Press Collection

[Adams, Charles F., editor]. **Correspondence between John Adams and Mercy Warren Relating to Her "History of the American Revolution," July-August, 1807.** With a new appendix of specimen pages from the "History." 1878.

[Arling], Emanie Sachs. **"The Terrible Siren": Victoria Woodhull, (1838-1927).** 1928.

Beard, Mary Ritter. **Woman's Work in Municipalities.** 1915.

Blanc, Madame [Marie Therese de Solms]. **The Condition of Woman in the United States.** 1895.

Bradford, Gamaliel. **Wives.** 1925.

Branagan, Thomas. **The Excellency of the Female Character Vindicated.** 1808.

Breckinridge, Sophonisba P. **Women in the Twentieth Century.** 1933.

Campbell, Helen. **Women Wage-Earners.** 1893.

Coolidge, Mary Roberts. **Why Women Are So.** 1912.

Dall, Caroline H. **The College, the Market, and the Court.** 1867.

[D'Arusmont], Frances Wright. **Life, Letters and Lectures: 1834, 1844.** 1972.

Davis, Almond H. **The Female Preacher, or Memoir of Salome Lincoln.** 1843.

Ellington, George. **The Women of New York.** 1869.

Farnham, Eliza W[oodson]. **Life in Prairie Land.** 1846.

Gage, Matilda Joslyn. **Woman, Church and State.** [1900].

Gilman, Charlotte Perkins. **The Living of Charlotte Perkins Gilman.** 1935.

Groves, Ernest R. **The American Woman.** 1944.

Hale, [Sarah J.] **Manners; or, Happy Homes and Good Society All the Year Round.** 1868.

Higginson, Thomas Wentworth. **Women and the Alphabet.** 1900.

Howe, Julia Ward, editor. **Sex and Education.** 1874.

La Follette, Suzanne. **Concerning Women.** 1926.

Leslie, Eliza . **Miss Leslie's Behaviour Book: A Guide and Manual for Ladies.** 1859.

Livermore, Mary A. **My Story of the War.** 1889.

Logan, Mrs. John A. (Mary S.) **The Part Taken By Women in American History.** 1912.

McGuire, Judith W. (A Lady of Virginia). **Diary of a Southern Refugee, During the War.** 1867.

Mann, Herman . **The Female Review: Life of Deborah Sampson.** 1866.

Meyer, Annie Nathan, editor.**Woman's Work in America.** 1891.

Myerson, Abraham. **The Nervous Housewife.** 1927.

Parsons, Elsie Clews. **The Old-Fashioned Woman.** 1913.

Porter, Sarah Harvey. **The Life and Times of Anne Royall.** 1909.

Pruette, Lorine. **Women and Leisure: A Study of Social Waste.** 1924.

Salmon, Lucy Maynard. **Domestic Service.** 1897.

Sanger, William W. **The History of Prostitution.** 1859.

Smith, Julia E. **Abby Smith and Her Cows.** 1877.

Spencer, Anna Garlin. **Woman's Share in Social Culture.** 1913.

Sprague, William Forrest. **Women and the West.** 1940.

Stanton, Elizabeth Cady. **The Woman's Bible** Parts I and II. 1895/1898.

Stewart, Mrs. Eliza Daniel . **Memories of the Crusade.** 1889.

Todd, John. **Woman's Rights.** 1867. [Dodge, Mary A.] (Gail Hamilton, pseud.) **Woman's Wrongs.** 1868.

Van Rensselaer, Mrs. John King. **The Goede Vrouw of Mana-ha-ta.** 1898.

Velazquez, Loreta Janeta. **The Woman in Battle.** 1876.

Vietor, Agnes C., editor. **A Woman's Quest: The Life of Marie E. Zakrzewska, M.D.** 1924.

Woodbury , Helen L. Sum n er. **Equal Suffrage.** 1909.

Young, Ann Eliza. **Wife No. 19.** 1875.